Are you interested in

a course management system that would

save you time & effort?

If the answer is *yes*, **CourseCompass is for you.**

Contact your local Allyn & Bacon/Longman sales representative for a free access code, or visit www.coursecompass.com, and take a tour of this course management system.

Technical support is available for faculty and students:

support@coursecompass.com
1-800-677-6337

CourseCompass is an online course management system designed to help you manage all the aspects of your course – communication, information distribution, testing and grading.

Let it help you:

- **Communicate directly with your students** via email, discussion boards, and announcement pages.

- **Post documents for your course,** eliminating the need for course packs or handouts.

- **Administer online tests,** with automatic grading and analysis.

- **Provide your students with 24/7 access** to key course information, such as syllabus, assignments, and additional resources – as well as check his/her grade instantly.

Demo CourseCompass today! www.coursecompass.com

Assessment Package

for

Woolfolk

Educational Psychology

Tenth Edition

prepared by

Gypsy M. Denzine
Northern Arizona University

Boston   New York   San Francisco
Mexico City   Montreal   Toronto   London   Madrid   Munich   Paris
Hong Kong   Singapore   Tokyo   Cape Town   Sydney

ISBN   0-205-50493-0

Printed in the United States of America

10 9 8 7 6 5 4 3 2   10 09 08 07 06

Contents

INTRODUCTION

Several features of the *Assessment Package* that accompanied Anita Woolfolk's 9th edition of *Educational Psychology* were well received by our readers. Therefore, we decided to retain the same features for the 10th edition of *Educational Psychology*. As was the case for the 9th edition's *Assessment Package*, the chapter feedback sections were arranged to follow their respective chapters in order to make it easier for you to locate the rationales for items that you will use for your tests. The 10th edition of the *Assessment Package* contains page numbers for the answers for all questions. We retained the feature of providing feedback for all case studies.

The revised *Assessment Package* contains items for new topics in the 10th edition of *Educational Psychology* such as the implication of the law No Child Left Behind, information on Annual Yearly Progress, more content related to diversity and multiculturalism, additional content in the area of technology, continued emphasis on self-regulated learning, and expanded coverage on individual differences and meeting the needs of students with special needs. In an effort to keep overall production cost increases to a minimum, the addition of new items necessitated the elimination of items contained in the previous edition of the *Assessment Package*. Removing items from the test bank was a daunting task that required careful consideration. Items were removed based on the following criteria: (a) topic was not heavily emphasized in the chapter; (b) item was based on a non-educational example, (c) correct answers required students to consider a negatively phrased question stem and a negatively framed answer (feedback has informed us students find "double negatives" to be confusing); and (d) the length of the question stem and possible answers was too long. In removing items, careful attention was paid to ensuring major topics had items assessing students' declarative, procedural, and conditional knowledge. Furthermore, the elimination of items was conducted equally across questions set in elementary, middle school, and high school settings. Items were not cut equally across all content areas; rather, items typically found to be on teacher certification tests were retained. Thus, the *Assessment Package* continues to contain a substantial number of questions related to topics such as student motivation, theories and principles of learning, human development, instructional objectives and strategies, and assessment of student learning. The *Assessment Package* for the 10th edition includes new items, which emphasize and reinforce Dr. Woolfolk's new book feature "**Connect** and **Extend** to **PRAXIS II™**." However, not all states require PRAXIS II so it will be important to point out to teacher candidates that the "Connect and Extend" notes may not have meaning for their respective teacher licensure exams.

Similar to the 8th edition's *Assessment Package*, item difficulty (**P**) and item discrimination (**D**) data are presented for a substantial number of items in each of the chapters. The discrimination power of these items was determined by the traditional Truman Kelly (1927) method that looks at the difference between high-scoring and low-scoring internal criterion groups. Kelly's item analysis method uses the following formulas for the difficulty index (**P**) and discrimination index (**D**):

P = Number of correct answers for the high-scoring group *plus* (+) the number of correct answers for the low scoring group *divided* by the total number of students in the **two** internal criterion groups.

D = Number of correct answers for the high-scoring group *minus* (-) the number of correct answers for the low-scoring group *divided* by the number of students in **one** internal criterion group.

The internal criterion groups for which the item data are presented here were formed by the students who scored in the highest and lowest one-third of the total group that responded to these items. The item data were derived from several hundred undergraduates in a basic educational psychology course in a large Midwestern university over a period of several years. The number of students that provided these data varies from one item to another, because not every item for which data are reported was used each semester. Moreover, the item data reported here are the averaged difficulty and discrimination indices derived across at least two semesters. For most of the items, the **P** and **D** indices are remarkably consistent across test administrations with different students. For your easy reference, interpretation of the **P** and **D** values is described as follows:

Difficulty Index	Interpretation
P = 0.75 to 1.00	Easy Items
P = 0.26 to 0.74	Average Items [0.61 to 0.73 = High average] [0.26 to 0.39 = Low average]
P = 0.00 to 0.25	Very Difficult Items

Discrimination Power	Interpretation
D = +.60 to 1.00	Very strong discrimination
D = +.40 to .59	Strong discrimination
D = +.20 to .39	Mild to moderate discrimination
D = -.19 to .19	Non-significant discrimination
D = -.20 to -1.00	Significantly negative discrimination

Clarification of the difficulty categories is quite arbitrary and can be redefined as the consumer wishes. However, this classification system is traditional. Items with difficulty values ranging from 0.40 to 0.60 tend to have the strongest potential for identifying individual differences (discrimination power). The descriptors for the discrimination power categories are also quite arbitrary but traditional. A 20% difference between high-scorers and low-scorers is viewed to be a significant difference ($p < .05$). The greater the difference is, the more power an item has to identify differences among individuals when differences do exist.

The *Assessment Package* also includes a Section containing items for Dr. Woolfolk's material on research methods that is located in the *Instructor's Resource Book* and on the Woolfolk Website. Several peopled contributed material for the authentic assessment section in the 7th and 8th editions, and their material has been retained in this edition:

> Dr. Gary G. Brannigan, State University of New York – Plattsburg
> Dr. William J. Gnagey, Illinois State University
> Dr. Diane Horgan, University of Memphis
> Dr. Elizabeth M. Penn, Thomas More College
> Dr. Jean R. Strait, Augsburg College.

Dr. Gypsy M. Denzine came on board the 9th edition *Assessment Package* and provided the content revisions for the current edition.

Special acknowledgement and thanks go to Kathryn Wolaver Linden, Professor Emerita at Purdue University, who provided so much of the material for previous editions of the Assessment Package, and, in particular, her contribution of the authentic assessment section.

Thanks also go to Adam Whitehurst, Rachel Lamson, and Lisa Joerin, who all helped in the process of bringing this project to publication.

Chapter 1 Teachers, Teaching, and Educational Psychology

Multiple-Choice Questions

1) According to the Woolfolk text, which of the following is true of expert teachers?

   A) They are more likely than novices to ignore students' wrong answers.

   B) They take more time to solve problems.

   C) They deal with new events as if they were new problems.

   D) They have a limited and focused knowledge base.

   Answer: C

   Explanation: A)

   C) It is **NOT** true that experts deal with new events as new problems. In fact, the opposite is true in the sense that experts employ their prior knowledge to come up with efficient solutions to new problems. They also make good use of students' wrong answers, are reflective about decisions, and have different ways of understanding the subject matter.

   Page Ref: 7
   Skill: Understanding
   P: .73
   D: .21

2) The "art vs. science" issue in teaching is probably best answered by the statement that teaching requires

   A) imagination and, therefore, is an art.

   B) learned skills and creativity.

   C) the ability to learn and apply specific rules.

   D) the use of scientific methods.

   Answer: B

   Explanation: B) Like medicine, teaching requires a combination of learned skills and creativity. Thus, teaching is considered to be *both an art and a science*.

   Page Ref: 6
   Skill: Understanding
   P: .75
   D: .26

3) According to James Popham, the law No Child Left Behind

    A) will not effect teachers in secondary education schools.

    B) will shorted the length of the school year.

    C) will effect the lives of teachers every day.

    D) relates to only teachers who teach in rural areas.

    E) will go into effect after January 2009.

Answer: C

Explanation: C) By the end of the 2005–2006 school year, all teachers must have core academic subjects and be "highly qualified." The NCLBA will effect the lives of teachers everyday.

Page Ref: 2
Skill: Understanding

4) Experienced teachers tend to judge their success by

    A) evaluations from their principals and peers.

    B) feedback from parents of students.

    C) their ability to establish discipline.

    D) the success demonstrated by their students.

Answer: D

Explanation: D) Research suggests that experienced teachers become more focused on students' needs and achievements. Consequently, they *judge their own success by the success demonstrated by their students*.

Page Ref: 15
Skill: Understanding
P: .72
D: .25

5) The concerns of educational psychology are distinctive in that they

    A) are limited to the classroom.

    B) do not overlap those of other fields of study.

    C) have no place in the laboratory.

    D) relate to improving learning and instruction.

Answer: D

Explanation: D) The concerns of educational psychology relate to *improving learning and instruction*. To achieve this objective, educational psychologists draw from other disciplines (e.g., psychology and sociology) and conduct research in both the classroom and the laboratory.

Page Ref: 9
Skill: Understanding
P: .83
D: .16

6) Use of the "common sense" approach to teaching is viewed by educational psychologists as

   A) appropriate in most circumstances.

   B) inappropriate unless supported by research.

   C) more reliable than scientific judgments.

   D) the main factor that differentiates experts from novices.

   Answer: B

   Explanation: B) Educational psychologists view the "common sense" approach to teaching as *inappropriate* or potentially misleading unless supported by research. As illustrated by the examples in the textbook, common sense ideas often do not work in the expected manner when applied in classrooms.

   Page Ref: 9
   Skill: Understanding
   P: .69
   D: .38

7) Research by Ogden, Brophy, and Evertson (1977) on selecting primary-grade students to read aloud suggests that the best method is to

   A) ask for volunteers to read.

   B) call on students in a prescribed order.

   C) call on students at random.

   D) have students read as a group (choral response).

   Answer: B

   Explanation: B) Research by Ogden, Brophy, and Evertson (1977) indicated that *first graders achieved better when they were called upon to read in a prescribed order.* Their interpretation was that the children would spend more time rehearsing when they were aware of the sections that they would be asked to read and would get more practice reading because they were not over-looked.

   Page Ref: 9
   Skill: Knowledge

8) Wong's research indicated that when individuals read a research result, they tended to

   A) become resistant toward using the strategy involved.

   B) find the results more obvious than originally thought.

   C) put the results into practice immediately.

   D) seek more information on the subject.

   Answer: B

   Explanation: B) Wong (1987) demonstrated that when subjects in her study were shown research results (whether or not correct) in writing, they had a greater tendency to believe that the results were *obviously true.*

   Page Ref: 10
   Skill: Knowledge

9) Research on acceleration for bright children suggests that acceleration is generally

    A) beneficial for these children at all age/grade levels.

    B) beneficial for younger children but detrimental for older children.

    C) detrimental for younger children but beneficial for older children.

    D) harmful for children at all age/grade levels.

Answer: A

Explanation: A) Research summarized by Kirk and his colleagues (1993) suggests that acceleration (skipping grades) is generally *beneficial (and, at least, not harmful) for bright children at all levels*.

Page Ref: 10
Skill: Knowledge

10) When studies are based only on observations, the results should be expressed as

    A) cause–and–effect relationships.

    B) descriptions.

    C) principles.

    D) theories.

Answer: B

Explanation: B) When studies are based only on observations, the results must be expressed as *descriptions of events. Descriptive studies rely on observational and subjective data.* Correlational studies identify the relationship(s) among two or more variables for a specific group of people. Experimental studies require controlled, objective data in order to establish causal relationships.

Page Ref: 10
Skill: Understanding
P: .56
D: .43

11) A case study is an investigation of

    A) a small group of people with similar backgrounds.

    B) different groups of people over a period of time.

    C) one person or group over a specific period of time.

    D) people from one geographic area.

Answer: C

Explanation: C) Case studies involve an intensive examination of real–life contexts (such as schools or classrooms) through direct observations, biographical data, school records, test results, peer ratings, and a wide variety of other observational tools. The researcher would investigate *one person or a group of people intensively over a relatively long period of time.*

Page Ref: 11
Skill: Knowledge
P: .83
D: .24

12) A correlation coefficient indicates the

   A) direction but not the strength of a relationship.

   B) direction and strength of a relationship.

   C) strength and direction of a treatment effect.

   D) strength but not the direction of a relationship.

Answer: B

Explanation: B) Correlation coefficients indicate *both the strength and direction of relationships*
                 (e.g., strong positive or weak negative). Treatment effects are not involved in
                 correlational research.

Page Ref: 11
Skill: Knowledge
P: .75
D: .28

13) In what specific type of research would a researcher be likely to serve as a
participant–observer?

   A) Correlational

   B) Descriptive

   C) Ethnographic

   D) Experimental

Answer: C

Explanation: C) Researchers sometimes serve as participant observers in *descriptive research,*
                 specifically ethnographic research. Their goal is to observe events in a classroom
                 or school by being part of the activities.

Page Ref: 11
Skill: Knowledge
P: .60
D: .44

14) A researcher participates in a class over a two-month period and analyzes the strategies the teacher employs to maintain discipline. This research is an example of what specific type of research study?

    A) Cross-sectional

    B) Ethnography

    C) Experimental

    D) Longitudinal

Answer: B

Explanation: B) *Ethnographic studies* involve an intensive examination of real-life contexts (such as schools or classrooms) through observations. In this example, the researcher spent two months observing the teacher and recording descriptions of the discipline techniques employed. There is no indication that the researcher is a participant observer in the research.

Page Ref: 10
Skill: Understanding

15) A researcher concludes from his study that, on a typical school day, students spend only 50 percent of their time engaged in learning. What specific type of research must have been conducted in order for this conclusion to be valid?

    A) Single-subject design

    B) Participant-observer

    C) Descriptive

    D) Experimental

Answer: C

Explanation: C) *Descriptive methods* would be used by a researcher to study how much time is spent on learning activities during a typical day. This would require observations for a number of days and might include students' self-reports and/or teacher ratings in order to identify a pattern for the amount of time actually spent in learning activities.

Page Ref: 10
Skill: Understanding
P: .72
D: .52

16) A positive correlation between two factors indicates that the factors

    A) are **NOT** necessarily related.

    B) are strongly related.

    C) decrease proportionately.

    D) tend to increase or decrease together.

Answer: D

Explanation: D) A positive correlation indicates that two factors *increase or decrease together*. As one increases so does the other; as one decreases so does the other. Therefore, the two factors for a positive correlation vary in the same direction. If the correlation is negative, one factor increases while the other factor decreases. [Note that, unless it is perfect, the correlation only suggests a tendency or pattern.]

Page Ref: 11
Skill: Knowledge
P: .59
D: .42

17) What size or direction of correlation coefficient is likely to be obtained between children's ages (from five to 13 years) and the distance that they can long jump?

    A) Close to zero

    B) Either +1.00 or −1.00

    C) Negative

    D) Positive

Answer: D

Explanation: D) A *positive relationship* is likely to exist between children's ages and the distance they can long jump. Due to their greater physical size, strength, and agility, older children will generally be able to jump farther than younger children. As age increases, jumping distance tends to increase, at least through adolescence.

Page Ref: 11
Skill: Understanding

18) Which one of the following correlation coefficients indicates the strongest relationship?

    A) –0.03

    B) –0.78

    C) +0.56

    D) +0.70

Answer: B

Explanation: B) The strongest correlation of the four choices is represented by –0.78. It is **NOT** the sign (direction) that determines strength; it is the closeness of the correlation to either +1.00 or –1.00. A *correlation of –0.78 represents a fairly strong negative relationship* between the factors being correlated.

Page Ref: 11
Skill: Understanding
P: .68
D: .64

19) What type of correlation coefficient is likely to be obtained between reading ability and running ability of high-school students?

    A) Close to zero

    B) Either +1.00 or –1.00

    C) Strong positive

    D) Weak negative

Answer: A

Explanation: A) A *correlation close to zero* is likely to exist between reading ability and running ability. The two factors are relatively independent. Better readers are not likely to be faster or slower runners than others and slower readers are not any better at running than their fast-reading peers.

Page Ref: 11
Skill: Understanding

20) When a correlation coefficient of –0.80 is found between factor A and factor B, the most accurate interpretation is that

    A) a decrease in factor A is strongly related to a decrease in factor B.

    B) a decrease in factor A is strongly related to an increase in factor B.

    C) there is **NO** significant relationship between the two factors.

    D) there is a very weak relationship between the two factors.

Answer: B

Explanation: B) A correlation of –0.80 indicates a strong negative relationship. *Decreases in factor A will be associated with increases in factor B.* Decreases in both factors will result in a positive relationship.

Page Ref: 11
Skill: Understanding
P: .66
D: .49

21) A correlation study indicates that teachers' interest in teaching and the amount of the day their students are engaged in learning correlate at +0.46. This coefficient would indicate that

    A) as teacher interest decreases, engaged time increases.

    B) as teacher interest increases, engaged time tends to increase.

    C) interest in teaching leads to a large increase in engaged time.

    D) there is virtually **NO** relationship between the two variables.

Answer: B

Explanation: B) The +0.46 correlation coefficient suggests a *moderately strong positive relationship* between teaching interest and engaged time. Teachers who have more interest in teaching tend to have students who are more engaged in learning, and vice versa.

Page Ref: 11
Skill: Understanding
P: .84
D: .25

22) A correlation coefficient of 0.90 indicates that

    A) one event has been caused by another event.

    B) one event is strongly related to another event.

    C) the two events are related 10 percent of the time.

    D) the two events are related 90 percent of the time.

Answer: B

Explanation: B) A correlation of 0.90 indicates a *strong positive relationship*. Correlations do not imply cause and effect, only that the two variables or factors are related.

Page Ref: 11
Skill: Understanding
P: .92
D: .21

23) A researcher reports that students who have the highest test scores in school tend to be more involved in extracurricular activities than are other students. What specific type of research study must have been conducted?

    A) Correlational

    B) Descriptive

    C) Ethnographic

    D) Experimental

Answer: A

Explanation: A) The researcher conducted a *correlational study*. The purpose is to determine the relationship between test scores and extracurricular activities. Ethnographic studies are another specific type of descriptive research. **NO** treatment is being manipulated; thus, the research is **NOT** experimental.

Page Ref: 11
Skill: Understanding

24) Random assignments would be most critical in what type of research?

   A) Case study

   B) Correlational

   C) Descriptive

   D) Experimental

Answer: D

Explanation: D) By randomly assigning subjects to treatments and evaluating the treatments, *experiments are designed to study cause and effect*. Unlike descriptive studies, changes made in an experimental study can be attributed to the treatments introduced, because all other relevant factors are intended to be controlled. In correlational studies, usually only one group of subjects is studied on a variety of factors. A cross-sectional study typically involves several groups of subjects who are then compared on a variety of factors. Such studies are not experimental.

Page Ref: 12
Skill: Knowledge
P: .57
D: .28

25) Which one of the following instances is **MOST** like a random sample for a class of thirty students?

   A) A coin is tossed in order to select students alternately one by one into the experimental and control groups.

   B) The first ten students who enter the classroom are placed into the experimental group and the next ten into the control group.

   C) The first twenty volunteers are selected from the physics class and alternately placed into experimental and control groups.

   D) The twenty students with the highest GPAs are selected and alternately placed into experimental and control groups.

Answer: A

Explanation: A) A random sample is one in which each subject has an equal opportunity to be selected for any group. The three situations described in the alternative answers to this question all concern special, rather than randomly composed, groups of students. Thus, identifying the experimental groups by *coin tossing* is the method that most closely approximates a random selection.

Page Ref: 12
Skill: Understanding

26) When a result from a research project involving an experimental design is reported in the literature as significant, this result

    A) contradicts the prevailing theoretical views.

    B) is unrelated to theory development.

    C) is unlikely to have occurred by chance.

    D) will indicate its practical importance.

Answer: C

Explanation: C) Statistical significance means that the result is *unlikely to have occurred by chance*. It does **NOT** necessarily imply that the result has either practical or theoretical importance.

Page Ref: 12
Skill: Understanding
P: .76
D: .38

27) What type of research participants should researchers use for studies of cause-and-effect relationships?

    A) Controlled samples

    B) Random samples

    C) Related samples

    D) Skilled samples

Answer: B

Explanation: B) *Random assignments* are critical for establishing cause-effect relationships. If such assignments are **NOT** employed, the researcher will be unable to determine whether treatment differences are caused by the treatments themselves or by the treatment groups being different in some important way that is related to the outcome being studied.

Page Ref: 12
Skill: Knowledge

28) Dr. Patterson concludes from her research that using a systematic study strategy **CAUSED** good grades for students assigned to a particular group. For this conclusion to be valid, the type of research that was performed must have been what type of study?

    A) Correlational

    B) Descriptive

    C) Experimental

    D) Observational

Answer: C

Explanation: C) Dr. Patterson can infer cause and effect only from *experimentation*. Correlational research and observational research provide descriptive results that do not support causal relations. However, these latter two types of research can often lead to questions that can be studied by means of experimental research.

Page Ref: 12
Skill: Understanding
P: .54
D: .41

29) A researcher finds that students who were given computers to use at home demonstrated greater independent learning skills than a comparable group that was not selected to receive home computers. What type of research study was probably designed for this conclusion to be valid?

    A) Correlational

    B) Descriptive

    C) Experimental

    D) Observation

Answer: C

Explanation: C) Apparently, an *experimental* approach was employed. The key factor is the manipulation and then comparison of different treatments: having computers vs. not having them.

Page Ref: 12
Skill: Understanding
P: .53
D: .30

30) An explanation of how we remember things that we have learned is called a

    A) construct.

    B) correlation.

    C) principle.

    D) theory.

Answer: D

Explanation: D) A *theory is an explanation of behavior or human functioning*, such as how we remember what we have learned or why we are motivated to do something.

Page Ref: 14
Skill: Knowledge

31) According to the law No Child Left Behind

    A) research is not important for improving schools.

    B) schools who receive federal funds must be consistent with "scientifically based research."

    C) initial hypotheses about education which have not been tested can still improve educational practices.

    D) mandates all teachers must conduct a research project on an annual basis.

Answer: B

Explanation: B) *According to NCLBA scientifically based research based on rigorous research can produce valid and reliable results for improving education.*

Page Ref: 13
Skill: Knowledge

Completion Questions

1) Schools are evaluated based on test schools, which indicate if their students are making _____.

Answer: Adequately Yearly Progress (AYP)
Page Ref: 2

2) Many educators believe that the mark of an expert teacher is the ability to be _____.

Answer: reflective
Page Ref: 7

3) When beginning teachers confront everyday classroom life, they often experience _____.

Answer: reality shock
Page Ref: 15

4) The study of the processes of teaching and learning is the focus of the discipline of _____.

Answer: educational psychology
Page Ref: 9

5) The type of research that attempts to record what happens in classrooms without attempting to manipulate any variables is called _____ research.

Answer: descriptive
Page Ref: 10

6) A researcher who becomes a working member of a class over a period of time in order to record and gain understanding of the class dynamics is a(n) _____.

Answer: participant observer
Page Ref: 11

7) Research that is designed to determine the relations between two variables is a(n) _____ study.

Answer: correlational
Page Ref: 11

8) The type of research that attempts to establish cause and effect relationships is a(n) _____ study.

Answer: experimental
Page Ref: 12

9) Each person is given an equal opportunity to be in a treatment or control group by means of _____ sampling.

Answer: random
Page Ref: 12

10) Findings considered statistically unlikely to have occurred by chance are described as _____.

Answer: significant
Page Ref: 12

11) Broad frameworks that attempt to explain relationships between sets of variables are called _____.

Answer: theories
Page Ref: 14

12) When findings in a given area repeatedly support the same conclusion, a(n) _____ can be derived.

Answer: principle
Page Ref: 13

True/False Questions

1) According to the law No Child Left Behind, paraprofessionals or teaching assistants are not required to be "highly qualified."

    Answer: FALSE

    Explanation: *No Child Left Behind* mandates all paraprofessionals and teaching assistants must be "highly qualified."
    Page Ref: 2

2) In general, educational experts believe being a "highly qualified teacher" as defined by the law No Child Left Behind is a good first step towards becoming an effective teacher.

    Answer: TRUE

    Explanation: Having content knowledge of one's subject area is a good first step to becoming a good teacher.
    Page Ref: 4

3) Sanders and River's (1996) research shows that the effects of good teaching produce additional achievement gains for lower-achieving students.

    Answer: TRUE

    Explanation: Researchers have found the effects of good teaching are cumulative and residual and have the most benefits for lower-achieving students.
    Page Ref: 4

4) Unlike playing chess, expertise in teaching is mainly a function of style rather than knowledge.

    Answer: FALSE
    Page Ref: 7

5) As teachers' experience grows, they tend to become more likely to judge their success by their students' successes.

    Answer: TRUE
    Page Ref: 15

6) Rigorous scientifically based research has been through a review by a journal or panel of experts

    Answer: TRUE

    Explanation: Reliable and valid results come from studies in which an independent group of experts review and evaluate the research question, methodology, and results.
    Page Ref: 13

7) The major concern of new teachers is that their knowledge of their subjects is limited.

Answer: FALSE
Page Ref: 15

8) Negative correlations are typically weaker than positive correlations.

Answer: FALSE
Page Ref: 11

9) A correlational study is a specific type of descriptive research.

Answer: TRUE
Page Ref: 11

10) Correlations provide a basis for making cause–effect interpretations.

Answer: FALSE
Page Ref: 11

11) A key element in a research experiment is random assignment of participants to groups.

Answer: TRUE
Page Ref: 12

12) A statistically significant result in experimental research indicates that the result is a true finding.

Answer: FALSE
Page Ref: 12

13) Principles are the product of consistency in research findings over time.

Answer: TRUE
Page Ref: 13

14) A theory is an explanation of occurrences in a given field.

Answer: TRUE
Page Ref: 14

15) David Olson has agreed with Robert Slavin's point of view and says experiments are the only or at least the best source of research for improving educational practices.

Answer: FALSE
Page Ref: 14

Short Answer Questions

1) How would you respond to someone who says "anyone can teach and a formal teacher preparation is unnecessary" based on the work of Linda Darling-Hammond?

   Answer: Research shows that in addition to teacher subject matter knowledge, teacher preparation and qualifications do make a difference in regards to student achievement.
   Page Ref: 4

2) Discuss the problems or issues that most concern beginning teachers today. Which of those concerns would be the most important to you personally? Explain your choice(s).

   Answer: New teachers may worry about their teaching skills, being liked by peers and students, making a good impression, and basically surviving. Specific concerns are maintaining discipline, motivating students, accommodating individual differences, evaluating students, and dealing with parents.
   Page Ref: 15

3) Explain how principles and theories are derived. Discuss how knowledge of a theory (e.g., classroom management) can be helpful to a classroom teacher.

   Answer: Principles come from seeing patterns in situations or research findings. For example a teacher may derive a principle after noticing the effect of a specific classroom management strategy on student achievement. A theory is a teacher's explicit explanation about a phenomenon. For example, a teacher might development a prediction about why the classroom management impacts student achievement. Principles help in solving specific problems, whereas, theories provide a more broad framework for deriving new solutions to problems.
   Page Ref: 7, 1-14

4) Differentiate between expert and novice teachers with regard to the approaches they use to teach knowledge of subject content. Use an example to illustrate how an expert and a novice teacher might approach this type of teaching differently.

   Answer: Shulman has identified seven areas of professional knowledge that experts have: academic subjects, general teaching strategies, curriculum materials and programs, subject-specific knowledge for teaching, characteristics and culture backgrounds of learners, settings for learners, and goals and purposes of teaching. Novices tend to be limited in these seven areas, particularly those involving how to relate learner characteristics to teaching strategies.
   Page Ref: 7, 13-14

5) Discuss the purposes and procedures of the discipline of educational psychology today. What are the interests of educational psychology with regard to theory vs. application and learning vs. teaching?

Answer: Educational psychology is concerned primarily with (a) understanding the processes of teaching and learning and (b) developing ways to improve these processes. Educational psychologists are interested in both learning and teaching. They recognize the distinction between learning as it is researched in the laboratory and teaching as it takes place in actual classroom settings. For this reason, they advocate testing the validity of learning theories outside the laboratory.

Page Ref: 8–10

6) Differentiate between descriptive and experimental research orientations with regard to purpose, methods, and the interpretation of results.

Answer: Descriptive research **CANNOT** show cause–and–effect relationships; it does **NOT** involve a change or treatment, and it uses observation to characterize things as they exist. Relationships between variables are described by correlations. Experimental research involves randomization and use of a dependent variable (outcome) and independent variable (treatment). Experimental research may indicate cause–and–effect relationships., for example, would provide a teacher with directions or basic guidelines for how to react to different problems that occur. [The theory would not, however, dictate specific solutions, because every situation is unique.]

Page Ref: 11–12

Case Studies

Jill received her Bachelor of Arts Degree in education in June and will be meeting her first class of second graders tomorrow at Briarview Elementary School. Her classroom will be adjacent to one assigned to Ms. Ferguson, a veteran first-grade teacher considered to be one of the most knowledgeable and skilled in the district. Ms. Ferguson will be starting her tenth year of teaching.

1) What are likely to be Jill's major concerns about her first months of teaching? Explain your choices.

Answer: As a novice teacher, Jill's primary concerns will most likely be related to classroom management. She may also be concerned about motivating students and teaching students with individual differences. Knowing how to evaluate student work and dealing with parents may be issues of concern for Jill.

Page Ref: 15

2) How might Jill prepare for the start of school and for a particular lesson differently than would Ms. Ferguson? Explain the plan for Jill.

Answer: Because Ms. Ferguson has automated many of the essential teaching skills, she will have more time in her preparation to explore new teaching methods or materials. Also, Ms. Ferguson will most likely begin her preparation for a specific lesson by focusing on her students' needs and how she will evaluate if the students are successful.

Page Ref: 15

3) Discuss how the two teachers might differ in using achievement results as information about (a) student learning and (b) their own success in teaching.

Answer: Compared to Jill, Ms. Ferguson is more likely to use information about student achievement to evaluate the extent to which her new teaching methods or materials allowed her to meet her instructional objectives. Whereas Jill might view her own success as a well-disciplined classroom environment, Ms. Ferguson is likely to view her own teaching success in relation to the achievements of her students.

Page Ref: 15

4) Discuss the areas of professional knowledge, based on Shulman's analysis, that Jill is likely to develop as she gains more experience as a teacher.

Answer: As Jill gains more experience she will know her academic subject area in more depth and will have more curriculum materials for teaching the subject areas. She will have adopted more general teaching strategies that apply in all subjects, while at the same time she will have more subject-specific teaching strategies. Jill will gain knowledge about the characteristics of her learners and a better understanding of the contexts in which students learn. Finally, she will become a much more reflective teacher and will have a more in-depth understanding of her goals and purposes of teaching.

Page Ref: 7

Ninth-grade teachers at Farmington Junior High School are interested in knowing whether using cooperative learning will increase student understanding of mathematics. They would like to conduct a research study to investigate whether this is truly the case.

5) Design an experimental study (basic elements, not detailed procedures) that could be used to answer the teachers' research question.

Answer: The researcher would randomly assign students to either the cooperative learning condition or the traditional lecture condition. Thus, the teacher is changing his or her approach and will note the results from the change. In this case, the change or "treatment" is the inclusion of cooperative learning. The traditional lecture group serves as the "control" condition. The researchers' goal is to compare the mathematical achievement scores from students in the cooperative learning condition with scores from students in the traditional lecture condition. If a difference between the two groups exists, then the researcher explores whether or not the difference is more than one might expect by chance (i.e., significance testing).

Page Ref: 12

6) How might descriptive research also be used in the above study? Describe an example.

Answer: The researcher would collect many types of information regarding the characteristics and background of the students in the cooperative learning situation. The researcher might report students' mathematics scores by gender, ethnicity, number of previous math courses, and students' level of math anxiety. The researcher could describe in detail the distribution of scores (how many earned very high or low math scores).

Page Ref: 10-12

7) One teacher speculates that students who are more social than others are likely to have greater appreciation of the cooperative learning method. What research approach should be used to answer this question? Use an example to illustrate an application of this type of research.

Answer: To answer this question the researcher would want to utilize a correlational design for the research project. The researcher could report how often and how much students socialize with other students during recess. Having a measure of social interaction, the research would explore whether mathematics scores for students in a cooperative learning setting relates to students' level of sociability. The hypothesis may be that students who are highly social will also have math test scores when they are taught in a cooperative learning setting. If this were to be true, we would expect a high and positive correlation coefficient (perhaps +.70 or higher).

Page Ref: 11

8) Briefly describe a study that would support a causal interpretation of the results. Explain why your study could be a cause-effect study.

Answer: A teacher may hypothesize that students' increase in math scores is not due to the cooperative learning situation, but that it is more closely related to students' reading ability. In this example, students would be randomly assigned to a cooperative learning group or a traditional lecture setting. In addition, students would be randomly assigned to a reading condition. In one reading condition the students had no additional reading assignments, while in the other condition students were required to read at least two books per week at home. Thus, the researcher can explore whether the cause of the difference in math scores is due to the teaching condition (cooperative learning or traditional lecture) or to the difference in reading.

Page Ref: 12

Chapter 2 Cognitive Development and Language

Multiple–Choice Questions

1) Which one of the following is an example of maturation?

    A) Gaining weight from age two to age three

    B) Losing weight due to exercise

    C) Losing weight during a brief illness

    D) Learning which foods produce the most weight

Answer: A

Explanation: A) *Maturation refers to changes that occur naturally and spontaneously* rather than as a result of environmental circumstances. An example would be gaining weight from age two to age three. [Note: losing weight due to illness or exercise is not a natural occurrence, but one that is caused by particular environmental events.]

Page Ref: 22
Skill: Understanding
P: .77
D: .28

2) As time goes on, Tina becomes a happier individual, more in touch with life, and content with her situation. This description emphasizes what kind of development for Tina?

    A) Cognitive

    B) Personal

    C) Physical

    D) Social

Answer: B

Explanation: B) In contrast with social development that involves relations with others, *personal development* is illustrated in the scenario on changes in Tina's personality (such as being happier, changes in self–concept, etc.).

Page Ref: 22
Skill: Understanding
P: .83
D: .24

3) All developmental theories have the following general principle in common

    A) Development is balanced.

    B) Development is gradual.

    C) Development occurs in a random way.

    D) Individuals develop at the same rate.

Answer: B

Explanation: A) Development is gradual, occurs in an orderly way, and occurs at variable rates. *Development is NOT considered to be balanced*, i.e., development is not balanced across physical, personal, social, and cognitive development.

Page Ref: 22
Skill: Knowledge
P: .83
D: .25

4) What part of the brain coordinates and orchestrates skilled movements?

    A) Cerebellum

    B) Cortex

    C) Cerebrum

    D) Frontal lobe

Answer: A

Explanation: A) The *cerebellum* is the part of the brain that coordinates and orchestrates skilled movements. The thalamus is associated with the ability to learn new information, while the cerebral cortex controls sensory input, the formation of associations, and voluntary movement.

Page Ref: 22
Skill: Knowledge

5) If John is introduced to the concept of fractions today, he will not be able to start adding and subtracting them tomorrow. What general principle of development is illustrated?

    A) Development proceeds through identifiable stages.

    B) Development takes place gradually.

    C) Maturation is the basis for development.

    D) John lacks personal development.

Answer: B

Explanation: B) *Development takes place gradually.* John will need to acquire more experience and skills with fractions before he can perform specific operations such as adding and subtracting. [He may, however, acquire those skills at different rates than others.]

Page Ref: 22
Skill: Understanding
P: .79
D: .24

6) The last part of the brain to develop fully is the

    A) cerebellum.

    B) cerebral cortex.

    C) frontal lobe.

    D) thalamus.

Answer: C

Explanation: C) The last section of the brain to develop fully is the *frontal lobe* in the cerebral cortex.

Page Ref: 23
Skill: Knowledge

7) The part of the cerebral cortex that matures first controls

    A) higher-order thinking processes.

    B) physical movements.

    C) the processing of language.

    D) the formation of associations.

Answer: B

Explanation: B) *Control of physical movements* matures in the cerebral cortex before other functions, such as activities that involve verbalization.

Page Ref: 23
Skill: Knowledge

8) Adults and children with ADHD have

    A) smaller frontal lobes than people without ADHD.

    B) tend to have great control of motor behavior compared to people without ADHD.

    C) have a greater amount of brain plasticity than people without ADHD.

    D) show no differences in brain activity when compared to people without ADHD.

Answer: A

Explanation: A) People with ADHD have smaller frontal lobes, basal ganglia, and cerebellums. As a result, people with ADHD tend to have difficulties with self-regulation of behavior, coordination, and control of motor behavior.

Page Ref: 25
Skill: Knowledge

9) Keith Stanovich is a researcher who has been vocal about calling the "left brain-right brain research"

    A) very important for improving educational practice.

    B) relevant only for female learners and not male learners.

    C) nonsense that has not improved educational research and/or practice.

    D) well grounded in scientific neuroscience.

Answer: D

Explanation: D) Stanovich has made strong statements about the misplaced brain research based on theories of "right brain versus left brain." Instead he argues no single part of the brain is solely responsible for specific activities and humans use all parts of their brain. He has challenged the simplistic interpretation of neuroscientific research.

Page Ref: 25
Skill: Understanding

10) Specialization of the two hemispheres of the brain involves

    A) Broca's area.

    B) lateralization.

    C) the primary auditory cortex.

    D) Wernicke's area.

Answer: B

Explanation: B) Specialization in the two hemispheres of the brain relates to *lateralization*.
Page Ref: 25
Skill: Knowledge

11) Messages sent by releasing chemicals that jump across synapses involve

    A) lateralization.

    B) myelination.

    C) neurons.

    D) transformations.

Answer: C

Explanation: C) *Neurons* send messages by releasing chemicals that jump across synapses in the brain.

Page Ref: 23
Skill: Knowledge

12) According to Piaget, the foundation for development in all humans is supplied by

    A) activity.

    B) exploration.

    C) maturation.

    D) social transmission.

Answer: C

Explanation: C) The fundamental basis for development in people is biological *maturation*, the characteristics that are genetically determined.

Page Ref: 27
Skill: Knowledge

13) Piaget's basic blocks of thinking and memory are

    A) actions.

    B) accommodations.

    C) adaptations.

    D) schemas.

Answer: D

Explanation: D) *Schemas* are Piaget's basic blocks of thinking. These schemas are an organized system of thought or action that permit us to represent objects and thoughts in our own words.

Page Ref: 28
Skill: Knowledge

14) The two processes involved in adaptation are

    A) assimilation and accommodation.

    B) assimilation and equilibration.

    C) equilibration and organization.

    D) social transmission and schema.

Answer: A

Explanation: A) The two processes of adaptation are *assimilation and accommodation*. Accommodation is defined by Piaget as the process of changing existing schemas to respond to a new situation. Assimilation is the process of changing what is learned to fit existing schemas.

Page Ref: 29
Skill: Knowledge
P: .91
D: .13

15) Which of the following pairs of factors that influence thinking is thought by Piaget to be genetic or inherited tendencies?

   A) Accommodation and assimilation

   B) Adaptation and organization

   C) Assimilation and schemas

   D) Schemas and equilibration

Answer: B

Explanation: B) Based on his work in biology, Piaget concluded that all species inherit two basic tendencies: *organization* (the combining of behaviors into coherent systems) and *adaptation* (adjusting to the environment).

Page Ref: 28
Skill: Knowledge

16) Which one of the following is the clearest example of Piaget's concept of assimilation?

   A) Learning that a green light means "go" and a red light means "stop."

   B) Learning to paint with a new type of brush.

   C) Looking at teachers as they lecture.

   D) Looking at a worm and thinking that it is a snake.

Answer: D

Explanation: D) The clearest example of assimilation of the choices given is *looking at a worm and thinking that it is a snake*. The observer is "fitting" the stimulus (worm) into her mental schema at the moment, which is apparently oriented to expect to see a snake or which assigns (based on experiences) greater saliency to a snake than to a worm. The environmental stimulus is being mentally "changed" in accord with the learner's existing schemas.

Page Ref: 29
Skill: Understanding
P: .61
D: .23

17) Jeannie observed rocks sinking in water and said, "I already knew that. All rocks sink." Then she saw a piece of pumice floating on water and was told that pumice is rock. Several days later, she was asked again if rocks sink in water. She replied, "Well, most do." In Piaget's terms, what process did Jeannie use to draw this conclusion?

A) Accommodation

B) Assimilation

C) Classification

D) Conservation

Answer: A

Explanation: A) Jeannie is using *accommodation* by changing her ideas about whether rocks sink or float based on her experience in observing a floating piece of pumice. Assimilation would have involved resisting the idea that rocks float, perhaps by failing to accept pumice as a type of rock.

Page Ref: 29
Skill: Understanding
P: .77
D: .37

18) According to Piaget, the process of searching for a balance between cognitive schemas and environmental information is called

A) accommodation.

B) adaptation.

C) assimilation.

D) equilibration.

Answer: D

Explanation: D) *Equilibration* is defined by Piaget as the process of searching for a balance between cognitive schemas and environmental information. When a balance occurs, equilibrium is felt; imbalance causes disequilibrium.

Page Ref: 29
Skill: Knowledge
P: .81
D: .29

19) When we try a particular strategy and it does not work, the discomfort we experience is called

    A) assimilation.

    B) centration.

    C) disequilibrium.

    D) non–adaptation.

Answer: C

Explanation: C) *Disequilibrium* is the discomfort we feel when a schema does not work as expected. It promotes new learning by motivating us to continue searching for a solution.

Page Ref: 29
Skill: Knowledge
P: .95
D: .12

20) According to Piaget, people pass through the four stages of cognitive development

    A) at the same levels of competence.

    B) at the same rates, adjusted for intelligence.

    C) in specifically determined ages.

    D) in the same sequence.

Answer: D

Explanation: D) Piaget theorized that people pass through the four stages of cognitive development *in the same sequence*. However, they do this at different rates, depending on individual development.

Page Ref: 29
Skill: Knowledge
P: .81
D: .18

21) The best way to determine what cognitive stage a person has reached is by

    A) interpreting the person's scores on a mental ability test.

    B) knowing the person's age.

    C) knowing the person's rate of development.

    D) observing how the person solves problems.

Answer: D

Explanation: D) The best way of determining the cognitive stage that a person has reached is to *observe how that individual solves problems*. The Piagetian stages concern ways of thinking, not particular age levels or levels of intelligence.

Page Ref: 29
Skill: Understanding

22) What of the following sayings best conveys a child's thinking before the notion of object permanence is acquired?

   A) "A bird in the hand is worth two in the bush."

   B) "A penny saved is a penny earned."

   C) "A stitch in time saves nine."

   D) "Out of sight, out of mind."

Answer: D

Explanation: D) Before object permanence is acquired, a child thinks that an object that is no longer visible has disappeared—out of sight, out of mind—as the saying goes.

Page Ref: 30
Skill: Understanding
P: .98
D: .05

23) In Piaget's theory, an understanding of object permanence is acquired during what period of development?

   A) Early preoperations

   B) Operations

   C) Late preoperations

   D) Sensorimotor

Answer: D

Explanation: D) Object permanence, the understanding that objects exist even if not visible, is acquired during the *sensorimotor period*.

Page Ref: 30
Skill: Knowledge

24) Michelle covers her own eyes, because she thinks her friends will not see her when playing a game of hide–and–seek. What stage of Piaget's cognitive theory does this account best illustrate?

   A) Concrete operations

   B) Formal operations

   C) Preoperational thought

   D) Sensorimotor

Answer: D

Explanation: D) Michelle is demonstrating an early form of egocentrism as well as a lack of object permanence. As is common during early stages of the *sensorimotor period*, she believes that if she can't see others, others can't see her.

Page Ref: 32
Skill: Understanding
P: .57
D: .27

25) In the sensorimotor stage of development, a child begins to develop

    A) goal–directed activities.

    B) mental operations.

    C) preoperational thought.

    D) semiotic functions.

Answer: A

Explanation: A) Toward the end of the *sensorimotor period*, children begin to use logical, goal–directed actions in which they play with objects in an orderly fashion (for a purpose, with a goal in mind). By the preoperations period, these types of actions are well established.

Page Ref: 30
Skill: Knowledge

26) Nathan is shown two balls of clay that he identifies as equal in quantity. When one of the balls is then rolled into a sausage, Nathan says that piece (i.e., sausage) now has more clay. In what stage of development is he likely to be?

    A) Concrete operations

    B) Goal–directed operations

    C) Preoperational thought

    D) Sensorimotor

Answer: C

Explanation: C) Nathan is probably in the *preoperational stage* because he is failing to demonstrate conservation. If he were in the concrete operations or formal operations stages, he would indicate that both pieces contain the same amount of clay because the quantity of the sausage-like piece has not changed.

Page Ref: 30–31
Skill: Understanding
P: .81
D: .30

27) Billy refuses to drink his orange juice from the 1/2 full glass that his mother gives to him. He wants her to pour the juice into his favorite cup and watches his mother fill it to the brim. Billy likes his cup better because he gets more juice in it. With what cognitive concept in Piaget's theory is Billy having trouble?

    A) Accommodation

    B) Assimilation

    C) Conservation

    D) Semiotic function

Answer: C

Explanation: C) The cognitive concept illustrated by Billy's thinking that he gets more juice in his small cup than in the half-full larger cup is an example of a child who has not yet developed Piaget's concept of *conservation*.

Page Ref: 31
Skill: Understanding
P: .89
D: .31

28) After stringing beads from a large necklace onto a smaller empty string, a child states that there are now more beads on the small string than there were on the larger string. What cognitive concept (Piaget's theory) does this behavior best illustrate?

    A) Accommodation

    B) Assimilation

    C) Conservation

    D) Equilibration

Answer: C

Explanation: C) The child is apparently preoperational. He or she is *failing to conserve quantity by thinking that the small string contains more beads* (because it "appears" more loaded with beads).

Page Ref: 31
Skill: Understanding
P: .68
D: .36

29) A teacher pours juice from a larger glass into two tiny glasses, and the child beams, happy now that he has "more juice." What cognitive stage (Piaget's theory) does the account best illustrate?

    A) Concrete operations

    B) Formal operational thought

    C) Preoperational thought

    D) Sensorimotor

Answer: C

Explanation: C) The child is in the *preoperational stage*. We can conclude this because he has *failed to demonstrate conservation* by thinking that the tiny glasses contain more juice.

Page Ref: 31
Skill: Understanding
P: .96
D: .05

30) In his first game of hide-and-seek, Andy covers his eyes so that his friends cannot see him. His thinking can be described as

    A) decentered.

    B) egocentric.

    C) schematic.

    D) seriation.

Answer: B

Explanation: B) Andy is acting in an *egocentric manner*. He assumes that just because he cannot see his friends, they cannot see him. [Ostriches are said to act the same way!]

Page Ref: 31
Skill: Understanding
P: .86
D: .28

31) A preoperational child's belief that a tall, narrow glass contains more liquid than a short, wide glass is probably due to difficulties in

    A) decentering.

    B) egocentrism.

    C) serration.

    D) object permanence.

Answer: A

Explanation: A) *Decentering* is the ability to focus on more than one aspect of a situation at a time. This occurs, for example, when the preoperational child perceives that, because a glass is taller, it must also have more liquid. In this case, the child is unable to see that the amount of liquid has not changed.

Page Ref: 31
Skill: Knowledge

32) Which one of the following situations illustrates what Piaget called "collective monologue"?

   A) A child sits in her room and talks to herself about a mixture of topics, one after the other.

   B) Children sitting in a circle actively engage in sharing ideas with one another.

   C) Students sit in the same room and talk aloud but with little attempt to involve their listeners.

   D) A teacher conducting a recitation exercise asks the students to call out the answer together.

Answer: C

Explanation: C) A *collective monologue* occurs when children sitting in a group talk enthusiastically but without the intention of conversing with others. They are most content to talk aloud to themselves.

Page Ref: 31
Skill: Understanding

33) Corinne has mastered this type of problem: "If the white house is bigger than the blue house, and the blue house is bigger than the red house, is the white house bigger or smaller than the red house?" What stage of Piaget's cognitive theory does this situation best illustrate?

   A) Concrete operations

   B) Formal operations

   C) Preoperational thought

   D) Sensorimotor

Answer: A

Explanation: A) By demonstrating an ability to understand ordering and seriation, Corinne is evidently in the *concrete operations stage*. She would be less capable at this task, however, if she were dealing with abstractions rather than with concrete objects (houses of different colors).

Page Ref: 32–34
Skill: Understanding
P: .73
D: .40

34) David has just purchased a car and is intensely interested in it. When the car has engine trouble, he is able systematically to locate the problem. What cognitive stage of Piaget's theory does this situation best illustrate?

    A) Concrete operations

    B) Formal operations

    C) Preoperational thought

    D) Sensorimotor

Answer: B

Explanation: B) David appears to be in the *formal operations stage*. He is able to use logical thinking to locate the engine trouble systematically. He is evidently using formal thought to solve unique problems.

Page Ref: 35–26
Skill: Understanding
P: .73
D: .30

35) What is the hallmark of Piaget's stage of formal operations?

    A) Semiotic function

    B) Hypothetical–deductive reasoning

    C) Organized thinking of dependent elements

    D) Reversible thinking

Answer: B

Explanation: B) The hallmark of Piaget's stage of formal operations is *hypothetical–deductive reasoning*. This ability involves both deductive and inductive reasoning to solve real as well as hypothetical problems.

Page Ref: 35
Skill: Knowledge

36) Janie was having some difficulty deciding how to organize her defense for the debate competition. She prepared several hypothetical arguments that her opponents might raise, and how she might reply. What cognitive stage of Piaget's theory does this account best illustrate?

    A) Concrete operations

    B) Formal operations

    C) Preoperational thought

    D) Sensorimotor

Answer: B

Explanation: B) Janie's problem with organizing her defense for the debate reflects the *characteristics of formal operations,* including hypothetical–deductive reasoning, problem solving, and scientific thought.

Page Ref: 35
Skill: Understanding
P: .71
D: .26

37) Perry is able to solve hypothetical problems by mentally working through a set of possibilities. What characteristic of cognitive development does Perry illustrate?

    A) Compensatory reasoning

    B) Inductive thinking

    C) Organized thinking

    D) Reversible reasoning

Answer: C

Explanation: C) Perry is probably in the *formal operations stage* because he is able to solve hypothetical problems by working through a set of possible actions. Such skills would be difficult for a concrete-minded child.

Page Ref: 35
Skill: Understanding
P: .81
D: .22

38) When Mary returned from the high-school prom, she complained, "Everyone hated my dress!" What specific concept does this account best illustrate?

    A) Adolescent egocentrism

    B) Interpsychological action

    C) Reversible thinking

    D) Semiotic function

Answer: A

Explanation: A) Mary is probably in the formal operations stage. She is demonstrating *adolescent egocentrism* by believing that everyone is focusing on her appearance.

Page Ref: 36
Skill: Understanding
P: .75
D: .22

39) Which one of the following statements best reflects Piaget's position on the question of speeding up cognitive development?

    A) Acceleration is both inefficient and useless.

    B) Acceleration is effective for only the brightest students.

    C) Keeping cognitive development "on track" is a teacher's role.

    D) Speeding up cognitive development is a teacher's role.

Answer: A

Explanation: A) Because biological maturation is genetically programmed, parents and teachers have little impact on this facet of cognitive development. Consequently, Piaget would contend that forced *acceleration is both inefficient and useless.* [See Point-Counterpoint.]

Page Ref: 36-37
Skill: Understanding

40) Current views about Piaget's theory generally support the idea that

   A) Piaget's tasks appear to have been invalid for judging cognitive ability.

   B) Piaget's tasks appear to have generally been too easy for subjects.

   C) Piaget tended to overestimate children's abilities and underestimate their social differences.

   D) Piaget tended to underestimate children's abilities and overlook the social and cultural issues.

Answer: D

Explanation: D) It appears that Piaget *underestimated children's abilities* by using tasks that were too difficult and directions that were too confusing. He also *overlooked social and cultural issues*. Recent studies have shown that children can reason at higher levels than Piaget had thought.

Page Ref: 38
Skill: Knowledge
P: .82
D: .33

41) According to Robbie Case, cognitive development in one domain of thought

   A) cannot be explained by assimilation and accommodation.

   B) differs from one domain to another.

   C) is similar from one domain to another.

   D) transfers from one domain to another.

Answer: B

Explanation: B) Cognitive development in one domain of thought *does not seem to transfer to other domains of thought*, according to Case. In other words, *development in one domain differs from development in other domains*. Development of mathematical thinking, for example, does not progress at the same pace as development of verbal thought.

Page Ref: 37
Skill: Knowledge

42) An increasingly influential view of cognitive development proposed by Vygotsky is based on

   A) concrete experiences.

   B) creation of complex schemas of thought.

   C) culture and socioculture theory.

   D) mastery of scientific thinking.

Answer: C

Explanation: C) *Culture and sociocultural theory* are becoming an increasingly more influential view of cognitive development than is Piaget's stage theory.

Page Ref: 39
Skill: Knowledge

43) According to Vygotsky, a child's cultural development is

A) co-constructed learning and shared experiences.

B) created by emphasis on private speech.

C) internalized by self-thinking.

D) intrapsychologically determined.

Answer: A

Explanation: A) A child's cultural development is the result of *co-constructed learning* (i.e., learning with others) *and shared experiences*.

Page Ref: 40
Skill: Knowledge

44) Vygotsky's view of cognitive development differs from Piaget's in the importance and emphasis placed on a person's

A) experience.

B) genetic factors.

C) interpersonal interactions.

D) private speech.

Answer: C

Explanation: C) Vygotsky places more emphasis on *interpersonal interactions* than Piaget. Vygotsky viewed language as playing important roles in cognitive development, both in the form of private speech (self-communication) and in the verbal transmission of guidance from other, more capable individuals.

Page Ref: 40
Skill: Knowledge
P: .70
D: .29

45) The role of cultural tools in cognitive development involves, according to Vygotsky,

A) both real and symbolic tools.

B) essentially real tools.

C) predominantly symbolic tools.

D) primarily psychological tools.

Answer: A

Explanation: A) According to Vygotsky, the role of cultural tools in cognitive development involves *both real and symbolic tools*.

Page Ref: 41
Skill: Knowledge

46) The role of "private speech" in Vygotsky's view is to

    A) call attention to oneself during play.

    B) guide one's activities in solving a problem.

    C) encourage children to learn new words.

    D) stimulate the development of language from simple words to full sentences.

Answer: B

Explanation: B) According to Vygotsky, *private speech* serves the beneficial function of *guiding activities in solving a problem*. Use of private speech is most common in the five- to seven-year range.

Page Ref: 42
Skill: Knowledge
P: .77
D: .40

47) Piaget called children's self-directed talk _____ while Vygotsky called the same behavior _____.

    A) egocentric speech; private speech

    B) private speech; egocentric speech

    C) private speech; social speech

    D) social speech; private speech

Answer: A

Explanation: A) Children's self-directed talk is Piaget's *egocentric speech* and Vygotsky's *private speech*.

Page Ref: 42–44
Skill: Knowledge

48) According to Vygotsky, scaffolding represents

    A) a barrier or a block to solving a problem.

    B) a plateau that children reach before progressing to a new stage.

    C) artificial support, such as notes, on which children can rely while learning.

    D) external support for helping children solve problems on their own.

Answer: D

Explanation: D) The zone of proximal development is the point at which a child cannot solve a problem alone but can do so *with support or scaffolding*. Teachers can help children move to higher reasoning levels by providing appropriate guidance during problem solving.

Page Ref: 48
Skill: Knowledge
P: .84
D: .30

49) The zone of proximal development is the area where students may solve a problem

    A) by themselves.

    B) with no disequilibrium.

    C) with support.

    D) without frustration.

Answer: C

Explanation: C) The zone of proximal development is the area between the learner's current development level and the level the learner could achieve with some support from a more capable peer or through adult guidance.

Page Ref: 44
Skill: Knowledge
P: .82
D: .31

50) Application of Vygotsky's zone of proximal development concept would include

    A) making new tasks slightly beyond the student's current level of ability.

    B) not introducing new tasks until prerequisite tasks are satisfactorily mastered.

    C) requiring the student to work completely independently, regardless of success or failure.

    D) using highly structured materials to introduce new content rather than semi-structured tasks.

Answer: A

Explanation: A) One implication of Vygotsky's zone of proximal development is to *make new tasks slightly beyond the child's current level of ability*. With support or "scaffolding" from others, where needed, this orientation will help the child progress to new levels of thinking.

Page Ref: 44
Skill: Understanding
P: .73
D: .38

51) The research of Luis Moll in Arizona has focused on the cultural "funds of knowledge," which include

    A) learning environments that require students to work on their own.

    B) the knowledge the families and communities have that can become the basis for teaching.

    C) learning activities funded under the law No Child Left Behind.

    D) learning activities that require the use of a computer.

Answer: B

Explanation: B) Moll's work involves families and communities by including their knowledge about agriculture, economics, manufacturing, medicine, cooking, and more in the teaching process. This model may also involve community experts to evaluate students' assignments.

Page Ref: 50
Skill: Knowledge
P: .26
D: .02

52) According to Kathleen Berger (2003), the best time for a child to learn a second language on his/her own is

    A) during early or middle childhood

    B) no one time is better than another

    C) early childhood

    D) adulthood when cognitive skills are developed

Answer: C

Explanation: C) Early childhood is the best time to *learn a second language* on one's own, however, early or middle childhood can be the best time to *teach a second language*. Also, there is no cognitive "penalty" for students who learn and speak a second language, in fact there may be long-term cognitive benefits.

Page Ref: 52
Skill: Knowledge

53) The period considered to be the most sensitive for language development occurs

   A) after puberty.

   B) about the time of puberty.

   C) during the first year of life.

   D) during the preschool years.

Answer: D

Explanation: D) The most sensitive period for language growth appears to be the period before puberty, *especially the preschool years*. For example, the average child between the ages of two and six learns from six to 10 words a day.

Page Ref: 52–54
Skill: Knowledge
P: .39
D: .36

54) The area of language that specifically deals with the ordering of words is called

   A) awareness.

   B) scaffolding.

   C) semantics.

   D) syntax.

Answer: D

Explanation: D) *Syntax* is the area of language that deals specifically with the ordering of words.

Page Ref: 54
Skill: Knowledge

55) Generally, students are not ready to study the rules of a language formally until about age five. This is when most students have started to gain

   A) literacy.

   B) metalinguistic awareness.

   C) semantic speech.

   D) syntax.

Answer: B

Explanation: B) *Metalinguistic awareness*, which develops at about age five, is knowledge about the rules and conventions of a language. At this stage, children are ready to begin to study the rules of a language. They can understand, for example, rules for past tense, capitalization, using plurals, and so on.

Page Ref: 55
Skill: Knowledge
P: .79
D: .42

Completion Questions

1) Developmental changes that are genetically programmed are a function of _____.

   Answer: maturation
   Page Ref: 22

2) The specialization of the two hemispheres of the brain is called _____.

   Answer: lateralization
   Page Ref: 25

3) According to Piaget, when environmental events cause changes in existing schemas, _____ occurs.

   Answer: accommodation
   Page Ref: 29

4) "Out of sight, out of mind" describes the behavior of children who have not acquired _____.

   Answer: object performance
   Page Ref: 30

5) When a schema produces an unsatisfactory result, a student experiences _____.

   Answer: disequilibrium
   Page Ref: 29

6) The principle that changing the shape of an object does not change the amount of the object is called _____.

   Answer: conservation
   Page Ref: 31

7) Having the ability to focus on more than one aspect of a situation at a time is called _____.

   Answer: decentering
   Page Ref: 31

8) The process of making an orderly arrangement of objects from large to small or vice versa is called _____.

   Answer: seriation
   Page Ref: 33

9) The ability to reason abstractly and deductively occurs during the Piagetian stage of _____.

   Answer: formal operations
   Page Ref: 35

10) The basis of formal operations is _____.

Answer: hypothetical–deductive reasoning
Page Ref: 35

11) An approach that teaches students to use private speech to guide their learning is called cognitive _____.

Answer: self–instruction
Page Ref: 44

12) Kathleen Berger (2006) refers to the space between what the learner already knows and what he or she is not yet ready to learn as the _____.

Answer: Magic middle

Explanation: Berger refers to the magic middle as the space between what the learner already knows and what the learner is not yet ready to learn as the *magic middle,* which is similar to Vygotsky's notion of the Zone of Proximal Development (ZPD).
Page Ref: 44

13) Guided participation in the classroom is an example of _____ learning.

Answer: assisted
Page Ref: 48–49

14) The area of language that deals specifically with word order is called _____.

Answer: syntax
Page Ref: 54

15) When a student understands language and how it works, the student is said to have _____.

Answer: metalinguistic awareness
Page Ref: 55

16) The support that children use to help them solve problems just beyond their capabilities is called _____.

Answer: scaffolding
Page Ref: 48

17) Both Piaget and Vygotsky would most likely agree students need to be taught in the "magic _____" or the place where they are neither bored or frustrated.

Answer: middle
Page Ref: 49

18) The Chinese educational system places heavy emphasis on math and science in the early grades. As a result, Chinese students typically solve Piagetian tasks that involve distance, time, and speed relationships about _____ years ahead of American students.

Answer: two
Page Ref: 57

True/False Questions

1) Developmental changes are genetically determined rather than environmentally determined.

Answer: FALSE
Page Ref: 22

2) The part of the brain directly associated with the coordination of physical movements is the cerebellum.

Answer: TRUE
Page Ref: 22

3) Assimilation takes place when a person uses existing schemas to respond to a new situation.

Answer: FALSE
Page Ref: 29

4) Understanding of object permanence occurs during the sensorimotor stage.

Answer: TRUE
Page Ref: 30

5) Seriation refers to the ability to work with symbols.

Answer: FALSE
Page Ref: 33

6) The cognitive stage associated with ability to understand hypothetical situations is formal operations.

Answer: TRUE
Page Ref: 35

7) Hypothetical–deductive reasoning is characteristic of adolescent egocentrism.

Answer: FALSE
Page Ref: 36

8) According to Piaget, most adults may be able to use formal operational thought in only a few areas in which they have the greatest interest or experience.

Answer: TRUE
Page Ref: 36

9) Neo–Piagetian theorists are concerned with how attention, memory, and strategy use relate to Piaget's theory of cognitive development.

Answer: TRUE
Page Ref: 37

10) One strategy for scaffolding complex learning is to use a reciprocal teaching approach, which requires students to play to role of the teacher by leading discussions and asking questions.

Answer: TRUE

Explanation: In reciprocal teaching, students rotate in playing the role of the teacher. The teacher becomes more of a facilitator of the learning process.
Page Ref: 49

11) The basic difference between Piaget and Vygotsky's views of cognitive development is in attention paid to genetic factors.

Answer: FALSE
Page Ref: 40–41

12) Vygotsky viewed children's private speech to be helpful for cognitive development.

Answer: TRUE
Page Ref: 42

13) When children are in a zone of proximal development, use of scaffolding is appropriate.

Answer: TRUE
Page Ref: 48

14) The development of language is associated with the concrete operational stage.

Answer: FALSE
Page Ref: 32–33

15) According to Luis Moll, medicine, agriculture, economics, and religion are funds of knowledge which should not be used in classroom instruction or serve as the basis of teaching.

Answer: FALSE

Explanation: Moll contends medicine, agriculture, economics, religion, and more can serve as knowledge that family and community members may have that can become the basis for teaching.
Page Ref: 50

16) Early childhood is the best time for a child to learn a second language on his/her own.

Answer: TRUE
Page Ref: 52

17) The basics of word orders, or *syntax,* are mastered by children well before they enter the first grade.

Answer: TRUE
Page Ref: 54

18) Metalinguistic awareness begins to develop at about the age of puberty.

Answer: FALSE
Page Ref: 55

Short Answer Questions

1) Define development and identify specific types of forms it can take. Then explain how maturation relates to development.

Answer: Development refers to orderly and relatively long-term changes that take place over one's life span. Physical development involves bodily changes, personal development changes in personality, social development changes in the way one relates to others, and cognitive development changes in one's thinking. Maturation is the part of development that involves genetically-based changes that are not influenced by environmental factors.
Page Ref: 22

2) How is the brain involved in adolescent behavior such as planning, risk-taking, and decision making?

Answer: Adolescents' prefrontal cortex controls impulsive thoughts and allows adolescents to engage in higher-order thinking processes. It is not until the high school years or maybe later that individuals can control some of the impulsive behavior by reasoning, planning, and/or delay of gratification.
Page Ref: 24

3) Describe Piaget's theoretical views on cognitive development using and defining the following terms in your answer: organization, adaptation, assimilation, accommodation, equilibration.

Answer: Humans inherit tendencies toward organization, arranging information into a coherent system, and adaptation, adjusting to the environment. The mental systems that are developed are called schemas. When existing schemas are used to interpret new information, assimilation takes place. When existing schemas are changed in response to new situations, accommodation takes place. We search for balance through the process of equilibration, making adjustments whenever dissonance or imbalance between our thinking and reality occurs.
Page Ref: 28-29

4) Name and define the basic aspects of reasoning that must be mastered before a child is able to solve problems of conservation.

   Answer: Conservation is mastered through the processes of *reversible thinking* (performing an operation and then "undoing" it), decentering (being able to focus on more than one property of a stimulus at a time), identity (knowing that changes in an object's shape do not change its quantity), and compensation (a change in one aspect, e.g., height, produces a compensating change in another aspect, e.g., width).

   Page Ref: 31

5) Define Vygotsky's zone of proximal development and explain how it relates to the problem of matching cognitive stages with instructional strategies.

   Answer: The zone of proximal development is the point when a child can master a task if given appropriate help and support. It suggests that students should have to reach a bit to understand, with the necessary support of parents, teachers, and peers. Such support is called scaffolding. Vygotsky's ideas suggest that students should be guided by explanations, demonstrations, and cooperative learning within their zone of proximal development. Use of private speech should also be encouraged in order to help organize thinking.

   Page Ref: 44

6) Describe the steps or stages that children go through in the process of developing language. Include reference to the different ways that children use words and sentences in these stages.

   Answer: Children begin to communicate through gestures and inarticulate sounds, followed by imitating sounds that they hear. During the early stages of language development, adults rarely correct pronunciation and grammar. In order to encourage children's new understanding, adults will simplify their language to stay a bit more advanced than the children's current level of development. Moreover, adults will provide the kind of support, or *scaffolding*, that Vygotsky has recommended. This support may also create *disequilibrium* that also encourages development. According to some psychologists, children are born with special capacity for processing, understanding, and creating language. Reward and correction undoubtedly play important roles in correct language use, but children's own thinking is very important in putting together the parts of this very complicated system. By age 5 or 6, most children have mastered the basics of language, or *syntax*, and begin to develop *metalinguistic awareness*—knowledge about rules and conventions of language, a process that continues throughout their lives.

   Page Ref: 54–55

Case Studies

Trip, a seventh-grader, is having difficulty learning principles of fractions, such as two out of five is 2/5, 3/5 is less than 2/3, and so on. While his classmates seem to follow most of the examples given in class and in the textbook, Trip feels overwhelmed and confused by them. He is good at other subjects (such as reading and social studies) but is falling behind rapidly in mathematics. Being familiar with Piaget's stages of development, you suspect that Trip is very concrete in his thinking about mathematical principles compared to many of his classmates.

1) Based on the above assessment of Trip's situation, what teaching approaches would Piaget's ideas suggest for making the principles of fractions more understandable to Trip?

Answer: The teacher will want to provide Trip with hands-on learning experiences. For example, the teacher could give Trip two apples to cut into pieces. Trip could cut one apple into five pieces and the other apple into three pieces. He could then compare the combined physical amount of two of the pieces from the five-piece cut apple to two of the pieces from the three-piece cut apple.

Page Ref: 34

2) If Trip is a concrete thinker in mathematics, is he likely to think in similar ways in other subjects? Explain using appropriate ideas from Piaget and Vygotsky.

Answer: According to Piagetian theory, Trip is also likely to think in concrete ways in other subject areas. For example, he may struggle with comparing the human brain to a computer. Neo-Piagetians, however, believe Trip may show general patterns of concrete thinking and yet be able to use some more advanced schemas within a particular domain. Trip may reason differently about social situations and numerical concepts. From Vygotsky's perspective, the teacher would want to consider Trip's sociocultural factors, such as how language is used, rather than focusing on whether or not Trip had surpassed a specific stage.

Page Ref: 32–34

Mason is another seventh grader who is having difficulty in math class. He stares blankly at the test paper asking him to compute fractions such as 5/7 and 9/12 as percentages. He can't remember at all how to determine whether 4/5 is larger or smaller than 5/8, so he makes a guess. He hopes that, with some luck, he might manage in the class. On the weekend, Mason is watching his favorite sport, basketball. He remarks to his sister, "Oh, this guy made eight out of 11 shots last week; he's close to an 80 percent shooter so he should be for these free throws." After the player makes both shots, Mason looks down at the statistics sheet he's been keeping on the local teams' shooting percentages, and updates the statistics.

3) Is the inconsistency between Mason's performances on school test problems and in working with basketball statistics a problem for Piaget's stage theory? That is, if Mason is at a particular stage of reasoning, shouldn't he be able to deal with the school problems as successfully as the basketball ones? Explain.

   Answer: The inconsistency noted in this case study is not a problem for Piaget's theory. According to Piaget, experience and interest can affect the stage one can reach. Mason should be able to solve the school-based math problems equally as well as the basketball ones. The teacher may need to help Mason see the connection between the two situations. Also, Mason's interest is likely to be influenced by the extent to which the student can move beyond rote memorization of mathematical principles. The teacher may want to introduce a math game to facilitate interest. Also, it is important for the teacher to explain why it is important for students to have an understanding of fractions and percentages in our society.

   Page Ref: 36

4) How might Vygotsky explain the role of other people in shaping Mason's math skills in the two contexts? Explain.

   Answer: First, the teacher may want to look at the statistics sheet Mason created. This sheet is viewed as a cultural tool and it would be important to find out if Mason shares the sheet with any other persons. For instance, what do the headings on the columns for the data communicate to others? In addition, from Vygotsky's perspective it would be important to know if Mason typically watches basketball alone or with his brother who is four years older. It may be that his brother is providing scaffolding (cues, encouragement) to Mason as they watch the game together.

   Page Ref: 41,48

5) Knowing Mason's behaviors, how might a teacher work with him to improve his performances on the fractions and percentages unit?

   Answer: The teacher may want to integrate a physical education unit on basketball with a mathematics lesson. Mason would get the concrete experience recommended by Piaget. He would also be involved in a highly social activity, which would be supported by both Piaget and Vygotsky's theories. The basketball team could be instructed to plan and monitor their basketball activities in order to solve the math problem.

   Page Ref: 32–34, 39

Chapter 3   Personal, Social, and Emotional Development

Multiple-Choice Questions

1) Erikson interprets development from the perspective of what theory?

   A) Psychosexual

   B) Psychosocial

   C) Psychosomatic

   D) Sociocultural

   Answer: B

   Explanation: B) Erikson's views of development are interpreted from the perspective of
   psychosocial theory that emphasizes individual changes and the individual's
   relationship with the cultural environment.

   Page Ref: 67
   Skill: Knowledge

2) The emphasis in Erikson's stage theory is on

   A) behaviors and their consequences.

   B) the development of moral values.

   C) the formation of a personal identity.

   D) the process of acculturation in school settings.

   Answer: C

   Explanation: C) According to Erikson's stage theory, emphasis is placed on the individual's
   formation of a self-image or personal identity as he/she resolves each crisis
   corresponding to the developmental stages. An unhealthy resolution of a crisis
   may have negative effects on the individual's self-identity later in life.

   Page Ref: 67
   Skill: Knowledge
   P: .64
   D: .25

3) According to Erikson, if a child fails to resolve a crisis at an early stage, the child is apt to

    A) encounter problems with resolutions of later crises.

    B) forget the crisis and progress normally.

    C) remain at the unresolved stage until the crisis is resolved.

    D) resolve the crisis at a later stage.

Answer: A

Explanation: A) Erikson theorized that individuals who fail to resolve a developmental crisis successfully at a particular stage will be *likely to encounter problems with resolutions of later crises*. Sometimes, the problem can be resolved later, but an unhealthy situation is generally expected.

Page Ref: 67
Skill: Knowledge
P: .63
D: .34

4) Erikson's notion of developmental crises can be defined as a

    A) concern with parental control and self-determination.

    B) conflict between a positive and an unhealthy alternative.

    C) conflict between physical growth and cognitive growth.

    D) puzzle that may assist a person's cognitive development.

Answer: B

Explanation: B) The crises that an individual faces at each developmental stage involve a *conflict between a positive alternative and a potentially unhealthy alternative*. An example is the *trust vs. mistrust* crisis during infancy. [Note: Equilibration is a process described by Piaget in which an individual attempts to obtain a state of balance.]

Page Ref: 67
Skill: Knowledge
P: .57
D: .39

5) Children experiencing the Eriksonian conflict of trust vs. mistrust are also in what Piagetian stage?

    A) Concrete operations

    B) Formal operations

    C) Preoperational thought

    D) Sensorimotor

Answer: D

Explanation: D) Erikson's *trust vs. mistrust* stage, that takes place during a child's first year, corresponds to the beginning of Piaget's *sensorimotor stage*, that occurs from ages zero to two years.

Page Ref: 68
Skill: Understanding
P: .80
D: .36

6) What does a conflict such as *initiative vs. guilt* represent in Erikson's theory?

    A) A developmental crisis

    B) Cognitive dissonance

    C) Disequilibration

    D) Equilibration

Answer: A

Explanation: A) According to Erikson's theory, a conflict such as *initiative vs. guilt* represents a *developmental crisis*.

Page Ref: 68
Skill: Knowledge

7) Sally is in the stage Erikson calls *initiative vs. guilt*. Her parents supervise her closely and direct all her activities. The danger is that Sally may

    A) develop an exaggerated sense of her own abilities.

    B) eventually grow to mistrust her parents.

    C) have difficulty trusting her own judgment.

    D) not learn that some things should never be done.

Answer: C

Explanation: C) Sally may have *difficulty trusting her own judgment*. By being overly controlling and strict, her parents are preventing her from developing initiative without experiencing guilt.

Page Ref: 68
Skill: Understanding
P: .86
D: .17

8) Children who experience autonomy are likely to become more

    A) aggressive.

    B) dependent.

    C) intelligent.

    D) self–reliant.

Answer: D

Explanation: D) Children who succeed in developing autonomy are likely to become more *self–reliant* by attempting to manage the world on their own terms.

Page Ref: 68
Skill: Understanding
P: .84
D: .19

9) The way that children resolve the *autonomy vs. shame and doubt* crisis influences their later sense of

    A) attachment to the family.

    B) confidence in their own abilities.

    C) cooperation in groups.

    D) evaluation of new ideas.

Answer: B

Explanation: B) During the *autonomy vs. shame and doubt* period, a child begins to assume responsibilities for self-care (dressing, feeding, etc.). If these activities are not reinforced by parents, children may begin *to lose confidence in their abilities to do things for themselves.*

Page Ref: 68
Skill: Knowledge
P: .89
D: .13

10) Francis is no longer satisfied with pretending he has a place of his own. He's in the third grade now and old enough to build a real playhouse. He sets to work with boards and cardboard, and takes great pleasure in the completed project. Francis is at the stage of

    A) autonomy vs. doubt and shame.

    B) generativity vs. self–absorption.

    C) identity vs. role diffusion.

    D) industry vs. inferiority.

Answer: D

Explanation: D) Francis is in the industry vs. inferiority stage. During this stage, children begin to branch out from the home world and cope with academics, group activities, and friends in developing a sense of industry. Accordingly, Francis wants to build the house for himself.

Page Ref: 69
Skill: Understanding
P: .81
D: .27

11) The school and the neighborhood first become highly important influences during what Eriksonian stage?

    A) Autonomy vs. shame

    B) Generativity vs. stagnation

    C) Industry vs. inferiority

    D) Intimacy vs. isolation

Answer: C

Explanation: C) The school and neighborhood first become highly important influences during the industry vs. inferiority stage. During this stage, children begin to branch out from the home world and cope with academics, group activities, and friends in developing a sense of industry.

Page Ref: 69
Skill: Knowledge
P: .67
D: .35

12) Martin now takes considerable pride in completing his fourth-grade homework assignments and in doing them well. He is quite disappointed when the teacher assigns an "A" to him for a project that he strongly felt deserved an A+ (or better!). According to Erikson's theory of psychosocial development, Martin is in what stage of development?

   A) Autonomy vs. doubt

   B) Initiative vs. guilt

   C) Identity vs. role diffusion

   D) Industry vs. inferiority

Answer: D

Explanation: D) During the industry vs. inferiority stage, children take considerable pride in their work (industry) and achievements. Here, Martin's school accomplishments become increasingly important relative to home activities.

Page Ref: 69-70
Skill: Understanding
P: .88
D: .22

13) As with most developmental crises, the resolution of the identity crisis

   A) does not depend on resolution of previous conflicts.

   B) is generally completed during a brief time period.

   C) may be an extended process.

   D) requires little conscious effort.

Answer: C

Explanation: C) Resolution of an identity crisis may be an *extended process*. In fact, many adolescents enter college experiencing an identity moratorium and do not realize identity achievement until sometime between their freshman and senior years.

Page Ref: 70
Skill: Understanding
P: .88
D: .18

14) Christine can't decide what she wants to pursue when she graduates from high school this year. "Life is so confusing," she thinks to herself. "Perhaps it is best not to think about these decisions at all." Christine is experiencing identity

    A) achievement.

    B) diffusion.

    C) foreclosure.

    D) moratorium.

Answer: B

Explanation: B) Christine is experiencing *identity diffusion* by delaying her commitment to personal and occupational choices. If extended too long, this can lead to an identity crisis and unhealthy outcomes. The healthy alternative is identifying achievement.

Page Ref: 71
Skill: Understanding
P: .62
D: .37

15) Seventeen-year-old Carl has considered several career options and has developed a firm career goal. Carl is experiencing identity

    A) achievement.

    B) diffusion.

    C) foreclosure.

    D) moratorium.

Answer: A

Explanation: A) Carl is experiencing *identity achievement* which, according to James Marcia, is a healthy outcome for adolescents. It involves considering realistic life options, making choices, and pursuing them.

Page Ref: 71
Skill: Understanding
P: .75
D: .38

16) Ever since Maida was a child, her parents talked about the possibility of her becoming a doctor. They brought her chemistry sets and equipment, such as stethoscopes and tongue depressors. When Maida entered college, she enrolled in the pre-medical program without even considering other options. According to James Marcia, Maida is exhibiting identity

   A) achievement.

   B) diffusion.

   C) foreclosure.

   D) moratorium.

Answer: C

Explanation: C) Maida is experiencing *identity foreclosure* by committing herself to an occupational choice of becoming a doctor that was made to satisfy her parents. A healthier approach to developing an identity is to consider all realistic options and select the one that best fits one's own interests and abilities.

Page Ref: 71
Skill: Understanding
P: .86
D: .22

17) June's mother always wanted to be an actress and started leading June in that direction at around age two. Now June sees herself as an actress and nothing else. In which of Erikson's stages is June?

   A) Identity achievement

   B) Identity diffusion

   C) Identity foreclosure

   D) Identity moratorium

Answer: C

Explanation: C) June is experiencing *identity foreclosure* by committing herself to an occupational choice made by her mother. A healthier approach to developing an identity is to consider all realistic options and select the one that best fits one's own interests and abilities.

Page Ref: 71
Skill: Understanding
P: .70
D: .31

18) Dependence on peers, parents, and others begins to change to independence during what identity status?

    A) Diffusion

    B) Conventional

    C) Foreclosure

    D) Moratorium

Answer: D

Explanation: D) Dependence on others begins to change to independence in adolescents during the *moratorium* stage of the identity status. In the foreclosure and diffusion states, dependence changes from being very dependent on others to some dependence on others. Independence and self-direction develop fully in the identity achievement state. [Also see Table 3.2.]

Page Ref: 71
Skill: Knowledge

19) Jerry has become active with a group working to save America's topsoil. He believes that steps must be taken to prevent food shortages 100 years from now. George's situation represents Erikson's concern for

    A) generativity.

    B) integrity.

    C) isolation.

    D) self-absorption.

Answer: A

Explanation: A) Jerry's concern involves *generativity,* or caring for future generations through his interests in ecology. By achieving generativity, he is avoiding the negative condition of stagnation.

Page Ref: 72
Skill: Understanding
P: .84
D: .21

20) Which one of Erikson's crises would you be **LEAST** likely to encounter in a K-12 classroom?

    A) Identity vs. inferiority

    B) Identity vs. role confusion

    C) Initiative vs. guilt

    D) Integrity vs. despair

Answer: D

Explanation: D) An individual is **LEAST** likely to encounter Erikson's *integrity vs. despair* in K–12 classrooms. This stage involves coming to terms with death and attaining a feeling of fulfillment and completeness with their achievements in life.

Page Ref: 72
Skill: Knowledge
P: .76
D: .25

21) The difference between self-concept and self-esteem is that

    A) self-concept is an affective reaction while self-esteem is a cognitive structure.

    B) self-concept is a cognitive structure while self-esteem is an affective reaction.

    C) self-esteem is a general concept while self-concept is specific to a given situation.

    D) there is actually little or no difference between self-esteem and self-concept.

Answer: B

Explanation: B) *Self-concept is a cognitive structure*, the composite of ideas, attitudes, and feelings that people have involving themselves. On the other hand, *self-esteem is an affective reaction* involving a person's evaluation of who he/she is.

Page Ref: 85–86
Skill: Knowledge

22) Which one of the following statements is **TRUE** regarding the development of self-concept?

    A) A person with a positive self-concept in one school subject is almost certain to have a positive self-concept in other subjects.

    B) Older children's academic self-concept may be quite different than their physical self-concept.

    C) Poor performance is most damaging to a student's self-concept in science and math courses.

    D) The developing self-concept remains quite stable throughout early and late childhood.

Answer: B

Explanation: B) Contemporary conceptions of self-concept stress an individual's differentiated view of self (or "multiple" self-concepts). Consequently, an *older students' school self-concept may be quite different than their "out-of-school" self-concept.*

Page Ref: 85–86
Skill: Understanding
P: .68
D: .24

23) The development of children's self-concept evolves by means of

    A) constant self-evaluation in many different situations.

    B) contrasting themselves with their peers.

    C) differentiating between their skills and those of their peers.

    D) gauging the verbal reactions of significant others.

Answer: A

Explanation: A) Development evolves by means of *constant self-evaluation in many different types of situations.*

Page Ref: 86
Skill: Knowledge

24) George attends a rural middle school in Virginia. On standardized achievement tests given in George's school, the school average is near the national average. George's friend Harold attends an elite private school in Washington, D.C. The average score of students at Harold's school on the same achievement measure is well above the national average. According to Marsh, George is more likely to feel better about his abilities than does Harold, even though both boys received high scores on the test. What developmental concept is illustrated?

    A) "Big Fish, Little Pond"

    B) Gradual development

    C) Identity diffusion

    D) Moratorium

Answer: A

Explanation: A) George will feel better about himself as a function of the "Big Fish, Little Pond Effect," described by Marsh. That is, excelling in a less competitive situation often boosts self-esteem more than performing as high as, but average in comparison to, a more competitive peer group.

Page Ref: 86
Skill: Understanding
P: .70
D: .40

25) The implication of the "Big Fish, Little Pond" idea is that

A) children in "average" schools may feel better about their own abilities than those in "high-ability" schools.

B) larger schools are likely to promote higher achievement than smaller schools.

C) self-concept is lower when competition is weaker than when it is stronger.

D) smaller schools offer limited opportunities for self-concept to develop.

Answer: A

Explanation: A) Students who *excel in a particular area at an "average" school tend to feel better about their abilities than those with the same ability who attend "high-ability" schools.* Marsh (1990) calls this the "Big Fish, Little Pond Effect."

Page Ref: 86
Skill: Knowledge
P: .86
D: .15

26) Research suggests that the relationship between self-esteem and success in school is a

A) causal relationship.

B) negative relationship.

C) positive relationship.

D) zero relationship.

Answer: C

Explanation: C) Research suggests that students with higher self-esteem are somewhat more likely to be successful in school than students with lower self-esteem. Thus, there is a *positive relationship* between the two variables (self-esteem and achievement). Note that this relationship does **NOT** imply that his/her self-esteem causes high achievement.

Page Ref: 86
Skill: Knowledge
P: .84
D: .18

27) Programs designed to increase students' self-esteem such as "Student of the Month" have

A) had little effect on increasing self-esteem.

B) are relevant only for certain ethnic cultures.

C) have a great influence on increasing students' self-esteem.

D) should be used only in special education classes.

Answer: A

Explanation: A) Research shows "Student of the Month" programs do little to increase students' self-esteem and collaborative and cooperative strategies are more effective.

Page Ref: 87
Skill: Knowledge

28) Which one of the following students is expected to have the highest self-esteem?

A) Charlene, who won the tennis tournament after the number one seed was injured

B) Jennifer, who scored highest in her class on the physics exam even though she hated physics

C) Richard, who won Best-of-Class in a statewide modeling competition

D) Terry, who became class president after the elected president moved to a new school

Answer: C

Explanation: C) Both Charlene and Terry succeeded only after something had happened to the winner, so it is unlikely that their success would enhance their self-esteem. In Jennifer's case, scoring highest on a test of a despised subject is also unlikely to enhance her self-esteem. Consequently, Richard's self-esteem is most likely to be enhanced by his recognition for a hobby that he apparently enjoys.

Page Ref: 86–87
Skill: Understanding
P: .65
D: .22

29) Woolfolk has suggested that self-esteem is probably increased the most by

A) demonstrating competence in valued knowledge domains.

B) demonstrating understanding in school subjects.

C) having a rich and diverse social life.

D) receiving public recognition and rewards.

Answer: A

Explanation: A) According to Woolfolk, increase in self-esteem is achieved mostly by *demonstrating competence in valued knowledge domains.*

Page Ref: 87
Skill: Knowledge
P: .60
D: .31

30) A recent study that followed 761 middle–class students from first grade through high school discovered the following about diversity and self–esteem:

    A) Boys are more confident than girls in their abilities in math and science

    B) There are no gender differences between boys and girls' self–esteem

    C) Girls feel more confidence than boys in math

    D) There are major differences between boys and girls in all subject areas

Answer: A

Explanation: A) Overall, the differences between boys and girls is small. However, some evidence suggests *boys are consistently more confident in their math and science abilities* compared to girls. In earlier grades girls are often more confident about their language arts abilities, however, by high school boys and girls are more equal in their perceptions of their language arts capabilities.

Page Ref: 89
Skill: Knowledge

31) The particular aspect of ethnic pride and heritage that affects schooling is instruction in

    A) bilingual language during the first three grades.

    B) heritage language during the first three grades.

    C) second language instruction throughout elementary school.

    D) the backgrounds of all students.

Answer: B

Explanation: B) Instruction in the *heritage language during the first three grades* is most influential for later achievement in school.

Page Ref: 92
Skill: Knowledge

32) Based on recent studies, which of the following children is likely to have the greatest difficulty with assessing the intention of others?

    A) Bart, a ten–year–old with high self–esteem

    B) Enid, an aggressive three–year–old

    C) Liliana, a passive five–year–old

    D) Philip, an aggressive nine–year–old

Answer: B

Explanation: B) Recent research suggests that younger children have more difficulty understanding the intentions of others than do older children. Further, aggressive children tend to have difficulty in this area. *An aggressive three-year-old* (Enid), therefore, would be likely to have limited capabilities for assessing intention.

Page Ref: 94
Skill: Understanding

33) Most people have developed societal perspective-taking ability during the

    A) early elementary grades.

    B) late elementary years.

    C) pre-school years.

    D) years between age 14 and adulthood.

Answer: D

Explanation: D) According to Selman, perspective-taking occurs from *about the age of three through adulthood*. Selman proposes a five-stage model that begins with undifferentiated perspective-taking (ages three to six) and concludes with societal perspective-taking (age 14 to adult).

Page Ref: 94
Skill: Knowledge

34) As children develop perspective-taking abilities, there is a gradual movement toward a state of

    A) moral dilemma.

    B) moral reason.

    C) morality of cooperation.

    D) personal reward orientation.

Answer: C

Explanation: C) There is a gradual movement in children toward the *morality of cooperation* as they develop their perspective-taking ability.

Page Ref: 95
Skill: Knowledge

35) During Kohlberg's stage of preconventional moral realism, a child is likely to believe that

    A) a person's intentions are really what matters, rather than results.

    B) hitting two children deserves a stronger punishment than hitting one child.

    C) misbehaving in school always merits punishment of some severe form.

    D) punishment is rarely justified even though the behavior was undesirable.

Answer: B

Explanation: B) During the stage of moral realism, children believe that rules are absolute and that punishment should be determined by the severity of the damage rather than by circumstance. *Hitting two children would, therefore, deserve a stronger punishment than hitting one child.*

Page Ref: 96
Skill: Understanding
P: .71
D: .30

36) Frank said, "If I were starving, I'd steal a loaf of bread, but it would be wrong and against the law." What level of moral reasoning does Frank demonstrate?

   A) Conventional

   B) Nonconventional

   C) Preconventional

   D) Postconventional

Answer: A

Explanation: A) At the *conventional level of moral reasoning*, laws become very important in determining what behaviors are right and wrong. Laws are viewed by Frank as absolute and unalterable regardless of the situation. At the postconventional level, the particular situation is taken into account.

Page Ref: 96
Skill: Understanding
P: .65
D: .27

37) Andrea is driving home from the library at 2:00 in the morning. She stops for a red light and waits, even though no one is in sight. After looking again carefully in all directions, she drives across against the light. According to Kohlberg, what level of moral reasoning is reflected by Andrea's decision to cross the intersection?

   A) Conventional

   B) Nonconventional

   C) Postconventional

   D) Preconventional

Answer: C

Explanation: C) Andrea is reasoning at the *postconventional level of moral reasoning*. By breaking the law to be on time, she is making a conscious decision with a clear understanding of the consequences. Although she probably appreciates the rationale for traffic laws, she perceives her situation as meriting an exception.

Page Ref: 96
Skill: Understanding
P: .57
D: .26

38) Vic was struggling with a difficult math exam. Abbey, an A+ student, was not covering her paper, so Vic decided to copy some of her answers in order to avoid having to try solving the rest of the problems himself. What level of moral reasoning did Vic demonstrate?

   A) Conventional

   B) Nonconventional

   C) Postconventional

   D) Preconventional

Answer: D

Explanation: D) Vic is reasoning at the *preconventional level* because he is concerned only with his personal needs and is apparently not concerned about cheating. Schab's (1980) study identified three primary reasons for why students cheat: too lazy, fear of failure, and parental pressure. In Vic's case, he is simply too lazy to figure out the problems himself.

Page Ref: 96
Skill: Understanding
P: .51
D: .50

39) Sue is presented with a moral dilemma and responds that she would act in a certain way to please her parents. The moral reasoning stage reflected is

   A) conventional.

   B) nonconventional.

   C) postconventional.

   D) preconventional.

Answer: A

Explanation: A) Sue is operating at the *conventional level*. A characteristic of thinking at this level is trying to behave in a way that will please authority figures, such as one's parents. This is the second of Kohlberg's three stages of moral reasoning.

Page Ref: 96
Skill: Understanding
P: .66
D: .38

40) Which one of the following statements is **TRUE** regarding how Kohlberg's theory treats social conventions relative to moral issues?

   A) Little differentiation between moral issues and social conventions is characteristic of this theory.

   B) Moral issues are regarded as more universally oriented than are social conventions.

   C) Social conventions are used as the basis for constructing dilemmas.

   D) Social conventions are viewed as inherently right or wrong and moral issues as arbitrary.

Answer: A

Explanation: A) Kohlberg's theory has been criticized for *having little differentiation between social conventions and moral issues.* Because children appear to make that differentiation as early as age three, the accuracy of completeness of moral stages can be questioned. [Moral issues involve the rights of people in general; social conventions are the arbitrary rules of a particular group or culture.]

Page Ref: 95–97
Skill: Knowledge

41) What is the important base for moral reasoning in both women and men, according to relevant research?

   A) Concern for caring and justice

   B) Emphasis on justice

   C) Importance of equality

   D) Sympathy for others

Answer: A

Explanation: A) Both male and female adults and children demonstrated a *morality of caring and a concern for justice,* according to research findings.

Page Ref: 97
Skill: Knowledge
P: .36
D: .29

42) One of the most hotly debated criticisms of Kohlberg's moral reasoning theory is that this theory is based on a longitudinal study of only

    A) adolescent females.

    B) adolescent males.

    C) adult females.

    D) adult males.

Answer: D

Explanation: D) Kohlberg's theory of the development of moral reasoning was derived from a *study of only males*. The criticism is that the stages are biased in favor of males and that the stages do not represent the way moral reasoning develops in women.

Page Ref: 97
Skill: Knowledge

43) In addition to reasoning, what other influences affect moral behavior?

    A) Caring and correction

    B) External standards and integration

    C) Internalization and modeling

    D) Valuing justice and sharing

Answer: C

Explanation: C) Moral behavior is affected by *internalization and modeling* in addition to cognitive reasoning.

Page Ref: 95–96
Skill: Knowledge

44) Research indicates that whether or not an individual cheats in school depends primarily on the

    A) individual's honesty.

    B) individual's personality.

    C) particular situation.

    D) subject matter involved.

Answer: C

Explanation: C) Research suggests that cheating is *more dependent on the situation* than on the personality or honesty of the individual.

Page Ref: 101–102
Skill: Knowledge
P: .78
D: .31

45) The first-grade students line up for recess according to a rotation system. When a mistake is made, Louise raises her hand and reminds the teacher that she is to be first today. Louise is being

   A) aggressive.

   B) assertive.

   C) independent.

   D) recalcitrant.

Answer: B

Explanation: B) Louise is being *assertive* by reminding the teacher of her rights. Aggressive behavior, in contrast, consists of actions designed to harm others.

Page Ref: 78–79
Skill: Understanding

46) Recent research suggests that victims of physical or verbal abuse tend to blame

   A) schoolmates.

   B) their abusers.

   C) their parents.

   D) themselves.

Answer: D

Explanation: D) According to research findings, victims of physical or verbal abuse tend to *blame themselves*, rather than their abusers or others.

Page Ref: 79–80
Skill: Knowledge

47) According to Pedro Noguero's research, adolescents in a "last chance" high school stated good teachers are those who are caring, teaching them something, and

   A) are strict and hold students accountable.

   B) allow students to turn in work late when needed.

   C) are overly rigid.

   D) use different rules for different students.

Answer: A

Explanation: A) Students want teachers who care about them and their learning and demonstrate this care by setting clear and high expectations.

Page Ref: 82
Skill: Knowledge

48) According to Urie Bronfenbrenner's Bioecological Model of Human Development

   A) the mesosystem is another word for the teacher.

   B) the microsystem refers to the society at large and how it influences the individual.

   C) The family is more important than the school environment for human development.

   D) the parent's work place (i.e., exosystem) influences the development of the child.

Answer: D

Explanation: D) The exosystem is based on social settings that affect the child, even though the
                child may not be a direct member of the social group.

Page Ref: 73
Skill: Knowledge
P: .97
D: .03

49) Research has shown that students who watch others behaving aggressively

   A) become more aggressive.

   B) become more passive.

   C) do not change their behavior.

   D) tolerate less aggression among peers.

Answer: A

Explanation: A) Studies of violence on television have shown that students who watch others
                behaving aggressively *become more aggressive*. Such findings reflect the
                powerful effects of modeling in the expression of aggression.

Page Ref: 78
Skill: Knowledge
P: .84
D: .05

50) Teachers today are more likely than teachers 10 years ago to have students who

   A) are middle–class rather than lower–class.

   B) are members of blended families.

   C) are white rather than African–American or Hispanic.

   D) live with large families.

Answer: B

Explanation: B) Teachers today are more likely than teachers of the past to have students who
                are part of *blended families*. A product of the higher incidence of divorce in
                today's society, blended families represent mixtures of step–relatives, parents,
                and siblings who live together.

Page Ref: 74
Skill: Knowledge
P: .99
D: .02

51) The term "blended family" refers to a family that

    A) consists of a working mother and father and their children.

    B) gets along well together, including parents and children.

    C) includes grandparents as well as parents and children living together.

    D) includes stepbrothers and stepsisters living together with perhaps one or more siblings.

Answer: D

Explanation: D) A blended family is one that combines, through new marriages, children from different parents. Thus, *stepbrothers and stepsisters live in the same household*.

Page Ref: 74
Skill: Knowledge
P: .98
D: .02

52) Long-term adjustment to a divorce appears to be

    A) equally difficult for both girls and boys.

    B) equally difficult for both older and younger children.

    C) generally more difficult for boys than girls.

    D) generally more difficult for girls than boys.

Answer: C

Explanation: C) Long-term adjustment to a divorce appears to be *more difficult for boys than for girls*. These difficulties are reflected in behavioral and interpersonal problems at home and in school.

Page Ref: 75
Skill: Knowledge
P: .24
D: .23

53) Adults who were rejected as children tend to have

    A) fewer problems than adults whose childhoods were without caring adults.

    B) friends who are socially competent and mature, even though their childhoods were essentially friendless.

    C) higher self-esteem than adults who were socially competent as children.

    D) more problems than adults who had close friends when they were children.

Answer: D

Explanation: D) Adults who were rejected as children tend to have more problems than adults who had close friends. The role of friendships during childhood is an important influence on social and emotional development. Lonely, friendless children tend to have more problems as adults such as committing crimes and other antisocial behaviors.

Page Ref: 77
Skill: Knowledge

54) Psychologists disagree about the commonly held belief that parents are the major influence on their children. What is the basis of this disagreement?

    A) Behavioral genetics

    B) Child rearing practices

    C) Peer influences

    D) Social environment

Answer: C

Explanation: C) The basis of the disagreement among psychologists concerning the common belief that parents are the major influence on children is the *influence of peers* on development.

Page Ref: 75–76
Skill: Knowledge

55) Relational aggression involves

    A) physical abuse between siblings.

    B) threatening or damaging social relationships.

    C) being assertive about one's rights.

    D) inflicting intentional harm.

Answer: B

Explanation: B) *Relational aggression* might involve gossip and rumors and is intended to hurt social relationships.

Page Ref: 78
Skill: Knowledge
P: .97
D: .03

56) Which one of the following symptoms of child abuse is a behavioral rather than a physical indicator of child abuse?

    A) Abandonment by parents

    B) Consistent lack of supervision

    C) Frequent absence or tardiness

    D) Unattended medical needs

Answer: C

Explanation: C) *Frequent absence* from school or tardiness are behavioral indicators of abuse rather than physical indicators.

Page Ref: 83
Skill: Knowledge

57) Nigresence refers to

   A) people who have been marginalized by the majority culture.

   B) a teacher's ability to build African-American students' self-esteem.

   C) the process of developing a Black identity.

   D) an identity concept that does not change much during one's lifespan.

Answer: C

Explanation: C) Nigresence is the process of developing an individual Black identity that
                develops over time.

Page Ref: 91
Skill: Understanding

58) According to Woolfolk, one of the best ways to prevent cheating in a classroom is to

   A) make every attempt to avoid placing learners in high-pressure situations.

   B) inform students you will call their parents if they are caught cheating.

   C) ignore the first cheating behavior because students typically do not cheat on a regular
      basis.

   D) emphasize why grades are so important to the learning process.

Answer: A

Explanation: A) Cheating is not always about individual differences and teachers can do a lot
                to prevent cheating by creating situations that are *not high-pressure*. Teachers
                are encouraged to emphasize the learning more than the grade.

Page Ref: 102
Skill: Knowledge

Completion Questions

1) Erikson interprets development based on the perspective of the _____ theory.

   Answer: psychosocial
   Page Ref: 69

2) The eating disorder that involves binge eating is _____.

   Answer: Bulimia
   Page Ref: 65

3) Children experiencing the Eriksonian conflict of trust vs. mistrust are in Piaget's _____
   stage.

   Answer: sensorimotor
   Page Ref: 69

4) Primary school students strive to avoid feeling _____ when they are not allowed to do certain things.

Answer: guilt
Page Ref: 69

5) The relationship between perseverance and a job completed is what Erikson calls _____.

Answer: industry
Page Ref: 70

6) Adolescents who fail to develop a strong identity are likely to experience _____.

Answer: role confusion
Page Ref: 70

7) According to Erikson, the main conflict for adolescents involves the search for _____.

Answer: identity
Page Ref: 76

8) Adolescents who do not experiment with different identities or consider a range of options experience identity _____.

Answer: foreclosure
Page Ref: 71

9) Individuals who reach no conclusion about who or what they are or what they want to do with their lives experience identity _____.

Answer: diffusion/moratorium
Page Ref: 71

10) In adulthood, one of the conflicts that people must face is *stagnation vs.* _____.

Answer: *generativity*
Page Ref: 72

11) Urie Bronfenbrenner's theory, which describes the social and cultural contexts of development is referred to as his _____ model of development.

Answer: bioecological

Explanation: Bronfenbrenner's *bioecological model* describes the nested social and cultural contexts that shape development.
Page Ref: 72

12) According to Urie Bronfenbrenner, families and teachers are part of a child's _____ system.

Answer: micro
Page Ref: 73

13) People who have a positive self-concept are said to have high _____.

Answer: self-esteem
Page Ref: 85

14) The relationship between self-esteem and academic success is _____.

Answer: positive
Page Ref: 87

15) According to Selman, people who perceive how different social and cultural values would influence the perceptions of a bystander are said to have _____ ability.

Answer: perspective-taking
Page Ref: 94

16) Situations in which people must make difficult decisions are called _____.

Answer: moral dilemmas
Page Ref: 95

17) A "punishment-obedience" orientation characterizes Kohlberg's stage of moral reasoning known as _____.

Answer: preconventional
Page Ref: 96

18) While moral issues involve the basic rights of individuals, rules and expectations of a particular group of people that are established arbitrarily are _____.

Answer: social conventions
Page Ref: 97-98

19) Two important influences on the development of moral behavior are internalization and _____.

Answer: modeling
Page Ref: 101

20) Whether or not a student cheats on a test or research paper in school depends on the _____.

Answer: particular situation
Page Ref: 101-102

21) Stepbrothers and half-sisters who live in the same household belong to _____ families.

Answer: blended
Page Ref: 74

22) Long-term adjustment to the divorce of a student's parents seems to be more difficult for
_____ than for _____.

Answer: boys; girls
Page Ref: 75

23) Because children with learning disabilities and mental retardation may respond
inappropriately to peers, they are at risk for developing feelings of _____.

Answer: loneliness
Page Ref: 82

24) Teachers who observe children with frequent, severe bruises and other signs of physical and
behavioral trauma should be alerted to the possibility of _____.

Answer: child abuse
Page Ref: 83

True/False Questions

1) Erikson, like Piaget, saw development as a passage through a series of interdependent stages.

Answer: TRUE
Page Ref: 67

2) Approximately two-thirds of people with eating disorders actually receive treatment and get
help.

Answer: FALSE
Page Ref: 66

3) According to Erikson, children's first development crisis is resolving *initiative vs. guilt.*

Answer: FALSE
Page Ref: 67

4) Children's failure to gain a sense of industry may result in feelings of inferiority.

Answer: TRUE
Page Ref: 67

5) Adolescents who do not experiment with different identities or consider a range of options are
experiencing identity diffusion.

Answer: FALSE
Page Ref: 71

6) According to Erikson, adolescents who are having difficulty with identity choices are
experiencing a moratorium.

Answer: TRUE
Page Ref: 71

7) A successful means of dealing with the adolescent identity crisis is identity foreclosure.

Answer: FALSE
Page Ref: 71

8) Children whose parents are divorcing can benefit from authoritative teachers.

Answer: TRUE

Explanation: *Authoritative teachers* are both warm and clear about requirements, which can be especially helpful for children experiencing the divorce of their parents.
Page Ref: 103

9) The basic difference between self–concept and self–esteem is that self–concept is a cognitive structure while self–esteem is an affective structure.

Answer: TRUE
Page Ref: 85

10) Learning in collaborative and cooperative settings affect self–esteem.

Answer: TRUE
Page Ref: 87

11) Research suggests boys' and girls' self–esteem slightly decreases as students transition to junior high.

Answer: TRUE
Page Ref: 90

12) Students' perceptions about their academic self–concepts are typically based on their actual abilities.

Answer: FALSE
Page Ref: 87

13) Some children from different ethnic groups hear and accept messages that devalue their own group.

Answer: TRUE
Page Ref: 91–92

14) Ethnic heritage and pride are especially important influences on self–esteem.

Answer: TRUE
Page Ref: 92

15) Selman's view is that the development of perspective-taking continues from early childhood to adulthood.

Answer: TRUE
Page Ref: 94

16) Being recognized as a "good" child by one's parents is especially important at the preconventional stage of moral reasoning.

Answer: FALSE
Page Ref: 96

17) Kohlberg's theory of moral development has been criticized because it does not differentiate between true moral issues and social conventions in the early stages.

Answer: TRUE
Page Ref: 96–97

18) When individuals adopt external standards as their own, they are internalizing those standards.

Answer: TRUE
Page Ref: 101

19) Internalization and modeling are important influences on the development of moral behavior.

Answer: TRUE
Page Ref: 101

20) Aggression and assertiveness are synonymous behaviors.

Answer: FALSE
Page Ref: 78

21) According to research conducted by Garbarino and deLara (2002) and estimated 100–200 students avoid school every day or drop out of school because they are afraid of their peers at school.

Answer: FALSE

Explanation: The researchers estimate 160,000 students avoid or drop out of school due to peer aggression and feelings of being victimized.
Page Ref: 80

22) Teachers should pay attention to which children are rejected and play alone

Answer: TRUE

Explanation: In addition to paying attention to children at risk for feelings of loneliness and/or victimization teachers should talk to parents about their child's experiences with peers.

Page Ref: 82

23) In order to promote emotional competence, teachers are encourages to help students keep their emotions to themselves and not self-disclose their feelings.

Answer: FALSE

Explanation: Teachers should help student find a vocabulary of emotions and appropriate emotive descriptors in order to encourage emotional competence.

Page Ref: 94

Short Answer Questions

1) What personal conflicts are most likely to be experienced by individuals of the following ages: (a) age of three; (b) age of 10; and (c) age of 15? What can parents or teachers do to help the individual achieve a healthy resolution?

Answer: At age three, conflicts concern achieving a balance between what one wants to do and what one can (is permitted to) do. Children want to "try out" adult roles and show initiative. Parents should encourage these interests by providing supervision without interference. At age 10, the conflict is between feeling accomplished or industrious vs. feeling inferior. Children become interested in excelling in academics and in interactions with peers. Teachers should provide students with opportunities to achieve and be independent, while supporting those who seem discouraged. At age 15, the major crisis is struggling to find an identity of sense of self that provides a basis for adulthood. Teachers need to provide models for career choices, allow students to express themselves in working out personal problems, and give students realistic feedback about themselves.

Page Ref: 64-66

2) Define the term "self-concept." How do school experiences affect the formation of self-concept? How is physical development related to school experiences and self-concept?

Answer: Self-concept is the composite of ideas, feelings, and attitudes people have about themselves. Children's early self-concepts relate to their appearance and, particularly later, to their actions. As children mature, their self-concepts vary from situation to situation. It is not clear whether positive self-concept leads to success in school or vice versa, but the two seem to be correlated. As self-concept is developed, so are relationships with others, as manifested in part through development of the senses of intention and perspective-taking (see Selman's five-step model). Also, time of physical development helps to influence the self-concept of adolescents.

Page Ref: 85-87

3) Outline Kohlberg's three levels of moral development and describe an example of reasoning at each level.

Answer: Kohlberg's Level 1 involves reasoning based on personal needs and others' rules. "If I'm not caught, it's okay to do." Level 2 involves adherence to others' approval, to the laws of society as absolute doctrines, and to the seeking of approval from others. "The rule says it's wrong, so Johnny was bad." Level 3 involves more abstract, philosophical analyses that judge individuals' idiosyncratic needs in particular situations relative to the laws that protect society as a whole. "Although Brenda broke the law, there were special circumstances that gave her little choice."

Page Ref: 95–96

4) Describe the four types of parenting styles according to the work of Diana Baumrind (1991).

Answer: The four types of parenting styles are based on the level of warmth and control provided by the parents:

Authoritarian parents (low warmth, high control) seem cold and controlling in their parenting.
Authoritative parents (high warmth, high control) set clear limits and enforce the rules in a caring manner.
Permissive parents (high warmth, low control) are warm and nurturing, but set few rules and/or consequences for misbehavior.
Rejecting/Neglecting parents (low warmth, low control) may appear to not care at all and may even be absents. They may appear to not want to be bothered with their parenting responsibilities.

Page Ref: 74

Case Studies

A member of your school board gives an impassioned speech regarding the need for "a dollar's worth of learning for every dollar spent." "The children of today are rarely challenged," he asserts. "We need to promote accelerated programs." For the next hour, he outlines a plan to introduce algebra in the sixth grade, physics in the seventh grade, reading in the preschool, and skipping grades for any student who scores at the 60th percentile on the State standardized achievement test. Some people in the audience look skeptical, others show strong displeasure, but a surprising number appear to agree with the sentiments expressed.

1) What is your general reaction to the speaker's arguments? Why do you feel that way?

Answer: Drawing upon Piaget's idea that we cannot necessarily speed up the cognitive process, we can provide students with the appropriate amount of challenge. In addition to achievement and cognitive growth, we must also explore the students' personal, social, and moral development. In chapter 2, Woolfolk notes that the brain is still developing in children and adolescents which creates some biological limitations on cognitive development. In chapter 3, Woolfolk points out the distinction between fluid and crystalized intelligence. Crystallized intelligence develops slowly over time and suggests we cannot force learning in too fast of a manner.

Page Ref: 66

2) Argue for or against the proposed program drawing from the ideas of (a) Piaget, (b) Erikson, and (c) Kohlberg.

Answer: All three theorists may be dissatisfied with the school board's new policy of allowing students to skip grades. The student may have the cognitive abilities and still be lacking in personal, social, and moral development. Thus, a student who had not successfully transitioned through Erikson's psychosocial stage of Industry vs. Inferiority may have a sense of inferiority, failure, and incompetence. It would be difficult for this student to be placed in an advanced classroom with older students, who are in Erikson's stage of Identity vs. Role Confusion. While the younger student is concerned with issues of competence, the older students may be focusing on issues such as gender equity, politics, and their career. We might also expect a difference in students' perspective-taking abilities due to their age and experience. As noted by Selman, there are developmental differences between young adolescents and late adolescents in regards to perspective-taking. Consistent with Selman's and Kohlberg's theories, the older adolescent has the ability to consider how social and cultural factors influence situations. We can imagine how these developmental differences would be important in a situation where a student observed another student cheating in class.

Page Ref: 67-70, 93-97

3) How might accelerated programs generally influence children's (a) self-concept and (b) social development?

Answer: One of the best ways to increase self-esteem is through students' accomplishments. Thus, a student who is an accelerated program has the awareness that they have surpassed the typical standards. They also know that they have legitimately succeeded in academic areas which are valued by important people in their environment. The accelerated program may increase students' academic self-concept and their self-concept for non-academic areas. In particular, students have self-concepts related to their physical ability, physical appearance, and peer relationships. Teachers will want to monitor the affects of the accelerated program on the student's self-concept for peer relationships, which can influence the student's social development. Beginning in the middle school years, children begin to make their self-evaluations in part by comparing themselves to other students. Of concern might be the student, who has a very low non-academic self-concept, and yet is placed in an advanced literature class with much older students who have very high self-concepts for peer relationships.

Page Ref: 85-87

4) In your opinion, in what ways can educational systems become more effective without developing moral dilemmas for children?

Answer: Teachers can be very intentional about what they model to their students. Specifically, they need to be careful not to use threats of aggression in order to maintain classroom discipline. They can also model appropriate assertiveness, nonviolent conflict resolution strategies, appropriate self-defense, and the benefits of cooperation. Teachers can design their classroom and learning activities to be based on principles on an ethic of care. For example, the classroom should contain enough of the highly valued toys/books so as not to cause conflicts related to limited resources. Learning activities can be based on group projects that require collaboration. Until children have internalized the moral rules, teachers will want to provide direct instruction regarding how to engage in positive social behaviors and how to avoid aggression, bullying, and the isolation of other students.

Page Ref: 95–97

Annie, a fifth-grade student in Mr. Baer's class, is being quiet and sullen for the fifth day in a row. "I just can't do this writing stuff," she finally says in an appeal to Mr. Baer. "I'm not a good student. Give me P.E. or art over this stuff any day!"

5) Discuss Annie's problem from the perspective of the development of self-concept and self-esteem.

Answer: It is important to note that in this case study we do not have any information about Annie's actual performance. She could be doing fine in the writing class and yet still have a low self-concept in the area of reading. The fact that Annie is a fifth-grader is relevant to this situation. Beginning in middle-school, students tend to evaluate their performance relative to their own standards and by making comparisons to other students. Annie may be an effective reader, but she is referencing her English skills to her exceptionally high math abilities. Also, she may be placed in an accelerated English class with many high-achieving students. The teacher will also want to listen carefully to Annie's feelings related to her low reading self-concept. In regards to self-esteem, Annie may be overcritical of herself and believe "I am a bad student (or bad daughter) if I cannot excel in reading." If she has low self-esteem, she may begin to ignore, deny, or devalue some of her other academic strengths.

Page Ref: 85–87

6) Analyze her views of self in the different subjects that she mentions in her interactions with people. For example, is her "writing" self-concept likely to influence her interaction or relationships with peers or parents? Explain.

Answer: The work of Marsh and Shavelson (1985) reveals that self-concept is a hierarchical construct. Thus, Annie's reading self-concept will be most related to her English self-concept. Research indicates students' academic self-concept is related to their parent relationships. Although indirectly related through one's general self-concept, a person's reading self-concept is less related to their self-concept for peer relationships. A student's self-concept is based on many experiences and events, so the teacher in this case study needs to realize it may take time to increase Annie's reading self-concept. It would be unrealistic for Mr. Baer to expect that one successful reading assignment or one statement of encouragement will immediately change Annie's self-concept.

Page Ref: 85–87

7) Based on the guidelines provided in your textbook, suggest some ways that Annie's teacher can help her to develop a more positive self-concept as a student in general and on writing tasks in particular.

Answer: First, Mr. Baer will want to obtain more information about Annie's goals and expectations for reading. Also, it would be useful to know the extent to which she values (and perceives others to value) reading achievement. It is important for Annie to experience success in the area of reading. However, the task must provide legitimate success and must be appropriately challenging. The teacher will want to avoid competitive reading assignments or projects that involve competition. He will also want to provide Annie with individual feedback rather than normative references (e.g., grades should not be posted publicly). Finally, specific reading tasks should be broken down into small measurable components so Annie can quickly begin experiencing success and self-reinforcement.

Page Ref: 85–87

Chapter 4 Learner Differences and Learning Needs

Multiple-Choice Questions

1) Woolfolk's position on the issue of labeling exceptional students is that such practices

   A) are clearly detrimental and should not be continued.

   B) are far more beneficial than harmful and definitely need to be continued.

   C) have both positive and negative effects and need to be exercised cautiously.

   D) should be used only with physical handicaps that do not affect mental or emotional functioning.

   Answer: C

   Explanation: C) The issue of labeling exceptional students is controversial. Such practices can become *self-fulfilling prophecies*. Because teachers may expect students to act like the label, they may treat them differently, thus reinforcing the very behaviors that need to be replaced with more adaptive behavior.

   Page Ref: 110
   Skill: Knowledge
   P: .96
   D: .02

2) The major difference between a *disability* and a *handicap* is that a *disability* is an inability to do something specific, such as being unable to hear or to walk, while a *handicap*

   A) has both advantages and disadvantages.

   B) is a disadvantage in certain situations.

   C) is a disadvantage in most situations.

   D) will become a disability.

   Answer: B

   Explanation: B) There is an important difference between a disability and a handicap. A *disability* is an inability to do something specific, such as walking or seeing or hearing. A *handicap* is a disadvantage in certain situations. Some educators have suggested that we drop the word *handicap* altogether because the source of the word is demeaning ("cap-in-hand" or begging to survive).

   Page Ref: 110
   Skill: Knowledge

3) Which one of the following statements is **TRUE** about intelligence?

   A) It is generally regarded today to be a poor predictor of academic achievement.

   B) It is theorized to be a collection of abilities by many psychologists.

   C) The first formal intelligence testing was conducted by Plato.

   D) Throughout history there has been general agreement about its meaning.

   Answer: B

   Explanation: B) Many psychologists theorize that *intelligence is a collection of abilities rather than one type of ability*. Still throughout history and today, there is little agreement about the specific meaning of intelligence.

   Page Ref: 111
   Skill: Knowledge
   P: .75
   D: .33

4) Alan performs well on most academic and learning tasks, but he has some difficulty on a test involving memorization of numbers. Spearman's explanation for Alan's test scores is expressed best by the statement that Alan

   A) has a high g factor but has problems with specific abilities.

   B) has good specific abilities but lacks a strong g factor.

   C) is skilled in learning but unskilled in memory.

   D) lacks the general intellectual capacity to perform math well.

   Answer: A

   Explanation: A) Spearman would interpret Alan to have a *high g factor, but problems with a specific ability*. The high *g* factor is indicated by his high performance on most academic tasks; the specific problem is reflected by his difficulties in memorizing numbers.

   Page Ref: 112
   Skill: Understanding
   P: .84
   D: .20

5) According to the work of Cattell and Horn (1963, 1988), there are two types of intelligence:

   A) Fluid and contextualized

   B) Fluid and crystallized

   C) Interpersonal and intrapersonal

   D) Global and verbal

Answer: B

Explanation: B) *Fluid intelligence is based on abilities related to mental efficiency,* nonverbal abilities grounded in brain development. Fluid intelligence involves non–verbal and culture-free types of mental abilities. *Crystallized intelligence involves verbal abilities, which are influenced by culture.* People who have high amounts of crystallized intelligence can apply culturally approved problem–solving methods.

Page Ref: 112
Skill: Knowledge

6) A teacher who knows how to effectively use cooperative learning in his or her classroom is demonstrating

   A) naturalist intelligence.

   B) speed of processing.

   C) linguistic intelligence.

   D) crystallized intelligence.

Answer: D

Explanation: D) *Crystallized intelligence is the ability to solve problems* or handle daily tasks with knowledge and abilities that have been developed over time with experience. Crystallized intelligence increases over the lifespan.

Page Ref: 112

7) The theory that defines intelligence as encompassing at least eight separate kinds of intelligence is

   A) Binet's theory of school–related intelligences.

   B) Gardner's theory of multiple intelligences.

   C) Spearman's g factor concept.

   D) Sternberg's components view of intelligence.

Answer: B

Explanation: B) *Gardner's theory of multiple intelligences* encompasses at least eight kinds of intelligence: linguistic, musical, spatial, logical–mathematical, bodily kinesthetic, intrapersonal, interpersonal, and naturalist.

Page Ref: 113
Skill: Knowledge
P: .76
D: .33

8) Based on the underlying idea of Gardner's theory, one might expect minor brain damage to

    A) affect all types of functioning with about the same degree of impact.

    B) cause more severe physical problems than mental problems.

    C) interfere with one type of functioning but not affect other areas.

    D) lower general intelligence but have less impact on specific types of intelligence.

Answer: C

Explanation: C) Based on Gardner's theory, one might expect minor brain damage to *interfere with one type of functioning but not to affect other areas.* Evidence showing that such occurs (i.e., localized or specific dysfunctions) provided a basis for Gardner's ideas about multiple intelligence.

Page Ref: 114
Skill: Understanding
P: .83
D: .24

9) Robert Sternberg's triarchic theory of intelligence includes what three distinct types of intelligence?

    A) Analytic, practical, and meta-components

    B) Creative, analytic, and practical

    C) Insight, creativity, and practical

    D) Performance, knowledge, and analytic components

Answer: B

Explanation: B) Robert Sternberg's triarchic theory of intelligence encompasses three distinct types of mental processes: *(1) analytic intelligence; (2) creativity; and (3) practical intelligence.*

Page Ref: 117–118
Skill: Knowledge
P: .77
D: .17

10) Stephanie has selected a problem-solving strategy and monitors her progress in applying it. She is using

    A) knowledge-acquisition components.

    B) meta-components.

    C) performance components.

    D) process and product components.

Answer: B

Explanation: B) According to Sternberg, Stephanie is using *meta-components* to perform the function of monitoring her progress in performing a task. Meta-components and performance components (executing strategies) are two types of mental processes (called "components") that led to Stephanie's intelligent behavior.

Page Ref: 118
Skill: Understanding
P: .26
D: .32

11) All children in Ms. Gray's math class can now solve subtraction problems, but Larry does them much more quickly and efficiently than most of his classmates. Sternberg would call this

    A) automaticity.

    B) flexibility.

    C) insight.

    D) meta-components.

Answer: A

Explanation: A) Larry is demonstrating *automaticity*, which according to Sternberg's theory is the ability to perform tasks quickly and efficiently, without much mental effort.

Page Ref: 118
Skill: Understanding
P: .67
D: .28

12) What psychologist developed the concept of *mental age*?

    A) Binet

    B) Gardner

    C) Sternberg

    D) Wechsler

Answer: A

Explanation: A) The concept of mental age was developed by *Binet*. Gardner and Sternberg proposed theories of intelligence and Wechsler created a series of individually administered intelligence tests.

Page Ref: 119
Skill: Knowledge

13) A five-year-old is found to have a mental age of seven on Binet's original IQ test. What is the estimate of the child's intelligence quotient?

   A) 115

   B) 130

   C) 140

   D) 170

Answer: C

Explanation: C) The original intelligence quotient was determined by dividing mental age by chronological age. For example, if a five-year-old child performed at a mental age of 7, his/her IQ would be *140 (7/5 ⇑ 100)*.

Page Ref: 119
Skill: Understanding
P: .63
D: .43

14) An intelligence quotient is a

   A) score comparing mental and chronological age.

   B) score derived from a group achievement test.

   C) way of expressing an individual's mental age.

   D) way to compare mental age with cognitive level.

Answer: A

Explanation: A) An intelligence quotient is a score *comparing mental age (MA) to chronological age (CA)*. It is the way that IQ was originally computed and is derived from the formula: (MA/CA) × 100.

Page Ref: 119
Skill: Knowledge
P: .80
D: .23

15) A deviation IQ score indicates

   A) how a person compares with others in his/her age group.

   B) how close mental age is to chronological age.

   C) the degree of how well mental age is related to a particular cognitive level.

   D) the difference between scores on group and individual IQ tests.

Answer: A

Explanation: A) The original intelligent quotient formula for determining IQ has been replaced by the concept of deviation IQ. This new concept bases IQ on *how individuals perform in relation to others (a norming sample) of the same age*.

Page Ref: 119
Skill: Knowledge
P: .66
D: .38

16) Compared to individual ability tests, a major limitation of group ability tests is that group tests

    A) are more expensive to administer and more difficult to interpret than individual ability tests.

    B) are less likely to produce an accurate picture of a person's abilities.

    C) provide a measure of general, but not specific, abilities.

    D) take much more skill on the part of the teacher to administer and interpret.

Answer: B

Explanation: B) Group intelligence tests are *less likely to produce an accurate picture of a person's ability* because such practices are susceptible to bias due to reading ability. That is, if a person is a poor reader, he/she may fail to answer questions correctly that would not be difficult if read orally by an examiner administering an individual intelligence test such as the Binet or the Wechsler series.

Page Ref: 119–120
Skill: Understanding
P: .49
D: .35

17) Approximately what percent of the general population scores over 100 on a standardized IQ test?

    A) 20

    B) 50

    C) 70

    D) 80

Answer: B

Explanation: B) About *50 percent* of a population scores 100 or higher on IQ tests, because IQ scores are normally distributed with 100 as the midpoint of the distribution. Half of the scores are 100 and above; half of the scores are below 100.

Page Ref: 120
Skill: Knowledge
P: .75
D: .31

18) Dianne's deviation IQ increased five points over her eighth-grade year. Her apparent improvement in deviation IQ score can be explained most validly

   A) as a significant improvement in her intellectual skills.

   B) as an exception to the general rule of IQ stability.

   C) by the influence of measurement error.

   D) by the relatively low validity of IQ tests.

Answer: C

Explanation: C) *Measurement error* can lead to fluctuations of a few points in students' IQ scores. Such error may reflect guessing, testing conditions, or internal conditions (how a student feels that day).

Page Ref: 119
Skill: Understanding
P: .60
D: .36

19) A major advantage of using standardized intelligence tests is that they

   A) are good indicators of the underlying cognitive processes needed for successful test performance.

   B) provide ways of comparing a child's performance with those of other children in the same situation.

   C) reward students for original and novel responses as opposed to school achievement.

   D) sample a wide variety of conditions under which intelligent behaviors can be observed.

Answer: B

Explanation: B) Standardized intelligence tests have the advantage of *comparing students who were tested in the same situation*. Unfortunately, they do not allow for diverse or creative responses or sample a wide range of conditions under which intelligent behavior can be observed.

Page Ref: 120–121
Skill: Understanding
P: .75
D: .21

20) What is the typical correlation between deviation IQ scores from an individual intelligence test and school achievement for the general population of school-age students?

   A) About zero

   B) Moderately positive

   C) Weak negative

   D) Weak positive

Answer: B

Explanation: B) The typical correlation or relationship between IQ and school achievement is usually approximately 0.65, *indicating a moderate and significant positive relationship.*

Page Ref: 121
Skill: Knowledge
P: .61
D: .52

21) Most psychologists today believe that intelligence is influenced

   A) about equally by heredity and environment.

   B) about 25 percent by heredity and 75 percent by environment.

   C) about 75 percent by heredity and 25 percent by environment.

   D) minimally by both heredity and environment.

Answer: A

Explanation: A) Psychologists today believe that intelligence is *influenced equally by heredity and environment.* Heredity determines one's potential, while environment shapes the level of intelligence that is actually attained. Therefore, both are important determinants of one's intellectual behaviors and often interact.

Page Ref: 121
Skill: Knowledge
P: .73
D: .44

22) What type of grouping is used in the Joplin Plan?

   A) Cross-grade

   B) Mixed-ability

   C) Tracking

   D) Within-class

Answer: A

Explanation: A) The Joplin Plan uses *cross-grade grouping* in which children are reassigned to classes in a certain subject (e.g., reading) solely on the basis of ability in that subject, regardless of grade level.

Page Ref: 122
Skill: Knowledge
P: .58
D: .57

23) At Meadow Lane Elementary School, there are four fifth-grade classes specifically arranged so that one contains high achievers only, one contains low achievers only, and two contain mid-range achievers. Based on research results, this type of orientation is most likely to be

   A) effective for high-achievers and low-achievers.

   B) ineffective for high-achievers.

   C) ineffective for low-achievers.

   D) neither better nor worse than conventional, mixed-ability groups.

Answer: C

Explanation: C) Research indicates that between-class ability grouping is *typically ineffective for low achievers*. When assigned to low-track classes, students are likely to receive less enthusiastic instruction and lose the opportunity to be stimulated by higher-achieving students. In addition, their self-esteem may suffer from the stigma of being in the "slow" class.

Page Ref: 122
Skill: Understanding

24) A disadvantage of segregated-ability classes is

   A) children in lower-ability classes may believe that they are less capable than other students.

   B) individual differences are too great to apply special programs.

   C) student performance in high-ability classes tends to decrease.

   D) teachers find it more difficult to teach this type of class than traditional classes.

Answer: A

Explanation: A) One disadvantage of segregated-ability classes is that *lower-ability students may feel that they are less capable* than other students. As a consequence, self-esteem and interest in learning may be reduced.

Page Ref: 122-123
Skill: Knowledge
P: .96
D: .05

25) A recommended procedure for within-class ability grouping is to

    A) establish competition among ability groups in order to increase motivation.

    B) keep the same groups for as many subject matter tasks as possible.

    C) make frequent changes in group placements when achievement levels change.

    D) place the highest achieving student together with the lowest achieving student.

Answer: C

Explanation: C) It is recommended that within-class ability groups should be formed and reformed on the basis of students' current performance in the subject being taught. This orientation implies *frequent changes in group placement as achievement levels change*.

Page Ref: 124
Skill: Knowledge
P: .81
D: .27

26) Terman's classic study found that children who are gifted tend to be

    A) larger and stronger as adults than their peers.

    B) less athletic than their peers.

    C) less socially skilled than their peers.

    D) teachers' pets.

Answer: A

Explanation: A) Terman's classic study found that gifted children tend to be *larger and stronger than their peers*. In general, the findings suggested that giftedness was associated with better adjustment and development than for non-gifted children.

Page Ref: 150
Skill: Knowledge

27) What affective characteristic has been added to Renzulli and Reis' definition of giftedness?

    A) Commitment

    B) Common sense

    C) Creativity

    D) Quick response

Answer: A

Explanation: A) Renzulli and Reis have defined giftedness as a combination of three basic characteristics: above-average ability, high level of creativity, and high *task commitment* as *an affective* characteristic. Quick responses and creativity are cognitive characteristics, while common sense is perhaps a combination of cognitive and affective characteristics (depending on the situation).

Page Ref: 149
Skill: Understanding

28) Research indicates that gifted students who were popular in school were

    A) less likely than their peers to be emotionally stable as adults.

    B) less likely to maintain serious intellectual interests as adults.

    C) more likely to experience social adjustment problems when accelerated.

    D) more likely to prefer the company of others of their own age.

Answer: B

Explanation: B) Research has indicated that gifted students who were popular in school were
                less likely than other gifted students to maintain serious intellectual interests as
                adults. None of the other options is true.

Page Ref: 150
Skill: Knowledge
P: .65
D: .44

29) Which one of the following assessments would provide the most valid basis for identifying
students who are academically gifted?

    A) A group achievement test

    B) A group intelligence test

    C) An individual IQ test

    D) Teacher observations and grades

Answer: C

Explanation: C) The most valid basis for identifying students who are gifted is an *individual IQ*
                test, such as the Binet tests and the Wechsler series. These tests, though not
                perfect predictors of giftedness, are more reliable indicators of high ability
                than are group tests, teacher observations, or group achievement tests.

Page Ref: 151
Skill: Knowledge

30) Current beliefs about teaching the gifted

    A) clearly favor acceleration over enrichment.

    B) clearly favor enrichment over acceleration.

    C) view both acceleration and enrichment as beneficial.

    D) view neither acceleration nor enrichment as beneficial.

Answer: C

Explanation: C) Experts on teaching students who are gifted now *view both acceleration and*
                enrichment as beneficial. Acceleration means skipping grades; enrichment
                means giving students more challenging and sophisticated work in their
                regular grades.

Page Ref: 152
Skill: Knowledge
P: .74
D: .39

31) Recent research has indicated that acceleration of students who are gifted

    A) has been unnecessarily discouraged in the past.

    B) is related to lower achievement.

    C) results in poor social and emotional adjustment.

    D) robs students of the companionship of their age group.

Answer: A

Explanation: A) Woolfolk's position is that acceleration for the gifted has been *discouraged*
                unnecessarily in the past. Research on acceleration indicates primarily positive
                effects or, at worst, no harmful effects of acceleration on gifted students.
                Acceleration is certainly **NOT** related to lower achievement for gifted
                students, nor does it result in poor social and emotional adjustment. Quite the
                opposite is true. Finally, gifted students, particularly the highly gifted, prefer
                the companionship of their intellectual peers to simply age–related peers.

Page Ref: 152
Skill: Knowledge
P: .58
D: .35

32) What type of learning style characterizes a person who is motivated to learn by external
rewards and the desire to be viewed in a good light by others?

    A) Analytic–processing

    B) Deep–processing

    C) Pattern–processing

    D) Surface–processing

Answer: D

Explanation: D) A person who is motivated to learn by external rewards and the desire to be
                viewed in a good light by others is said to have a *surface-processing* learning
                style, rather than deep processing, analytic processing, or pattern processing
                styles.

Page Ref: 125
Skill: Knowledge
P: .88
D: .18

33) Zero reject is a basic principle meaning

A) children with disabilities who come from low income families must receive more federal funding than those who come from high income families.

B) aggressive children who bully other children must be removed from the class immediately.

C) it is acceptable to write an IEP for children with profound disabilities every other year rather than on an annual basis.

D) no students with a disability can be denied a free public education.

Answer: D

Explanation: D) Zero reject means there are no exceptions and all students, no how severe there disability, must be provided a free public education.

Page Ref: 127
Skill: Knowledge

34) An implication of the regular education initiative is that

A) more special education teachers will need to be trained for these classrooms.

B) special education classrooms will require additional resources.

C) teachers will need to be more knowledgeable about teaching handicapped children.

D) 10 to 20 percent increases in student to teacher ratios in regular classes are necessary.

Answer: C

Explanation: C) An implication of the regular education initiative is that regular teachers will need to take more responsibility for teaching children with disabilities who are increasingly being "mainstreamed" into regular classes. *Regular teachers will need to become more knowledgeable about teaching children with disabilities.*

Page Ref: 127–128
Skill: Knowledge
P: .91
D: .12

35) *Inclusion*, as it relates to special education, means that students will

    A) be included in regular classrooms for each activity in the daily routine of the school.

    B) become involved in the development and implementation of his/her IEP.

    C) demonstrate normal ability within his/her handicapping condition.

    D) participate in the typical subject–matter lessons in the school's regular classrooms.

Answer: D

Explanation: D) The concept of inclusion schools means that students with exceptional qualities will *participate in the typical subject matter lessons in regular classrooms*. These students will be integrated with all students in classrooms of an inclusion school. Inclusion does not, however, require students with exceptional abilities to participate in every activity in the daily routine of the school.

Page Ref: 128
Skill: Knowledge
P: .54
D: .34

36) An IEP is a written plan for a specific student's education, and it must include

    A) career goals.

    B) needed transitional services.

    C) specific educational goals.

    D) specific educational goals, current functioning level, and career goals.

Answer: C

Explanation: C) Each IEP is unique for a given student and *must include specific educational goals for that student*. Career goals are not usually a part of an IEP, and a statement of needed transitional goals is relevant only for students 16 years old (although sometimes for 14–year–old students).

Page Ref: 127–128
Skill: Knowledge
P: .81
D: .29

37) What is the largest category of students with disabilities?

    A) Students who are slow learners

    B) Students with a physical disability

    C) Students with an emotional handicap

    D) Students with a learning disability

Answer: D

Explanation: D) Almost 50 percent of all students who receive some type of special education services is diagnosed as *having a learning disability*. This group of students is the largest single category of students with disabilities.

Page Ref: 131
Skill: Knowledge
P: .86
D: .15

38) Bill, age 16, is bright and articulate. His classmates watch him with great interest because he "will try almost anything." Unfortunately, his reading level is very low, probably no higher than fourth–grade level, and he does not succeed in most courses. This description of Bill would lead one to think first about the possibility of

    A) a learning disability.

    B) an emotional disturbance.

    C) giftedness.

    D) mental retardation.

Answer: A

Explanation: A) Because Bill is bright and popular, mental retardation and emotional disturbance would be ruled out. His reading difficulty also rules out being a student who is gifted. Moreover, Bill's problem with reading suggests that he is a student with a *specific learning disability*.

Page Ref: 131–132
Skill: Understanding
P: .80
D: .18

39) Tammy received her fourth *F* in her math class. She accepted the grade and believes that there is nothing she can do to improve her scores. Tammy appears to be experiencing

    A) a math ability problem.

    B) a passive learning problem.

    C) learned helplessness.

    D) poor study and attention skills.

Answer: C

Explanation: C) Tammy appears to be experiencing *learned helplessness*. She thinks that no matter what she does, it is wrong, so she quits trying. None of the other response choices fits Tammy's situation.

Page Ref: 131–132
Skill: Understanding
P: .92
D: .17

40) Charlene's school records indicate that she has been diagnosed with a learning disability. Mr. Fredericksen, her teacher for the new school year, will want to learn more about Charlene. However, his first reaction, based on the literature, is that Charlene will have problems

    A) controlling her emotions.

    B) paying attention.

    C) reading at grade level.

    D) thinking in a logical way.

Answer: C

Explanation: C) A student with a learning disability, such as Charlene, is most likely to have *reading problems,* as opposed to problems with attention, emotions, or thinking logically.

Page Ref: 132
Skill: Understanding

41) Hyperactivity can be most accurately described as a

    A) disease characterized by excessive nervousness.

    B) neurological disorder causing short attention spans.

    C) variable set of conditions with differing sets of causes.

    D) variable set of conditions with a single cause.

Answer: C

Explanation: C) Hyperactivity can be most accurately described as a *variable set of conditions with a variable set of causes*. Although hyperactive children have short attention spans and are restless, these behaviors will differ qualitatively from case to case.

Page Ref: 134
Skill: Knowledge

42) Peter is a student at Mainstreet High School. He has had problems in the past maintaining appropriate behavior in his science class. Mrs. Brady, a ninth-grade science teacher, observes Peter during a laboratory experiment in her class. Peter is very calm and composed since he began taking his medication for Attention Deficit Hyperactive Disorder. A problem with using drug therapy in treating this disorder is that

    A) neither Peter's behavior nor his participation in learning activities has improved.

    B) Peter's learning may not have improved even though his behavior improved.

    C) Peter may develop chemical dependency for the medicine used to treat this disorder.

    D) the expense of having to take the drug therapy may outweigh the benefits for Peter.

Answer: B

Explanation: B) The problem with using drug therapy to treat Peter's hyperactivity is that, *although behavior improves, learning may not*. Motivation training programs can be useful in filling this void if combined with instruction in learning and memory strategies. There is no evidence presented in Peter's scenario to indicate that neither his behavior nor his participation in learning activities has improved, nor is there evidence of developing a chemical dependency for his medication.

Page Ref: 134
Skill: Understanding
P: .71
D: .29

43) In treating hyperactivity, the medication that seems to work best is

    A) common aspirin.

    B) depressants.

    C) placebo prescriptions.

    D) stimulants.

Answer: D

Explanation: D) Ironically, *stimulants* (e.g., Ritalin) are used as medication in treating hyperactivity. Drug therapy, however, seems to be only a short-term remedy that deals with symptoms rather than with the causes of the condition.

Page Ref: 134
Skill: Knowledge
P: .81
D: .41

44) What type of intervention appears to be the most successful in helping students with attention deficits?

    A) Behavior management strategies

    B) Cognitive management training

    C) Cooperative learning strategies

    D) Socialization skills training

Answer: A

Explanation: A) *Behavior management strategies* seem to be the most effective in helping students with attention deficits. Such strategies supplement (or replace) drug therapy by teaching students strategies for learning.

Page Ref: 135–136
Skill: Knowledge
P: .56
D: .32

45) Attention Deficit Disorder refers to a condition that

    A) affects an individual's ability to focus on tasks and/or be patient.

    B) affects an individual's physical and language abilities.

    C) is characterized by excessive nervousness.

    D) is described as a type of learning disability.

Answer: A

Explanation: A) Attention Deficit Disorder refers to a *condition that affects a person's ability to focus on tasks and/or be patient.* It is not necessarily characterized by excessive nervousness and does not affect physical and language abilities, nor is this condition considered to be a learning disorder.

Page Ref: 134–135
Skill: Knowledge
P: .97
D: .07

46) Which one of the following behaviors is an example of an articulation disorder?

    A) Repeating a word several times in an utterance

    B) Saying "wike" for "like"

    C) Speaking in an inappropriate pitch

    D) Speaking too slowly or too rapidly

Answer: B

Explanation: B) An articulation disorder is characterized by the substitution of one sound for another. An example would be saying *"wike "* for *"like."*

Page Ref: 138
Skill: Understanding
P: .92
D: .07

47) Which of the following statements is **TRUE** regarding stuttering?

A) It affects girls more frequently than boys.

B) It is more likely to occur in preschool than in adolescence.

C) It is not classified as a speech impairment.

D) The causes are well known, but treatments are not.

Answer: B

Explanation: B) Stuttering is much more likely to occur in *preschool than in adolescence.* By adolescence, the incidence and severity of stuttering substantially decrease. Stuttering affects boys more than girls, and the causes are generally unknown.

Page Ref: 138
Skill: Knowledge
P: .81
D: .31

48) Students often complain about Debbie. Debbie is always speaking very loudly even when circumstances do not call for such behavior. What type of problem is she demonstrating?

A) Articulation

B) Oral language

C) Stuttering

D) Voicing

Answer: D

Explanation: D) Students, such as Debbie, who speak much too loudly for the circumstances would be described as having a *voicing* problem. Other indications of this type of problem are inappropriate pitch or quality of voice.

Page Ref: 138
Skill: Understanding
P: .99
D: .01

49) Which one of the following situations is considered a language *difference* rather than a language *disorder*?

A) Delayed language development

B) Failing to adapt language to the context

C) Interrupted language development

D) Speaking in a strong dialect

Answer: D

Explanation: D) Language differences primarily represent variations due to experiences in a particular society or culture and are not necessarily a disorder. An example would be *speaking in a strong dialect.*

Page Ref: 138
Skill: Understanding
P: .59
D: .22

50) Almost every definition of mental retardation includes the idea that individuals with mental retardation

    A) are functionally immature.

    B) cannot adapt adequately to their environment.

    C) have deviation IQ scores below 75.

    D) have limited verbal abilities.

Answer: B

Explanation: B) Almost every definition of mental retardation includes the idea that *individuals with mental retardation cannot adapt to their environment*. Specific deficiencies such as immaturity or poor verbal skills are considered less important than ability to adapt.

Page Ref: 139
Skill: Understanding
P: .42
D: .37

51) Rachele achieved an IQ score of 73 and has demonstrated difficulty with independent living and personal hygiene. Her doctor believes that Rachele's condition is the result of inadequate prenatal care. Which one of the following disabilities **BEST** reflects Rachele's condition?

    A) Attention deficit disorder

    B) Independent living disorder

    C) Learning disabled

    D) Mental retardation

Answer: D

Explanation: D) Rachele's condition fits the definition of *mental retardation* according the AAMR's definition. Poor prenatal care is one source of mental retardation.

Page Ref: 139–140
Skill: Understanding
P: .64
D: .32

52) Mr. Nowicki has learned that Jacqueline has moderate mental retardation. When presenting instructions to her, he states objectives and presents the same material in different ways. What is another strategy that can be useful?

   A) Develop a sizable list of target behaviors.

   B) Do not interfere with social development.

   C) Move quickly from one objective to the next.

   D) Work on practical skills based on the demands of adult life.

Answer: D

Explanation: D) Mr. Nowicki should not move quickly between objectives or develop a sizable list of objectives. A good strategy would be to *emphasize practical skills acquisition,* an orientation consistent with transition programming.

Page Ref: 140
Skill: Understanding
P: .88
D: .03

53) The trend today in educating students with mental retardation involves giving greater emphasis to what type of skill(s)?

   A) Aesthetic appreciation

   B) Psychomotor

   C) Self-help and domestic

   D) Sensory

Answer: C

Explanation: C) The trend today in educating mentally retarded students involves giving increased emphasis to *self-help and domestic skills.* This emphasis is called transition programming.

Page Ref: 140
Skill: Knowledge
P: .85
D: .25

54) Greta is experiencing difficulty in Mr. Popanopoulous' class because she has different needs than many of the other students. Greta must use a variable-speed tape recorder to record the lessons, she often struggles with spasticity, and she frequently uses finger spelling as a method of communication. Which of the following disorders does **NOT** appear to describe Greta's possible condition?

    A) Cerebral palsy

    B) Epilepsy

    C) Hearing impairment

    D) Visual impairment

Answer: A

Explanation: A) Greta's disabilities suggest the possibility of hearing impairment, visual impairment, or cerebral palsy (spasticity). Because there are no seizures involved, *epilepsy is not suggested.*

Page Ref: 148
Skill: Understanding
P: .34
D: .29

55) A student is having a generalized epileptic seizure. Your first response as the teacher should be to

    A) insert a pen or pencil in his mouth to protect the tongue.

    B) move hard objects away from the student.

    C) seek medical assistance immediately.

    D) try to restrain the student's movements.

Answer: B

Explanation: B) When a student has a generalized epileptic seizure, the teacher should *move hard objects away* to prevent the student from getting hurt. The teacher should remain calm and not attempt to intervene directly.

Page Ref: 146
Skill: Knowledge
P: .84
D: .22

56) Troy is frequently accused of day-dreaming during class. The problem has become annoying enough that his teacher has requested medical testing. These behaviors suggest the possible occurrence of

    A) a generalized epileptic seizure.

    B) a tonic-chronic seizure.

    C) an absence seizure.

    D) generalized cerebral palsy.

Answer: C

Explanation: C) Troy may be having an *absence seizure*. Absence seizures, in contrast to the more serious generalized seizures, are characterized by a brief loss of awareness or consciousness. The student may stare and look blank during this period which usually lasts from about one to 30 seconds.

Page Ref: 146
Skill: Understanding
P: .80
D: .29

57) What type of approach to understanding language seems best for students with hearing impairments?

    A) A combination of speech and manual reading methods

    B) Finger spelling only

    C) Sign language only

    D) Speech reading only

Answer: A

Explanation: A) Today, the trend is to *combine speech reading and manual methods of communication* when teaching hearing impaired students. Either strategy or finger spelling alone will **NOT** be very helpful.

Page Ref: 147
Skill: Knowledge

58) Loni has a vision impairment and you notice that she seems to have fewer problems working from photocopied material than from materials copied by hand. This difference is likely due to the

    A) better quality of the photocopied print.

    B) difference in print colors.

    C) kind of material being copied.

    D) size of the printing.

Answer: A

Explanation: A) For students with visual problems, the quality of the print is usually more important than the size. Thus, Loni is probably doing better *with the photocopied material because of its higher quality print.*

Page Ref: 147
Skill: Understanding

59) All of the following student conditions are covered under Section 504 **EXCEPT**

    A) diabetes.

    B) alcoholism.

    C) poverty.

    D) students with attention–deficit/hyperactivity disorder.

Answer: C

Explanation: C) *Section 504 covers students with medical or health needs* such as diabetes, drug addiction, severe allergies, temporary disabilities due to a n accident, alcoholism, and ADHD.

Page Ref: 129–130
Skill: Knowledge

60) According to Woolfolk's writing about individual differences and diversity

    A) differences among individuals are actually quite minimal compared to all of the characteristics we share.

    B) about 50% of the alphabetic sequence we share in genetic code is due to race.

    C) there really are no differences in learning preferences.

    D) most differences in abilities disappear by the time students begin adolescents.

Answer: A

Explanation: A) Myers (2005) research reveals the differences between races is actually very small (only about .012% of the alphabetic sequence in genetic code).

Page Ref: 154
Skill: Knowledge

Completion Questions

1) The type of language that teachers and others should use when referring to students with disabilities is _____.

Answer: person-first
Page Ref: 110

2) The theory of multiple intelligences consisting of at least eight separate entities was proposed by _____.

Answer: Gardner
Page Ref: 113

3) Having the ability to apply culturally accepted problem-solving methods is referred to as _____.

Answer: crystallized intelligence
Page Ref: 112

4) The type of intelligence that increases until adolescence and then gradually declines with age is _____.

Answer: fluid intelligence
Page Ref: 112

5) At the top of Carroll's three-tiered intelligence model is _____.

Answer: general intelligence (G)
Page Ref: 113

6) A multiple-part description of intelligence that emphasizes competence and coping with new experiences and the environment is the theory of _____ intelligence.

Answer: triarchic
Page Ref: 117

7) When a student identifies a problem-solving strategy and then monitors his progress toward solving the problem, the student is using _____.

Answer: meta-components
Page Ref: 118

8) The French psychologist credited with developing the first intelligence test is _____.

Answer: Binet
Page Ref: 119

9) The average deviation IQ score for the general population is _____.

Answer: 100
Page Ref: 119

10) The Joplin Plan utilizes _____ grouping.

Answer: cross-grade
Page Ref: 122

11) In their definition of giftedness, Renzulli and Reis added the affective characteristic of

_____.

Answer: task commitment
Page Ref: 149

12) Students who tend to be motivated by rewards and external standards take a
_____-processing approach to learning.

Answer: surface
Page Ref: 125

13) Classrooms in which teachers of students with disabilities and teachers of other students are involved in cooperative teaching are called _____ classrooms.

Answer: inclusion
Page Ref: 128

14) The unique instructional plan developed for each student with a disability is called a(n)

_____.

Answer: IEP
Page Ref: 127

15) The largest category of students with disabilities consists of students with _____.

Answer: learning disabilities
Page Ref: 131

16) A strong belief that one is unable to succeed or make a difference in achievement is called

_____.

Answer: learned helplessness
Page Ref: 133

17) Students who continually move about and do not sit still for any length of time are described
as _____.

Answer: hyperactive
Page Ref: 134

18) Students with learning disabilities also face another challenge in that they often have _____.

Answer: attention disorders
Page Ref: 136

19) A type of speech impairment that is characterized by difficulty in producing sounds is a(n) _____.

Answer: articulation disorder
Page Ref: 138

20) In educating children with mental retardation, a modern orientation that stresses adaptation to community living is _____ programming.

Answer: transition
Page Ref: 140

21) A disorder characterized by uncontrolled seizures is called _____.

Answer: epilepsy
Page Ref: 146

22) Cerebral palsy is commonly characterized by overly tense muscles or _____.

Answer: spasticity
Page Ref: 146

23) A student who repeats stories over and over or share obscure facts about topics peers may find boring may have _____ or Asperger syndrome.

Answer: autism

Explanation: *Autistic* students may not appreciate the thoughts and feelings of others and therefore struggle with understanding that peers may be bored with his or her repeated stories or trivial facts.
Page Ref: 148

24) Gifted children are typically, above average in general ability, highly creative, and have high levels of _____.

Answer: motivation.

Explanation: *Gifted learners* have above average general abilities, high levels of creativity, and maintain a high level of task commitment or motivation to achieve.
Page Ref: 149

True/False Questions

1) The practice of labeling exceptional students is clearly detrimental and should be discontinued.

Answer: FALSE
Page Ref: 110

2) According to Gardner, minor brain damage can be expected to affect all types of functioning with fairly equal impact.

Answer: FALSE
Page Ref: 113–114

3) Carroll's intelligence model contains over 70 specific abilities.

Answer: TRUE
Page Ref: 113

4) Solving a geometry problem will require students to use both their fluid and crystallized intelligences.

Answer: TRUE
Page Ref: 112

5) An individual who can retrieve information from his or her memory with great speed is demonstrating a high level of crystallized intelligence.

Answer: FALSE
Page Ref: 112

6) Intelligence scores are computed today as deviation IQs rather than ratio scores.

Answer: TRUE
Page Ref: 119

7) A relatively small positive change in deviation IQ scores can often be explained as a real improvement in intellectual skills.

Answer: FALSE
Page Ref: 119

8) Using the Joplin Plan might involve students from different grades working together.

Answer: TRUE
Page Ref: 122

9) Compared to field–independent learners, field–dependent learners are likely to see patterns as individual components.

Answer: FALSE
Page Ref: 110

10) A *disability* and a *handicap* refer to the same condition.

Answer: FALSE
Page Ref: 110

11) The *inclusion* concept requires that even students with severe handicaps must be placed in a regular classroom for at least part of the school day.

Answer: FALSE
Page Ref: 128

12) An IEP should be prepared by a team that includes the child's parents or guardians.

Answer: TRUE
Page Ref: 127

13) The largest category of students with disabilities includes students who are emotionally disabled.

Answer: FALSE
Page Ref: 131

14) More boys than girls are classified as hyperactive.

Answer: TRUE
Page Ref: 134

15) Many children with hyperactivity are made more manageable by being given stimulant drugs.

Answer: TRUE
Page Ref: 135

16) An "oral" approach to communicating with children who have hearing impairments is speech reading.

Answer: TRUE
Page Ref: 146–147

17) A student with mild retardation will be unlikely to read above the first-grade level.

Answer: FALSE
Page Ref: 139

18) The six dimensions of emotional/behavioral disorders include psychotic behavior.

Answer: TRUE
Page Ref: 142

19) Section 504 is a state law (found in most states) that protects students against any type of discrimination.

Answer: FALSE
Page Ref: 129

20) Providing books on tape would be considered a reasonable accommodation under Section 504.

   Answer: TRUE
   Page Ref: 130

21) Schools who receive federal funds must develop a plan for students who want to participate in school activities but have participation limits due to a diagnosed medical or health disability.

   Answer: TRUE
   Page Ref: 129–130

22) A student can be both gifted and learning disabled.

   Answer: TRUE

   Explanation: It is estimated there may be more than 180,000 American students who are both gifted and learning disabled.
   Page Ref: 151

23) Teachers are usually extremely accurate in identifying students who are gifted and talented.

   Answer: FALSE

   Explanation: Approximately 10% to 50% of teachers are not accurate in recognizing the gifted children in their classrooms.
   Page Ref: 151

Short Answer Questions

1) The use of labels to describe exceptional children has both positive and negative consequences. Discuss those consequences in terms of their impact on the students and the regular classroom teacher.

   Answer: Labels are necessary so that students may receive the protection offered by special programs and by PL 94–142, but labels may limit the students as well. Teachers may be uncomfortable about having the student in class, and other students may shun the labeled child. Teachers may tend to lower their expectations and to blame all difficulties the child has on the handicapping condition. Students may develop low self-esteem and may feel alienated from their peers. Students may also attempt to "use" the condition to avoid unpleasant tasks.
   Page Ref: 110–111

2) What are some of the many distinctive collection of talents, abilities, and limitations that comprise the concept *exceptional students*?

   Answer: *Exceptional students* is a term used to describe students who may have very high special talents or they may have a learning disability, communication disorder, emotional or behavioral disorder, vision impairment, autism, traumatic brain injury, or a some combination of behavioral skills or abilities which differ substantially form the norm (either higher or lower).
   Page Ref: 119

3) Helen is a student in your class. You think she may be gifted enough to warrant special treatment. Describe the measures you might use to assess her and the way you should instruct her.

Answer: There is no sure way to identify a gifted child such as Helen, but many districts and schools have set up guidelines for identifying who qualifies for their gifted programs. IQ tests are often used together with teacher observations. Walton (1961) listed seven questions that are useful in identifying giftedness. Creativity tests may also be used to help in the identification process, as well as exhibitions and projects. Problem solving and divergent thinking skills should be stressed when working with gifted students. Long-term projects and activities are appropriate alternatives. Often, the gifted student is able to be highly involved in planning his/her own educational activities. Intrinsic reinforcement is often used and advanced materials should be made available.

Page Ref: 148-153

4) Using the models of intelligence given by the text as a guide, define what is meant by intelligence. What are some factors that affect the reliability of intelligence tests?

Answer: Some people think intelligence to be a global ability, while others think it is a collection of separate abilities, and still others think it is simply the ability to do well on an IQ test. Intelligence tests vary in their reliability according to 1) whether the test is given to a group or individual and 2) the culture and SES of the student. It might be noted that individual IQs vary over the years. Recent conceptions of intelligence, namely those by Gardner and Sternberg, stress its multiple dimensions, suggesting that intelligence is not a unitary construct. People may be high in some types of intelligent thinking but low in others.

Page Ref: 111-113

5) Describe different approaches to ability grouping. Based on the results of research, what approaches seem most effective for low-ability students?

Answer: There are two main ways that students are grouped by ability: 1) assign student to classes based on ability; and 2) form small ability-based groups within classes. Research has consistently shown that the use of separate classes or "tracks" is very ineffective for lower-ability students. The second method seems to have positive effects when groups are formed and reformed as needed, comparisons are avoided, and the number of groups is kept small. Alternative concepts are non-graded elementary schools and the Joplin Plan. In these arrangements, students are grouped by ability in particular subjects.

Page Ref: 122

6) You suspect that Brenda, a student in your fourth-grade class, might have a hearing impairment. What signs should you look for and what are the teaching strategies that might be effective to use with her?

Answer: Symptoms of possible hearing problems: turning one ear to the speaker; misunderstanding conversation when the speaker's face cannot be seen; not following directions; asking others to repeat teachers' directions; and mispronouncing new words and names. A student such as Brenda should be referred to a specialist for testing. If an impairment is found, you should continue to speak naturally and in complete sentences, avoiding distractions that may draw attention away from your face while you are speaking with a hearing-impaired student.

Page Ref: 146

7) Define what generally constitutes an emotional behavior disorder. Describe four out of the six categories of disorders presented in Woolfolk's text.

Answer: *Conduct disorders* involve behaviors that are aggressive, destructive, and disobedient. The offending students create negative impressions among both their peers and adults. Typically, such students have been corrected and punished multiple times for the same behavior. Children with *anxiety-withdrawal disorders* have poor social skills and few friends. They are anxious, withdrawn, and lack self-confidence. *Immaturity* includes a short attention span, daydreaming, poor concentration, and generally being behind others. *Socialized aggression* is associated with students' membership in organized gangs that commit crimes and antisocial acts. *Motor excess* is related to immaturity (attention problem). These students are restless, tense, and constantly moving. *Psychotic behavior* is reflected by bizarre ideas and unnatural behaviors and perceptions.

Page Ref: 140-142

8) How are you, as a regular teacher, likely to be affected by Public Laws 94-142 and 99-457, the Individuals with Disabilities Act, and the notion of least restrictive environment? Under these laws, you may participate in developing an IEP. Describe the major elements of an IEP.

Answer: *PL 94-142, PL 99-457,* and the *Individuals with Disabilities Education Act (IDEA)* have the goal of giving all handicapped students a free and appropriate public education in the least restrictive environment. [IDEA replaced the word "handicapped" with "disabled" and expanded services for the latter children.] Least restrictive placement requires that as much of the student's day as possible should be within the regular classroom, with appropriate support services offered by means of resource teachers and modifications as necessary. An IEP is a written plan for a specific student's education, with specific goals for that student. Parents, teachers, and special education personnel will be involved in the team process of writing and implementing the goals. This plan is updated yearly and describes current functioning and evaluation procedures, as well as the specific plan for educating the student.

Page Ref: 127-128

Case Studies

The superintendent of Country Pike school system decides to implement group IQ testing of all first and second graders in the schools. In the spring, all children are tested in class by their teachers. When the results come back from the test developers, they are listed by class and used by the school principals and teachers to develop "tracked" second and third grades the following fall. That is, based on scores, the children are assigned to high or low (and medium, where enrollment is sufficient) classes in each grade. Teachers of the classes are also shown the scores at the beginning of the year to help them adapt teaching methods to individual needs.

1) What is your overall reaction to the superintendent's program? What aspects, if any do you like? What aspects, if any, do you dislike?

Answer: It is a positive approach to pay attention to individual differences in learners. IQ scores can provide one piece of information, which can help educators make an informed decision about student readiness and placement. One concern is that the school system may be overly relying upon scores from standardized tests. It is also useful to get teachers' and parents' ratings of the child's behavior, attitudes, and abilities. It is equally important to know if a child can positively interact with his or her peers during recess. IQ scores are limited in that they only provide a glimpse of part of a students' intelligence profile. For example, traditional IQ tests do not measure the eight aspects of Gardner's theory of multiple intelligences. Nor do they assess Sternberg's knowledge–acquisition component.

Page Ref: 111–115

2) Evaluate the use of group IQ tests for making educational decisions about children. What are the advantages and disadvantages?

Answer: There are two problems with the testing procedure described in this case study. First, scores from group administration of intelligence tests are not recommended for making decisions about individuals. A student may lose their place on the bubble sheet, misunderstand the directions, or be distracted by another test–taker. These factors can go unnoticed and negatively influence a student's score. Second, intelligence tests are best administered by a trained school psychologist instead of a teacher. Group tests are often given because an individual test typically takes about two hours to administer. However, accuracy should not be substituted for efficiency.

Page Ref: 119–120

3) React specifically to the idea of using between–class ability grouping. Suggest and defend an alternative orientation (or modification) that would be more desirable for helping low–ability students.

Answer: Between–class ability grouping or tracking occurs when students are assigned to classes based on their measured ability or their achievement. Although a common practice in American education systems, this approach is problematic for low–ability students in part because they tend to receive lower quality instruction. Unfortunately, students placed in the low–ability group are given less rigorous tasks, lower expectations, and routine procedures. This type of learning environment does not provide students with the appropriate amount of challenge and can be boring. Thus, students in this situation tend to act out more and teachers experience more classroom management problems. Oakes and Wells (2002) have recently called upon educators to eliminate tracking and suggest the elimination of remedial classes. Instead, they argue for one regular and one advanced course (or honors assignment option). Tutoring should be provided to assist students who need additional assistance. Researchers suggest providing students with additional resources rather than decreasing standards or expectations.

Page Ref: 122

4) Your school district recently instituted a new program for students who have demonstrated aggressive behaviors towards teachers or other students. You have accepted the responsibility of designing the program to reduce aggression among the students in the program.

What approach would you take in an effort to increase the amount of emotional intelligence of students in this program?

Answer: One model is Susan Graham's program, which helps children learn how to perceive the intention of others. This program involves having the students read a statement about another person's emotions and engage in role–play activities. The focus of this program is to decrease students' aggression by increasing their empathy skills. For very young children, Feshbach encourages teachers to help their students by imagining how others feel. One example cited in the textbook suggests teachers could ask the children to write down what each person in their family might want for a birthday present. In addition to increasing positive behaviors, you will want to develop a behavioral plan for decreasing aggressive behaviors such as bullying and the use of slurs. You could show a videotape of children playing and ask your students to identify the behaviors of the characters which they would classify as bullying. Ask the children to state why they classified specific behaviors of the characters as bullying.

A note of caution: increasing students' empathic reasoning or emotional intelligence may appear to be a simple task. Yet Woolfolk notes that emotional intelligence is often a misinterpreted idea and may have been popularized by the media. Prior to designing any type of intervention program or curriculum designed to increase emotional intelligence, educators are encouraged to read the authoritative information on this topic.

Page Ref: 116–117

Micah is a first grader who has earned a deviation IQ score of 116 on the Stanford –Binet Ability Test. The problem is that he is doing very poorly academically due to his very limited attention span and uncontrolled physical activity. For much of the day, Micah is out of his seat wandering around the room. When he's in his seat, he is almost certain to be fidgeting or moving in some way. His parents recently took him to a psychiatrist who suggested beginning drug therapy. [Note: The Binet series has a scaled score mean of 100 and
a standard deviation of 16. The Wechsler series utilizes a standard deviation of 15.]

5) What appears to be the nature of the problem? What type of disorder is suggested? What is the likely prognosis for Micah's academic and social development, if the problem is not treated? What about the longevity of the problem?

   Answer: Micah appears to be demonstrating behaviors typical of those common to students with attention–deficit/hyperactivity disorder (ADHD). If Micah does in fact have diagnosed ADHD, he is at risk to have several academic problems. Specifically, he may struggle with meeting deadlines, forgetting assignments, prioritizing his goals, remaining focused for even short periods of time, and listening to instructions. He may also experience negative social implications due to his ADHD. Children with ADHD have difficulty controlling their impulses and sustaining attention during play activities. This situation may be frustrating for peers during play. Researchers do not agree about the duration of ADHD. Although once believed to decrease after childhood, today researchers are finding evidence to suggest ADHD can persist through adolescence and even into adulthood.
   Page Ref: 119, 134

6) React to the psychiatrist's suggestion of drug therapy. What are the advantages of using drug therapy at this point? What are the limitations?

   Answer: The amount of children on medication in American schools is of great concern. Because research reveals about 80 percent of the children are more manageable, medication should not be completely dismissed as an intervention. However, children on medication primarily improve in the areas of cooperation, sustained attention, and compliance. Although they may be easier for parents and teachers to deal with, there is less convincing evidence from research indicating children on medication improve in the areas of learning and/or peer relations. A major concern is the health risks related to children taking medication to control ADHD. They are at risk for increased heart rate and blood pressure and other negative side effects. Also, there is very little research regarding the long–term health implications of taking ADHD medication in earlier years.
   Page Ref: 135–136

7) What other interventions would you suggest to help Micah?

   Answer: A new intervention suggested by David Nylund (2000) is the SMART approach. The SMART approach focuses on the students' strengths and stresses personal agency. The child is coached on seeing the problem (attention, boredom) as being outside of themselves. From this perspective, the child is instructed in putting themselves in control and reclaiming their special abilities. In addition, some researchers encourage the teaching of specific academic and social skills. All of these interventions are recommended by Dr. Woolfolk prior to using solely drug therapy.
   Page Ref: 136

Chapter 5   Culture and Diversity

Multiple-Choice Questions

1) Educational practices in American schools during the twentieth century have tended to be based on

   A) a cultural deficit model.

   B) lower-class, non-sectarian, rationalistic values.

   C) middle-class, sectarian values.

   D) the melting pot philosophy.

Answer: C

Explanation: C) During the 20th century, educational practices in American schools typically reflected *middle class, sectarian values*. The melting pot philosophy involved bringing students from different cultures into the mainstream of American society.

Page Ref: 162
Skill: Understanding

2) The cultural-deficit model suggests that immigrant students

   A) achieve higher than American students because of their greater motivation.

   B) are just as prepared for school as students who are born in this country.

   C) come from an inferior culture that leaves them at a disadvantage.

   D) deserve special treatment given the obstacles they have overcome.

Answer: C

Explanation: C) The traditional philosophy was that immigrant students *come from an inferior culture that leaves them at a disadvantage*. This philosophy engendered the cultural deficit model for educating these students.

Page Ref: 162
Skill: Knowledge

3) The rules and traditions that guide the behavior of a group comprise its

   A) culture.

   B) ethnic heritage.

   C) racial identity.

   D) social status.

   Answer: A

   Explanation: A) *Culture* is defined as the rules and traditions that guide the behavior of a
                   group. People are members of groups, not of cultures. The multicultural
                   education movement strongly supports valuing diverse cultures in our
                   society.

   Page Ref: 162
   Skill: Knowledge
   P: .75
   D: .20

4) Ivan is a male Caucasian of Russian heritage who is living in an upper-middle-class
   neighborhood. Knowing this information would give his teacher

   A) accurate data about the types of interventions that Ivan needs.

   B) motivation for creating a self-fulfilling prophesy.

   C) nothing of value for understanding Ivan's needs.

   D) some useful information about how Ivan is likely to behave.

   Answer: D

   Explanation: D) The description of Ivan's characteristics is hardly conclusive for knowing him
                   as a person or predicting how he will behave. *Knowing Ivan's cultural
                   background does, however, provide some useful information about how he is likely to
                   behave.* This information needs to be viewed cautiously, but it is still useful for
                   planning for Ivan's needs.

   Page Ref: 164–165
   Skill: Understanding
   P: .68
   D: .37

5) Membership in what cultural group is the best predictor of cultural differences?

    A) Ethnicity

    B) Gender

    C) Race

    D) Social class

Answer: D

Explanation: D) No one variable is the single predictor of cultural differences, but *social class* is the variable that seems to have the strongest relationship with cultural differences. Ethnicity, gender, and level of intellectual functioning are variables that also contribute to cultural differences, depending on the specific situation, but social class remains the strongest predictor.

Page Ref: 164
Skill: Knowledge

6) Which one of the following students **BEST** illustrates the concept of learned helplessness as an explanation for failure by low socioeconomic status children?

    A) Trina seeks help from her older sister in completing practically all of her homework assignments.

    B) Michael decides that he has no chance of passing the seventh grade or getting out of school.

    C) Brook never volunteers an answer, but hopes that the teacher will call on her.

    D) Josh will only compete against smaller children while playing sports after school.

Answer: B

Explanation: B) Learned helplessness is a condition characterized by accepting failure as inevitable. An example would be a student (Michael, in this instance) *deciding that he has no chance of passing*.

Page Ref: 167
Skill: Understanding
P: .79
D: .21

7) Mark decides that he doesn't want to be like the "rich kids who sell themselves out to the system." Accordingly, he prides himself on not learning what the school is trying to teach. Which of the following concepts best characterizes his behavior?

   A) Academic anti-socialization

   B) Learned helplessness

   C) Resistance culture

   D) Tracking

Answer: C

Explanation: C) A *resistance culture* is represented by lower-class students' rejection of middle-class values. This behavior is exemplified by Marko's purposeful attempt to not learn what the school is trying to teach (to "the rich kids").

Page Ref: 167
Skill: Understanding
P: .82
D: .35

8) Which one of the following student situations is predictive of tracking practices?

   A) Andy, who continued to be a low achiever throughout grade school, remains in school after reaching the age of 16.

   B) Marie, who was placed in the low reading group in the third grade, is counseled in the eighth grade into home economics instead of beginning algebra.

   C) Sylvia, who experienced considerable academic success in elementary school, is admitted to a prestigious university on an athletic scholarship.

   D) Vincent, who was accelerated from second to fourth grade because of his outstanding ability test score, had difficulty with social interaction in high school.

Answer: B

Explanation: B) Tracking is predictive of students' success and academic choices in later grades. Accordingly, *Marie, who was placed in the low reading group as a third grader, becomes identified five years later as being better served by a less academic program (home economics as opposed to algebra)*.

Page Ref: 167-168
Skill: Understanding
P: .75
D: .32

9) Which one of the following variables is **MOST** likely to correlate positively and highest with children's school achievement?

    A) Ethnicity of the family

    B) Level of the parents' education

    C) Parents' attitudes toward education

    D) Total family income

Answer: C

Explanation: C) The strongest correlations between SES and school achievement occur when SES is measured in terms of family atmosphere variables such as *parents' attitudes toward education*. Variables such as family income, parents' education, and parents' occupations correlate positively, but more weakly, with school achievement.

Page Ref: 166
Skill: Knowledge
P: .77
D: .20

10) Which one of the following statements is technically **TRUE** regarding the term *minority group*?

    A) It is a category composed of people who have biologically transmitted traits.

    B) It is a term that refers to a numerical minority compared to the total population.

    C) It refers to a group of people who receives unequal or discriminatory treatment.

    D) The number of these groups is decreasing slightly in nearly every one of the states.

Answer: B

Explanation: B) The term minority group technically refers to a numerical minority in a population compared to the total population. *Sociologists use the term to label a group of people who receive discriminatory treatment.*

Page Ref: 168
Skill: Knowledge

11) By the year 2020 it is predicted nearly two-thirds of the school-age population

    A) will be African-Americans.

    B) will be Asians.

    C) will be from African American, Asian, Latina/Latino, or other ethnic groups.

    D) will be English language learners or English as a second language learners.

Answer: C

Explanation: B) As discussed by Woolfolk, the minority group that has had the largest percentage of growth increase in the United States since 1980 *consists* of Asians. The second highest increase has been for Hispanics.

    C) There will be a continued large percentage of growth increase in the United States in regards to diverse cultures and ethnic groups.

Page Ref: 169
Skill: Knowledge

12) Researchers generally believe that differences between ethnic groups in cognitive abilities occur primarily as a result of

    A) biases inherent in most standardized tests.

    B) different experiences in and out of school.

    C) different levels of motivation among the groups.

    D) natural abilities of the various groups.

Answer: B

Explanation: B) Researchers generally believe that differences between ethnic groups in cognitive abilities mainly occur as a result of *different experiences in and out of school*. For example, minority groups must contend with fewer resources and discriminating practices. These factors make it more difficult for them to be successful in school compared with white students.

Page Ref: 171
Skill: Knowledge
P: .69
D: .31

13) The outcomes of the *Brown vs. Board of Education* case relative to the original goals for the ruling are generally viewed today as

    A) favorable for minorities who are high in SES.

    B) highly negative.

    C) highly successful.

    D) only slightly successful.

Answer: D

Explanation: D) The outcomes of the *Brown vs. Board of Education* case have been only *slightly successful*. The problem is that, despite segregation being declared illegal, many of today's students attend schools in which the student body is predominantly of one race. This is called *de facto* segregation.

Page Ref: 171
Skill: Knowledge

14) What is the major reason for the development of prejudice?

    A) Dislike of certain people or groups

    B) Economic competition among different groups

    C) Instinctive mistrust of people who are different

    D) Learning cultural values

Answer: D

Explanation: D) Prejudice develops as a result of *learning certain cultural values of a certain cultural group*. Typically, prejudice produces negative views.

Page Ref: 172
Skill: Knowledge

15) Mr. Kennedy, a middle-class Caucasian teacher, assigns lower grades when evaluating the work of two Native American students in his high-school physics class than he does for comparable work from other students. The most valid interpretation of Mr. Kennedy's behavior is that he appears to

    A) be conforming to conventional ethnic values.

    B) be demonstrating a laissez-faire personality.

    C) have a negative schema regarding Native Americans.

    D) mistrust people who are culturally inferior.

Answer: C

Explanation: C) Mr. Kennedy appears to have a *negative schema (stereotype) regarding Native Americans*. As a result, he is discriminating against them (perhaps unknowingly) in his grading practices.

Page Ref: 173
Skill: Understanding
P: .86
D: .12

16) Which one of the following quotations **MOST** clearly represents the concept of stereotyping?

    A) "Boys should line up to the right and girls to the left."

    B) "If he's one of your friends, tell him not to apply."

    C) "Matthew just doesn't seem interested in spelling."

    D) "People from that region just aren't ambitious."

Answer: D

Explanation: D) *Stereotyping* is a schema for viewing a particular group. It does not necessarily invoke negative perceptions, as would be the case for prejudice. An example is thinking that people from a particular region are not ambitious. The other examples are descriptions of behavior or rules or of a prejudicial attitude ("If he's one of those people...").

Page Ref: 173
Skill: Understanding
P: .98
D: .03

17) Studies of educational discrimination against minority ethnic groups today show that

    A) African–American and Hispanic students are now entering science fields at close to the same rate as white students.

    B) discrimination on the basis of minority and ethnicity has virtually been eliminated.

    C) Hispanic and Asian students lose out on opportunities to enter science careers due to lack of interest.

    D) there are still fewer opportunities for minority students to enter top–level professions.

Answer: D

Explanation: D) Studies of educational discrimination show that *there are still fewer opportunities for minority students to enter top-level professions.* For example, minority students are selected less often for gifted classes and for programs that lead to careers in science, engineering, and medicine.

Page Ref: 173
Skill: Understanding
P: .61
D: .38

18) As opposed to the term *prejudice*, the term *discrimination* refers to

    A) attitudes.

    B) beliefs.

    C) behavior.

    D) feelings.

Answer: C

Explanation: C) As Woolfolk has pointed out, prejudice is based on an individual's attitudes, feelings, and beliefs concerning an entire category of people, not certain individuals. *Discrimination involves behavior* — that is, treating particular categories of people unequally.

Page Ref: 172–172
Skill: Knowledge

19) One way of inoculating students against stereotype threats is to

    A) be assertive about defining success as "uncool."

    B) believe that intelligence can be improved.

    C) disidentify from success in academics.

    D) psychologically disengage from success in academics.

Answer: B

Explanation: B) Although stereotypes are pervasive and difficult to change, the *belief that intelligence can be changed* might be able to protect students against stereotype threats. The other three response choices encourage stereotype threats.

Page Ref: 174
Skill: Knowledge

20) Barbara has a strong feminine identity, whereas Charles has a strong masculine identity. However, Alex's identity tends to be more androgynous. Based on research on gender-role identities, it would be predicted that Alex is likely to

    A) be relatively forceful and competitive compared to the others.

    B) have higher self-esteem than Barbara.

    C) have lower self-esteem than either Barbara or Charles.

    D) have low masculine and feminine traits compared to others.

Answer: B

Explanation: B) Research on gender-role identities suggests that self-esteem is highest for masculine and androgynous identities and lowest for a feminine identity. Accordingly, *Alex is likely to have higher self-esteem than Barbara.*

Page Ref: 177–178
Skill: Understanding
P: .74
D: .33

21) The term *gender* is associated with judgments influenced by culture and

    A) androgynous characteristics.

    B) biological differences.

    C) context.

    D) schemas.

Answer: C

Explanation: C) Judgments influenced by *culture and context* are encompassed in the term gender. Biological differences refer to sex. Androgynous characteristics are related to gender identity, and gender schemas are organized networks of knowledge about what it means to be male or female.

Page Ref: 176
Skill: Knowledge

22) What is a *gender schema*?

    A) A means of identifying the differences among the three types of gender roles

    B) A method of determining who is masculine and who is feminine

    C) An organized network of knowledge about gender-role identity

    D) A stereotype of a masculine or feminine sex role

Answer: C

Explanation: C) A gender schema is an *organized network of knowledge about gender-role identity.* These schemata guide students' perceptions of themselves and how they behave.

Page Ref: 178
Skill: Knowledge

23) What group of people have the most stereotyped notions of gender roles?

    A) Elementary school children

    B) College students

    C) High school students

    D) Preschool children

Answer: D

Explanation: D) The most stereotypical notions of gender-role identity are expressed by *young children* because of how they are treated by adults; girls are encouraged to be affectionate and tender while boys are encouraged to be more physically active than girls.

Page Ref: 178–179
Skill: Knowledge

24) According to research evidence, which of the following statements about gender differences is **TRUE**?

    A) Females are more likely than males to initiate comments in college classes.

    B) Gender differences in social and cognitive abilities are large.

    C) Public school teachers tend to interact more with boys than with girls.

    D) Textbooks today tend to be free of gender stereotypes.

Answer: C

Explanation: C) Research on teacher behaviors shows a tendency for *public-school teachers to interact more with boys than with girls*. It is also the case that, although gender differences in cognition tend to be small, textbooks still reflect some gender biases, and men are more likely than women to initiate comments in college classes.

Page Ref: 180
Skill: Knowledge
P: .88
D: .24

25) Differences between males and females in cognitive abilities are

    A) attributed more to genetic than environmental factors.

    B) considered to be very small and insignificant.

    C) reported to be larger today than was the case in earlier studies.

    D) small in the past decade but steadily increasing.

Answer: B

Explanation: B) Differences between males and females in cognitive abilities are considered to be *small or nonexistent*. When differences are found, they may be attributed primarily to environmental factors (e.g., boys receive more encouragement than girls do to take mathematics courses).

Page Ref: 180–181
Skill: Knowledge
P: .92
D: .18

26) What type(s) of learning approaches would be the most helpful in eliminating gender bias in the classroom?

    A) Balance competitive and cooperative approaches.

    B) Emphasize cooperative approaches.

    C) Emphasize competitive approaches.

    D) Use both approaches but emphasize competitive approaches.

Answer: A

Explanation: A) The potentially most helpful learning strategy for eliminating gender bias in classrooms is to *balance both cooperative and competitive learning methods*, so that students who learn best with one or the other method have equal opportunities to learn.

Page Ref: 182
Skill: Knowledge

27) In applying our knowledge of the differences in mathematical abilities between boys and girls, we should remember that

    A) boys have superior mathematical skills compared to girls.

    B) boys' skills are limited by their general cognitive abilities.

    C) differences are based on averages, not on individual students.

    D) girls tend to excel in math story problems compared to boys.

Answer: C

Explanation: C) In applying our knowledge of gender differences in mathematical abilities, it is important to remember that *the differences are based on averages, not on individuals*. Thus, teachers need to deal with the individual student, based on his or her needs, not based on a basic stereotype about a small overall group difference.

Page Ref: 181
Skill: Understanding
P: .91
D: .22

28) Which one of the following differences in test scores between males and females is most clearly documented in the current research literature?

    A) Females are significantly superior in spatial abilities.

    B) Females have a strong advantage in verbal skills.

    C) Males are highly superior in spatial abilities.

    D) Males tend to score highest and lowest on various tests.

Answer: D

Explanation: D) The scores of males on tests tend to be more variable than those of females. *More males than females score very high and very low*. Still, most studies of gender differences do not take into account such variables as race and socioeconomic status. Research shows that there is much overlap between the sexes in most ability areas, and everyone can improve in any area with practice and appropriate education.

Page Ref: 181
Skill: Knowledge

29) A language variation spoken by a particular ethnic, social, or regional group is called a

   A) dialect.

   B) language disorder.

   C) pronunciation problem.

   D) standard speech.

   Answer: A

   Explanation: A) A *dialect* is a variation of language spoken by a particular social, ethnic, or regional group that is an element of the group's collective identity. A dialect may sometimes cause a pronunciation problem in certain situations and could even be regarded as a language disorder in other situations, but a dialect is never regarded as an element of Standard English. Nevertheless, a dialect is always a language variation of a particular group.

   Page Ref: 184
   Skill: Knowledge

30) Darnel, an African–American second grader who uses nonstandard English, complained about his partner in spelling practice. "Fred not say nothin' today." Which of the following would be the most relevant reply that the teacher could make?

   A) "If he's not saying anything today, do you think something is bothering him?"

   B) "In school language we should say 'Fred is not saying anything today.'"

   C) "Darnel, please remember: 'not' goes with 'anything.' We don't use it with 'nothing.'"

   D) "Why don't you ask Fred what the matter is? Maybe something is wrong."

   Answer: A

   Explanation: A) The teacher's most relevant reply would be: *"If he's not saying anything today, do you think that something is bothering him?"* In this way, the *teacher models good speaking without making the student feel inferior and shows respect for the student's language while allowing him/her to communicate freely.* When interacting with children who speak in a nonstandard dialect, teachers are encouraged to *accept the dialect but teach Standard English.* Learning Standard English also seems fairly easy for most of these students provided they have good models.

   Page Ref: 184–185
   Skill: Understanding
   P: .54
   D: .21

31) In order to reduce the possible negative stereotypes about students who speak a different dialect, teachers should

    A) accept students' dialects as a valid and correct language system, but teach standard English as well.

    B) expect to find more homonyms in the students' language than usual.

    C) focus on teaching "standard" or "formal" English to all students.

    D) promote "heritage" English rather than "formal" English for all students.

Answer: A

Explanation: A) Teachers should reduce the possible negative stereotypes about students who speak different dialects by *accepting their dialects as a valid and correct language system*, show respect for the students' language variations, and strive to teach the standard form of English (or whatever the dominant language might be in the country of interest) as an alternative language that is necessary for effective communications in the world of work. It appears that learning the standard speech (Dimientieff's "Formal English") is easy for most students whose original language is a dialect (or "Heritage English," for example) provided that students have good role models, clear instruction, and opportunities for authentic practice (Woolfolk, p. 39).

Page Ref: 184
Skill: Knowledge

32) What is the primary reason why bilingualism has generated such heated debates in recent years?

    A) Changing demographics

    B) Failure of many students to use standard English

    C) Increased numbers of students who must take summer school

    D) Rising numbers of college freshmen with poor reading skills

Answer: A

Explanation: A) Because the number of non–native–speaking students is expected to double (to over five million) by the year 2000, the major reason for the heated debates over bilingualism is *changing demographics*. [Although the other response choices may also contribute to the debates, changing demographics is the primary reason.]

Page Ref: 185
Skill: Knowledge

33) Research on bilingualism suggests that

    A) the division of students into separate English classes according to the primary language is desirable.

    B) learning a second language interferes with use of the first language.

    C) the more skilled the individual is in the first language, the faster he/she will learn a second language.

    D) the more skilled the individual is in the first language, the slower he/she will learn a second language.

Answer: C

Explanation: C) Research on bilingualism suggests that the *more skilled the individual is in the first language, the faster he/she will learn a second language*. Although there are periods during which an individual may confuse the two languages, generally the progression is smooth and results in proficiency in both languages.

Page Ref: 187–188
Skill: Knowledge
P: .76
D: .05

34) According to Woolfolk, the most desirable approach to the "language problem" in today's bilingual schools is to

    A) divide students into separate language classes according to the primary language that they speak.

    B) try to make students fluent in both languages.

    C) employ monolingual educational strategies.

    D) try to make students at least semi-lingual in their second language.

Answer: B

Explanation: B) Woolfolk suggests that the "language problem" should be approached by *trying to make students proficient in both languages*. This may be accomplished by creating classes that mix students who are learning a second language with students who are native speakers of that language. Having bilingual teachers also seems critical for this approach to be successful.

Page Ref: 187–188
Skill: Knowledge

35) Nikolas is an eleventh grader who came to America from Russia with his parents one year ago. He has gradually developed his fluency in the English language, but he continues to have some difficulty using English during classroom activities. What should Nikolas' teacher do to help him with his English language acquisition?

   A) Encourage Nikolas to use English in the classroom and save his Russian for use at home.

   B) Promote Nikolas' bilingualism in both Russian and English.

   C) Refer Nikolas to the English-as-a-Second-Language program in the local magnet school.

   D) Respond positively to Nikolas only when he makes accurate attempts with English.

Answer: B

Explanation: B) Research on bilingualism (e.g., Garcia, 1992) supports the idea that children benefit from becoming proficient speakers of both their native language and the dominant language of the country. Therefore, Nikolas' teacher should *promote his bilingualism in both Russian and English.*

Page Ref: 187–188
Skill: Understanding
P: .69
D: .45

36) Which of the following illustrations is characteristic of a culturally compatible classroom?

   A) Mr. Buhr regularly demonstrated the correct procedures for borrowing school materials during his homeroom period.

   B) Mr. Denver gave each biology student the same laboratory worksheet in order to determine what misconceptions in handling a microscope could be identified.

   C) Ms. Hayes assigned an article on euthanasia for her social studies class to read prior to their exam, although the topic had not been discussed.

   D) Ms. Rosen organized her English class into homogeneous groups during small group discussions.

Answer: A

Explanation: A) Homogeneous groupings or "tracks" are clearly not recommended for creating culturally compatible classrooms. Such groupings create segregated classrooms in which high-achieving students from the same ethnic or cultural groups are clustered together. Positive strategies are cross-cultural group "study buddies," explicit teaching of participation structures, and use of a wide range of teaching methods to accommodate cultural differences and learning styles. An example of teaching participation structures is *Ms. Buhr's demonstration of the proper procedures for borrowing school materials.*

Page Ref: 190–191
Skill: Understanding
P: .55
D: .24

37) Resilience children not only survive in difficult times, they also

    A) are less likely to need social or emotional support.

    B) lack strong family support systems.

    C) maintain a positive outlook even though they lack confidence in their own abilities.

    D) thrive in spite of the difficult circumstances.

Answer: D

Explanation: D) Resilient individuals *thrive* in difficult times and can adapt even though there
                may be events that threaten their development.

Page Ref: 191
Skill: Understanding

38) According to Borman and Overman (2004), teachers can do the following to create resilient
classrooms:

    A) increase class size so that students can build up a tolerance to challenging circumstances.

    B) set the learning goals for the students.

    C) provide a safe and orderly classroom and develop positive teacher–student relationships.

    D) focus mostly on test scores so that students can experience academic self–efficacy.

Answer: C

Explanation: C) The two characteristics of schools associated with academic resilience are *safe
                and orderly classrooms* and *positive teacher–student relationships*.

Page Ref: 192
Skill: Knowledge

39) What group of students tends to work best in small same–sex groups?

    A) African–American children

    B) Hawaiian children

    C) Hispanic children

    D) Navajo children

Answer: D

Explanation: D) According to the research of Roland Tharp (1989), Navajo children are
                socialized to be quite solitary and not interested in playing with children of
                the opposite sex. Consequently, teachers can encourage Navajo children to
                work together by *setting up same–sex groups of only two or three children* and
                having them work together. Children in Hawaiian society depend heavily on
                cooperation and collaboration in their activities, while Hispanic students also
                prefer cooperative activities and dislike competition with their peers.
                African–American students want emphasis on small–group learning activities
                and hands–on contact with the teacher (Hale–Benson, 1986).

Page Ref: 195
Skill: Knowledge

40) Research on African–American students suggests that the typical learning style of this group is

    A) field–independent.

    B) reflective.

    C) verbal/analytic.

    D) visual/global.

Answer: D

Explanation: D) Research on African–American students suggests that a common learning style is *visual/global rather than verbal/analytic*. Hale–Benson (1986) recommended teaching young black children using methods that emphasize nonverbal cues, equal "talking time," and small–group learning strategies.

Page Ref: 195–196
Skill: Knowledge

41) The learning style of Native Americans appears to be

    A) field–independent.

    B) global, analytic.

    C) global, visual.

    D) reasoning by inference.

Answer: C

Explanation: C) The learning style favored by many Native Americans appears to be a *global and visual style*. The style of African Americans tends to be visual and global. Research suggests that Mexican Americans tend to be field–dependent and oriented toward family and group loyalty rather than being individualistic. The learning styles of Asian Americans are unclear due to few research studies.

Page Ref: 196
Skill: Knowledge

42) The prevailing view regarding the use of learning styles research for identifying ethnic group differences is that such information

   A) has very little validity and, therefore, should be ignored by teachers.

   B) is both highly valid and valuable and should be recognized by teachers.

   C) needs to be considered cautiously as it may promote stereotyping.

   D) promotes the idea that ethnic groups in the U.S. are more similar than different.

Answer: C

Explanation: C) A current concern regarding the use of learning styles research is that such information *needs to be considered cautiously as it may promote stereotyping*. The evidence that associates ethnic group membership with different learning styles is correlational and indicative, at best, of *tendencies* of an overall group and **NOT** an individual's needs.

Page Ref: 196
Skill: Knowledge
P: .64
D: .22

43) Participation structures in a classroom would generally dictate

   A) grading policies, including alternative assessments as well as paper-pencil tests.

   B) the student-teacher ratio in classrooms as well as extra-curricular activities.

   C) when it is appropriate to talk to another student as well as to respond to the teacher.

   D) whether the primary teaching method is lecture-recitation or discussion.

Answer: C

Explanation: C) The activity rules for a classroom are dictated by *participation structures*. A example of such structure is when it is appropriate to talk to other students. Most classrooms have many different participation structures that vary for subjects and tasks.

Page Ref: 196
Skill: Knowledge

44) Mary, a student who cannot afford a computer is caught in the

   A) magic middle

   B) digital divide.

   C) participation structure.

   D) semilingual.

Answer: B

Explanation: B) The *digital divide* is the term used to describe the disparity between poor and more affluent students and families in regards to access to technology.

Page Ref: 197
Skill: Understanding

Completion Questions

1) The assumption that students' home culture is inferior because it has not prepared them to fit well into schools is called the _____ model.

   Answer: cultural deficit
   Page Ref: 162

2) According to James Banks, the notion that all students, regardless of race or background, should have equal opportunities to learn in school is directly supported by the _____ education movement.

   Answer: multicultural
   Page Ref: 163

3) The knowledge, rules, traditions, and attitudes that guide behavior in a particular group of people represent the _____ of that group.

   Answer: culture
   Page Ref: 169

4) The commonly used index of wealth, power, and influence is _____.

   Answer: socioeconomic status (SES)
   Page Ref: 165

5) Both low socioeconomic status students and others who fail continually may be the victims of learned _____.

   Answer: helplessness
   Page Ref: 167

6) A group of people who are discriminated against by the dominant culture is called a(n) _____ group by sociologists.

   Answer: minority
   Page Ref: 168

7) When members of a different culture are perceived as slow, rude, or disrespectful, these perceptions may be caused by _____.

   Answer: cultural conflicts
   Page Ref: 169

8) Joyce Epstein described six types of family/school/community _____ designed to reduce the impact of cultural conflicts and discrimination on school achievement.

   Answer: partnerships
   Page Ref: 193

9) Differences among ethnic groups on tests of cognitive abilities are primarily the product of cultural mismatches, growing up in a low SES environment, or the legacy of _____.

Answer: discrimination
Page Ref: 171

10) Discrimination is the behavior that often accompanies the affective component (feelings, attitudes, etc.) called _____.

Answer: prejudice
Page Ref: 172

11) Organized bodies of knowledge about groups of people that affect how we react to them are called _____.

Answer: stereotypes
Page Ref: 173

12) Aronson and Fried identified "a social predicament rooted in the prevailing American image of African–Americans as intellectually inferior" as being a _____.

Answer: stereotype threat
Page Ref: 174

13) Organized networks of knowledge about what it means to be a male or female are called

_____.

Answer: gender schemas
Page Ref: 178

14) Individuals who speak two languages are said to be _____.

Answer: bilingual
Page Ref: 185

15) Most bilingual programs in the United States use the _____ approach for learning standard English.

Answer: transition
Page Ref: 185

16) People who are inadequate speakers of both their native language and their second language are called _____.

Answer: semilingual
Page Ref: 186

17) The study of the courtesies and conventions of communication across different cultures is called _____.

Answer: sociolinguistics
Page Ref: 196

18) A child who knows how and when to raise her or his hand in class is demonstrating an understanding of the _____ of the classroom.

Answer: pragmatics

Explanation: *Pragmatics* are the rules for how and when to use language in order to be an effective communicator in a particular culture.

Page Ref: 196

True/False Questions

1) The number of minority group students in the United States has been increasing steadily over the years.

Answer: TRUE
Page Ref: 162

2) The assumption underlying the cultural deficit model was that many ethnic groups did not want to assimilate completely into mainstream American society.

Answer: FALSE
Page Ref: 162

3) Both traditional and ethnocentric approaches should be emphasized in multicultural education.

Answer: TRUE
Page Ref: 163

4) Membership in a particular group determines behavior as well as increases the probability of certain types of behavior.

Answer: TRUE
Page Ref: 164

5) Socioeconomic status (SES) is positively correlated with school achievement.

Answer: TRUE
Page Ref: 166

6) The majority of poor children in the schools of the United States are African-American.

Answer: FALSE
Page Ref: 166

7) Differences in cultural values as well as the dangers of neighborhoods may make the strategy of less parental control both appropriate and useful for children's learning.

Answer: FALSE
Page Ref: 168

8) The purposes of creating culturally compatible classrooms are to lessen ethnic prejudice, racism, and sexism and, at the same time, provide equal opportunities for all students.

Answer: TRUE
Page Ref: 170

9) Segregation was declared illegal by the *Brown vs. Board of Education of Topeka* ruling.

Answer: TRUE
Page Ref: 171

10) Discrimination and prejudice are the same negative behaviors.

Answer: FALSE
Page Ref: 171-172

11) In a study of the effects of a negative stereotype on college students' standardized test performances, similar results were found for both African-American and Caucasian students.

Answer: FALSE
Page Ref: 174

12) Comparisons between males and females on mental ability tests generally show small or no differences.

Answer: TRUE
Page Ref: 174

13) Gender differences in mathematics achievement are generally the same for all racial groups.

Answer: FALSE
Page Ref: 174

14) It is difficult for most students whose original language is a dialect to learn the standard speech of their country.

Answer: FALSE
Page Ref: 184

15) Recent studies show that speaking two languages is detrimental to cognitive development.

Answer: FALSE
Page Ref: 185-186

16) Proponents of the native language maintenance approach for bilingual education believe that valuable learning time is lost when students are taught in their native language.

Answer: FALSE
Page Ref: 187

17) Resilient children typically have parents who are supportive but have low expectations of their success.

Answer: FALSE

Explanation: Parents of resilient students tend to support learning and place *high expectations* on their children.
Page Ref: 192

18) According to Woolfolk, results from learning styles research are generally considered highly valid for adapting instruction to culturally diverse groups.

Answer: FALSE

Explanation: Woolfolk cautions people about the lack of rigorous research in support of the existence of *learning styles*. She further claims the idea of "deficits" can be especially problematic for labeling minority students.
Page Ref: 196

19) The pragmatics of a classroom involve differentiative activity rules that are called participation structures.

Answer: FALSE

Explanation: *Pragmatics* refer to the rules for how and when to use language to be an effective communicator in a particular culture.
Page Ref: 196

20) David knows exactly when he should take part in a certain classroom activity. David has an understanding of the classroom's **participation structures**.

Answer: TRUE

Explanation: *Participation structures* are the informal and formal rules for how one should take part in a given activity.
Page Ref: 196

21) Culturally relevant pedagogy is a method that has been used successfully with students of color and students in poverty.

Answer: TRUE
Page Ref: 189

22) The digital divide is greater for Latino Americans compared to White individuals.

Answer: TRUE

Explanation: Approximately 13% of Latino American children have broadband access at home compared to 26% of White children. The lack of broadband access contributes to the *digital divide* among students.

Page Ref: 197

Short Answer Questions

1) Define *culture* and discuss the issues that prompted belief in the *cultural deficit* model. What are the prevailing beliefs of educational researchers and theorists today about this issue?

Answer: *Culture* refers to the knowledge, rules, traditions, and attitudes that guide behavior in a particular group of people. The assumption of the *cultural deficit* model, supported by some educators in the 1960s and 1970s, was that minority students and others from different backgrounds than white students were culturally disadvantaged. Today, this idea is rejected in favor of the belief that no culture is deficient. Rather, there may be some incompatibility between the students' culture and the dominant culture of the school.

Page Ref: 162

2) Discuss the assumptions and goals of multicultural education.

Answer: The idea of multicultural education is that all students should have an equal opportunity to learn in school and be respected. Multicultural education is also a reform movement that attempts to promote acceptance of all cultures in what is taught in schools. Recently, Banks (1994) has proposed that multicultural education is more than a change in the curriculum. It must involve content integration, the knowledge construction process, an equity pedagogy, prejudice reduction, and an empowering school culture and social culture.

Page Ref: 163

3) Identify some of the factors that may lead low–income students to perform less well in school than middle–income students with the same abilities.

Answer: Factors that may lead low–income students to perform less successfully in school than middle–income children of the same abilities are: (a) poor health; (b) limited resources; (c) low self–esteem; (d) learned helplessness; (e) resistance cultures; (f) tracking practices; (g) child rearing practices that do not promote independent thinking; and (h) low expectations.

Page Ref: 165–167

4) Define gender bias and describe how it has been expressed in school.

   Answer: Gender bias occurs when males and females are treated differently, mainly due to stereotypes ascribed to each sex. For example, male infants are treated more physically by parents whereas female infants are protected more. In general, males are encouraged to become more independent, females to become more dependent. At school, textbooks frequently portray females in roles that depict them as passive or domestic. Teachers are more likely to verbally interact with males and assign them more active classroom responsibilities. Expectancies to do well in math and science are more likely to be conveyed to males than to females.

   Page Ref: 179–180

5) Compare alternative approaches to teaching bilingual children. Should a child's use of his/her non-English language in classroom learning be discouraged or directly integrated with learning in Standard English?

   Answer: Most bilingual programs today attempt to introduce the use of English as early a possible. However, there are concerns that forcing children to learn a difficult subject in an unfamiliar language may be detrimental. Students may also feel that their language is not valued if they are not permitted to use it. The best approach, it appears, is to integrate the use of both the natural language and Standard English. If possible, classes might be created that mix students who are trying to learn a second language with native speakers of that language. The goal would be to produce fluent speakers of both languages.

   Page Ref: 185–186

6) Discuss major findings from learning styles research regarding Hispanic, African-American, and Native American students. Specifically, what types of learning styles appear dominant or more common for each of these groups?

   Answer: The major findings of learning styles research are as follows:

   A. Hispanic-Americans: field-dependent and people-oriented
   B. African-Americans: visual/global, not verbal/analytic, focus on people, and nonverbal communication
   C. Native Americans: visual/global and preference for learning privately
   D. Asian-Americans: field-dependent, global, and do well with cooperative learning

   Cautions are suggested regarding the use of learning styles results to adapt instruction. First, the research is not highly conclusive. Second, there is the danger of stereotyping. Third, individual differences may be greater than cultural differences.

   Page Ref: 195–196

Case Studies

Two Cambodian students who speak very little English move to your school district three weeks after school begins and are assigned to your sixth-grade class. Because a small Cambodian community has been established in the area, you already have five bilingual students in class who speak both Cambodian and English. You are having difficulty communicating with the new students and suspect that they are following very little of what is being taught in your class.

1) What are the likely outcomes (academic, social, personal) for the new students if no additional interventions or strategies are employed?

Answer: If the Cambodian students in this class receive no additional interventions or support they are likely to have short and long-term academic problems. Students who receive good quality intervention(s) will need about two to three years to be able to effectively communicate face-to-face in a second language (i.e., contextualized language skills). Becoming proficient in academic language skills in a second language (i.e., decontextualized language skills) can take five to seven years. It would certainly take a much longer amount of time for students to master decontextualized language skills if they were not participating in a high quality language program. Some educators caution students who do not receive adequate bilingual education may be at risk to become semilingual, which means they cannot speak proficiently in any language. There are also social affects for students who cannot adequately speak English due in part because they may be placed in special classes away from their peers. Woolfolk suggests all students benefit when classes mix students who are learning a second language with students who are native speakers. For example, English speakers who want to learn Spanish could be placed with Spanish speaking students. In regards to personal implications, researchers claim some students may come to believe that their home language is "second class", which can lead to a sense of shame. There is some research to support the finding that students who were taught in their native language had increased levels of self-esteem.

Page Ref: 185-187

2) What strategy or strategies might you use to help the new students succeed in your class?

Answer: In order to help the next students be successful it is important to take a broad multicultural education approach rather than simply addressing language issues. In particular, James Banks argues a comprehensive multicultural education includes the following: integrating content for a variety of cultures and groups; helping students understand how the discipline–specific implicit cultural assumptions influence knowledge constructed within the discipline; reducing prejudice by identifying and modifying students' racial attitudes; examining school culture and social structure and creating a school culture that empowers students from all groups; and providing an equity pedagogy that matches teaching styles to students' learning styles and individual differences. In regards to specific classrooms, Banks suggests teachers use examples and content from many cultures and groups to illustrate key concepts, principles, and general theories in their subject area. Researchers also recommend teachers become familiar with stereotype threat, which is the extra emotional and cognitive burden that that a student of a minority group may experience when feeling apprehensive about confirming a stereotype. This burden can induce a student's test anxiety and undermine their academic performance. Woolfolk suggests the strategies teachers use for decreasing test anxiety (e.g., no time limit for exams) can also be useful for helping students resist stereotype threat. A final strategy for a teacher in this situation is to ensure the Cambodian students in this case study have access to good models, are given clear instructions for all learning tasks, and have opportunities for practicing their English skills.

Page Ref: 163, 174

3) In your opinion, whose responsibility is it to teach the children to communicate fluently in English (the school's, the families', or both)? Explain.

Answer: It is very important for teachers to involve family members in language instructional strategies. In this example, as the Cambodian children learn English they are likely to adopt standard speech and may rely less upon their dialect. Standard speech is the most generally accepted and used form of language. A dialect is the language variation, which may be spoken in the child's home and is an important part of the group's collective identity. While it is the teachers' and school's responsibility to deal with linguistic diversity in their classroom, it is also their responsibility to work collaboratively with students' family members. During parent–teacher conferences, the teacher can validate that he or she accepts others who speak a different dialect. It is also crucial for teachers to communicate with family members in order to encourage parents to provide a sufficient amount of practice for the child learning English. Also, the teacher can discuss with the family members the importance of supporting the student, who is often required to engage in code–switching. Code–switching is when the child successfully switches from one language, dialect, or non–verbal behavior to another depending on the situation. Language is also influenced by culture. Therefore, in addition to focusing on increasing the English skills of all students, teachers and school personnel are responsible for creating culturally compatible classrooms. Culturally compatible classrooms are based on rules, procedures, and grouping strategies that do not cause conflicts with student's cultural differences.

Page Ref: 183–187

Cannon Elementary School has always held a school-wide Christmas show. The school is in a suburb of a large city and draws from a diverse, multicultural student population. While the Christmas show has always been presented without incident, this year four sets of parents of different religious orientations complain that they feel it is inappropriate for their children to be singing songs that celebrate a particular faith (Christianity). All indicate that they enjoy the holiday season; their objection is with the religious aspect.

4) What would you say to these parents? Explain why you would give these answers.

Answer: The first thing to do would be to thank the parents for coming to see you and sharing their concerns. You will want to explicitly state to the parents that it is your goal to engage in culturally relevant teaching. In regards to the celebration of holidays and special events, it may be necessary to evaluate the extent to which you have relied on the celebration of a particular faith (Christianity in this example) at the potential neglect of other faiths. If you believe you have not included other faiths, you may want to ask the parents who came to see you if they would be willing to assist you in using holidays as a chance to discuss the origins and meanings of traditions. Let the parents know you are genuinely interested in learning about the customs, traditions, and values of all of your students. One strategy might be to design a curriculum unit that analyzes different traditions for common themes.

Page Ref: 189

5) What are some things schools and teachers can do in this instance to accommodate cultural diversity?

Answer: In addition to evaluating your holiday celebrations, you will also want to reflect upon your curriculum and grouping arrangements to ensure you are engaging in culturally relevant teaching. You will want to analyze your curriculum for any potential cultural biases. Woolfolk suggests teachers can also encourage their students to become "bias detectors", especially for critiquing information from the media. In regards to grouping arrangements, you could try "study buddies" or pairs, which will encourage students to interact with others who may be culturally different from them selves. Another strategy recommended by Woolfolk for dealing with cultural diversity is for teachers to attend community fairs and cultural festivals. Cultural diversity requires teachers to know their own biases, stereotypes, traditions, and values. It is also important for teachers to know the cultural beliefs, values, and norms of their students. According to Ladson–Billings research, the best teachers are those who provide culturally relevant pedagogy for students of color. Culturally relevant pedagogy includes the following components: student experience authentic academic success; student develop and maintain their cultural competence; students develop a critical consciousness to challenge the status quo and social inequities.

Page Ref: 191, 198, 189

Chapter 6   Behavioral Views of Learning

Multiple-Choice Questions

1) Behavioral theories of learning emphasize

    A) development.

    B) nature over nurture.

    C) observable actions.

    D) thinking.

Answer: C

Explanation: C) Behavioral theories *emphasize external events or observable actions*. They ignore or de–emphasize internal events such as thinking. The key element is whether the behavior can be directly observed.

Page Ref: 206
Skill: Knowledge
P: .75
D: .32

2) Strict behaviorists, such as J.B. Watson, would most likely say that cognitive theorists

    A) are too mechanical in their approach.

    B) are unable to account for complex mental tasks.

    C) fail to account for internal processes.

    D) speculate about invisible and unprovable concepts.

Answer: D

Explanation: D) Strict behaviorists would most likely say that cognitive psychologists *speculate about invisible and unprovable concepts*. Behaviorists focus on observable stimuli and behavior; they would view "cognition" as not observable and subjective.

Page Ref: 206–207
Skill: Understanding
P: .74
D: .31

3) The principle of contiguity involves an association between

   A) a negative and a positive stimulus.

   B) emotion and behavior.

   C) two events through pairing.

   D) two events through reinforcement.

   Answer: C

   Explanation: C) The principle of contiguity involves an association between *two events through pairing*. For example, the response "stopping" and the stimulus "red light" become associated by being paired. When the driver subsequently sees a red light, the stopping response is the one likely to be selected. (For some drivers, unfortunately, stopping is not always the strongest response in that situation.)

   Page Ref: 208
   Skill: Knowledge
   P: .70
   D: .37

4) During music class, Lisa enthusiastically sings aloud with her class, but the teacher comments, "Lisa, please...you sound like an owl in a torture chamber." Lisa turns bright red. The next week she feels ill when it is time to go to music class again. Feeling anxiety at the prospect of going to music class is an example of

   A) an unconditioned stimulus.

   B) classical conditioning.

   C) cognitive learning.

   D) social learning.

   Answer: B

   Explanation: B) Lisa's reaction most clearly illustrates *classical conditioning*. Evidently, she is now associating music class with embarrassment due to the earlier pairing of her singing (and music class) with the teacher's public criticism of her performance.

   Page Ref: 208
   Skill: Understanding
   P: .61
   D: .30

5) In the above example involving Lisa, feeling ill at the prospect of going to the music class served as the

   A) conditioned response.

   B) conditioned stimulus.

   C) unconditioned response.

   D) unconditioned stimulus.

Answer: A

Explanation: A) For Lisa, feeling ill at the prospect of going to music class served as the *conditioned response*. This response did not occur naturally, but was produced by the teacher's inadvertent pairing of the previously neutral stimulus, music class, with feelings of embarrassment.

Page Ref: 209
Skill: Understanding

6) In classical conditioning, the conditioned stimulus and the unconditioned stimulus must be

   A) dependent upon reward.

   B) equivalent stimuli.

   C) in a contiguous relationship.

   D) in a noncontiguous relationship.

Answer: C

Explanation: C) In classical conditioning, the conditioned stimulus (e.g., tuning fork tone) and unconditioned stimulus (e.g., meat powder) must be in a *contiguous relationship*. Such a relationship means they occur together, with the CS appearing immediately prior to the UCS.

Page Ref: 208
Skill: Knowledge
P: .81
D: .36

7) Which of the following is a practical implication of contiguity theory?

   A) Avoid the use of punishment whenever humanly possible.

   B) Make sure that the last response to a stimulus is the correct response.

   C) Use continuous reinforcement rather than intermittent reinforcement.

   D) Use intermittent reinforcement instead of continuous reinforcement.

Answer: B

Explanation: B) Contiguity theory views learning as dependent on the association of a response with a stimulus. By *making sure that the last response is correct*, the probability is increased that the correct response will be the one associated and emitted the next time that the same stimulus occurs.

Page Ref: 208
Skill: Understanding

8) A neutral stimulus is paired with an unconditioned stimulus that brings about an unconditioned response. Through repeated pairings of the neutral stimulus and the unconditioned stimulus, the

A) conditioned stimulus will trigger a conditioned response.

B) neutral stimulus will come to be ignored.

C) unconditioned response will become extinct.

D) unconditioned response becomes its own stimulus.

Answer: A

Explanation: A) A neutral stimulus (e.g., a tuning fork tone) is paired repeatedly with an unconditioned stimulus (e.g., meat powder) which brings about an unconditioned response (e.g., salivating to food). The likely result is that the *neutral stimulus will trigger a conditioned stimulus that brings about a conditioned response* (e.g., salivating in response to the tone). This process is called classical conditioning.

Page Ref: 208
Skill: Understanding
P: .56
D: .44

9) In an experiment, an electric can opener is used to open a can, and no salivation by the subject is detected. After a number of pairings between the can opener's operation and food, any time the can opener is used, the subject salivates. The conditioned response in this study is the

A) can opener.

B) food.

C) salivation to the can opener.

D) salivation to the food.

Answer: C

Explanation: C) The conditioned response (CS) in this experiment would be *salivation to the can opener*. Prior to the pairing of the neutral stimulus, can opener, with the unconditioned stimulus, food, this response did not occur. It needed to be learned or "conditioned."

Page Ref: 209
Skill: Understanding
P: .94
D: .15

10) Ray's temper tantrums have finally driven his mother to her "wits' end." Ray's mother resolves that she will ignore the tantrums no matter what. This plan is an example of

    A) classical conditioning.

    B) discrimination.

    C) extinction.

    D) shaping.

Answer: C

Explanation: C) By ignoring Ray's tantrums, his mother is using *extinction*. This approach involves withholding reinforcement (attention) for behavior, resulting in the behavior decreasing in frequency and intensity.

Page Ref: 214
Skill: Understanding
P: .60
D: .28

11) The law of effect in Thorndike's theory of learning is related to the concept of

    A) antecedents.

    B) consequences.

    C) patterns.

    D) punishments.

Answer: B

Explanation: B) A behavior that produces satisfying *consequences* in a given situation will tend be repeated given a repeat of the same situation. This statement refers to Thorndike's law of effect. In Skinner's approach, Thorndike's law of effect would be reflected as a consequence of a behavior and the relationship is expressed as antecedent–behavior–consequence (A–B–C).

Page Ref: 210
Skill: Knowledge

12) B. F. Skinner is to _____, as Ivan Pavlov is to _____.

    A) classical conditioning; cognitive learning

    B) classical conditioning; operant conditioning

    C) cognitive learning; classical conditioning

    D) operant conditioning; classical conditioning

Answer: D

Explanation: D) B.F. Skinner is to *operant conditioning* as Ivan Pavlov is to *classical conditioning*. Each scientist is associated with the development of the respective behavioral theories.

Page Ref: 208, 210
Skill: Understanding

13) Operant conditioning differs from classical conditioning by

    A) dealing primarily with reflexive types of responses.

    B) focusing on animal behavior to a much greater extent than on human behavior.

    C) focusing on the consequences of voluntary behavior.

    D) treating learners as passive rather then active agents.

Answer: C

Explanation: C) Operant conditioning differs from classical conditioning by focusing on goal–directed actions and the *consequences of behavior*. Learners, therefore, respond in order to obtain or avoid certain consequences (e.g., rewards and punishments, respectively).

Page Ref: 210
Skill: Knowledge
P: .86
D: .29

14) A consequence is defined by Skinner as a reinforcer or a punisher depending on whether it

    A) increases or decreases the frequency of the behavior that it follows.

    B) is designed to promote desirable behavior or suppress undesirable behavior.

    C) is pleasurable or uncomfortable for the subject receiving the consequence.

    D) occurs antecedent to or as a consequence of the behavior.

Answer: A

Explanation: A) According to Skinner, whether a stimulus is a reinforcer or a punisher depends on whether *the stimulus increases or decreases the behavior that it follows*. If the consequence increases the behavior that it follows, it is a reinforcer. If the consequence decreases or suppresses the behavior, the consequence is a punishment.

Page Ref: 210–211
Skill: Understanding
P: .48
D: .47

15) Mr. Lynch always uses his "mean" face to stop undesirable behavior in his first–period class. However, even though he looks at Tommy with his mean face each time Tommy talks out of turn, Tommy is talking out of turn more and more frequently. For Tommy, the mean face is apparently a

   A) cue.

   B) model.

   C) negative reinforcer.

   D) positive reinforcer.

Answer: D

Explanation: D) For Tommy, the mean face of Mr. Lynch is a *positive reinforcer*. A reinforcer is a stimulus or event that increases the tendency to make a particular response. In this case, Mr. Lynch's mean face reinforces Tommy's talking out of turn.

Page Ref: 211
Skill: Understanding
P: .63
D: .33

16) Removing an aversive stimulus to increase the frequency of a behavior exemplifies

   A) negative reinforcement.

   B) positive reinforcement.

   C) presentation punishment.

   D) removal punishment.

Answer: A

Explanation: A) Removing an aversive stimulus to increase the frequency of a behavior is *negative reinforcement*. The key element is "reinforcement," that occurs in this case by taking something "negative" away.

Page Ref: 211
Skill: Knowledge

17) You finally take out the garbage in order to get your father to stop pestering you. Your behavior is being influenced by

   A) negative reinforcement.

   B) positive reinforcement.

   C) presentation punishment.

   D) removal punishment.

Answer: A

Explanation: A) Your behavior is being influenced by *negative reinforcement*. By taking out the garbage, you are removing a negative stimulus (father's nagging).

Page Ref: 211
Skill: Understanding
P: .59
D: .37

18) The essential difference between negative reinforcement and punishment is that

   A) negative reinforcement decreases misbehavior rather quickly.

   B) punishment decreases the behavior while negative reinforcement increases it.

   C) punishment is more effective in bringing about a positive change in behavior.

   D) punishment is presented after, and reinforcement before, the behavior has occurred.

Answer: B

Explanation: B) The essential difference between negative reinforcers and punishment is that *punishment decreases behavior while negative reinforcement increases it* (by removing an aversive stimulus). Negative reinforcement is a reinforcing, not punishing, condition.

Page Ref: 211–212
Skill: Knowledge

19) 17–year–old Kelly receives a ticket for speeding. Her parents take away the privilege of using the car. Her parents are using

   A) negative reinforcement.

   B) positive reinforcement.

   C) presentation punishment.

   D) removal punishment.

Answer: D

Explanation: D) Kelly's parents are using *removal punishment,* which is defined as taking something positive (car use) away as a consequence for misbehavior (the speeding ticket).

Page Ref: 212
Skill: Understanding

20) Mr. Smith uses a token economy system in his history class. Whenever Bill breaks a rule, he lose a "chip." If the infraction is major, Bill loses several chips. This is an example of

   A) cueing.

   B) presentation punishment.

   C) removal punishment.

   D) satiation.

Answer: C

Explanation: C) Bill is experiencing *removal punishment.* Mr. Smith takes a positive stimulus (a chip) away as a consequence of Bill's rule infraction.

Page Ref: 212
Skill: Understanding
P: .83
D: .22

21) Yancey turns on the water faucet to get a drink. What schedule of reinforcement typically prevails?

    A) Continuous

    B) Fixed–interval

    C) Variable–interval

    D) Variable–ratio

Answer: A

Explanation: A) When Yancey turns on the faucet to get a drink, a *continuous schedule of reinforcement* typically prevails. (It is probably rare that the faucet would fail to produce the water.)

Page Ref: 213
Skill: Understanding

22) Slot machines that pay off after an indeterminate number of uses illustrate what schedule of reinforcement?

    A) Fixed–interval

    B) Fixed–ratio

    C) Variable–interval

    D) Variable–ratio

Answer: D

Explanation: D) Slot machines use a *variable-ratio schedule of reinforcement* by rewarding the gambler after a variable (indeterminate) number of plays that change rapidly and consistently from trial to trial. This schedule will motivate many gamblers to respond consistently, a very reinforcing schedule for casinos!

Page Ref: 213
Skill: Understanding
P: .84
D: .33

23) What schedule of reinforcement is most likely to be involved when teachers give "pop" quizzes?

    A) Fixed–interval

    B) Fixed–ratio

    C) Variable–interval

    D) Variable–ratio

Answer: C

Explanation: C) Pop quizzing employs a *variable-interval schedule*. Students never know when the time for the quiz will be. This schedule fosters consistent responding:studying each night for a possible quiz the next day.

Page Ref: 213
Skill: Understanding
P: .75
D: .26

24) Mr. Saunders hates sending in his income tax forms each year and constantly worries that his return will be the "one" selected for auditing. Therefore, he completes the forms carefully and honestly in order to avoid a possible penalty, but he continues to worry about being audited. What reinforcement schedule is most likely to be involved?

 A) Fixed–interval

 B) Fixed–ratio

 C) Variable–interval

 D) Variable–ratio

Answer: D

Explanation: D) A *variable–ratio schedule* is affecting Mr. Saunders because Internal Revenue tax audits occur randomly. Mr. Saunders' income tax return could be one that is selected in any given year, but he doesn't know if or when it might be selected. Because the schedule is unpredictable, Mr. Saunders remains honest in case he is chosen for an audit.

Page Ref: 213
Skill: Understanding

25) The schedule of reinforcement that is the most appropriate to use in the classroom because it encourages persistence and high rates of response is what type of schedule?

 A) Fixed–interval

 B) Fixed–ratio

 C) Variable–interval

 D) Variable–ratio

Answer: D

Explanation: D) A *variable–ratio (VR) schedule encourages persistence and high rates of response*. Consequently, teachers are advised to use a variable–ratio schedule whenever reinforcement is needed. A variable–interval schedule also encourages persistence but is predictable when the individual figures out the interval timing.

Page Ref: 213
Skill: Understanding
P: .43
D: .43

26) Persistence in responding is increased by what type of reinforcement schedule?

   A) Fixed

   B) Interval

   C) Ratio

   D) Variable

Answer: D

Explanation: D) Persistence in responding is likely to be most directly strengthened by *variable schedules (both ratio and interval types)*. Variable schedules, especially variable-ratio schedules, are unpredictable and consequently "keep you on your toes." You never can be certain when the reinforcement or punishment may be coming.

Page Ref: 213
Skill: Knowledge

27) Bart uses an old cigarette lighter that has become unreliable. It usually takes from one to 10 flicks to make it work. When the lighter is out of fluid, it will not work at all. By the time that Bart figures out the problem, he has tried flicking it 15 to 20 times. This situation illustrates the principle that

   A) fixed-reinforcement schedules will produce the fastest performance.

   B) intermittent-reinforcement schedules will aid prior learning.

   C) interval-reinforcement schedules will produce the fastest performance.

   D) variable-reinforcement schedules will produce the greatest persistence.

Answer: D

Explanation: D) *Variable-reinforcement schedules produce the greatest persistence.* Bart has learned not to expect the lighter to work every time. Thus, if he flicks it and it doesn't light, he is conditioned to continue to flick it until it does.

Page Ref: 213
Skill: Understanding
P: .70
D: .28

28) Kathy frequently makes faces at her classmates. Instead of punishing her for making faces, the teacher has the students totally ignore Kathy. This example illustrates the teacher's attempt at

    A) cuing.

    B) extinction.

    C) modeling.

    D) shaping.

Answer: B

Explanation: B) The teacher is attempting to extinguish Kathy's making faces behavior by ignoring her behavior. If the students as well as the teacher can ignore Kathy long enough, their *attempt at extinction* should be successful.

Page Ref: 214
Skill: Understanding
P: .65
D: .25

29) Which one of the following statements is an example of cueing?

    A) "Please remember to put your name on each page."

    B) "Today's lesson was much too noisy."

    C) "Why didn't you remember to do your homework?"

    D) "Why didn't you clean up before you left?"

Answer: A

Explanation: A) Cueing is providing an antecedent stimulus before a behavior should occur. It is used in classroom management to help students remember the behavior. An example is *"Please remember to write your names on each page."*

Page Ref: 214
Skill: Understanding
P: .89
D: .18

30) During the first few days of class, Mr. Brackman noticed some isolated instances of minor misbehavior such as talking out of turn. His initial approach to dealing with this should probably be to use

    A) praise–and–ignore techniques.

    B) prompting and cueing.

    C) response cost.

    D) shaping.

Answer: A

Explanation: A) A general rule for teachers such as Mr. Brackman is to employ the least restrictive, least disruptive strategies first. Therefore, *praise–and–ignore techniques are recommended* as an initial response to minor misbehavior.

Page Ref: 216
Skill: Understanding
P: .30
D: .31

31) The teacher says to Marty, "Good job," but frowns as he looks at her. According to O'Leary and O'Leary, the teacher's praise is **NOT**

    A) believable.

    B) contingent.

    C) identified with the behavior.

    D) salient.

Answer: A

Explanation: A) O'Leary and O'Leary (1977) proposed that praise must be *believable* in order for it to be effective. Frowning at Marty while saying "good job"to Marty would clearly lack this quality.

Page Ref: 217
Skill: Understanding

32) The Premack Principle states that

    A) a less–preferred activity is postponed until after a preferred activity.

    B) a preferred activity is withheld until rewards are earned.

    C) a preferred activity is a reinforcer for a less–preferred activity.

    D) less–preferred activities can be very effective as punishment activities.

Answer: C

Explanation: C) The Premack Principle uses a *preferred activity as a reinforcer for a less preferred activity.* An example is, "Clean your room and then you can watch T.V."

Page Ref: 217–218
Skill: Knowledge
P: .88
D: .22

33) According to Woolfolk, the best way to determine potential reinforcers is to

    A) ask the experienced teachers for their suggestions.

    B) establish a student committee and have them vote.

    C) observe what students choose to do in their free time.

    D) set up activities to see if students enjoy them.

Answer: C

Explanation: C) Woolfolk suggests that the best way to determine appropriate reinforcers for students is to observe *what they choose to do in their free time*. If, for example, you observe that they frequently try to play computer games, it is a good bet that free time to engage in that activity will be an effective reinforcer for good behavior.

Page Ref: 217–218
Skill: Knowledge
P: .87
D: .15

34) During math lessons, Ms. Olson continually observed Jim reading stories from his English anthology. She has probably found

    A) a short attention span to be a problem for Jim.

    B) an effective reinforcer for Jim.

    C) that her lessons are too hard for Jim.

    D) that Jim dislikes authority figures.

Answer: B

Explanation: B) Ms. Olson probably found an *effective reinforcer* for Jimmy. It is suggested in the Woolfolk textbook that the best way to determine appropriate reinforcers is to determine what students like to do in their spare time.

Page Ref: 217–218
Skill: Understanding
P: .79
D: .21

35) Ms. Johnson's sixth graders complained about diagramming sentences, and they were able convince her to show a movie first. Ms. Johnson made the common error of

    A) bribing the students in order to gain their cooperation.

    B) promising a reward for an unfavored activity.

    C) providing an incompatible alternative to the lesson.

    D) using a reinforcer before a low-frequency behavior.

Answer: D

Explanation: D) Ms. Johnson violated the Premack Principle by *using the reinforcer (movie) before the low-frequency behavior (diagramming sentences)*. The reverse ordering should have been employed instead.

Page Ref: 217–218
Skill: Understanding
P: .61
D: .38

36) Shaping is an appropriate method for developing new behavior when

    A) no appropriate reinforcers can be found.

    B) performance is otherwise too poor to gain reinforcement.

    C) students are capable of the behavior but seldom perform it.

    D) there is no one available to model the appropriate behavior.

Answer: B

Explanation: B) Shaping, also called successive approximations, involves reinforcing progress toward a response rather than requiring the complete response. This procedure may be particularly effective when *performance is otherwise too poor to gain reinforcement* (i.e., the learner is making progress but is unlikely to be capable of performing the full response).

Page Ref: 218
Skill: Knowledge
P: .27
D: .34

37) Which one of the following is a major advantage of task analysis?

   A) Allows for creativity in student responses.

   B) Describes the sequence of skills leading to a goal.

   C) Reduces the need for expository presentations.

   D) Requires only minimal time to use.

Answer: B

Explanation: B) Task analysis has the advantage of *defining the sequence of skills needed to complete a more complex task or goal*. With the sequence defined, it is easier to concentrate on teaching the component skills leading to mastery of the task.

Page Ref: 218–219
Skill: Knowledge
P: .83
D: .28

38) An example of the use of positive practice is having students

   A) develop sentences using commonly misused words.

   B) ignore mistakes and practice the items they know.

   C) study a list of commonly misspelled words.

   D) write "I will not chew gum" 100 times.

Answer: A

Explanation: A) Positive practice is a strategy that makes students correct a mistake by practicing the correct response. An example would be *using a misspelled word in new sentences*.

Page Ref: 219
Skill: Understanding
P: .61
D: .28

39) Mrs. Lever allows Nathaniel to be the first to leave the uncomfortable bus because he has behaved so well on the trip. The technique being used is

   A) cuing.

   B) negative reinforcement.

   C) positive practice.

   D) shaping.

Answer: B

Explanation: B) Mrs. Lever is using *negative reinforcement* by taking away an aversive condition (staying on the uncomfortable bus) as a consequence for Nathaniel's good behavior.

Page Ref: 211
Skill: Understanding

40) Dan enters the classroom, puts his foot in the wastebasket, and drags it around the room to the delight of his peers. When the teacher insists that Dan continue this same behavior, the teacher is attempting to use

    A) negative reinforcement.

    B) positive reinforcement.

    C) satiation.

    D) shaping.

Answer: C

Explanation: C) *Satiation is a form of extinction.* It involves having students repeat a misbehavior (e.g., Dan's dragging the wastepaper basket) until they grow tired of it and the undesired behavior stops.

Page Ref: 221
Skill: Understanding
P: .82
D: .28

41) Which one of the following students is an example of the use of "satiation?"

    A) John disrupts the class and then is sent out of the room.

    B) Louise makes a rude noise and is forced to continue until she becomes bored.

    C) Randy finally becomes quiet and is then allowed to leave for recess.

    D) Whitney loses thirty minutes of recess because she had been misbehaving.

Answer: B

Explanation: B) The teacher is using *satiation.* By having Louise repeat the misbehavior, the teacher is hoping that she will tire of it and then be less likely to do it on her own in the future. In this way, stopping her misbehavior rather than doing it becomes reinforcing for Louise.

Page Ref: 221
Skill: Understanding
P: .86
D: .22

42) Wendy, a fifth-grade child, just loves to throw paper airplanes during class. To change Wendy's behavior, the teacher insisted that Wendy throw paper airplanes continually for one hour. What behavioral concept does this illustrate?

   A) Modeling

   B) Response cost

   C) Satiation

   D) Shaping

Answer: C

Explanation: C) Wendy is experiencing *satiation*. She is being required to repeat a misbehavior (throwing the airplanes) until she becomes tired of it (satiated). In a sense, she is being conditioned **NOT** to want to engage in that behavior.

Page Ref: 221
Skill: Understanding
P: .88
D: .36

43) The most effective reprimands are those that are

   A) sharp and private.

   B) sharp and public.

   C) soft and private.

   D) soft and public.

Answer: C

Explanation: C) O'Leary and his associates found that *soft, private reprimands were more effective* in decreasing disruptive behavior than loud, public reprimands. The likely reason is that soft reprimands neither disrupt the class nor make the student the center of attention.

Page Ref: 221–222
Skill: Knowledge
P: .76
D: .20

44) Each time Robert fails to do his homework, five points are deducted from his total course points. The procedure being used by the teacher is

   A) negative reinforcement.

   B) presentation punishment.

   C) response cost.

   D) satiation.

Answer: C

Explanation: C) Robert is receiving *response cost*, a form of removal punishment, by losing something positive (points) for undesired behavior (not doing homework).

Page Ref: 222
Skill: Understanding
P: .71
D: .37

45) Mr. Lubinetti sends students to a "time-out" box when they become too physically aggressive during hockey practice. Once they have been seated quietly for at least five minutes, they are allowed to re-enter the game. The chance *to leave the "time-out" box* is an example of what type of consequence?

   A) Negative reinforcement

   B) Positive reinforcement

   C) Presentation punishment

   D) Removal punishment

Answer: A

Explanation: A) The chance to leave the "time-out" box is *negative reinforcement*. Mr. Lubinetti is removing a negative stimulus (the "time out" box), thus providing reinforcement for good behavior (quietly waiting out the time). Losing the opportunity to play is an example of removal punishment, while being sent to the "box" is presentation punishment, and being allowed to play after five minutes in the "box" is positive reinforcement. However, the question asks for the type of consequence exemplified by the *chance to leave the "box"*, which is negative reinforcement.

Page Ref: 222
Skill: Understanding
P: .43
D: .32

46) The Good Behavior Game is based on the application of

    A) contingency contracts.

    B) group consequences.

    C) peer tutoring.

    D) primary reinforcers.

Answer: B

Explanation: B) The Good Behavior Game employs *group consequences as a strategy by making*
                team rewards dependent upon how team members behave. Specifically, each time a
                student breaks a behavior rule, his/her team loses a point. The issue here is to
                have peer pressure to conform be a motivating force for good behavior.

Page Ref: 226
Skill: Knowledge

47) Woolfolk suggests that programs for promoting group responsibility may be particularly hard
on

    A) popular students who must perform well for everyone.

    B) students who try to sabotage the system.

    C) teachers who must monitor the entire class.

    D) unpopular students who are unable to perform well.

Answer: D

Explanation: D) A disadvantage of programs intended to promote group responsibility is that
                a whole group may suffer because of the misbehavior or mistakes of one
                individual. This result could be *particularly difficult for unpopular students who*
                are unable to perform (or even choose to misbehave in order to obtain attention),
                because it can provoke even further rejection by teammates.

Page Ref: 226
Skill: Knowledge

48) Which one of the following statements is **TRUE** regarding the use of peer pressure in applying
group consequences? Peer pressure

    A) can be effectively monitored by the teacher.

    B) has little effect on most misbehavior.

    C) may be both a positive and a negative influence.

    D) should be eliminated as much as possible.

Answer: C

Explanation: C) When group consequences are used, peer pressure can become the key factor
                in influencing behavior. Although peer pressure can have powerful effects on
                students, unfortunately, *the effects of peer pressure can be positive or negative*.
                Negative effects occur when peers put unfair pressure on, or tease, an
                individual who has cost the team points by making a mistake.

Page Ref: 226
Skill: Knowledge

49) Mr. Bennett's student teacher suggested using a token reinforcement strategy with his disruptive sixth-grade class. The token system was received well by students and soon the class was following the classroom rules. Now that this strategy is working well, the tokens should be distributed

   A) by the students rather than the teacher.

   B) on a continuous schedule.

   C) on an intermittent schedule.

   D) so that they gradually increase in value.

Answer: C

Explanation: C) Principles of operant conditioning suggest that, once a token reinforcement system is working well as it is for Mr. Bennett's student teacher, the tokens should then be distributed on an *intermittent schedule*. The reason is that intermittent schedules make responses more resistant to extinction.

Page Ref: 213
Skill: Understanding
P: .73
D: .40

50) Rewards to be purchased with earned tokens should be

   A) gradually decreased in cost over time.

   B) limited to consumable items.

   C) limited to school-related items and supplies.

   D) varied in price so that all students may be rewarded.

Answer: D

Explanation: D) One guideline for establishing a token reinforcement system is to *offer a variety of rewards with different prices*. As a result, both the lower- and higher-achievers will be able to earn rewards commensurate with their individual levels of performance. Over time, the requirements (prices) for rewards should be increased.

Page Ref: 227-228
Skill: Knowledge

51) The position taken by Woolfolk on token reinforcement systems is they should be used primarily

   A) as an incentive program to reward classes that have met unit objectives.

   B) by science or math teachers, due to the objective nature of their subjects.

   C) in situations where students are not making progress with conventional methods.

   D) with gifted classes or older students who are self-motivated.

Answer: C

Explanation: C) Woolfolk has taken the position that token economies are difficult and time-consuming to implement. Therefore, their usage should be reserved for situations in which students *are* **NOT** *progressing satisfactorily with conventional methods* (e.g., students who are unmotivated or low-achieving).

Page Ref: 227-228
Skill: Knowledge

52) In a contingency contract program, teachers set up

   A) a group performance contract with each class.

   B) individual performance contracts with each student.

   C) "reward contracts" as models for misbehaving students.

   D) punishment contracts with students who misbehave.

Answer: B

Explanation: B) Contingency contract programs involve *setting up an individual contract with each student* (not just those who misbehave). The contract specifies what the individual must do to earn a privilege or reward.

Page Ref: 226-227
Skill: Knowledge

53) Lionel was humiliated when he forgot his lines in a play. Now he refuses to take part in any function of the speech class. Based on the behavioral principles discussed by Woolfolk, the best strategy for Lionel's teacher would be to

   A) assign Lionel jobs that do not involve any speaking.

   B) assign Lionel to work with another student until the feeling becomes extinguished.

   C) bring Lionel back into class participation in small steps.

   D) help Lionel regain his confidence by assigning him a major role in a play.

Answer: C

Explanation: C) The teacher needs to involve Lionel in acting or else take the chance that he will continue to avoid such activities. However, asking him to do too much may be overly threatening. The best approach, therefore, would be to use *shaping, or involving him in a task using small steps.*

Page Ref: 217-218
Skill: Understanding
P: .78
D: .30

54) The concluding step of the self-management process is

    A) evaluating progress.

    B) goal-setting.

    C) recording progress.

    D) self-reinforcement.

Answer: D

Explanation: D) Although there is some disagreement about its necessity, the last step in the self-management process is *self-reinforcement*. It involves rewarding oneself for completing a task.

Page Ref: 234–235
Skill: Knowledge

55) Cognitive behavior modification adds what to the management process?

    A) Parent intervention

    B) Response cost

    C) Self-instruction

    D) Self-reinforcement

Answer: C

Explanation: C) Cognitive behavior modification adds *self-verbalization to the self-management process*. The purpose of self-verbalization is to guide behavior as one works through a task. (This notion is similar to Vygotsky's private speech.)

Page Ref: 215–216
Skill: Knowledge

56) Which one of the following in the correct sequence of phases for Bandura's model of observational learning?

    A) Attention, retention, motivation, and production

    B) Attention, retention, production, motivation

    C) Motivation, attention, production, retention

    D) Motivation, retention, reduction, attention

Answer: B

Explanation: B) The correct sequence of steps in Bandura's model is *attention, retention, production, and motivation*. We pay attention to something, remember it, produce it, and are then motivated to repeat it.

Page Ref: 230–231
Skill: Knowledge

57) Ms. Jackson's perception of her capabilities to effectively deal with a particular task is her sense of

   A) modeling.

   B) self–efficacy.

   C) self–reinforcement.

   D) vicarious reinforcement.

Answer: B

Explanation: B) *Self–efficacy* is defined as a person's sense of being able to deal effectively with a particular task.

Page Ref: 232
Skill: Understanding

58) The "ripple effect" involves

   A) peer tutoring that helps other students to learn.

   B) teacher modeling to demonstrate good behaviors to students.

   C) the contiguous spreading of behaviors by imitation.

   D) the emotional reactions of students to establish attitudes toward new materials.

Answer: C

Explanation: C) The "ripple effect" uses *imitation to spread behaviors*. A positive example is when the teacher disciplines a high status individual and everyone immediately behaves properly. The good behavior "ripples" through the class.

Page Ref: 233
Skill: Knowledge

59) Ms. Gibbs, the physics teacher, explains her thinking processes to her students and shows them the exact steps she took to solve the problem. What technique is she using?

   A) Associating

   B) Cueing

   C) Modeling

   D) Shaping

Answer: C

Explanation: C) Ms. Gibbs is using *modeling*. By explaining her own behaviors, she is demonstrating to the class how to solve the problem.

Page Ref: 233
Skill: Understanding

Completion Questions

1) A relatively permanent change in a person's knowledge or behavior that results from experiences is called _____.

Answer: learning
Page Ref: 206

2) The influences of external events or behavior are the focus of _____ learning theories.

Answer: behavioral
Page Ref: 206

3) The association between a stimulus and a response that occur together is the basis for _____ learning.

Answer: contiguity
Page Ref: 208

4) In classical conditioning, the response made to the unconditioned stimulus before conditioning occurs is the _____ response.

Answer: unconditioned
Page Ref: 208

5) When a particular tone is presented repeatedly but is not followed by a conditioned stimulus, _____ has occurred, if there had been no response earlier with no previous conditioning.

Answer: extinction
Page Ref: 214

6) Any consequence that strengthens the behavior it follows is a(n) _____.

Answer: reinforcer
Page Ref: 210

7) When an aversive stimulus is removed following a behavior and the reinforcement behavior increases, the type of consequence that occurs is _____.

Answer: negative reinforcement
Page Ref: 211

8) When teachers take away privileges for students' inappropriate behavior, they are applying _____ punishment.

Answer: removal
Page Ref: 212

9) The schedule of reinforcement that produces the highest and most consistent response rate is the _____ schedule.

Answer: variable–ratio
Page Ref: 213

10) Removal of a given reinforcement leads to _____.

Answer: extinction
Page Ref: 214

11) The act of providing an antecedent stimulus just before a particular behavior is to take place is _____.

Answer: cueing
Page Ref: 214

12) The application of learning principles to change behavior is called applied behavioral analysis or _____.

Answer: behavior modification
Page Ref: 215

13) Reinforcing completion of a less–preferred activity by allowing participation in a desired activity illustrates the use of the _____.

Answer: Premack Principle
Page Ref: 217–219

14) The behavioral strategy of successive approximations is called _____.

Answer: shaping
Page Ref: 218–219

15) Breaking complex performances into sub–skills and sub–processes is part of a systematic procedure called _____.

Answer: task analysis
Page Ref: 218

16) A means of suppressing inappropriate behavior by making students repeat the behavior until they become tired of doing it is _____.

Answer: satiation
Page Ref: 221

17) For certain infractions of the rules, people must lose a reinforcer (e.g., privileges, time, etc.) and suffer _____.

Answer: response cost
Page Ref: 222

18) Interventions designed to replace problem behaviors with new behaviors that serve the same purpose for the students are called _____.

Answer: positive behavioral supports

Explanation: *Positive behavioral supports* are interventions designed to replace problems behaviors with new actions that serve the same purpose for the student.

Page Ref: 223

19) Mr. Crutch divides his class into groups and each group has points taken away if students do not behavior. He is employing the _____ game.

Answer: good behavior

Explanation: The *good behavior game* is used for holding students accountable for good behavior. Assigned teams loose points if students break the rules fo good behavior.

Page Ref: 226

20) Crediting all students to earn a reward for both academic work and positive classroom behavior is a _____ system.

Answer: token reinforcement
Page Ref: 227–228

21) In order for students to gain control of their own learning, they must be able to set their own goals, participate in self-evaluation, and achieve self-_____, although there is some disagreement about whether this last step is really necessary.

Answer: reinforcement
Page Ref: 225

22) Lucia observes Martin flawlessly read his poem for the class, and she says to herself "I can do that." Lucia is demonstrating what Bandura refers to as _____.

Answer: self-efficacy

Explanation: *Self-efficacy* refers to an individual's sense of being able to deal effectively with a specific task.

Page Ref: 232

23) An important element in cognitive behavior modification while performing a task is _____.

Answer: self-verbalization
Page Ref: 236

24) In Bandura's social cognitive theory, "learning by doing" is referred to as _____ learning.

Answer: enactive

Explanation: *Enactive learning* is "learning by doing" and experiencing the consequences of one's actions.

Page Ref: 230

True/False Questions

1) Learning is defined as a deliberate action that produces a positive result.

Answer: FALSE
Page Ref: 206

2) In Pavlov's experiment the conditioned stimulus was the tuning fork tone.

Answer: TRUE
Page Ref: 208

3) Extinction in classical conditioning occurs when the conditioned stimulus is presented repeatedly without the unconditioned stimulus.

Answer: TRUE
Page Ref: 214

4) B.F. Skinner established the basis for operant conditioning and E.L. Thorndike was responsible for developing the concept of operant conditioning.

Answer: FALSE
Page Ref: 210

5) Negative reinforcement introduces an aversive stimulus to decrease the frequency of a behavior.

Answer: FALSE
Page Ref: 211

6) Detention after school is an example of both presentation and removal punishment.

Answer: TRUE
Page Ref: 212

7) The act of providing an antecedent stimulus immediately before a particular behavior is to take place is called *prompting*.

Answer: FALSE
Page Ref: 214

8) In using the Premack Principle, it is important that the higher frequency behavior happens first.

Answer: FALSE
Page Ref: 217–218

9) Positive practice involves having students give correct responses several times immediately following errors.

Answer: TRUE
Page Ref: 219

10) Removing something aversive as soon as the desired behavior occurs is an example of punishment.

Answer: FALSE
Page Ref: 212

11) Woolfolk agrees asking a student to repeat a problem behavior past the point of interest or motivation is an effective strategy for eliminating disruptive behaviors.

Answer: FALSE

Explanation: Requiring a student to repeat a problem behavior past the point of interest or motivation is referred to as *satiation* and is not recommended.
Page Ref: 221

12) Ms. Tolleson is effectively using social isolation when she removes Mark, who is being disruptive, for a period of 60 minutes.

Answer: FALSE

Explanation: Effective use of *social isolation* typically involves removing the disruptive student from his or her peers for about 5 to 10 minutes.
Page Ref: 222

13) Mr. Matin interviews a student about her disruptive behavior to learn about her reasons for the behavior. This approach is an example of doing functional behavioral assessment.

Answer: TRUE

Explanation: Although there are may procedures for conducting *functional behavioral assessments,* interviewing students about their behavior is an acceptable approach.
Page Ref: 224

14) A contingency contract is an example of a system for rewarding positive group consequences.

Answer: FALSE
Page Ref: 226–227

15) Reinforcement is an important concept in operant conditioning theory but is irrelevant to Bandura's social cognitive theory.

Answer: FALSE

Explanation: *Reinforcement* plays an important part in the motivation phase of observational learning, which is the final step in Bandura's model of observational learning.
Page Ref: 231

16) Researchers agree goals-setting is most beneficial for self-management when students keep their goals private.

Answer: FALSE

Explanation: Researchers recommend *goals* should be made public in order to best support self-management and behavioral change.
Page Ref: 235

17) Self-talk for students is one of the cognitive behavior modification strategies proposed by Meichenbaum.

Answer: TRUE

Explanation: In cognitive behavior modification, students are taught to think and engage in *self-talk* in order to guide themselves through the steps of a task.
Page Ref: 236

18) Over time, student-set goals tend to become higher with regard to performance standards.

Answer: FALSE
Page Ref: 235

19) Ethical questions related to the use of the strategies described in this chapter are comparable to those raised by any process that seeks to influence people.

Answer: TRUE
Page Ref: 238-239

20) The first step in Meichenbaum's self-instruction model is to have the student perform the task while using private speech.

Answer: FALSE

Explanation: The first step in *self-instruction* is to have an adult perform the task while talking to him- or herself out loud. This step is also referred to as cognitive modeling.
Page Ref: 236

Short Answer Questions

1) Define "learning" and discuss how it differs from other forms of behavior.

Answer: Learning occurs when experience causes a relatively permanent change in an individual's knowledge or behavior. It may be intentional or unintentional or positive or negative in its consequences. It is not, however, due to maturation or to temporary changes due to illness, fatigue, or hunger.
Page Ref: 206-207

2) Describe Pavlov's experiment in classical conditioning, identifying and defining all the major components of the conditioning model.

Answer: Pavlov was studying digestion in dogs when he noted that dogs began to salivate when they saw food. He called the food an unconditioned stimulus (US) and the salivation an unconditioned response (UR). Pavlov paired a tone with the food for a period of time and found that the tone alone (a conditioned stimulus) would bring on salivation (now a conditioned response).

Page Ref: 208

3) List the basic types of reinforcement schedules and describe the performances that they are likely to produce. Include performance patterns, rates, and effects of persistence.

Answer: Continuous reinforcement produces the fastest learning but least persistence. Several types of intermittent schedules exist: fixed–ratio (reinforce after a set number of responses); fixed–interval (reinforce after a set period of time); variable–ratio (reinforce after a variable number of responses); and variable–interval (reinforce after a variable amount of time). Pauses after reinforcement are found in fixed schedules. Ratio schedules produce the highest performance rates, and variable schedules produce the greatest persistence.

Page Ref: 212–213

4) Contrast reinforcement and punishment and describe the various categories of each. How can we tell if something is a reinforcer or a punisher?

Answer: Reinforcement is a stimulus that increases the frequency of the behavior it follows. Punishment is a stimulus that decreases the frequency of the behavior it follows. In order to tell the two apart, we must look to the associated behavior. Reinforcement can be positive (something is presented) or negative (an aversive stimulus is removed). Punishment can be presentation of an aversive stimulus or removal of a desired one.

Page Ref: 211–212

5) Describe what is meant by the "praise–and–ignore" approach to classroom management. What are the strengths and limitations of this approach? Give several examples of the types of incidents to which it might be applied appropriately.

Answer: Praise–and–ignore involves accentuating the positive and **NOT** giving attention to negative behaviors. The advantage is creating a positive classroom atmosphere in which punishment and unpleasant events are minimized. The disadvantage is that, although the praise–and–ignore strategy is effective in certain circumstances, it does not solve all classroom management problems. Disruptive behaviors may persist unless negative contingencies (punishments) are also applied.

Page Ref: 216–217

6) Give classroom–related examples of how teacher attention can increase a particular desirable student behavior and an undesirable student behavior.

Answer: Examples should include, at a minimum, a description of a classroom situation, the behavior, and the form of teacher attention that affects the behavior. For example, a student talks out of turn, the teacher loudly reprimands the student, and other students laugh. The student likes the attention and is motivated to misbehave again. [Use a comparable structure for positive examples.]

Page Ref: 216–222

7) Compare and contrast the strategies of cueing and shaping as methods for developing desirable behaviors.

Answer: *Cueing*: Indicates when a particular behavior will be reinforced. The cue may be supported with a prompt, and the prompt faded. This method requires that students already know and are capable of the behavior. *Shaping*: A very time–consuming strategy. It allows the development of behavior when the behavior does not appear by other strategies. Shaping requires that the behavior be broken down into small steps and approximations of the desired behavior. Consequently, *task analysis* is needed in order to identify the small steps and their appropriate sequence in the learning task.

Page Ref: 214

8) Discuss the ethical issues involving uses of punishment in the classroom, including when each may be appropriate, what the likely outcomes are, and any cautions with their use.

Answer: The major ethical issues are ensuring that positive and negative consequences are applied correctly and are directed toward effective ends. Emphasis needs to be placed on academic improvement, not just conditioning students to behave properly. Important ethical considerations come into play, particularly in the case of applying punishment that can cause negative reactions, inappropriate modeling, and an unpleasant classroom atmosphere. For this reason, "least restrictive and intrusive" procedures should be used to suppress improper behaviors.

Page Ref: 211–212, 222

9) What is **functional behavioral assessment** (FBA) and how would a teacher use FBA?

Answer: *Functional behavioral assessment* is a collection of methods and procedures for identifying problem behaviors. Teachers who use FBA are most interested in the determining the reason or function of the problem behavior. FBA procedures provide information to the teacher about the antecedents, behaviors, and consequences related to the problem behavior. In addition to assessment, teachers who use FBA also develop an intervention strategy for eliminating the problem behaviors.

Page Ref: 223

3) In the cognitive approach to learning, learning

    A) depends a great deal on individual perception.

    B) is dependent on elicited responses.

    C) is determined by acquired traits.

    D) is primarily a consequence of other people's actions.

Answer: A

Explanation: A) Cognitive theorists view learning as the result of an individual's attempts to make sense of the world and these theorists believe that *learning depends a great deal on individual perception*.

Page Ref: 250
Skill: Knowledge

4) Maria has excellent study habits. She seems to know just what to review and how long to spend on each part of every course. Maria is applying what type of knowledge?

    A) Conditional

    B) Declarative

    C) Domain-specific

    D) Procedural

Answer: A

Explanation: A) *Conditional knowledge* provides the "when and why" for applying other types of knowledge. In this example, it helps Maria to identify and use good strategies.

Page Ref: 258
Skill: Understanding
P: .32
D: .32

5) Alec still remembers how to touch-type, even though it has been three years since he has practiced. The memory system most directly involved here is

    A) episodic.

    B) procedural.

    C) semantic.

    D) short-term.

Answer: B

Explanation: B) *Procedural memory* is memory for how to do things, such as to roller skate, translate a paragraph into a second language, or ride a bicycle. In this example, Alec remembers touch typing. [Episodic memory concerns events in our lives, not procedures.]

Page Ref: 258
Skill: Understanding
P: .83
D: .27

6) Cliff is good at solving math problems, but has difficulty solving problems in his computer class. His problem-solving ability in math represents what type of knowledge?

   A) Conditional

   B) Declarative

   C) Domain-specific

   D) Procedural

Answer: C

Explanation: C) Cliff has *domain-specific knowledge* because he is able to solve problems in a particular subject-math. He is weaker at general problem-solving knowledge given his difficulty in computer class.

Page Ref: 249
Skill: Understanding
P: .67
D: .10

7) A jogger is startled by the feeling of a moving object on his right side. It could have been a ferocious dog, but it turns out to be a newspaper page blown by the wind. What memory component was most directly involved?

   A) Episodic

   B) Schematic

   C) Sensory memory

   D) Working memory

Answer: C

Explanation: C) The *sensory memory* records the immediate sensation of the object. If the jogger now attends to the "moving object," it will be perceived as a particular thing (the newspaper, hopefully, but perhaps the ferocious dog).

Page Ref: 250–251
Skill: Understanding

8) One of the educational implications of sensory memory is that

    A) attention is necessary if children are to remember information.

    B) children can take in and comprehend almost a limitless amount of information.

    C) information seen is brought into consciousness almost immediately.

    D) reinforcement is a requirement if children are to retain information.

Answer: A

Explanation: A) The key implication of sensory memory and perception is that our senses are constantly bombarded by a multitude of stimuli. We only learn the limited amount we attend to. The rest are not perceived and fade from sensory memory after a few seconds. *Attention* is, therefore, *necessary for learning and remembering.*

Page Ref: 250–251
Skill: Understanding
P: .51
D: .37

9) A photographer shoots a flashbulb directly into your eyes. For the next few seconds, all you can see are big blue dots everywhere you look. What type of memory is most directly involved in this phenomenon?

    A) Long–term

    B) Semantic

    C) Sensory

    D) Working

Answer: C

Explanation: C) The image of the flashbulb would reside in *sensory memory*. The content of sensory memory resembles the sensations from the original stimulus, with visual sensations coded as images that fade rapidly.

Page Ref: 250–251
Skill: Understanding
P: .80
D: .13

10) While Mr. Lindsey was explaining the social studies assignment, Missy was finishing homework due for her next class. When the class began the assignment, Missy did not know what to do. According to the information processing model of cognitive learning, Missy was lost because

    A) her perception of the activity was different from that of other students.

    B) she did not pay attention to the instructions that were given.

    C) the instructions for the assignment were out of context.

    D) the instructions were not transferred from working to long-term memory.

Answer: B

Explanation: B) Missy was apparently lost because she *did not pay attention to the instructions* given by Mr. Lindsey. Attention is necessary for perception (and learning) to occur, but it is a limited resource. That is, we can pay attention to only one demanding task at a time.

Page Ref: 250–251
Skill: Understanding
P: .57
D: .17

11) Top-down processing is distinguished by its reliance on a(n)

    A) assembly of elements into a meaningful pattern.

    B) downward scanning of the eyes.

    C) search for familiar features or elements.

    D) understanding of the context of a situation.

Answer: D

Explanation: D) Top-down processing involves using the *context of the situation* as a basis for recognizing (or perceiving) something. In contrast, bottom-up processing bases perception on analyzing specific features of the stimulus and "mentally assembling" the whole from the parts.

Page Ref: 252
Skill: Knowledge

12) What you are thinking about right now is being held in what type of memory?

   A) Long-term

   B) Schematic

   C) Sensory

   D) Working

Answer: D

Explanation: D) Your *working memory* contains the information that you are thinking about at the present moment. Due to this function, it is frequently called "working memory."

Page Ref: 253–254
Skill: Understanding
P: .79
D: .18

13) Bottom-up processing refers to the way people examine a new stimulus for

   A) contextual cues.

   B) contrasting details.

   C) perceptual closure.

   D) recognizable features.

Answer: D

Explanation: D) Bottom-up processing involves analyzing the *recognizable features of incoming stimuli*. We then mentally "build" the pattern or whole from the parts. In contrast, top-down processing involves using the context of a situation to recognize a stimulus.

Page Ref: 251
Skill: Knowledge

14) Mr. Kawicki is teaching his sixth-grade science students about the scientific method. Students are instructed about each component of the method first in order to understand the whole process. This instructional strategy is based on what concept?

    A) Bottom-up processing

    B) Memory strength

    C) Propositional network

    D) Top-down processing

Answer: A

Explanation: A) *Bottom-up processing*, called "feature analysis," involves analyzing a stimulus into components and assembling the components into a whole pattern. This process is exemplified by Mr. Kawicki's expecting his science students to achieve understanding of the scientific method by first learning each component.

Page Ref: 251
Skill: Understanding
P: .65
D: .28

15) Megan tries to remember the address, 10 Anchor Street, by imagining a ten-dollar bill attached to the anchor of a ship. She is using a memory strategy called

    A) chunking.

    B) elaborative rehearsal.

    C) maintenance rehearsal.

    D) part learning.

Answer: B

Explanation: B) *Elaborative rehearsal* involves associating the information one is trying to remember with existing knowledge in long-term memory. In this example, Megan is relating the address to a mental image combining familiar objects.

Page Ref: 256
Skill: Understanding
P: .73
D: .24

16) Items can typically be stored in working memory for approximately how long?

    A) About 20 seconds

    B) A day

    C) One minute

    D) One week

Answer: A

Explanation: A) Working memory, with its limited duration, can hold information for *about 20 to 30 seconds*. By comparison, long-term memory is assumed to be permanent; the problem there is retrieving the information.

Page Ref: 255–256
Skill: Knowledge
P: .84
D: .21

17) Research has shown that the capacity of the working memory is limited to about how many chunks?

    A) Two to four

    B) Five to nine

    C) 11 to 12

    D) 13 to 15

Answer: B

Explanation: B) The capacity of working memory is from *five to nine separate "bits"* or chunks of information. By comparison, long-term memory is theorized to have an unlimited capacity.

Page Ref: 256
Skill: Knowledge
P: .88
D: .22

18) Our ability to conserve something in working memory is most directly affected by the

    A) executive control processes.

    B) perceptual factors that we apply to the stimulus.

    C) reinforcement of information.

    D) strength and intensity of the initial stimulus.

Answer: A

Explanation: A) The *executive control processes such as rehearsal* increase our ability to maintain information in our working memory.

Page Ref: 254
Skill: Knowledge
P: .92
D: .18

19) The basic purpose of chunking as a memory strategy is to

    A) increase the capacity of information in all of the sensory registers.

    B) increase the amount of information to be stored in the long–term memory.

    C) reduce the amount of information to be stored in the working memory.

    D) reduce the amount of time for processing information in long–term memory.

Answer: C

Explanation: C) By grouping individual bits of information in a meaningful way (as when letters are combined to form words), chunking *reduces the amount of information to be stored in working memory.*

Page Ref: 256
Skill: Knowledge
P: .46
D: .30

 20) Which one of the following persons most clearly illustrates the concept of elaboration?

    A) Alicia asks the teacher to define percentages in a different way than how they were defined in the text.

    B) Bart calculates percentages for the homework problems assigned by the teacher.

    C) John recognizes that he can use percentages in calculating his team's batting average.

    D) Mary rehearses the steps for computing the statistics needed to describe the school population.

Answer: C

Explanation: C) *John is relating his study of percentages* to his existing knowledge about baseball. As a result of this elaboration, the material on percentages will be better connected with other information in long–term memory, and thus be more easily remembered.

Page Ref: 263
Skill: Understanding
P: .72
D: .28

21) You are given a math problem to solve. As you try to remember the formula involved, what memory system is being searched?

    A) Long-term semantic

    B) Schematic

    C) Sensory register

    D) Working procedural

Answer: A

Explanation: A) *Schemas, or schemes*, are structures or patterns that people must develop in order to understand large amounts of information inherent in complex concepts and problems. Therefore, *schematic memory* is a feature of long-term memory.

Page Ref: 260–261
Skill: Understanding
P: .58
D: .21

22) Long-term memory that is memory for meaning is called

    A) episodic.

    B) procedural.

    C) semantic.

    D) working.

Answer: C

Explanation: C) The *long-term semantic memory* is our memory for meaning. This information represents our knowledge of the world (formulas, facts, scripts, words, etc.).

Page Ref: 257–258
Skill: Knowledge

23) Mark can answer the physics problem because of patterns of knowledge stored in his long-term memory, which he did not intentionally try to learn. This situation involves Mark using his

    A) explicit memory.

    B) implicit memory.

    C) short-term memory.

    D) episodic memory.

Answer: B

Explanation: B) *Implicit memory is knowledge that is not readily available to conscious recall,* however, it does influence one's behavior or thought without awareness.

Page Ref: 259
Skill: Understanding

24) Propositional networks are defined most accurately as

    A) a process by which verbal information reaches short-term memory.

    B) a technique used to increase the capacity of short-term memory.

    C) the organization of information according to its meaning.

    D) the process by means of which information reaches the sensory register.

Answer: C

Explanation: C) A proposition is defined as the smallest unit of information that can be judged true or false. The sentence, "The truck is red," represents one proposition. Propositional networking involves the *organization of such information according to its meaning.*

Page Ref: 260
Skill: Knowledge
P: .70
D: .33

25) When we intentionally try to learn something new, we are involving what type of long-term memory?

    A) Crystallized memory

    B) Episodic memory

    C) Working memory

    D) Explicit memory

Answer: D

Explanation: D) *Explicit memory is knowledge from long-term memory that can be recalled and consciously considered.* It involves knowledge that was gained through deliberate or intentional learning processes.

Page Ref: 259
Skill: Understanding

26) Because memories are organized in propositional networks, recall of one bit of information often

    A) blocks the recall of other information.

    B) leads to recall of another bit of information.

    C) leads to the integration of organized patterns.

    D) requires specific, external memory cues.

Answer: B

Explanation: B) A propositional network is an interconnected set of bits of information. Because the bits are meaningfully related to one another in the network, recall of one bit (e.g., thinking of a spoon) may trigger the *recall of another bit of information* (e.g., fork).

Page Ref: 260–261
Skill: Knowledge
P: .91
D: .03

27) In order to understand the large amounts of information inherent in complex concepts, people must develop structures or patterns called

    A) levels.

    B) mnemonics.

    C) propositions.

    D) schemas.

Answer: D

Explanation: D) *Schemas* are defined by cognitive psychologists as mental patterns, structures, or guides for understanding events, concepts, or ideas. [Mnemonics are memory devices; propositions are units of information.]

Page Ref: 260–261
Skill: Knowledge
P: .77
D: .25

28) A *script* is viewed by cognitive theorists as useful

    A) as a note–taking strategy in lecture classes.

    B) in directing everyday activities in different situations.

    C) in formalizing interactions between students.

    D) in outlining the main ideas of a story.

Answer: B

Explanation: B) Scripts are schemas representing the typical *sequence of events in everyday situations*. For example, most adults have different scripts for weekdays than for Saturdays and Sundays.

Page Ref: 262
Skill: Knowledge

29) Long–term memory for how to do things is called

    A) elaboration.

    B) episodic memory.

    C) procedural memory.

    D) productions.

Answer: C

Explanation: C) Long–term memory for how to do things is called *procedural memory*.
Page Ref: 262
Skill: Knowledge

30) According to current cognitive theories, information may be lost from long-term memory in all of the following ways **EXCEPT** by

    A) interference.

    B) lack of use.

    C) substitution.

    D) time decay.

Answer: C

Explanation: C) *Substitution* has nothing to do with why information may be lost from long-term memory. Current explanations emphasize interference and time decay. Also, when not used, neural connections grow weak over time.

Page Ref: 263–266
Skill: Knowledge

31) Based on studies of context, in what location would a student be likely to perform best on an educational psychology test?

    A) In a familiar room such as a dorm room

    B) In a small comfortable room with soft music playing

    C) In a very quiet area, such as a library

    D) In an educational psychology classroom

Answer: D

Explanation: D) Studies of context indicate that aspects of the physical surroundings (e.g., the room we are in; the time of day) become associated with other information that we are attending to. Thus, theoretically, students would perform best if they took their exams in the *same room in which they studied the material being tested* (e.g, the educational psychology class).

Page Ref: 262–263
Skill: Understanding
P: .74
D: .31

32) Ms. Gentry took her tenth-grade biology students to the Horticulture Garden. The students were able to observe and classify a wide variety of exotic plants. Students in her class are likely to remember the names and characteristics of those plants because of

    A) automaticity.

    B) context.

    C) meta-components.

    D) retrieval.

Answer: B

Explanation: B) *Context* represents the physical environment and our emotional states. It is learned together (associated) with other information. Learning the names of plants in a realistic setting, such as Ms. Gentry's class is in, should provide contextual cues to facilitate memory of the names.

Page Ref: 262-263
Skill: Understanding
P: .69
D: .50

33) According to the levels of processing theory, the length of time information is remembered is determined by

    A) how completely the initial learning was accomplished.

    B) when we first encountered the information.

    C) where it is stored in our memory.

    D) why we have chosen to attend to the information.

Answer: A

Explanation: A) Levels of processing theory propose that *the more completely we learn something initially and analyze the information, the longer we retain it.* Deeper processing leads to stronger connections in long-term memory.

Page Ref: 263-264
Skill: Knowledge
P: .70
D: .20

34) Marc starts talking to Wynoma about the field trip to the zoo, which reminds him of the book he read on tigers last week. He concludes by telling Wynoma that the new library is very easy to use. This phenomenon illustrates the concept of

    A) construction of the working memory.

    B) deactivation of the active memory.

    C) reconstruction of the working memory.

    D) spread of activation.

Answer: D

Explanation: D) When a particular proposition or image is active, closely associated knowledge can be activated as well. Talk about the field trip activated Marc's memory of reading the book about tigers. This process is called the *spread of activation.*

Page Ref: 264
Skill: Understanding
P: .70
D: .41

35) A student provides an explanation of why water evaporates, but his description leaves out some of the details the teacher provided, while including some new information. Cognitive theorists would attribute this to

    A) elaboration.

    B) reconstruction.

    C) repression.

    D) time decay.

Answer: B

Explanation: B) *Reconstruction* involves recalling information based on what we actually remember, what we fill in based on related experiences, or what seems logical to us. Because of these variables, different people will often remember very different things after experiencing the same event.

Page Ref: 264–265
Skill: Understanding
P: .59
D: .26

36) Metacognition deals with knowledge about our own

   A) cognitive development.

   B) cognitive stage.

   C) memory capacities.

   D) thinking processes.

Answer: D

Explanation: D) Metacognition means knowledge about cognition. It deals with *knowledge about our thinking processes*.

Page Ref: 267
Skill: Knowledge
P: .65
D: .29

37) Which one of the following behaviors does **NOT** encompass the meaning of metacognition?

   A) Awareness of resources

   B) Awareness of strategies

   C) Knowledge of facts concerning a subject

   D) Knowledge of how to perform a strategy

Answer: C

Explanation: C) Knowledge about cognition—the processes of learning—is the definition of metacognition. This domain would encompass awareness of context (or resources), strategies, and how to perform strategies. It would *NOT include knowledge of facts concerning a subject*.

Page Ref: 267–268
Skill: Understanding
P: .48
D: .41

38) Metacognition requires three essential skills: (1) to plan; (2) to monitor; and (3) to

   A) comprehend.

   B) evaluate.

   C) use mnemonic strategies.

   D) problem solve.

Answer: B

Explanation: B) The three essential skills involved in metacognition are to plan, to monitor, and *to evaluate*. Mnemonic strategies, comprehension, and problem solving are specific strategies that are involved in each of the three essential skills of metacognition.

Page Ref: 267–268
Skill: Knowledge
P: .84
D: .25

39) Willis concludes that he is having difficulty remembering the material because of the teacher's lecture style. Willis thinks that he would remember better with a recitation-style presentation. Willis' thinking illustrates

    A) cognitive monitoring.

    B) episodic memory.

    C) pathway monitoring.

    D) procedural memory.

Answer: A

Explanation: A) Metacognition involves the use of regulatory abilities called *cognitive monitoring*. As illustrated by Willis' analysis of his needs, these processes help learners decide what to do, how to do it, and when to do it.

Page Ref: 267–278
Skill: Understanding
P: .68
D: .49

40) Claire, a three-year-old, has difficulty remembering her street address. According to research on short-term memory use, what is a likely cause of Claire's problem?

    A) Both limited memory capacity and ineffective strategy use

    B) Ineffective strategy use, but not limited memory capacity

    C) Limited memory capacity, but not ineffective strategy use

    D) Neither limited memory capacity nor effective strategy use

Answer: A

Explanation: A) A three-year-old child such as Claire is likely to have *limited working memory capacity and to use strategies for remembering ineffectively*. By age five or six, Claire will naturally begin to use other strategies including rehearsal.

Page Ref: 269
Skill: Understanding
P: .33
D: .25

41) Josh's history teacher wants Josh to learn important events that occurred during the Civil War. What type of knowledge would be most directly involved in this learning?

  A) Conditional declarative

  B) Domain-specific declarative

  C) General declarative

  D) Procedural declarative

Answer: B

Explanation: B) Knowing information about a particular area (Civil War), as is expected of Josh, is *domain-specific declarative knowledge*. General declarative knowledge is knowing general information, such as the reason that lists are often alphabetized. Conditional knowledge is knowing when and why to apply information.

Page Ref: 249–250
Skill: Understanding
P: .81
D: .20

42) While taking his final exam, Jerry recalled one item of information that caused him to remember another piece of information related to the question. What phenomenon has he just experienced?

  A) Distributed recall

  B) Massed practice

  C) Serial-position effect

  D) Spread of activation

Answer: D

Explanation: D) Jerry's recall of one bit of information that led him to associate it with another piece of information is called the of *spread of activation* phenomenon. None of the other three response choices relates to this phenomenon.

Page Ref: 264
Skill: Understanding
P: .71
D: .50

43) Forgetting due to the serial-position effect can be reduced through the use of

    A) massed practice.

    B) part learning.

    C) relearning.

    D) rote memorization.

Answer: B

Explanation: B) *Part learning* breaks up a long list of items into a shorter list. As a result, there
                are fewer items in the middle that, due to the serial-position effect, are more
                difficult to remember than items at the beginning or end of a list.

Page Ref: 274
Skill: Knowledge
P: .46
D: .56

44) You are asked to learn the 50 U.S. states, so you divide the country into geographic areas and
set about your task. You are more likely to succeed than someone who begins to learn the
states at random, because your system

    A) capitalizes on the serial-position effect by fragmenting the task.

    B) employs cues to organize your transfer from sensory memory.

    C) helps you encode the names of states at the time of recall.

    D) minimizes proactive interference through the 'blocking' effect.

Answer: A

Explanation: A) The *serial-position effect* is that recall of items at the beginning and the end of a
                list is higher than of items in the middle of a list. Part learning, as occurs in
                this geography example, reduces the number of items in the middle.
                Consequently, verbal recall should increase.

Page Ref: 274
Skill: Understanding
P: .54
D: .44

45) An educational application designed to reduce the impact of the serial-position effect is to

   A) begin teaching important materials at the beginning of class and deal with administrative tasks later.

   B) break down the lesson into small parts that can be handled quite easily.

   C) provide a preview of the next period at the end of class rather than a review of what was covered today.

   D) start a class with seatwork, teach new information, and then end the class with seatwork whenever possible.

Answer: B

Explanation: B) In order to reduce the impact of the serial-position effect, it is important for the teacher *to break down the information or concept into small parts that can be handled easily by students.* It is meaningful to teach important content at the beginning of the class period and leave administrative tasks for later, but it is even more crucial to break down the information to be learned into small parts.

Page Ref: 274
Skill: Knowledge

46) Based on the serial-position effect, what group of letters of the alphabet should be the most difficult to remember for someone who is first learning the alphabet?

   A) ABC

   B) MNO

   C) XYZ

   D) All of the above groups should be of equal difficulty.

Answer: B

Explanation: B) The letters *MNO* would be most different to learn because they occur in the middle of the alphabet. The serial-position effect makes beginning or ending letters easier to remember.

Page Ref: 274
Skill: Knowledge

47) According to Woolfolk, the basic purpose of mnemonic aids is to

    A) increase students' motivation to learn material requiring rote memorization.

    B) make connections between the information to be memorized.

    C) rehearse old information in order to implant it in the working memory.

    D) set up a system of rewards for remembering items that are not connected.

Answer: B

Improve memory

Explanation: B) The main function of mnemonic aids is to help us *make connections between information to be memorized*. Commonly used strategies involve imagery and verbal associations (e.g., acronyms).

Page Ref: 271
Skill: Knowledge
P: .49
D: .13

48) The first step in peg–type mnemonics is to

    A) associate new material with a familiar place or location.

    B) memorize a random list of places, words, or facts.

    C) organize the new material into meaningful patterns.

    D) visualize each element of the new material.

Answer: B

Explanation: B) Peg–type mnemonics first require that you *memorize a random list of places, words, or facts*. This process works to serve as pegs to which new information can be associated.

Page Ref: 271
Skill: Knowledge

49) Dr. Beach used to be a typical 'absent minded professor.' However, she found that she could remember the things her husband asked her to pick up at the grocery store by imagining the items she needed placed on her desk, bookshelf, and file cabinet. The mnemonic device that she used is

    A) an acronym.

    B) chunking.

    C) the keyword method.

    D) the loci method.

Answer: D

Explanation: D) Dr. Beach is using the *loci method*. Specifically, she is associating an already learned set of locations (or pegs) through imagery with the new information (the items to purchase).

Page Ref: 272
Skill: Understanding
P: .91
D: .21

50) "*I* before *E* except after *C*" is an example of the use of what memory method?

    A) Chain

    B) Loci

    C) Keyword

    D) Peg-type

Answer: A

Explanation: A) One application of the *chain mnemonics* method is to incorporate all items to be memorized into a jingle, such as "I before E except after C." Consequently, the information becomes easier to recall.

Page Ref: 272
Skill: Knowledge

51) In order to avoid confusing entomology (the study of insects) with etymology (the study of the history of words), Vicky associates the sound "en" of entomology with the sound "in" of insects. What specific type of mnemonic is she using?

    A) Acronym

    B) Chain

    C) Keyword

    D) Peg-type

Answer: C

Explanation: C) Vicky is using the *keyword* approach to avoid the confusion of terms. She is using a common English word ("insects") to associate with the new word ("entomology"). Further elaboration might also invoke images to strengthen the association.

Page Ref: 272
Skill: Understanding
P: .49
D: .30

52) Consuela is a fourth-grade student who is studying geography. Tomorrow, she has a quiz over the Great Lakes. She creates a mnemonic device, HOMES (Huron, Ontario, Michigan, Erie, Superior), to help her remember the names of the lakes. What type of mnemonic device is she using?

   A) Acronym

   B) Chain

   C) Keyword

   D) Peg-type

Answer: A

Explanation: A) Consuela is using an *acronym*, which is a word formed from the first letter of each word or phrase. In contrast, a chain involves using the same procedure to create a sentence or jingle.

Page Ref: 271
Skill: Understanding
P: .92
D: .20

53) The use of imagery techniques of learning, such as the keyword method, seems most appropriate for what age group?

   A) Early elementary school

   B) Kindergarten

   C) Late elementary school and older

   D) Preschool

Answer: C

Explanation: C) Because younger students have difficulty forming their own images, the use of the keyword method is more appropriate for children in *late elementary school and beyond*. Younger children seem more successful with rhymes and chaining methods.

Page Ref: 270–271
Skill: Knowledge

54) Stacey is trying to learn the abbreviations and names for the chemical elements, such as Au (gold). He connects the Au with a mental picture of Auric Goldfinger, the villain in a James Bond novel. This is an example of using what learning strategy?

    A) Chaining

    B) Keyword

    C) Loci

    D) Metacognitive

Answer: B

Explanation: B) Stacey is using the *keyword method* by linking a new item to be remembered (AU) with an image that incorporates the item (an image of Auric Goldfinger, the James Bond villain).

Page Ref: 272
Skill: Understanding
P: .56
D: .36

55) Within the information processing perspective, learning declarative knowledge involves

    A) applying rules for the purpose of categorizing specific objects or ideas.

    B) developing new strategies for performing various cognitive activities.

    C) generating ways to organize thoughts and actions in order to meet a goal.

    D) integrating new ideas with existing knowledge to create an understanding.

Answer: D

Explanation: D) According to the information–processing perspective, learning declarative knowledge involves *integrating new ideas with existing knowledge to create an understanding*. In this manner, learning becomes meaningful instead of rote.

Page Ref: 258
Skill: Knowledge

56) What type of knowledge do experts have that involves an understanding of how to perform various cognitive activities?

    A) Conditional

    B) Declarative

    C) Organizational

    D) Procedural

Answer: D

Explanation: D) The type of knowledge that involves an understanding of how to perform various cognitive activities is *procedural knowledge*. Declarative knowledge involves verbal information and facts, while conditional knowledge involves manipulating declarative and procedural knowledge to solve problems.

Page Ref: 258
Skill: Knowledge
P: .78
D: .21

57) Anita began her answer with a long historical background of legal precedents. Mr. Cartwright interrupted her and requested that she remain within the facts of the specific case for this kind of question. What type of knowledge is the instructor requesting for Anita to utilize?

   A) Conditional

   B) Declarative

   C) Organizational

   D) Procedural

Answer: A

Explanation: A) Mr. Cartwright is requesting that Anita attend to the problems of the legal case, rather than expound on historical background. This type of knowledge is *conditional* knowledge that involves manipulating declarative and procedural knowledge to solve the problem of the legal case in this scenario.

Page Ref: 258
Skill: Understanding
P: .51
D: .22

58) What can teachers do to help their students develop an automated basic skill?

   A) Ensure that students have the necessary prerequisite knowledge and provide practice with feedback.

   B) Focus on executive control processes in order to guide the flow of information through students' information processing systems.

   C) Teach domain-specific strategies for solving problems and control processes for guiding knowledge.

   D) Train students to use a variety of strategies for retrieving knowledge from long-term memory.

Answer: A

Explanation: A) Most psychologists identify three stages in the development of an automated skill. In order to help students pass through these stages, it appears that two factors are critical: *prerequisite knowledge and practice with feedback.*

Page Ref: 274–275
Skill: Knowledge
P: .61
D: .30

59) In order to help students become better learners, it is recommended that they

    A) be provided a variety of strategies and practices.

    B) be taught strategies, but not specific tactics.

    C) master one effective strategy before introducing another.

    D) receive strategies training that focuses on procedures.

Answer: A

Explanation: A) Research has suggested that students should be exposed to a *variety of different strategies*. Also, specific tactics, such as mnemonic techniques, should be learned.

Page Ref: 274–276
Skill: Knowledge
P: .92
D: .13

Bill is having considerable difficulty remembering names, terms, and facts in his American History class. On the last exam, he identified General Sherman as a Vietnam War hero, and Saigon as the capitol of Japan. Historical dates are so confusing to him that he does not even try to remember them. The result is that, although he typically does satisfactorily on essay questions (he purposely leaves out any names that he is uncertain about and always omits dates), his scores are extremely low on objective items such as multiple–choice and fill–in–the–blank items. Given this scenario, answer the following items:

60) If Bill wants to begin memorizing specific historical events, what strategy would prove to be most useful?

    A) Distributed practice

    B) Figurative learning

    C) Metacognitive differentiation

    D) Procedural memory

Answer: A

Explanation: A) Bill's problem with memorizing would be assisted by using *distributed practice* in addition to using mnemonic strategies (not a response choice for this item).

Page Ref: 274
Skill: Understanding
P: .44
D: .56

61) With what type of knowledge is Bill having difficulty?

   A) Conditional

   B) Declarative

   C) General

   D) Procedural

Answer: B

Explanation: B) Bill's learning difficulty is with *declarative knowledge*, i.e., the ability to integrate existing knowledge to construct understanding of American history. Rote learning methods, mnemonics, and distributed practice are methods for aiding declarative knowledge.

Page Ref: 258
Skill: Understanding
P: .72
D: .36

62) What type of learning should Bill's teacher be most concerned about in order for Bill to be able to use consciously applied skills of organizing thoughts and actions to reach a learning goal?

   A) Condition–action strategies

   B) Domain–specific strategies

   C) General strategies

   D) Production strategies

Answer: B

Explanation: B) The specific type of learning with which Bill's teacher is most concerned is with *domain–specific strategies*. These strategies involve consciously applied skills of organizing thoughts and actions to reach a goal. In this scenario, the goal involves Jerry learning names, terms, and facts of American history. The teacher needs to provide many opportunities for Jerry to practice these learning skills.

Page Ref: 275
Skill: Understanding
P: .78
D: .22

Completion Questions

1) Older cognitive views of learning emphasized the acquisition of knowledge, although newer approaches stress _____ of knowledge.

Answer: construction
Page Ref: 248

2) Knowing specific facts or knowing how to do something is called verbal information or _____ knowledge.

Answer: declarative
Page Ref: 258

3) Knowing when to apply a particular procedure and when to apply a different one is _____ knowledge.

Answer: conditional
Page Ref: 258

4) The information processing model of memory involves encoding, storage, and _____ of information.

Answer: retrieval
Page Ref: 263

5) The memory system that initially receives stimuli from the environment is the _____.

Answer: sensory memory
Page Ref: 250–251

6) The process of detecting a stimulus and assigning meaning to it is called _____.

Answer: perception
Page Ref: 251

7) The type of processing that involves identifying stimuli by analyzing their features is called _____ processing.

Answer: bottom up
Page Ref: 251–252

8) Short–term memory is often called _____, because it is where our current thinking or "consciousness" takes place.

Answer: working
Page Ref: 253–254

9) Information may be lost from working memory by decay or _____.

Answer: interference
Page Ref: 265

10) Knowledge stored in long–term memory that **CANNOT** be recalled upon demand is referred to as _____.

Answer: Implicit Memory
Page Ref: 259

11) _____ memories involve knowledge that we can deliberately recall when we need the information.

Answer: Explicit
Page Ref: 259

12) The smallest unit of knowledge that can be judged true or false is called a _____.

   Answer: proposition
   Page Ref: 265

13) Information regarding events of our lives is stored in _____ long-term memory.

   Answer: episodic
   Page Ref: 263

14) The theory that strongly emphasizes as a determinant of memory the degree to which information is analyzed and associated with other information is _____ theory.

   Answer: levels of processing
   Page Ref: 263

15) The process that occurs when remembering certain information is hampered by the presence of other information is called _____.

   Answer: interference
   Page Ref: 265

16) According to current theories of memory, the flow of information through information processing systems is guided by the _____ processes.

   Answer: executive control
   Page Ref: 254

17) The concept of knowledge about knowing that is used to monitor and regulate cognitive processes is called _____.

   Answer: metacognition
   Page Ref: 267-268

18) Knowing about the characteristics and images of a concept is _____ knowledge.

   Answer: declarative
   Page Ref: 258

19) Knowing how to apply rules to categorize objects and ideas is _____ knowledge.

   Answer: procedural
   Page Ref: 258

20) The greater difficulty of remembering items in the middle of a list, compared to beginning or ending items, is referred to as the _____ effect.

   Answer: serial-position
   Page Ref: 274

21) One of the specific methods used to improve memory that derives its name from the plural of the Latin word meaning "place" is the _____ method.

Answer: loci
Page Ref: 271

22) The mnemonic technique that involves associating a familiar word with a known word through an image or sentence is the _____ method.

Answer: keyword
Page Ref: 272

23) The three stages in the development of an automated skill are cognitive, associative, and _____.

Answer: autonomous
Page Ref: 275

24) Consciously applied skills of organizing thoughts and actions to reach a goal are _____ strategies.

Answer: domain-specific
Page Ref: 275

True/False Questions

1) Current cognitive psychologists view learning more as the construction of knowledge than as the acquisition of knowledge.

Answer: TRUE
Page Ref: 248-249

2) Knowing when to skim a text rather than reading every word is an example of using one's conditional knowledge.

Answer: TRUE
Page Ref: 258

3) Recognizing stimuli by feature analysis is a form of bottom-up processing.

Answer: TRUE
Page Ref: 261

4) Stimuli from the environment are theorized to first enter working memory.

Answer: FALSE
Page Ref: 250

5) Only about 14 items may be stored in short-term memory at any given time.

Answer: FALSE
Page Ref: 254

6) It appears that the capacity of long-term memory is unlimited.

Answer: TRUE
Page Ref: 246–247

7) Long-term memory holds information that is currently activated.

Answer: FALSE
Page Ref: 257

8) "Memory for meaning" is semantic memory.

Answer: TRUE
Page Ref: 259

9) Schemas provide the structures or guides that enable people to understand an event.

Answer: TRUE
Page Ref: 260

10) The element of processing that influences the physical and emotional environment in which learning takes place is elaboration.

Answer: FALSE
Page Ref: 263

11) A story grammar is a type of schema for text.

Answer: TRUE
Page Ref: 261

12) The "spread of activation" phenomenon is basically a short-term memory process.

Answer: FALSE
Page Ref: 264

13) The key to maintaining information in long-term memory is rehearsal.

Answer: FALSE
Page Ref: 256

14) The primary difference between implicit and explicit memories is in the amount of information that can be stored in the different types of memories.

Answer: FALSE
Page Ref: 259

15) If a student tries very hard to remember the name of a book author, he or she is searching knowledge stored as an explicit memory.

Answer: TRUE
Page Ref: 259

16) "Reconstructed memory" means "accurate memory."

Answer: FALSE
Page Ref: 264

17) Metacognitive abilities begin to develop in children when they are about five to seven years of age.

Answer: TRUE
Page Ref: 267

18) Most children will discover the value of using organizational strategies when they are about six years of age.

Answer: TRUE
Page Ref: 267

19) The serial-position effect suggests that forgetting the middle of a list is more likely than forgetting the beginning or end of a list.

Answer: TRUE
Page Ref: 274

20) The keyword method involves memorizing a standard list of words as a basis for forming associations with new items.

Answer: FALSE
Page Ref: 272

21) The typical student who "crams" the night before an important exam is attempting to use massed practice.

Answer: TRUE
Page Ref: 274

22) Consciously applied skills of organizing thoughts and actions to reach a learning goal are called domain-specific strategies.

Answer: TRUE
Page Ref: 275

Short Answer Questions

1) Describe what is meant by the "cognitive perspective" and discuss how this perspective differs from behavioral orientations to learning.

Answer: The cognitive perspective is a philosophical orientation that views learning as a attempt to make sense out of the world through active processing of information. Specifically, we relate new information to what we already know, and in the process change the information and our knowledge structures to achieve a consistent fit. Older cognitive views stressed the acquisition of knowledge, whereas current views stress the construction of knowledge. In contrast, behavioral views focus on the effects of reinforcement in strengthening responses and the overt behavior that represents those responses.

Page Ref: 248–249

2) Compare and contrast long–term and working memory with regard to storage, capacity, and retrieval.

Answer: Short-term memory is limited to five to nine items and is subject to time decay, though items can be held indefinitely through rehearsal. Maintenance rehearsal, for example, involves repeating information in one's mind. Elaborative rehearsal involves trying to associate new information with existing knowledge. Items enter immediately and are immediately available with little distortion, but items forgotten are lost forever. Short-term memory is also called working memory. Long-term memory has unlimited duration and capacity. Information is much more reliant on organization and schemata. Recall may depend on reconstruction and cues. There is more possibility of distortion than for short-term memory. Types of long-term memory are semantic, episodic, and procedural.

Page Ref: 253–257

3) Do we ever truly forget anything? Describe how information is retrieved from long–term memories and the processes that prevent or limit accurate recall.

Answer: Information lost from sensory memory or working memory is lost forever. In long-term memory, however, information may never be truly lost. Some theories attribute long-term forgetting to suppression or fading of the memory trace. Interference may also inhibit memory, but in principle it should be possible to reconstruct information from the organizational structures of long-term memory. Interference occurs when the learning of new information makes it more difficult to remember what was previously learned or when previous learning makes it more difficult to remember new information.

Page Ref: 263–266

4) Explain the role of attention in learning, giving suggestions for teachers to increase student attentiveness to the lesson.

   Answer: Our senses are continually bombarded with stimuli. Consequently, attending to every change in the environment is impossible. To be helpful, attention must be selective. Students need to attend to the lesson and to ignore other stimuli. Teachers can help assure student attention by focusing attention through the use of colorful or unusual lesson starters. They can tell students the purpose of the lesson is to arouse curiosity and use an animated style to improve students' attention.

   Page Ref: 252–253

5) Define and give examples of metacognitive strategies. How does the use of metacognitive strategies facilitate classroom learning?

   Answer: Metacognition is knowledge about one's own cognitive processes and products. The ability to monitor one's performance and the effectiveness of the strategy one is using greatly influences classroom performance. Metacognition appears to involve at least two components: declarative and procedural knowledge (knowing what to do and how to do it) and conditional knowledge (knowing when to do it). Among other things, such monitoring can direct the apportionment of time and effort, isolate those things that are known and knowable, change strategies when necessary, and predict the outcome of a particular strategy in a given situation. Metacognitive skills can and should be taught, though it seems that such instruction is effective in the first years of schooling.

   Page Ref: 267–268

6) Do children of different ages tend to use working memory in the same way? Discuss developmental differences in working memory.

   Answer: Research indicates that young children have very limited working memories, but that memory span improves. The differences may be due to changes in memory capacity or improvements in strategy use. As children grow older, they develop more effective strategies for remembering, such as rehearsing (about age five or six). Not until they are 10- to 11-years-old do children have adult-like working memories. Organization strategies begin at about age 6 and are used spontaneously at about age 8 or 9. It also seems to be the case that some people, regardless of development, have more efficient short-term memories than do others.

   Page Ref: 253–257

7) Identify and describe the procedures of three different mnemonic strategies.

   Answer: *Peg-type mnemonics* involve memorizing a standard list of places or words. New items are mentally associated with these "pegs." The method of loci and acronym are two examples. *Chain mnemonics* involve connecting each new item on a list to a previous one using imagery or a verbal jingle (e.g., "I before E except after C"). The *keyword method* involves associating a new word (such as a foreign word) with a known word through an image or sentence. All three of these mnemonic strategies attempt to increase the meaningfulness of material by relating the new items to information already in memory (e.g., image, word, or verbal jingle). The new information is learned in association with existing knowledge rather than as isolated rote memorization.

   Page Ref: 271–272

8) Define what is meant by automated skills, and describe the stages assumed to be involved in developing them.

Answer: Skills that are applied without conscious thought are called automated basic skills. Most psychologists describe three stages in the development of an automated skill: cognitive, associative, and autonomous. At the cognitive stage, we rely on declarative knowledge and general problem-solving strategies. There is much trial-and-error learning. At the associative stage, individual steps are combined or chunked into larger units. At the autonomous stage, the whole procedure is accomplished without much attention. Teachers can help students pass through these stages by providing them with prerequisite knowledge and practice with feedback.

Page Ref: 274–275

Case Studies

Ramona and Ann were walking home from school when they heard the screeching of brakes and the blare of a horn. Then, just 30 feet in front of them, they saw the crash of a white car and a blue pickup truck. The next day the children were excitedly telling their friends about what they saw. "That white car was traveling real fast and swerving from side to side," Ramona said. "I don't remember that," corrected Ann. "It seemed to me that the truck didn't stop fast enough at the stop sign." "What stop sign?" asked Ramona. "It was on the other street–the white car's side. Don't you remember?" said Ann. The discussion continued this way for the next five minutes, until the audience of increasingly impatient listeners dwindled down to one faithful friend. Ramona and Ann weren't trying to argue, but they couldn't seem to agree on anything.

1) Discuss how the following memory systems would be involved in perceiving and remembering the accident: sensory, working, long–term.

Answer: The information from the accident scene entered Ramona and Ann's sensory memory through their own senses of hearing, seeing, smelling and feeling. For example, both girls heard the screeching of the car brakes and smelled the burnt rubber of the tires as the driver tried to slow down. Although this stimuli from the environment remained in the sensory register for less than a split second, this initial process is required for taking information into memory. Due to the loud sound, both girls paid careful attention to the events over the next few seconds. Because they knew of the severity of the situation, they were almost hyper-alert and did not pay attention to any other stimuli in the environment. During this phase, the information was stored and processed in working memory. The girls stored the information in working memory for probably about 15–20 seconds, which was sufficient time to connect their newly stored information with knowledge previously stored in their long-term memory. For example, they may have memories of car crashes from television shows and movies. Most likely the girls would have utilized their central executive, which is a specific component of working memory. Knowing that they may need to provide a police report later, the girls relied upon their central executive aspect of their working memory to focus their attention and plan for how they would remember minor details of the accident. Because they could repeat specific details related to the accident later (i.e., color of the truck, etc.), we know that some of the information is stored in their long-term memory. However, because they do not have a lot of expertise relative to being a witness to a car accident, we would expect some of their knowledge in their long-term memories would not be integrated or translated into accurate images.

Page Ref: 250–263

2) In trying to remember the events of the preceding day, were the children mainly using semantic memory or episodic memory? Explain.

Answer: When verbalizing events that took place the previous day the girls would most likely use knowledge stored as episodic memories. When repeating information tied to the specific car accident, they are relying upon memories connected to their own personal life. If they were not able to describe the specific event in that they observed, but were relying upon knowledge about car accidents in general, then they would be utilizing semantic memories.

Page Ref: 259, 262

3) What is the role of schemas in influencing the children's recollections?

Answer: Ramona and Ann each have a schema for how car accidents take place. Thus, they have a representation of this event, which would guide their later recollection of the specific car accident they observed. For example, Ann has a driving schema which includes the knowledge that when a car slows down it should be because there is a stop sign. Therefore, Ann believes she saw a stop sign at the scene of the accident. Whereas, Ramona did not have the stop sign in her "driving schema" and does not remember a stop sign at the accident scene.

Page Ref: 260–261

4) Discuss the children's disagreements in terms of reconstructive memory. Is the variance in their recollections likely to increase or decrease over time? Explain.

Answer: When knowledge is missing, we typically "fill in the gaps" with other information that seems reasonable to the situation. For example, Ramona cannot correctly remember exactly what the white car was doing during the accident. Thus, it seems logical that it was swerving from side to side. In contrast, Ann was paying focused attention to the white car during the accident. She does not have any missing information in her memory and this may explain why she disagrees with Ramona that the white car was swerving. As Ramona and Ann both talk to different people about the accident, they are likely to encounter questions that reveal more parts of their missing memories. Thus, they are likely to engage in additional memory reconstruction over time which would account for the expected increase in variance in their recollections.

Page Ref: 264–265

Taylor is having considerable difficulty remembering terms, names, and facts in his English Literature class. On his last exam, he identified Shakespeare as the author of *The Canterbury Tales* and Paris as the location of the *Tales*. Historical authors and their works are so confusing to him that he doesn't even try to remember them. The result is that, although he typically does satisfactorily on essays (he purposefully leaves out connecting authors with their works that he is uncertain about), his scores are extremely low on objective items such as multiple-choice and fill-in-the-blank items.

5) With what type of learning is Taylor having difficulty? What implications do the special properties of this type of material have for learning and retention?

Answer: Taylor is struggling with processing declarative knowledge, which is knowledge about facts and is referred to as "knowing that." By lacking declarative knowledge about authors and other facts about literature, Taylor will have limited capabilities for organizing smaller facts into larger units of knowledge (i.e., broad principles about English literature).
Page Ref: 258

6) Apply the concepts of massed vs. distributed practice to suggest an effective strategy that Taylor might employ to improve his performance.

Answer: One way to approach Taylor's learning difficulty is to have him engage in distributed practice, which means requiring him to memorize dates and authors in brief periods with short rest intervals. Because Taylor has lost interest in the subject matter, he tends to study English literature in a single study period of four straight hours (i.e., massed practice). Research shows Taylor will have better retention and retrieval of material if he were to study one hour for four consecutive nights. By distributing Taylor's study efforts, he will have more of an opportunity to engage in deeper processing, which increases the probability that they information will be moved into long-term memory.
Page Ref: 274

7) Identify at least two mnemonic strategies that he could employ and briefly describe how each might be used.

Answer: The first step in using mnemonics is that Taylor will need to rely upon information stored as procedural and conditional knowledge. He will need to know how to use a specific mnemonic (procedural) and when to employ the mnemonic (conditional). You could recommend Taylor try the keyword method for memorizing the fact that The Canterbury Tales takes place in London. In this example, Taylor might memorize the sentence "The cat buried his tail in London." The keyword here is "buried" which is a part of Canterbury. Using a "cat" in this sentence will cue Taylor to the letter "c." He can remember "Cat buried", which sounds somewhat familiar to "Canterbury." In addition, to the keyword method he could use visual imagery techniques to imagine a cat buring his tail in a hole in a London street. Building on the cat theme, you could assist Taylor in creating an acronym for remembering the author's name. For example, Taylor could remember "C.A.T.", which stands for "Chaucer – Author of Tales."
Page Ref: 271-272

Chapter 8 Complex Cognitive Processes

Multiple-Choice Questions

1) Which one of the following students best illustrates the simplest and most practical definition of understanding?

    A) Ava figures out how to finance her project within her current budget.

    B) Mike contemplates four different shell shapes of oysters.

    C) Robert answers the teacher's question correctly and rapidly.

    D) Samantha's concept of multicultural education is similar to that of most of her classmates.

Answer: A

Explanation: A) According to Gardner, understanding involves knowing when to apply and when not to apply knowledge. *Ava's figuring out how to finance her project within the budget is an example of understanding.*

Page Ref: 285
Skill: Knowledge

2) Traditional views of concept learning suggest that we recognize examples of a concept by

    A) deductive reasoning.

    B) identifying defining features.

    C) imaging prototypes.

    D) top-down processing.

Answer: B

Explanation: B) For many years, it was thought that examples of concepts were recognized by identifying their *distinctive attributes or defining features*. The traditional view emphasizes bottom-up processing over top-down processing.

Page Ref: 286
Skill: Knowledge
P: .67
D: .24

3) Which one of the following behaviors is a defining attribute for the concept "bird"?

    A) Building nests

    B) Eating insects

    C) Growing feathers

    D) Vocalizing its territorial boundaries

Answer: C

Explanation: C) A defining attribute of a concept is a distinctive feature. For birds, the *growth of feathers* is the only distinctive feature of the choices listed. Building nests, eating insects, and territorial vocalization apply to many other animals.

Page Ref: 286
Skill: Understanding

4) Noah counted the legs on a bug and came up with eight. He then decided the bug was an arachnid (spider) because an arachnid has eight legs. His decision was based upon what aspect of concept learning?

    A) Algorithm

    B) Defining attribute

    C) Heuristic

    D) Prototype

Answer: B

Explanation: B) Noah determined that a *defining attribute* of arachnids is having eight legs. Defining attributes are distinctive features that characterize all members of the concept category.

Page Ref: 286
Skill: Understanding
P: .69
D: .26

5) When you mention "dogs," both Bethany and Ashley would picture collies. In relation to the concept "dog," what would the image of a collie be?

    A) Algorithm

    B) Attribute

    C) Heuristic

    D) Prototype

Answer: D

Explanation: D) A *prototype* is the best representative of a category for individuals. Apparently Bethany's and Ashley's experiences with dogs have frequently involved collies, because both girls view collies as a prototype of the concept "dogs."

Page Ref: 286
Skill: Understanding
P: .82
D: .36

6) Little Billy was accustomed to seeing Officer Sam O'Reilly walking around the block, but then one day he met Officer Sally Murdock. Billy gave her a suspicious look and said, "You can't be an officer, you're a lady." Billy's concept of a police officer was probably

  A) based on a male prototype.

  B) derived primarily from defining attributes.

  C) refined from a complex schema.

  D) verbal rather than intellectual.

Answer: A

Explanation: A) Billy's conception of a police officer was probably *based on a male prototype,* as a consequence of seeing only male exemplars. Thus, he failed to recognize Sally as a police officer because she was female.

Page Ref: 286
Skill: Understanding
P: .73
D: .26

7) When Mr. Wilson wants his students to learn about a familiar concept and practice thinking skills at the same time, he should stress

  A) concept attainment.

  B) exemplar of the concept.

  C) nonexamples of the concept.

  D) positive instances of the concept.

Answer: A

Explanation: A) The strategy that Mr. Wilson should use is to stress *concept attainment.* This strategy is focused on methods of helping students to construct an understanding of specific concepts and, at the same time, practice thinking skills such as hypothesis testing.

Page Ref: 288
Skill: Understanding
P: .38
D: .30

8) In discussing the concept "fruit," the teacher says "...and fruits come in practically all colors."
The teacher is identifying a(n)

A) defining attribute.

B) irrelevant attribute.

C) nonexample.

D) prototype.

Answer: B

Explanation: B) The attribute, color, is an *irrelevant attribute* in this case because it cannot be
used to determine which objects are fruit and which are something else. For
example, if you know that an object is green, you are no better off than you
were without this information in guessing whether it's a fruit, a vegetable, or a
refrigerator.

Page Ref: 288
Skill: Understanding

9) In teaching the concept "language," Mr. Cartlow has included hand signs and computer
software as examples. His choice of examples is designed to avoid

A) defining attributes.

B) negative transfer.

C) undergeneralization.

D) underlearning.

Answer: C

Explanation: C) *Undergeneralization* occurs when students fail to include valid instances in a
concept category. Therefore, Mr. Cartlow is using different types of stimuli
(hand signs and computer software) to reduce the possibility of
undergeneralization. In another example, exposing students to different types
of language would prevent undergeneralization for language as a concept.

Page Ref: 289
Skill: Understanding
P: .83
D: .31

10) Which one of the following is the sequence of procedures recommended by Woolfolk for teaching concepts?

    A) Less obvious examples, nonexamples, then prototypes

    B) Less obvious examples, prototypes, then nonexamples

    C) Nonexamples, less obvious examples, then prototypes

    D) Prototypes, less obvious examples, then nonexamples

Answer: D

Explanation: D) To help students establish the concept category, start with a *prototype* or best example. Then present *less obvious examples to reduce tendencies for undergeneralization*. Finally, present *nonexamples to reduce tendencies for overgeneralization*.

Page Ref: 289
Skill: Knowledge
P: .68
D: .36

11) In identifying marsupials, a student excludes the koala, thinking it is a cuddly little bear. With regard to the marsupial category, what has taken place?

    A) Overgeneralization

    B) Retroactive inhibition

    C) Subsumption

    D) Undergeneralization

Answer: D

Explanation: D) *Undergeneralization* is the tendency to exclude valid instances of a concept category. In this case, Koala is a valid instance of the category "marsupial."

Page Ref: 289
Skill: Understanding

12) A child hopefully, but erroneously, argues that an orange soda qualifies as a type of fruit juice. This event illustrates the concept of

    A) overgeneralization.

    B) retroactive inhibition.

    C) subsumption.

    D) undergeneralization.

Answer: A

Explanation: A) *Overgeneralization* has occurred in this situation. The child incorrectly classified orange soda as an instance of the category "fruit juice." Orange soda may be similar to orange juice, but it lacks the critical defining attributes for the fruit juice category.

Page Ref: 289
Skill: Understanding

13) When teaching a concept, teachers should present "nonexamples" in order to help students avoid

    A) irrelevant attributes.

    B) negative instances.

    C) overgeneralization.

    D) undergeneralization.

Answer: C

Explanation: C) *Overgeneralization* occurs when non–instances of a concept are included as members of that concept category (such as thinking that a bat is a type of bird). Presenting non–examples reduces overgeneralization by showing that not all related or similar instances (e.g., things that fly) belong to the same concept category.

Page Ref: 289
Skill: Knowledge
P: .80
D: .26

14) In what phase of the concept attainment model does the teacher have the students generate examples of the concept?

    A) Analyzing thinking strategies

    B) Identification of the concept

    C) Presentation of defining attributes

    D) Testing understanding of the concept

Answer: D

Explanation: D) Having students generate examples of a concept is a strategy used in Phase Two of the Concept Attainment Model: *Testing attainment, or understanding, of the concept.*

Page Ref: 288
Skill: Knowledge
P: .48
D: .34

15) Which one of the following phrases **BEST** contrasts concept learning with discovery teaching methods?

    A) Concept mapping vs. information processing

    B) Facts vs. concepts

    C) Knowledge vs. application

    D) Reception vs. inquiry

Answer: D

Explanation: D) *Reception vs. inquiry* is the phrase that best contrasts concept learning (reception) with discovery teaching (inquiry) methods. *Expository learning is sometimes called reception learning* because students "receive" information from teachers. Discovery learning involves inquiry, i.e., exploratory activities by students to construct knowledge and make intuitive guesses.

Page Ref: 290–291
Skill: Understanding
P: .64
D: .42

16) Dr. Alvarez presented several cases involving liability to her business law class. She then asked the class to develop a general rule based on the cases. What type of learning was involved?

    A) Cognitive strategy

    B) Deductive reasoning

    C) Inductive reasoning

    D) Structured ideas

Answer: C

Explanation: C) *Inductive reasoning* involves progressing from specific examples (in the situation involving Dr. Alverez, developing a rule based on liability cases) to a general principle. Deductive reasoning involves the opposite type of progression (rule to specific examples).

Page Ref: 290
Skill: Understanding
P: .50
D: .41

17) Ms. McDonald's class learns to list the names of all the U.S. Vice Presidents in order. Asusbel would consider this type of learning to be rote learning because it

   A) involves nonessential information.

   B) is not connected to existing knowledge.

   C) is not inductive reasoning.

   D) meets no behavioral objective.

Answer: B

Explanation: B) Learning to list the Vice Presidents in order is a *rote memorization task*. That is, students generally approach such tasks without needing to have relevant knowledge that would help them to learn.

Page Ref: 295
Skill: Understanding
P: .45
D: .21

18) Ms. Louis begins her sixth–grade science class by making an egg drop through the neck of a bottle. She then presents some questions about this and encourages students to solve them. This activity is most consistent with that used in

   A) deductive analysis.

   B) eg–rule learning.

   C) guided discovery.

   D) expository learning.

Answer: C

Explanation: C) *Guided discovery* presents students with intriguing questions and interesting problems while challenging them to come up with relevant solutions. Teachers, such as Ms. Louis, provide direction (as in the demonstration) to ensure more control over the activity. [Imagine 25 students trying to push eggs through bottles on their own!]

Page Ref: 291
Skill: Understanding
P: .74
D: .33

19) Expository teaching is to discovery learning as

    A) induction is to deduction.

    B) negative instances are to positive instances.

    C) relevant attributes are to irrelevant attributes.

    D) rule–eg methods are to eg–rule methods.

Answer: D

Explanation: D) Expository teaching is to discovery learning as *rule–eg methods are to eg–rule methods*. Both expository teaching and rule–eg methods involve moving from rule to specific examples. Discovery and eg–rule involve moving from specific examples to a rule.

Page Ref: 292
Skill: Understanding
P: .59
D: .26

20) Which one of the following is the best example of using an advance organizer?

    A) Having the appropriate learning behavior reinforced vicariously

    B) Relating prior knowledge of the American Revolution to introduce the French Revolution

    C) Remembering that the first initials of the five key words in a passage spell "**TULIP**"

    D) Underlining the important passages in a reading assignment that is due tomorrow

Answer: B

Explanation: B) An advance organizer is illustrated by *relating prior knowledge of the American Revolution to introduce the French Revolution*. The important idea is to use previous knowledge (American Revolution) to provide a framework or knowledge base to which new material (French Revolution) can be meaningfully related.

Page Ref: 292
Skill: Understanding
P: .82
D: .33

21) Mr. Stanley began his lesson with "plate tectonics refer to the gradual movement of vast segments of the earth's crust. Picture paper plates floating in a pool of water. Continents float on the earth's mantle in just the same way." This illustrates a(n)

   A) advance organizer.

   B) positive instance of the concept.

   C) prototypic example.

   D) response set.

Answer: A

Explanation: A) An *advance organizer* is being used to activate students' knowledge of paper plates and how they might look when floating on water. This image will provide useful scaffolding for understanding the principles of geology that Mr. Stanley is now teaching.

Page Ref: 292
Skill: Understanding
P: .57
D: .33

22) Consider the following sequence for a lesson about communism and socialism: (1) Tell the students in general terms about what you will be covering. (2) Present examples of some basic similarities and differences between communism and socialism. (3) Help students relate the examples to their everyday lives. This lesson is best characterized as teaching what type of learning?

   A) Conditional

   B) Discovery

   C) Expository

   D) Rote

Answer: C

Explanation: C) The lesson on communism and socialism represents *expository teaching*. It includes an overview, comparison of major concepts, examples, and an attempt to relate the material to students' lives (make the material meaningful). There is no discovery or rote or vicarious learning involved here.

Page Ref: 292
Skill: Understanding
P: .76
D: .30

23) Current beliefs about problem-solving techniques suggest that domain-specific strategies are

   A) more useful than general problem-solving strategies.

   B) likely to be used increasingly as experience with a particular subject increases.

   C) highly transferable to other domains.

   D) unlikely to be used in well-defined subject areas such as mathematics.

Answer: B

Explanation: B) Most psychologists believe that people switch between general and domain-specific approaches to problem solving. When we become involved in a new area we primarily rely on the general strategies. As we gain more experience, we *increasingly use domain-specific strategies as experience with a particular subject increases,* because these strategies apply directly to typical problems in the area concerned.

Page Ref: 304
Skill: Knowledge
P: .63
D: .26

24) In using the **IDEAL** approach to problem solving, the first step is to

   A) identify the problem.

   B) introduce the problem.

   C) isolate the problem.

   D) probe for solutions to the problem.

Answer: A

Explanation: A) The IDEAL model, developed by Bransford and Stern, begins with *identifying the problem.* The model includes Identify, Define, Explore, Act, and Look Back.

Page Ref: 295
Skill: Knowledge
P: .90
D: .21

25) The main difficulty that occurs when students are too quick to decide what a problem asks is that they may

    A) activate an inappropriate schema.

    B) become too reflective.

    C) experience overgeneralization.

    D) rely on heuristics instead of algorithms to solve it.

Answer: A

Explanation: A) Research shows that students often *activate an inappropriate schema* when they work too quickly on problems. Typically, a problem is categorized after reading only the first few sentences. Cognitive theory suggests that representing problems involves activating appropriate schema. Students who use the wrong schema can overlook critical information, use irrelevant information, or may even misread critical information. Changing one's interpretation of experiences could activate relevant schema.

Page Ref: 296
Skill: Knowledge

26) You remember that, when you lost your billfold last semester, campus security found it for you. You lost it again this morning and decided to call campus security. The method used to solve this problem is called a(n)

    A) heuristic search.

    B) means–ends analysis.

    C) pattern matching.

    D) schema–driven route.

Answer: D

Explanation: D) A *schema–driven route* is a previously used approach to solving a problem. When a similar situation later occurs, the same schema may be activated and suggest the use of the former solution strategy (in this case, calling campus security).

Page Ref: 298
Skill: Understanding
P: .41
D: .32

27) The strategy of solving a crossword puzzle by doing "down" items before "across" items is an example of

    A) a heuristic.

    B) metacognition.

    C) patterning.

    D) top–down processing.

Answer: A

Explanation: A) The strategy of solving a crossword puzzle by doing "down" items before "across" items is an example of a heuristic. A *heuristic is a strategy that may not guarantee a correct solution but it provides a reasonable approach to problem solving that, if successful, will reduce the steps to a solution.*

Page Ref: 299
Skill: Understanding
P: .55
D: .46

28) A procedure that is guaranteed to accomplish a particular goal when correctly implemented is called a(n)

    A) algorithm.

    B) heuristic.

    C) theorem.

    D) working–backward strategy.

Answer: A

Explanation: A) An *algorithm* is a step–by–step procedure that guarantees a correct answer. The limitation is that students often apply algorithms haphazardly without understanding how the correct answer was obtained.

Page Ref: 298–299
Skill: Knowledge
P: .70
D: .45

29) Which one of the following concepts is consistent with the notion of a heuristic?

   A) Analogical thinking

   B) Domain specific

   C) Exhaustive

   D) Guaranteed solution

Answer: A

Explanation: A) *Analogical thinking* is a type of heuristic approach. Employing a general
                strategy previously used in a similar situation, even though analogical
                thinking does not guarantee a solution, provides a reasonable approach that
                has a good chance of working.

Page Ref: 300
Skill: Knowledge
P: .67
D: .39

30) Sgt. York couldn't get a shot at the enemy, who was keeping his head down in a foxhole.
    "Why, he's acting just like the turkeys back in Kentucky!" Sgt.York thought and yelled out his
    best turkey gobble. The enemy stuck up his head to see what the noise was and found a bullet.
    What cognition process did the sergeant use?

   A) Analogical thinking

   B) Deductive logic

   C) Overlearning

   D) The generate–test method

Answer: A

Explanation: A) *Analogical thinking* involves solving a new problem by thinking of a strategy
                employed in some similar situation. In this example, Sgt. York made a turkey
                out of the enemy with his "gobble" cries. What worked in Kentucky worked
                during the battle in World War I.

Page Ref: 300
Skill: Understanding
P: .58
D: .32

31) Means–ends analysis in problem solving involves

    A) beginning at the goal and moving backwards to the unsolved initial problem.

    B) distance reduction and dividing a problem into subgoals.

    C) limiting the search for solutions having something in common with the problem.

    D) using analogical reasoning and heuristics.

Answer: B

Explanation: B) Means–ends analysis involves identifying the final goal and then *achieving distance reduction between the starting place and the goal by dividing the problem into subgoals.* Each of the subgoals is then addressed systematically.

Page Ref: 299
Skill: Knowledge

32) Hernando looked at the problem and exclaimed: "Aha! This is just like when Ahab was obsessed with the great white whale, Moby Dick!" This comment is the result of

    A) analogical thinking.

    B) deductive logic.

    C) overlearning.

    D) the generate–test method.

Answer: A

Explanation: A) Hernando's sudden recognition that the present problem was similar to the analogy of Ahab and Moby Dick is an example of *analogical thinking*.

Page Ref: 300
Skill: Understanding
P: .66
D: .43

33) Which one of the following students **BEST** illustrates the state of functional fixedness?

    A) Nathaniel, a student who is using a ruler for drawing lines, fails to realize that he can use its metal edge as a scraper to remove paint from his desk.

    B) Kathy, a student who is trying to solve a math problem, explores many different strategies until she finds a reasonable answer.

    C) Rebecca, a third–grade teacher, sees the second–grade achievement scores for her new class and begins to form expectancies about individuals' abilities.

    D) Wendell, who is used to making "d" look like "b," continues to make the same error.

Answer: A

Explanation: A) The ruler can be used as a scraper as well as a tool for drawing lines. *Due to functional fixedness, however, Nathaniel recognizes only the latter, more common function.* The other students represent other strategies for concept learning, except for Wendell who may have a perceptual problem.

Page Ref: 302–303
Skill: Understanding
P: .81
D: .40

34) Greg ponders over a math problem. He looks, frowns, and several minutes pass as he continues to study and shuffle his papers. All at once, he smiles, picks up his pencil, and writes down the correct answer. The suddenness of Greg's solution best exemplifies

   A) functional fixedness.

   B) insight.

   C) problem representation.

   D) transfer.

Answer: B

Explanation: B) Greg is demonstrating *insight* in his attempt to solve math problems. Insight is the sudden recognition of a solution to a problem; it is often fostered by mental restructuring and analysis of the problem.

Page Ref: 303
Skill: Understanding
P: .76
D: .40

35) Frank was supposed to push three wheelbarrows back to the barn, and he wasn't relishing the idea of three trips. Then in a flash he reorganized the problem. He loaded two wheelbarrows onto the third and made one trip. In doing this, he demonstrated

   A) flexibility.

   B) functional fixedness.

   C) insight.

   D) response set.

Answer: C

Explanation: C) *Insight* is defined as the sudden reconceptualization of a problem. In this instance, Frank acquired the insight that one wheelbarrow can be used to carry the other two. Note that Frank also avoided functional fixedness by realizing that a wheelbarrow can be a cart as well as a carrier.

Page Ref: 303
Skill: Understanding
P: .85
D: .29

36) Gloria thinks about the solution to a problem regarding welfare in her American Problems course. She asks herself what she needs to know in order to solve the problem. She tries to think about the problem in different and, possibly, creative ways. She is then able to clarify the problem and propose a potentially useful solution. The aspect of problem solving that Gloria's strategy exemplifies is

A) flexibility.

B) functional fixedness.

C) response set.

D) transfer.

Answer: A

Explanation: A) The strategy of asking herself what it is that she needs in order to solve the problem is an example of Gloria's using *flexibility* in helping herself solve the problem. She is using flexibility to help her think about the problem in different and perhaps creative ways. This permits her to clarify the problem and propose a potentially useful solution.

Page Ref: 303
Skill: Understanding
P: .81
D: .38

37) Studies of expertise have discovered that chess masters are superior to nonexpert players in

A) conscious analytical thought.

B) domain knowledge.

C) random chess pattern recognition.

D) recognition of meaningful chess patterns.

Answer: D

Explanation: D) Chess masters have superior memory for *meaningful chess patterns*. When pieces are placed on a board randomly, the masters are no better than other people at remembering the positions of the pieces. Nor are they considered to be superior at conscious analytical thought.

Page Ref: 304–305
Skill: Knowledge
P: .63
D: .29

38) Creativity is thought be be associated directly with what type of thinking?

   A) Convergent

   B) Deductive reasoning

   C) Divergent thinking

   D) Intuitive

Answer: C

Explanation: C) Creativity is sometimes associated with *divergent thinking,* which involves
                  coming up with many different ideas or answers. In contrast, convergent
                  thinking involves generating a particular answer.

Page Ref: 308
Skill: Knowledge

39) Michael was asked to devise as many uses for a brick as he could. After taking the assignment
    home to work on further, he came up with over 30 ideas, many of which were not proposed by
    any other student. All of Michael's ideas dealt with using a brick to break things. In what
    aspect of creativity proposed by Torrence is Michael lacking?

   A) Flexibility

   B) Fluency

   C) Incubation

   D) Originality

Answer: A

Explanation: A) On Torrence's tests, fluency is the measure of the total number of different
                  responses given. Flexibility is a count of the number of different categories of
                  responses. Originality is the number of responses given by fewer than five
                  people out of every 100 who take the test. Michael's task included fluency
                  (many ideas on uses of a brick), and incubation (worked on the problem
                  overnight). However, all of Michael's ideas represented only one category
                  (using a brick to break things), so flexibility was NOT represented in Michael's
                  task behavior.

Page Ref: 308
Skill: Understanding

40) Ms. Cricket gave a creative writing assignment on today's film. She allows 10 minutes today and 10 minutes tomorrow to work on it. What component of the creative process is she fostering?

 A) Automaticity

 B) Elaboration

 C) Flexibility

 D) Restructuring

Answer: D

Explanation: D) Ms. Cricket is fostering *restructuring or breaking set* in order to see a problem in a new way. On the other hand, restructuring has the disadvantage of removing the student from active problem–solving.

Page Ref: 307
Skill: Knowledge

41) Which one of the following people illustrates the best example of creative behavior?

 A) Billy uses and established method to solve an algebraic equation on a test.

 B) Calita uses an encyclopedia to find the significance of the date July 4, 1776.

 C) Jack pours a solution of acid into a breaker of water in the chemistry lab.

 D) Sheryl generates a list of solutions for the recycling problem.

Answer: D

Explanation: D) The best example of creativity is Sheryl's *compilation of a list of solutions* for the recycling problem in her school. Sheryl is trying to come up with unusual and diverse ideas, as opposed to the students in the other response alternatives who are applying knowledge in a straightforward, uncreative manner.

Page Ref: 307–309
Skill: Understanding

42) In order to encourage student creativity, teachers are advised to

 A) enhance each student's reliance on authorities for response accuracy.

 B) promote convergent thinking and problem–solving skills.

 C) reinforce unusual solutions, even if the product is not perfect.

 D) work on increasing the speed with which students can identify solutions to problems.

Answer: C

Explanation: C) In order to encourage creativity, teachers are advised to *reinforce unusual solutions* even if the products are not perfect. In this way, they will convey to students that divergent thinking is desirable and the "correct" answers are not as important for the given task as creative thinking.

Page Ref: 309–311
Skill: Knowledge

43) Expert teachers don't have to think as hard as beginning teachers due to an ability to

   A) access short-term memory.

   B) memorize many details.

   C) recognize patterns in problems.

   D) use logical reasoning.

Answer: C

Explanation: C) A critical distinction between the thinking processes used by novices and experts *is that experts recognize patterns in problems*. Consequently, they rely less on bottom–up (feature analysis) processing and put less strain on working memory.

Page Ref: 293
Skill: Knowledge
P: .63
D: .29

44) Research indicates that science students are frequently inhibited in problem solving by their

   A) difficulties in evaluating their own work.

   B) erroneous models of the physical world.

   C) errors in applying solutions.

   D) lack of motivation.

Answer: B

Explanation: B) Science students form intuitive models of basic concepts. These models are based on what they "think" happens and are often *erroneous models of the world*.

Page Ref: 293
Skill: Knowledge

45) Ms. Cricket gave a creative writing assignment on today's film. She allows 10 minutes today and 10 minutes tomorrow to work on it. What component of the creative process is she fostering?

   A) Automaticity

   B) Elaboration

   C) Flexibility

   D) Restructuring

Answer: A, D

Explanation: D) Mr. Cricket is fostering *restructuring* or breaking set in order to see a problem in a new way. On the other hand, restructuring has the disadvantage of removing the student from active problem solving.

Page Ref: 307
Skill: Understanding

46) You are teaching a class of students who are very inexperienced in solving problems on their own. What is the most useful strategy for the teacher to use in order to help students solve the problems for a particular unit?

    A) Combine the use of guidelines for problem solving with student self-monitoring.

    B) Provide an algorithm that specifies the steps for one of the specific problems.

    C) Supply general guidelines for problem solving and have students experiment through trial and error.

    D) Use teacher demonstrations in conjunction with partner learning.

Answer: A

Explanation: A) In working with inexperienced problem solvers, it is recommended that teachers *combine the use of guidelines for problem solving with student self-monitoring.* Providing an algorithm specifying the steps for specific problems (response b) does not help the problem solver to transfer effective strategies to new situations. Allowing students to experiment through trial and error, even though they may have guidelines (response c), is not only very time consuming but also an ineffective way to deal with new problems. Using teacher demonstrations could be a "spoon feeding" solution, although partner learning might be helpful (response d). Woolfolk emphasized letting students do the thinking, both individually and in groups, in order that each student has a chance to practice problem solving.

Page Ref: 312
Skill: Understanding

47) Use of the *READS* method would probably have questionable benefits for

    A) children in early elementary school.

    B) encouraging a distributed practice schedule.

    C) high school students.

    D) improving recall of information from the text.

Answer: A

Explanation: A) Although the READS method improves recall and encourages a distributed practice schedule, it is not recommended for children in early elementary school. *Young children may lack the metacognitive skills and discipline to use it effectively.*

Page Ref: 314–315
Skill: Knowledge

48) One of the conditions for using good learning strategies is that students must

    A) be able to work independently

    B) understand that ability is more important than effort

    C) value and care about learning

    D) have speed of learning

Answer: C

Explanation: C) Students who have sophisticated learning strategies, and know when to use them, also tend to *value and care about learning and understanding.* Their learning goals are related to the fact that they value the learning task.

Page Ref: 317
Skill: Understanding

49) All of the following are aspects of epistemological beliefs **EXCEPT**

    A) certainty of knowledge.

    B) academic self-concept.

    C) ability to learn.

    D) speed of learning.

Answer: B

Explanation: B) Epistemological beliefs are what students believe about knowledge and learning. For example, they involve what students believe to be the source of knowledge or beliefs about whether or not knowledge can be gaining quickly. Student's *beliefs about knowing and learning c*an influence their use of learning strategies, which ultimately effects their quality of learning.

Page Ref: 318
Skill: Knowledge

50) Cheryl gets good grades in her language class but uses incorrect grammar and punctuation in her written work in other classes. This situation suggests a problem with

    A) assimilation.

    B) encoding.

    C) integration.

    D) transfer.

Answer: D

Explanation: D) Cheryl apparently has a problem with *transfer,* which is using previous learning to influence new learning. Specifically, her learning in language class is not being effectively applied to her usage of grammar and punctuation in writing.

Page Ref: 319
Skill: Understanding
P: .78
D: .40

51) Rory learned about divergent rays in physics class when he was studying the effects of lenses. Later, in his psychology class, he immediately understood the concept of "divergent thinking." What learning experience did Rory have?

   A) A response set

   B) Functional fixedness

   C) General transfer

   D) Negative transfer

Answer: C

Explanation: C) Rory's learning of the concept of divergent rays in physics class has transferred to his learning of divergent thinking in psychology class. This outcome illustrates *general transfer*—applying previous learning to new problems in other, often dissimilar, situations.

Page Ref: 319
Skill: Understanding
P: .90
D: .15

52) Jennifer had her stomach pumped after she ingested part of an unknown compound in chemistry class. "But at home we always taste things to find out whether they're sugar or salt," she said. Jennifer is a victim of

   A) negative transfer.

   B) improper coding.

   C) intuitive thinking.

Answer: A

Explanation: A) Transfer occurs when something learned previously influences current learning. In the present example, the transfer was *negative* because the prior learning interfered with Jennifer's adaptation in a new context.

Page Ref: 320
Skill: Understanding
P: .74
D: .30

53) Low-road transfer is exemplified by

    A) critical thinking skills to derive an innovative solution to a problem.

    B) driving an automatic shift car and forgetting how to drive a standard transmission.

    C) relating chess strategy to developing a military battle strategy.

    D) using two different hammers to drive nails on different projects.

Answer: D

Explanation: D) *Using the two hammers would illustrate low-road transfer*, which is a spontaneous, automatic application of highly practiced skills in new situations. Once you have learned to use one hammer, use of another hammer is typically automatic.

Page Ref: 319
Skill: Understanding
P: .41
D: .37

54) As she tries to bandage Fang, who was grazed by Mr. Simpson's car, Mary Beth reflects on the principles of pressure and clotting that she learned long ago in a Girl Scout first-aid lecture. This attempt to apply previous learning illustrates

    A) high-road transfer.

    B) low-road transfer.

    C) overlearning.

    D) subject structure.

Answer: A

Explanation: A) Mary Beth is using *high-road transfer*, as she consciously attempts to apply former general knowledge (about blood clotting) to a new situation (bandaging Fang). Unlike low-road transfer, this is a "mindful" effort rather than an automatic type of response.

Page Ref: 319
Skill: Understanding
P: .59
D: .25

55) Learning Latin to improve basic intelligence would possibly be inefficient due to

    A) general rather than specific transfer taking place.

    B) specific rather than general transfer taking place.

    C) the impracticality of disciplining mental processes.

    D) the irrelevance of the subject.

Answer: B

Explanation: B) The transfer that occurs from learning subjects such as Latin and mathematics is probably *specific, not general*. The result is likely to be better performance in those areas, but not in learning other subjects.

Page Ref: 319
Skill: Understanding

56) Because an individual is looking to apply knowledge gained in one situation to a new situation, the transfer is

    A) automatic transfer.

    B) backward–reaching transfer.

    C) forward–reaching transfer.

    D) low–road transfer.

Answer: C

Explanation: C) *Forward–reaching transfer* is the type of transfer involved when an individual wants to apply previously learned knowledge to a new situation.

Page Ref: 319
Skill: Knowledge

57) What is the key to high–road transfer?

    A) Analogical thinking

    B) Automated transfer of highly practiced skills

    C) Mindful abstraction

    D) Overlearning

Answer: C

Explanation: C) The key to high–road transfer is *mindful abstraction,* or the deliberate identification of a principle, main idea, strategy, or procedure that is not tied to one specific problem or situation but could apply to many.

Page Ref: 320
Skill: Knowledge

58) Overlearning is the process of practicing a skill

    A) for too long, such that retroactive inhibition develops.

    B) for too long, such that proactive inhibition develops.

    C) past the point of mastery, such that retention is improved.

    D) similar to one previously learned, so that positive transfer is realized.

Answer: C

Explanation: C) The definition of overlearning is that it is the process of practicing a skill *beyond the point of mastery in order to facilitate retention of that skill.*

Page Ref: 321
Skill: Knowledge
P: .68
D: .46

59) Before pulling off the bank job, Bugsy had his gang recite the steps of the operation. "Do we hafta, Bugsy?" complained Willy. "We must have been over them steps fifty times already." Bugsy is aware of the benefits of

　　A) general transfer.

　　B) making learning meaningful.

　　C) modeling.

　　D) overlearning.

Answer: D

Explanation:　　D) By repeatedly reciting the steps of the bank operation, the robbers are being forced into *overlearning*. Chances of remembering the steps for doing the job correctly will increase. [In fact, the men will probably still remember them in prison later on.]

Page Ref: 321
Skill: Understanding
P: .85
D: .26

60) Which one of the following transfer stages is **NOT** one of Gary Phyte's stages in developing strategic transfer of learning?

　　A) Acquisition phase

　　B) Overlearning phase

　　C) Retention phase

　　D) Transfer phase

Answer: B

Explanation:　　B) Transfer of learning strategies can be thought of as a tool for solving problems in a "mindful" way, according to Gary Phyte (1992, 1994). Phyte's three stages in the development of transfer are (1) acquisition phase; (2) retention phase; and (3) transfer phase. *Overlearning is NOT* specifically included in Phyte's transfer strategies.

Page Ref: 322
Skill: Knowledge

61) The stage of transfer for strategies in which the teacher should provide new problems that can be solved with the same strategy is the stage of

   A) acquisition.

   B) overlearning.

   C) retention.

   D) transfer.

Answer: D

Explanation: D) The stage of transfer in which teachers should provide new problems that can be solved using the same strategy is the *transfer stage.*

Page Ref: 322
Skill: Knowledge

The eighth grade is preparing for its annual "School Scam Skit," in which students parody amusing school events during the year. Alonzo, the class President, discovers that the class has mistakenly sold 500 tickets for an auditorium with a seating capacity of only 200. The auditorium is not available for any other night, and the class does not have the funds available to rent a suitable room elsewhere. Numerous possible solutions may exist, but the class is feeling panicked. The class officers are meeting in order to attempt to find a solution to this problem. What type of cognitive approach is each class officer using?

62) Gwen, the class Vice President, suggested that they organize committees that would be responsible for (1) checking the calendar to see if the program could be held on two consecutive nights; (2) checking with other junior or senior high schools in the community to find out about availability of their facilities; and (3) checking on the possibility of using the high school's football stadium to construct a stage and lighting system for an outdoor program.

   A) Analogical thinking

   B) Brainstorming

   C) Means–end analysis

   D) Response set

   E) Working backwards

Answer: E

Explanation: E) The suggestions presented by Gwen reflect *the working backwards problem–solving strategy.* She was systematically searching backwards from the goal of presenting the school skit as scheduled initially to the beginning of the problem as a strategy for finding a workable solution to the problem.

Page Ref: 299
Skill: Understanding
P: .50
D: .39

63) Nephi, the class Treasurer, told the class officers that this situation reminded him of the *Titanic* sinking. Accordingly, the *Titanic* officers could have preserved three times the number of people had they allowed the passengers to lay alongside the life boats and support themselves by holding onto the gunnels. Perhaps the solution to the current problem is embedded in the *Titanic* problem.

    A) Analogical thinking

    B) Brainstorming

    C) Means–end analysis

    D) Response set

    E) Working backwards

Answer: A

Explanation: A) Nephi's analogy of the sinking of the *Titanic* reflects *analogical thinking*. However, analogical thinking can lead to faulty problem solving as well as successful problem solving. Given only the analogy of the sinking of the *Titanic*, it is rather difficult to see how his analogy will lead to a successful solution for finding appropriate space to hold the annual "School Scam Skit"on the night originally scheduled. People need knowledge in both the problem domain as well as the analogical domain in order to reach a successful solution to this problem.

Page Ref: 300
Skill: Understanding
P: .61
D: .33

Completion Questions

1) Categories that group similar events or things are called _____.

Answer: concepts
Page Ref: 286

2) The term used to describe the best example of a particular concept category is a(n) _____.

Answer: prototype
Page Ref: 286

3) When instances that do not belong to a concept category are mistakenly associated with that category, _____ is said to occur.

Answer: overgeneralization
Page Ref: 289

4) Jerome Bruner believes that classroom learning should take place by means of _____ reasoning.

Answer: inductive
Page Ref: 290

5) In order to encourage meaningful rather than rote reception learning, Ausubel proposed a model for _____ teaching.

Answer: expository
Page Ref: 292

6) Introductory statements of a relationship or high-level concept that is broad enough to encompass all of the information to follow are _____.

Answer: advance organizers
Page Ref: 292

7) Formulating new answers by going beyond the simple application of previously learned rules to reach a goal is _____.

Answer: problem solving
Page Ref: 294–295

8) The acronym IDEAL identifies the five steps involved in strategies for _____ problem solving.

Answer: general
Page Ref: 295

9) Providing students with practice in recognizing and categorizing a variety of problem types involves _____.

Answer: schema training
Page Ref: 298

10) An exhaustive, step-by-step approach for solving a problem, in which a solution is virtually guaranteed is a(n) _____.

Answer: algorithm
Page Ref: 298

11) Dividing a problem into a number of intermediate goals and then identifying a means of solving each subgoal is called _____.

Answer: means–ends analysis
Page Ref: 299

12) The inability to recognize unconventional uses of familiar objects represents a barrier to problem solving that is referred to as _____.

Answer: functional fixedness
Page Ref: 302

13) The sudden re–conceptualization or reorganization of a problem that clarifies it and suggests a possible solution is _____.

Answer: insight
Page Ref: 303

14) An important part of becoming an expert in a field is _____ knowledge.

Answer: domain–specific
Page Ref: 303–304

15) Teaching about the where, when, and why of using various strategies reflects _____ learning strategies.

Answer: conditional
Page Ref: 304

16) Making certain that you have the necessary declarative knowledge to understand new information will help to make you a(n) _____ student.

Answer: expert
Page Ref: 304

17) Creativity is often equated with _____ thinking or the ability to generate many different ideas.

Answer: Divergent
Page Ref: 308

18) Creative work is original, appropriate, and _____.

Answer: useful
Page Ref: 306–307

19) In addition to having originality, creativity involves _____ motivation.

Answer: instrinsic task
Page Ref: 307

20) Ms. Winn developed a new method of math instruction, which had a wide spread impact on education and revolutionized the field of mathematics education. Ms. Winn is noted for her _____ or innovation.

Answer: big–C creativity
Page Ref: 310

21) Students' beliefs about knowledge and learning are called _____ beliefs.

Answer: Epistemological
Page Ref: 318

22) The spontaneous, automatic transfer of highly practiced skills is called _____ transfer.

Answer: low-road
Page Ref: 319

23) A conscious and deliberate attempt to apply abstract knowledge learned in one situation in a new situation comprises _____ transfer.

Answer: high-road
Page Ref: 319

24) An example of backward-reaching transfer in which you search for other, related situations is _____ thinking.

Answer: analogical
Page Ref: 319

True/False Questions

1) All members of a concept category have clearly identifiable defining attributes.

Answer: FALSE
Page Ref: 286

2) A prototype is a false instance of a concept.

Answer: FALSE
Page Ref: 286

3) Failing to include instances that belong to a particular concept is called overgeneralization.

Answer: FALSE
Page Ref: 289

4) There are three major phases in the Concept Attainment Model.

Answer: TRUE
Page Ref: 288

5) A basic tenet of discovery learning is deductive reasoning.

Answer: FALSE
Page Ref: 292

6) Meaningful verbal learning is a basic principle of expository teaching.

Answer: TRUE
Page Ref: 292

7) Advance organizers provide new knowledge that students will need in order to understand the information to follow.

Answer: FALSE
Page Ref: 292

8) The two types of advance organizers are comparative and expository organizers.

Answer: TRUE
Page Ref: 292–293

9) As domain–specific knowledge increases, general problem–solving strategies are used more frequently.

Answer: FALSE
Page Ref: 295–296

10) When students do not have existing schemas that suggest an immediate solution to the problem, they must take a schema–driven route to solve the problem.

Answer: FALSE
Page Ref: 296–297

11) An algorithm is a general strategy that might lead to the right answer to a problem.

Answer: FALSE
Page Ref: 298

12) Recognizing a problem as a "disguised" version of an old problem for which one has a solution already is called schema–driven problem solving.

Answer: TRUE
Page Ref: 298

13) The aspect of means–end analysis that involves distance reduction means pursuing a path that moves directly to the goal.

Answer: TRUE
Page Ref: 299

14) A heuristic is a step–by–step prescription for achieving a goal that usually is domain–specific.

Answer: FALSE
Page Ref: 299

15) Means–ends analysis, analogical thinking, functional fixedness, and verbalization are all examples of heuristics.

Answer: FALSE
Page Ref: 299

16) A heuristic that limits one's search for solutions to problems that have something in common is analogical thinking.

Answer: TRUE
Page Ref: 299

17) The working backward strategy is sometimes an effective heuristic for solving certain mathematical problems.

Answer: TRUE
Page Ref: 299–300

18) Functional fixedness is a strategy for using an object in an unconventional way.

Answer: FALSE
Page Ref: 302

19) The tendency to respond in the most familiar or rigid way is a response set.

Answer: TRUE
Page Ref: 302

20) Experts excel relative to novices in applying domain-specific knowledge.

Answer: TRUE
Page Ref: 303–304

21) Diagramming relationships by noting causal connections, comparison/contrast connections, and examples is the specific strategy of textual organization.

Answer: FALSE
Page Ref: 290

22) One of the visual tools that students can use to enhance understanding of a concept is a Venn diagram or a graphic map or chart.

Answer: TRUE
Page Ref: 290

23) Learning domain-specific information is now considered to be an effective orientation for promoting general transfer.

Answer: FALSE
Page Ref: 319

24) Practicing a skill beyond the point of mastery ensures the enhancement of general transfer of problem-solving skills.

Answer: TRUE
Page Ref: 319–320

25) Students who have sophisticated learning strategies, and know when to use them, also tend to have high self–efficacy for the learning task.

Answer: TRUE
Page Ref: 318

26) A students' epistemological belief related to how quickly knowledge can be gained is an aspect of the students' epistemological dimension of *Ability to Learn?*

Answer: FALSE
Page Ref: 318

27) Epistemological beliefs are what students believe to be their own greatest learning strengths and weaknesses.

Answer: FALSE
Page Ref: 318

28) In the retention phase of transfer, teachers should provide plenty of practice with feedback in order for students to hone their strategy use.

Answer: TRUE
Page Ref: 311

29) According to Woolfolk, bringing in familiar cultural folk tales with diverse students is not a good use of a teacher's time because students regardless of their cultural backgrounds typically bring similar beliefs and prior knowledge to the classroom.

Answer: FALSE
Page Ref: 322

30) Researchers have found that exposing individuals to other cultures may increase their creativity.

Answer: TRUE
Page Ref: 323

Short Answer Questions

1) Discuss contemporary views about how concepts are learned and the implication of those views for teaching.

Answer: The traditional view of concept learning was that all members of a category share defining attributes or distinctive features. Today it is believed that, in learning concepts, people are often unaware of these attributes and instead focus on a prototype or "best representative" of a concept category. It is also assumed that we identify members of a category by referring to *exemplars*—actual memories of specific examples to which we compare new stimuli for possible membership. Recommended strategies for teaching concepts use both *distinctive features and prototypes*. Lessons should include (a) the concept name, (b) a definition, (c) relevant and irrelevant attributes, and (d) examples and nonexamples. Starting with prototypes is encouraged, as is the use of pictures to illustrate similarities and differences between examples and nonexamples.

Page Ref: 286–287

2) Explain Bruner's idea of discovery learning. How might his ideas be applied to teaching methods in your future classroom?

Answer: Bruner's *discovery teaching* is focused on students being presented with a problem or question and the teacher providing materials and encouraging students to observe, form hypotheses, and test solutions. Discovery learning employs an *inductive,* or *eg-rule, learning* approach in which rules are derived from experiences with examples. [Answers for the application of discovery learning to individual students will vary.

Page Ref: 290

3) List the major characteristics of Ausubel's expository approach and explain how they relate to his beliefs about learning. How might you use Ausubel's ideas in planning a lesson in your own subject area?

Answer: Ausubel's expository teaching involves the following characteristics: (1) high level of student–teacher interaction; (2) use of many examples; (3) deductive reasoning; and (4) sequential presentation of material. Ausubel has indicated that information will be acquired if the instruction proceeds from general to specific. The teacher provides a lot of information that is organized deductively. Examples are presented to demonstrate similarities in teaching new material and differences to distinguish the new from the old. *Advance organizers* are used to provide a knowledge base to which new information can be meaningfully related. Ausubel stresses *meaningful verbal learning*.

Page Ref: 292–293

4) What is meant by problem solving? Identify some of the factors that inhibit problem solving and suggest strategies for reducing their effects.

Answer: Problem solving involves formulating new answers to create a solution. Because the problem situation is novel for the learner, it does not involve a straightforward or mechanical application of previously learned rules. One of the factors that inhibits problem solving is *functional fixedness*, which is the failure to consider unconventional uses of materials. Another factor is *response set* in which an inappropriate solution strategy is rigidly applied. The effects of these debilitating orientations can be reduced through the application of algorithms and heuristics. One useful heuristic is *means–ends analysis*, which involves dividing the problem into sub–problems and working on each part. Another strategy is *analogical reasoning* based on problems in other domains. *Verbalizing the problem–solving steps* can also be effective. Expert problem solvers, compared to novices, have a richer supply of knowledge and strategies. They are more persistent and better able to employ *top–down processing*. They have a larger store of *condition–action schemata* that guide their actions in each situation. There is also a debate over whether problem-solving strategies are generalizable to different domains or are domain– specific. As we gain more expertise in an area, it seems that we use domain–specific strategies more and more frequently.

Page Ref: 294–300

5) What has research determined about the ways experts solve problems? How can students use this information to make themselves learn more like experts?

Answer: Research shows that experts organize their knowledge around principles rather than details and that they learn to recognize patterns in solutions. These findings point out the importance of organizing knowledge. Novices often approach problem solving with considerable misinformation and apprehension. They often rely on what seems "intuitively correct," rather than on a fundamental understanding of the basic concepts. It is very important for teachers to understand their students' intuitive models of basic concepts because, in order to learn new information and solve problems, students must sometimes "unlearn" common sense ideas. [Researchers with the Elementary Science Project at Michigan State University found that, when new materials were designed that directly confronted fifth–grade students' misconceptions about light, the number of students who failed to comprehend the concept was greatly reduced.]

Page Ref: 303–304

6) Mr. Tolbert comes to you because he is concerned about this son Jack. He describes Jack as being a risk–taker, easily bored, susceptible to day dreaming, intensely curious, and at times silly. He is concerned Jack may have some learning difficulties. What else might be going on with Jack?

Answer: As noted by Torrence (1972), the characteristics described by Mr. Tolbert are also factors associated with high levels of creativity. Specifically, creative students often have the following characteristics: curiosity and playfulness, adaptability, high energy, humor, risk–taking, willingness to fantasize, interest in the mysterious, and intolerance for boredom. Although these are individual characteristics, it is important to point out that creativity is also influenced by social factors (Amabile, 1996).

Page Ref: 309

7) Describe the purpose of the PQ4R method of learning. Explain the five steps involved in this method. How could you use this learning strategy in your teaching area? How is this method similar or different from READS, KWL (KWL Plus), and CAPS?

Answer: The purpose of the *PQ4R* method is to help students study more effectively and, as a consequence, to enhance remembering and understanding of what they read. Step 1 is *Preview*, which involves surveying the chapter to be read to obtain an impression of the purposes and topics and how they relate to existing knowledge. Step 2 is *Question*, which involves generating questions that come to mind as one reads. Step 3 is *Read*, which means the questions formulated in Step 2 can be answered by paying attention to the main ideas, supporting details, and other data in keeping with your purposes. Step 4 is *Reflect*, which involves thinking about examples or images of the material for the purposes of connecting it with existing knowledge. Step 5 is *Recite*, which involves trying to remember information and answers without looking at the book. Reciting is typically done after each headed section. Step 6 is *Review*, which involves rereading and answering questions without looking at the answer feedback. [The description of how this method could be used for a given teaching area will vary with each student.]

READS (**R**eview, **E**xamine, **A**sk, **D**o it, and **S**ummarize) is similar to the PQ4R method. READS starts out with reviewing headings and subheadings, a similar strategy to the fourth R (Review) in that READS requires students to use their own words to pull together the main ideas of the material that they have studied. Review in the PQ4R method is intended to incorporate new material more thoroughly into students' long-term memory but not necessarily requiring students to use their own words. READS is a strategy for use in any grade above the later elementary years, while the PQ4R method can be used with younger students.

CAPS is a strategy for reading literature, while both PQ4R and READS are useful for multiple subjects. The **C** in CAPS asks "Who are the *characters*?" **A** stands for "What is the *aim* of the story?" or the purpose of the story. **P** is "What *problem* happens?" and **S** asks "How is the problem *solved*?"

The *KWL* strategy is used by many of the cooperating teachers that Professor Woolfolk works with to guide reading and inquiry in general. The general framework of this strategy can be used with most grade levels, as can the PQ4R method. The steps in the KWL method include: **K** — "What do I already *know* about this subject?"; **W** — "What do I *want* to know?"; and **L** — "At the end of the reading or inquiry, what have I *learned*?"

Although these four reading strategies differ slightly from each other, students have to be taught how to use the strategies. Direct teaching, explanation, modeling, and practice with feedback are necessary for implementing each of the strategies.

Page Ref: 314–315

8) Define the different types of transfer and create new examples of each.

Answer: Transfer occurs whenever something previously learned in one situation is applied in another situation. *Specific transfer* occurs when a fact, rule, concept, or skill learned in one situation is applied in another, very similar, situation. When the effect of past learning on present learning is **NOT** positive, negative transfer may take place. Response set and functional fixedness are examples of negative transfer. *General transfer* involves applying the principles and attitudes learned in one situation to new problems. Salomon and Perkins (1989) differentiated between *low-road transfer* (the automatic and spontaneous application of well-practiced skills) and *high-road transfer* (the conscious application of abstract knowledge in a new situation). High-road transfer is the more difficult of the two types. It can be forward reaching or backwards reaching. The key to high-road transfer is mindful abstraction, or the deliberate identification of a strategy, main idea, principle, or procedure that could be applied to many situations or problems, not to only one. Student examples of these types of transfer will vary but should reflect the basic concepts of each type of transfer.

Page Ref: 319–321

Case Studies

The eighth-grade class is preparing for its annual "School Scam Skit" in which it parodies amusing school events during the year. Alonzo discovers that, by mistake, the class has sold 500 tickets for an auditorium that has a seating capacity of 200. The auditorium is not available any other night, and the class doesn't have funds available to rent a suitable room elsewhere. Numerous possible solutions may exist, but the class is feeling panicked. Describe how a class committee might attempt to approach the problem using each of the following strategies. [Note: Some strategies might not be effective. Also, you do not need to derive a solution, given that you do not have all the information needed. The main interest is the procedures that you use.]

1) Response set:

Answer: Members of the planning group may hold on to the initial structure dictating that they can only hold one live performance for one group on a given night. Their rigid thinking may limit their potential to see other creative solutions to this problem.

Page Ref: 302

2) Means–ends analysis:

Answer: Using a means–ends analysis approach to solve this problem means that the planning committee could break the problem down into subgoals and solve each subgoal at an intermediate step. For example, even though they initially sold 500 tickets in advance, perhaps with the passage of time some ticket holders can no longer attend the performance on that night. Thus, they might need to find a solution for 450 tickets rather than 500 tickets. Effective means–analysis would also involve distance reduction, or taking the path that leads most directly to the end goal state. This also involves resisting approaches that initially might sound promising but are unlikely to move directly and quickly towards the goal. For example, the committee might consider placing additional chairs in the aisles in order to increase the seating capacity of the facility. However, they would resist this idea knowing that the fire department would not approve this plan.

Page Ref: 299–300

3) Working backwards:

Answer: By working backwards, Alonzo's planning committee might consider the fact that many people just want to see the performance. Some people may not care if they actually see the live performance and would be satisfied with seeing a live video stream delivered over the Internet. Some people may in fact enjoy being able to stay home and invite other people over to view the performance via the Internet. Using this approach, the committee begins with the end goal of showing the performance to a large number of people, who may be physically distributed.

Page Ref: 299

4) Analogical thinking:

Answer: Alonzo brings up the the fact that a similar situation took place last year in their school. The technology instructor had a class with 28 students and only 15 computer work stations. By using this analogy Alonzo limits the search for solutions to the problem, because he has defined it as a space problem which requires a creative solution to how instruction (or performances) are delivered.

Page Ref: 294

5) Overlearning

Answer: Overlearning involves practicing a skill past the point of mastery and is really not relevant to the nature of Alonzo's problem.

Page Ref: 321

6) Negative transfer:

Answer: Alonzo had remembered a situation in the past when a teacher said too many students chose the same topic for a term paper. Hence, the teacher said the last three students who informed her of their topic needed to select another topic. Thinking this was a good principle, Alonzo decided the last 300 tickets purchased would be refunded. This is an example of negative transfer in that the strategy to solve an earlier problem may not be appropriate for the new situation. Instead Alonzo might consider a random selection process for determining how to refund the tickets.

Page Ref: 319

Joe Cunningham and Mary Nesbit are novice English teachers who have been hired at Bison Central High School. Mr. Frank Robinson, a designated Master Teacher, has been assigned as their mentor and supervisor. Both Mary and Joe were selected for their positions from a pool of nearly 70 applicants. Although they have been trained well and are strong academically in their discipline, they do have concerns about how to teach problem-solving strategies to their students. Mary will teach both regular and honors English and literature to sophomores, and Joe will have both honors students and regular students in his junior English and literature classes. The two novice teachers are also expected to team-teach one class of freshmen remedial students.

7) How do you expect Mary and Joe to differ from Mr. Robinson at this stage in their careers? Can you make some assumptions regarding Mary's and Joe's own problem-solving skills?

Answer: It can be assumed Mary and Joe will differ greatly from Mr. Robinson given their limited declarative, procedural, and conditional knowledge base. Mary and Joe's lectures may appear disorganized because they do not have the extensive knowledge base with rich examples and case studies. They may make simplistic summaries of the characters in a book because they do not see the more complex patterns between the characters. As another example, when diagramming sentence structures they will take longer and make more errors compared to Mr. Robinson. Given his expertise, Mr. Robinson will be able to read the short stories written by his students and be able to monitor his own teaching progress. In contrast, Mary and Joe will have more difficulty monitoring their own progress and may be at risk to only focus on students' abilities.

Page Ref: 303–304, 311–312

8) Describe some of the learning strategies that Joe and Mary might use to enhance the problem-solving skills of their students. Will their strategies differ for regular vs. honors students?

Answer: All students, including both regular and honors, should receive direct instruction about how and when to use specific learning strategies. One strategy Joe and Mary could use is to ask students to prepare summaries of the content. As recommended by Ormrod, students would identify the *big ideas* and the *supporting information* related to each big idea. In addition, students would eliminate any *redundant or irrelevant information*. The actual learning strategies might be similar for regular and honors students, but honors students may require less motivational training compared to regular students.

Page Ref: 292–294

9) Do you think Mr. Robinson will suggest some different strategies for the remedial freshman class? If so, what might these strategies be? Would the PQ4R model be helpful for all of these students? What are the merits of using READS or the KWL programs to promote learning? Might one of these programs work better for one type of student than for another (e.g., honors vs. remedial or regular)? Explain your choice(s).

Answer: The *READS* approach requires students to **R**eview headings; **E**xamine boldface words; **A**sk "What do I expect to learn?"; **D**o it — read; **S**ummarize in their own words. READS is quite similar to the *PQ4R* strategy, which involves Preview, Question, Reflect, Recite, and Review. A somewhat simpler approach is the *KWL* reading strategy, in which students ask themselves three questions: What do I already **K**now about this subject?; What do I **W**ant to know?; At the end of the reading or inquiry, what have I **L**earned? All students (honors, remedial, regular) can benefit from these metacognitive strategies. It will be important for Mary and Joe to model to students how to use the various reading and inquiry strategies. In addition, students will need sufficient practice, and Mary and Joe should provide feedback to students about their use of the learning and reading strategies. The appropriate amount of practice and feedback is most likely more important than the choice of one strategy over another.

Page Ref: 314–316

Chapter 9 Social Cognitive and Constructivist Views of Learning

Multiple-Choice Questions

1) Bandura challenged and expanded his early work on behavioral conceptions of learning by focusing on

   A) acquisition of knowledge.

   B) observable performances.

   C) principles of reinforcement and punishment.

   D) social learning theory.

Answer: D

Explanation: D) Bandura challenged and expanded on early work on behavioral aspects of learning by focusing on social behaviors that resulted in his *social learning theory*.

Page Ref: 330
Skill: Knowledge

2) Bandura suggested that the main limitation of traditional views of learning is that these views are

   A) inaccurate.

   B) incomplete.

   C) too abstract.

   D) too classroom-based.

Answer: B

Explanation: B) Bandura suggested that traditional learning theories, though accurate, are *incomplete*. Their limitation is failing to take into account cognitive processes that cannot be directly observed.

Page Ref: 330
Skill: Knowledge

3) Which one of the following perspectives would be the **MOST** consistent with a social view of learning?

    A) Be sure that every student has the proper materials and is ready to work.

    B) Expect each student to process the lesson material somewhat differently.

    C) Teach to the middle of the class in order to achieve the best results.

    D) Use mnemonics and other devices to make learning as simple as possible.

Answer: B

Explanation: B) Constructivists emphasize the unique perspectives that individuals bring to learning situations. Because of these unique perspectives, *each student is expected to process the lesson somewhat differently.*

Page Ref: 330
Skill: Understanding
P: .65
D: .39

4) Ms. Jackson's perception of her capabilities to effectively deal with a particular task is her sense of

    A) modeling.

    B) self–efficacy.

    C) self–reinforcement.

    D) vicarious reinforcement.

Answer: B

Explanation: B) *Self–efficacy* is defined as a person's sense of being able to deal effectively with a particular task.

Page Ref: 332
Skill: Knowledge

5) The following statement is **true** about the relation between self–efficacy and self–esteem.

    A) There appears to be direct relationship between self–efficacy and self–esteem.

    B) There is a strong negative correlation between self–efficacy and self–esteem. As self–efficacy increases, self–esteem decreases.

    C) There is a strong positive correlation between self–efficacy and self–esteem. As self–efficacy increases, self–esteem increases.

    D) There is a strong relationship between self–efficacy and self–esteem only for non–academic tasks. There is no relationship between self–efficacy and self–esteem for academic tasks.

Answer: A

Explanation: A) Self–efficacy is a person's sense of their ability to competently perform a specific task, whereas self–esteem is concerned with judgments of self–worth. Researchers have found the two self constructs are unrelated.

Page Ref: 332
Skill: Understanding

6) In Bandura's social cognitive learning theory, the interaction among personal factors, environmental events, and behaviors is called

    A) enactive learning.

    B) reciprocal determinism.

    C) self–efficacy.

    D) vicarious learning.

Answer: B

Explanation: B) *Reciprocal determinism* is the name Bandura uses for the interaction between the environment, internal factors, and behaviors. By including these three domains, Bandura promoted a strict behavioristic account of learning.

Page Ref: 330
Skill: Knowledge
P: .38
D: .47

7) According to Bandura, expectations are part of which one of the elements that comprise reciprocal determinism?

    A) Behavioral factors

    B) Environmental factors

    C) Personal factors

    D) Social factors

Answer: C

Explanation: C) In Bandura's reciprocal determinism concept, expectations, beliefs, attitudes, and knowledge are examples of his *personal factors dimension*. His environment dimension includes resources, physical settings, and consequences of actions, while the behavior dimension includes individual actions, choices, and verbal statements.

Page Ref: 330
Skill: Knowledge

8) According to Bandura's theory of self–efficacy, the most important and influential source of self–efficacy information comes from

    A) modeling

    B) social persuasion

    C) volition

    D) mastery experiences

Answer: D

Explanation: D) *Mastery experiences* are the student's own direct experiences, which provide useful information about successes and failures and shape the student's sense of self–efficacy.

Page Ref: 333
Skill: Knowledge

9) In addition to academic learning skills, self-regulated learners have

    A) more time to learn new tasks

    B) good self-control abilities

    C) the belief that problem-solving is easy

    D) a tendency to set unrealistic goals

Answer: B

Explanation: B) *Self-regulated learners* have both "will and skill." They have a combination of good academic learning strategies and self-control that makes learning easier. They also are highly motivated and have a good sense of self-discipline.

Page Ref: 335
Skill: Understanding

10) Mr. Snow, the math teacher, asks parents to facilitate their child's self-regulation by

    A) rewarding only large improvements in math skills.

    B) encouraging the student not to engage in self-evaluation.

    C) linking success to natural born abilities.

    D) modeling how to set specific goals.

Answer: D

Explanation: D) Parents and teachers can model *self-regulated learning by showing good planning skills, self-monitoring, self-reflection, and self-evaluation.* They can model how to self-reinforce oneself for meeting his or her goals and the importance of being persistent in order to meet one's goals.

Page Ref: 335-336
Skill: Understanding

11) When failure does occur, self-regulated learners are **LESS** likely to

    A) get defensive.

    B) be persistent.

    C) ask for help.

    D) stay motivated.

Answer: A

Explanation: A) Their strong sense of self-efficacy serves as a buffer for how self-regulated learners perceive failure. When they do fail, they are more likely to reflect upon how much effort they put toward the task, whereas *students who lack self-regulation skills are more likely to get defensive* and adopt face-saving and/or self-defeating behaviors.

Page Ref: 336
Skill: Knowledge

12) Which one of the following teaching approaches does Lynn Fuch (2003) recommend for incorporating self-regulated learning strategies into math-problem solving?

   A) Self-regulated learning strategies should not be taught in math classes until high school because younger students do not have the cognitive maturity to employ the appropriate learning strategies.

   B) Teachers should assess student's level of volition.

   C) Students should not discuss their problem-solving strategies with other students because this can lead to cheating and students not solving the problem on his or her own.

   D) At the beginning of each session, students should set new goals based on their previous math performance.

Answer: D

Explanation: D) Students should inspect their work from the previous session, chart their progress, and *set new goals* based on their previous work.

Page Ref: 339
Skill: Knowledge

13) Woolfolk suggests the following strategy for teachers in an effort to involve parents in supporting self-regulation within their child:

   A) Ask parents to focus on large, overall learning goals

   B) Do not bias parents by sharing the area most challenging for their child

   C) Ask families to keep records in support of the students' self-evaluation of progress

   D) Remind families that children need immediate help, thus children should utilize the answers in the back of their book when doing homework

Answer: C

Explanation: C) Parents can provide self-evaluation guides by *using record-keeping sheets to log assignments*. Teachers are encouraged to provide examples of record-keeping materials during parent-teacher conferences. Parents are encouraged to target small steps for improving students' academic skills rather than focusing on large goals or skills. Woolfolk suggests teachers will want to share with parents what is challenging for their child. Finally, parents are to be reminded of the importance of not turning immediately to the answers in the back of the book when doing homework.

Page Ref: 340
Skill: Understanding

14) What are the steps involved in self-regulated learning?

    A) Modeling, reflection, self-evaluation, devising plans

    B) Teaching, practice, goal-setting, reflective task analysis

    C) Analyzing the task, setting goals, devising plans, enacting strategies

    D) Self-efficacy, strategy use, volition

Answer: C

Explanation: C) In the *forethought stage*, self-regulated learners set clear and reasonable plans and goals for their learning tasks. Their plans and goals are influenced by their sense of self-efficacy for the task. During the *performance stage*, self-regulated learners must employ their self-discipline and ability to stay focused on the task at hand. While performing they also engage in self-observation and monitor their progress frequently to see if they need to make an adaptations. In the final stage, *reflection*, self-regulated learners look back at their performance and think about what happened. Their strong sense of self-efficacy allows them to evaluate their performance in terms of the effort they expended, rather than viewing a "failure" as a sign of weakness or lack of ability. Hence, self-regulated learners are not likely to get defensive in failure situations.

Page Ref: 337
Skill: Knowledge

15) Constructivist views of learning are grounded in the research of

    A) curriculum designers.

    B) Gestalt psychologists.

    C) many psychologists and educators.

    D) Piaget and Vygotsky primarily.

Answer: C

Explanation: C) *Many psychologists and educators have contributed to constructivist views of learning,* including Gestalt psychologists, Piaget, Vygotsky, John Dewey, and others.

Page Ref: 344
Skill: Knowledge

16) Sociological constructivists are concerned primarily with how

    A) cognition creates culture.

    B) cultural context explains learning.

    C) individuals create knowledge.

    D) public knowledge is created.

Answer: D

Explanation: D) Sociological constructivists are concerned primarily with *how public knowledge is created.*

Page Ref: 344–345
Skill: Knowledge

17) Vygotsky's approach to learning is an example of what type of constructivism?

    A) Both externally and internally directed

    B) Externally directed

    C) Internally directed

    D) Logically directed

Answer: A

Explanation: A) Vygotsky's approach to learning is an example of *both internally–directed and externally–directed constructivism,* or situated learning. Learning is viewed as the collaborative construction of socially–defined knowledge and values that occurs by means of socially–constructed opportunities. Moreover, teachers co-construct knowledge with students and act as facilitators of learning and co-participants in the learning process.

Page Ref: 346
Skill: Knowledge

18) Which one of the following student factors influences the extent to which a student will engage in self–regulated learning?

    A) Having knowledge about the teacher

    B) Believing that knowledge is absolute

    C) Knowing about one's own interests and talents

    D) Having the knowledge that all learning tasks require a similar approach

Answer: C

Explanation: C) Self-regulated learners have a great deal of knowledge about their own strengths and needs. They also have good content knowledge about the subject and know the requirements of the task. Finally, they have sufficient contextual knowledge and know what the specific situation calls for in order to apply their learning. Thus, they have both procedural ("how to") and condition knowledge ("when to") relative to their own approaches to learning.

Page Ref: 335–336
Skill: Understanding

19) Mr. Jacoby is very effective at encouraging his students to become self-regulated learners because he includes the following in his teaching:

   A) Direct instruction on the aspects of self-regulated learning

   B) Minimal feedback so that his students can evaluate their own work

   C) Cooperative learning activities

   D) Opportunities for students to develop their creative abilities

Answer: A

Explanation: A) *Teachers can facilitate self-regulated learning among their students by providing direct instruction,* modeling, coaching, and providing students an opportunity to practice their developing self-regulation skills.

Page Ref: 340–341
Skill: Understanding

20) Piaget's approach to learning is an example of what type of constructivism?

   A) Both externally and internally directed

   B) Externally directed

   C) Internally directed

   D) Logically directed

Answer: B

Explanation: B) Piaget's approach to learning is an example of *internally-directed constructivism,* because learning is viewed as occurring by means of multiple opportunities and diverse processes to connect what is already known to the new information. The teacher is viewed to be a facilitator of learning who challenges learners and guides them toward more complete understanding.

Page Ref: 345
Skill: Knowledge

21) Adopting the norms, behaviors, skills, beliefs, language, and attitudes of a particular community is called

   A) enculturation.

   B) general constructivism.

   C) radical constructivism.

   D) social construction of knowledge.

Answer: A

Explanation: A) Adopting the norms, behaviors, skills, language, and attitudes of a particular community is called *enculturation,* a description often applied to situated learning.

Page Ref: 359
Skill: Knowledge

22) Vygotsky's notion that learning is inherently social and embedded in a particular cultural setting is consistent with

    A) guided learning.

    B) relativistic learning.

    C) situated learning.

    D) sociological learning.

Answer: C

Explanation: C) Vygotsky's idea that learning is inherently social and embedded in a particular social or cultural setting is consistent with *situated learning,* because both Vygotsky and situated learning acknowledge the role of context in learning.

Page Ref: 346
Skill: Knowledge

23) Which one of the following ways of learning an applied skill is most consistent with a constructivist approach?

    A) Have the teacher "walk" the students step–by–step through the process.

    B) Provide well-constructed worksheets with which students can practice individually.

    C) Use simplified, artificial materials in order to make the task easier for students.

    D) Use realistic materials and a group format to provide support for individuals.

Answer: D

Explanation: D) *Using realistic materials and a group format* are most consistent with the constructivist approach to learning an applied skill. The other three response choices reflect a more direct instruction orientation rather than a constructivist orientation.

Page Ref: 350–354
Skill: Understanding
P: .68
D: .33

24) The principal characteristics of constructivist teaching are complex, real–life learning environments and

A) guided discovery and feedback.

B) inquiry methods and discovery strategies.

C) social negotiation and shared responsibility.

D) testing hypotheses and forming conclusions.

Answer: C

Explanation: C) Two of the principle characteristics of constructivist teaching approaches are complex, real–life environments and *social negotiation and shared responsibility among learners*. Other characteristics include multiple representations of content, understanding that knowledge is constructed, and student–centered instruction. Inquiry and other problem–based learning approaches are examples of constructivist models.

Page Ref: 350
Skill: Knowledge

25) A structure for teaching, developed by Jerome Bruner, that introduces the fundamental structure of all subjects during the early school years and then revisits the subjects in increasingly more complex forms over time, is called what type of curriculum?

A) Advanced

B) Cultural

C) Spiral

D) Vicarious

Answer: C

Explanation: C) Bruner's model for teaching that introduces the fundamental structure of all subjects during the early school years followed by revisiting the subjects in increasingly more complex form over time is called the *spiral curriculum*.

Page Ref: 350
Skill: Knowledge

26) Ms. French would like to have her students, while experimenting with their own structured materials, discover some key principles of gravity. Which one of the following teaching methods should be most appropriate for this purpose?

   A) Discussion

   B) Inquiry

   C) Lecture

   D) Reciprocal learning

Answer: B

Explanation: B) *The inquiry approach would be best choice for Ms. French to use.* Inquiry would involve her students in questioning how growth works and in actively experimenting and gathering data to test their hypotheses. Discussion, lecture, and mastery learning strategies are direct models that do not involve inquiry.

Page Ref: 351–352
Skill: Understanding
P: .75
D: .30

27) When students encounter only one method of understanding complex content, it is important for the teacher to

   A) have students engage in cooperative learning activities.

   B) present a guided discovery approach to the problem.

   C) revisit the same material from a similar perspective.

   D) use different analogies, examples, and metaphors.

Answer: D

Explanation: D) It is always important for a teacher to *use different analogies, examples, and metaphors* in teaching complex content. Students learn in different ways, so it is very important for the teacher to use different approaches in teaching a complex learning task.

Page Ref: 354–355
Skill: Understanding

28) The guided inquiry model developed by Magnusson, Palincsar, and their colleagues involves both firsthand investigations and

   A) discovery methods.

   B) pattern investigations.

   C) secondhand investigations.

   D) sequences of inquiry.

Answer: C

Explanation: C) The guided inquiry model developed by Palincsar and her colleagues involved both first-hand and *secondhand investigations*. Discovery methods, pattern investigations, and inquiry, as well as other thinking processes, may be subsumed under both firsthand and secondhand investigations.

Page Ref: 351–352
Skill: Knowledge

29) Which one of the following behaviors is one of the teacher's roles in problem-based learning?

   A) Avoid assisting groups and independent investigations.

   B) Demonstrate the steps in scientific investigations.

   C) Discourage students to conduct experiments.

   D) Help students to reflect on their investigations.

Answer: D

Explanation: B) In problem-based learning, the teacher assists group and independent investigations, encourages students to conduct experiments, helps students to reflect on their investigations, and provides other student-centered assistance. *The teacher does NOT* demonstrate the steps involved in scientific investigations when engaging in problem-based learning.

Page Ref: 352–354
Skill: Knowledge

30) Using instructional conversations as a teaching tool is designed to provide a means for

   A) arranging the environment so that students can discover on their own.

   B) grappling with problems in students' zones of proximal development and providing scaffolding.

   C) guiding learning by expectations and demonstrations of the students.

   D) placing students in situations where they have to reach for understanding.

Answer: B

Explanation: B) Using instructional conversations as a teaching tool provides a means for *grappling with problems in students' zones of proximal development and providing scaffolding*. Elements of instructional conversations include a thematic focus, activation and use of background, direct teaching, promotion of expression, and promotion of bases for statements.

Page Ref: 355–356
Skill: Knowledge
P: .58
D: .30

31) Which one of the following factors is an element of the *instructional* aspect of instructional conversations?

   A) Challenging but non-threatening atmosphere

   B) General participation, including self-selected turns

   C) Promotion of complex language and expressions

   D) Responsiveness to student contributions

Answer: C

Explanation: C) *Promotion of complex language and expressions* is an element of the instructional aspect of instructional conversations. The conversational factors of instructional conversations are reflected by the three other response options.

Page Ref: 355–356
Skill: Knowledge

32) An example of a "stand-alone thinking skills" program is

    A) brainstorming.

    B) CoRT.

    C) IDEAL.

    D) PQ4R.

Answer: B

Explanation: B) An example of a stand-alone-thinking program for teaching thinking skills directly is the CoRT program developed by deBono. The advantage of such programs as CoRT is that students do not need extensive subject matter knowledge in order to master the skills. The other three response options are programs or techniques that are **NOT** stand-alone programs.

Page Ref: 360
Skill: Knowledge

33) A broad and complex process of acquiring knowledge and understanding that is consistent with Vygotsky's theory of mediated learning is

    A) direct instruction.

    B) enculturation.

    C) inquiry training.

    D) stand-alone thinking programs.

Answer: B

Explanation: B) David Perkins and his colleagues proposed encouraging analysis, problem solving, and reasoning through a process called *enculturation* that is consistent with Vygotsky's theory of mediated learning. The classroom culture provides models of good thinking, direct instruction, practice, and interactions with others.

Page Ref: 359
Skill: Knowledge

34) Research on the question of whether schools should teach critical thinking and problem-solving skills

    A) favors the teaching of these skills.

    B) recommends direct teaching to poor/novice readers.

    C) remain subjects for debate.

    D) suggests that CoRT programs provide evidence of success.

Answer: C

Explanation: C) Whether schools should teach critical thinking skills and problem-solving skills has **NOT** been resolved by the findings of research studies (see Point-Counter Point Section). Therefore, the correct response is that *teaching these skills remain subjects for debate.*

Page Ref: 360
Skill: Knowledge

35) Which one of the following critical thinking skills is involved in defining and clarifying a problem?

   A) Comparing differences and similarities

   B) Distinguishing between fact and opinion

   C) Identifying unstated assumptions

   D) Recognizing different value systems and ideologies

Answer: A

Explanation: A) One of the thinking skills involved in the stage of defining and clarifying the problem is *comparing differences and similarities*. Distinguishing between fact and opinion, identifying unstated assumptions, and recognizing different value systems and ideologies are skills related to judging the information related to the problem

Page Ref: 359–361
Skill: Knowledge

Completion Questions

1) In recent years, Bandura focused on cognitive factors such as self-perceptions, expectations, and beliefs, so his theory is now called a _____ theory.

   Answer: social cognitive
   Page Ref: 330

2) In social cognitive theory, the interaction of forces that influence learning is called _____.

   Answer: reciprocal determinism
   Page Ref: 330

3) Mr. Kain believes he can teach any student in his class regardless of the student's background. Mr. Kain demonstrates a teacher who has a strong sense of _____.

   Answer: Teacher self-efficacy

   Explanation: *Teachers' sense of efficacy* refers to a teacher's belief that he or she can reach even the most difficult students and help them learn and grow.
   Page Ref: 334

4) Vygotsky's notion that learning is inherently social and embedded within a particular cultural setting is consistent with _____.

   Answer: situated learning
   Page Ref: 346–347

5) Social constructivist theorists view learning as occurring within a specific _____.

   Answer: community of practice
   Page Ref: 347

6) The alternative conception of learning based on the view that students actively create their own knowledge through their interactions with tasks and resources is the _____ perspective.

Answer: constructivist
Page Ref: 344

7) Martha strongly believes that the world was in fact flat prior to Christopher Columbus's journal of the world. Martha's teacher does not correct Martha's construction of this knowledge because she wants to validate Martha's current understanding of the world. In this example, the teacher is most aligned with _____ constructivist teaching perspectives.

Answer: radical

Explanation: *Radical constructivists* believe that knowledge is assumed to the student's individual construction and therefore cannot be judged or proven to be wright or wrong.
Page Ref: 345

8) Two major characteristics of constructivist teaching are complex learning environments and _____.

Answer: social interaction
Page Ref: 346

9) When pre-service teachers engage in a student teaching or capstone experience they are learning with the support and guidance of an expert teacher, which is based on that knowledge and skills are best learned in the context in which they will be lated used in the real world setting. This model of teacher preparation emphasizes _____ learning.

Answer: situated

Explanation: *Situated learning* emphasizes learning in which the knowledge and skills are tied to the situation in which they were learned. Situation learning is a constructivist notion that recognizes it is difficult to transfer learning to new settings.
Page Ref: 347

10) Regarding negotiation and joint construction of meaning, a commitment to build shared meaning by finding a common ground and exchanging interpretations is called a(n) _____ attitude.

Answer: intersubjective
Page Ref: 349

11) Collaboration with others in learning is believed by many constructivists to involve working together to co-construct meaning through _____.

Answer: social negotiation
Page Ref: 349

12) Bruner's notion of teaching, in which more complex forms of learning build upon fundamental concepts taught early in the school years, is called the _____ curriculum.

Answer: spiral
Page Ref: 350

13) A teaching strategy in which the teacher presents a problem and students ask yes/no questions to gather data and test hypotheses is called _____ learning.

Answer: inquiry
Page Ref: 351–352

14) When students are confronted with real situations that have meaning for them, the learning is _____.

Answer: problem–based
Page Ref: 352–354

15) A teaching strategy, based on Vygotsky's theory, that involves active learning is _____.

Answer: conversations
Page Ref: 355

16) The teacher's goal to keep everyone cognitively engaged in a substantive discussion is involved in _____ conversations.

Answer: instructional
Page Ref: 355

17) In the Key School (Indianapolis, Indiana), students of different ages work side by side in a "pod" as part of a program called cognitive _____.

Answer: apprenticeships
Page Ref: 356–357

18) Programs that teach thinking skills directly are called _____ programs.

Answer: stand–alone thinking
Page Ref: 360

19) A complex, broad process of acquiring knowledge and understanding consistent with Vygotsky's theory of mediated learning is _____.

Answer: enculturation
Page Ref: 359

20) Skills in defining and clarifying the problem, judging the information related to the problem, solving the problem, and drawing conclusions are examples of _____ skills.

Answer: critical thinking
Page Ref: 359

True/False Questions

1) Bandura's model of reciprocal determinism is based on the notion of agency and personal control, therefore social influences are not part of his model of reciprocal determinism.

Answer: FALSE

Explanation: Bandura's model of *reciprocal determinism* places equal emphasis on social influences, self–influences, and achievement outcomes.
Page Ref: 330

2) Bandura's observational learning involves paying attention, retaining information or impressions, producing behaviors, and being motivated.

Answer: TRUE
Page Ref: 333–334

3) Self–efficacy is an important influence on observational learning.

Answer: TRUE
Page Ref: 333–334

4) The interaction of environmental events, personal factors, and behaviors is called reciprocal determinism.

Answer: TRUE
Page Ref: 330

5) When a teacher gives a "pep talk" to a student and says "you can do it," the teacher may be able to influence a student's self–efficacy for a task.

Answer: TRUE

Explanation: Social persuasion, if from a credible source, can influence a person's self–efficacy. However, social persuasion in of itself is typically not a powerful enough source of self–efficacy information to create change in belief systems. The pep talk usually needs to be combined with mastery or vicarious experiences in order to have an effect on a student's level of self–efficacy.
Page Ref: 333

6) In order to move from the forethought phase to the performance stage in Barry Zimmerman's (2002) self–regulated learning model it is important for students to have self–control.

Answer: TRUE

Explanation: In Zimmerman's self–regulated learning model, students need to have volition and self–control in order to move from the *forethought stage* to *performance stage*.
Page Ref: 338

7) The externally-directed constructivist view emphasizes that learners construct their own knowledge by means of transforming and reorganizing their existing cognitive structures.

Answer: FALSE
Page Ref: 344–345

8) Locating the source of knowledge in the interaction between learners and their environment is the internally-directed constructivist view of learning.

Answer: FALSE
Page Ref: 345

9) Inquiry teaching methods are very similar to expository teaching methods.

Answer: FALSE
Page Ref: 351

10) The videodisc-based learning environment developed by the Vanderbilt University Group is a problem-based approach called anchored instruction.

Answer: TRUE
Page Ref: 354

11) Although there are many cognitive apprenticeship models, they all share the feature of conceptual scaffolding that is gradually reduced as students become more competent and proficient.

Answer: TRUE
Page Ref: 356–357

12) Once effective cooperative learning groups are established for problem-based learning activities, the teacher's role is primarily that of observer.

Answer: FALSE
Page Ref: 353

13) Instructional conversations are designed to promote learning by means of traditional discussions.

Answer: FALSE
Page Ref: 355–356

14) Stand-alone thinking programs require negligible subject matter knowledge to master the skills.

Answer: TRUE
Page Ref: 359

15) Psychologists are in general agreement on the skills that constitute critical thinking.

Answer: FALSE
Page Ref: 350–351

16) Cognitive apprenticeships are appropriate for nearly all subject areas, but are not appropriate for learning mathematics.

Answer: FALSE

Explanation: Schoenfeld's (1994) research shows *cognitive apprenticeships* can be effective in learning mathematics. He states cognitive apprenticeships are useful in helping novice learners move towards expertise as they asked "What are you doing?", "Why are you doing this?", and "How will success in what you are doing help you find a solution to the problem?"

Page Ref: 358

Short Answer Questions

1) Students who have good learning skills and can control their own thoughts and behaviors are referred to as _____.

Answer: self-regulated learners
Page Ref: 335

2) Self-regulated learners are _____ to learn.

Answer: motivated
Page Ref: 335

3) Self-regulation involves activating and maintaining one's _____, behaviors, and emotions.

Answer: thoughts
Page Ref: 335

4) A student with willpower or self-discipline is said to have _____.

Answer: volition
Page Ref: 336

5) In an effort to encourage students to become self-regulated learners, teachers will want to be very careful about the types of behaviors they _____.

Answer: model
Page Ref: 340

6) Describe the major elements of inquiry and problem-based learning. Describe how you could implement these ideas in planning a lesson in your subject area. How could you know that your efforts were successful?

Answer: The many adaptations of the basic learning inquiry format usually include the following major elements after the teacher formulates a puzzling question, event, or problem. Students (1) formulate hypotheses to explain the event, answer the question, or solve the problem, (2) collect data to test the hypotheses, (3) draw conclusions, and (4) reflect on the original question or problem and the thinking processes needed to solve it. In creating their own plans, students should demonstrate clearly how they would implement each of these phases in responding to whatever problem or question that the students would devise for their hypothetical future students.

Page Ref: 350–351

7) What is the role of teachers today in teaching thinking skills? Discuss your opinion with reference to the specific areas of creating a "culture of thinking" in classrooms and teaching critical thinking skills.

Answer: One way of developing a "culture of thinking" is to teach lessons about thinking. Possible strategies include: (1) using models of good thinking; (2) providing direct instruction in thinking processes; (3) encouraging practice of those thinking processes; and (4) using interactions with others. Critical thinking skills can also be developed by means of practice that emphasizes defining and clarifying problems, judging information related to problems, and solving problems/drawing conclusions.

Page Ref: 359–361

8) What are some of the challenges and dilemmas related to teaching from a constructivist perspective?

Answer: Mark Windschitl (2002) says teachers struggle with implementing constructivist teaching practices because it can be difficult to resolve theoretical assumptions from cognitive and social perspectives. It can also be challenging to balance one's desire to make sure students are thinking creatively and constructing their own knowledge, yet still have an accurate understanding of the information to be learned. Cultural dilemmas will also add to the complexities of teacher's abilities to engage in constructivist practices. Finally, according to Windshitl, the realities and requirements related to the law No Child Left Behind can make it difficult for teachers to teach for deep understanding and student construction of knowledge when test scores are high-stakes and highly emphasized.

Page Ref: 362

Case Studies

John Butler is a skilled and charismatic teacher of high-school chemistry. He sees himself as a proponent of the constructivist theory of learning, while having elements of social cognitive views of learning reflected in some of his teaching strategies. The make-up of this year's class poses some problems for Mr. Butler in that approximately half the class has a strong background in science while the other half has a weak background.

1) How might Bandura's observational learning model be used by Mr. Butler to promote student learning in his classroom?

Answer: First, Mr. Butler would design a very innovative example of a principle of chemistry to get his student's attention. He would explicitly say to students, "You need to pay attention and watch what I do at every step." Next, Mr. Butler would show his students how to solve a chemistry problem. While solving the problem, Mr. Butler would model high self-efficacy by repeating "This is a challenging task, but I know I can do it." He could also provide encouragement to his students by stating "I am certain you can do it too." Mr. Butler would provide multiple opportunities for student practice and build in activities that allow students to engage in self-reinforcement. Mr. Butler might also allow for peer presentations, which would facilitate a peer modeling process.

Page Ref: 330–333

2) Would the use of social negotiation and shared responsibility help Mr. Butler to create a cohesive group among the students? Explain.

Answer: The use of social negotiation and shared responsibility are most likely to help Mr. Butler create a cohesive group if he emphasizes a situated learning approach. Thus, Mr. Butler would ask the students to solve a real life problem, which will require them to utilize their knowledge about the principles and theories of chemistry. In solving the real world problem, the students would be asked to reflect upon the norms, beliefs, language, and attitudes of all participants in their learning group. Students would be asked to share what identity they brought to the group and what tools they relied upon in order to solve the problem. In addition, students could be asked to state to what extent they thought they were a novice or expert relative to the skills needed for solving the problem or completing the task. In this example, Mr. Butler would select a problem that would take the students several weeks or months to solve. The cohesive group would result from social negotiation, which must be developed over time.

Page Ref: 349–350

3) How might the use of cooperative learning strategies help students to overcome the diverseness in their science backgrounds?

Answer: First, the problem may serve as an "instructional anchor" as suggested by the Vanderbilt group's approach to problem-based learning. The anchored instructional approach can develop student interest and provide a reason for the participants to set a group goal. Goals are also an important part of Dr. Bandura's social cognitive theory. A learner's goals influences who he or she is likely to pay attention to and will impact the observational learning process. Second, well-designed cooperative learning groups can be used to overcome student differences in prior knowledge by creating learning communities that require students to engage in active and reflective learning. The strategies suggested by Brown and Campione (1996) would allow Mr. Butler to guide students through a major project that would require the group to research, share information, and perform a consequential task. The performance aspect of a cooperative learning group (or community of learners) is what makes this instructional approach different than standard practices of "teach and test." Students will always have varying levels of declarative and procedural knowledge, however, cooperative learning strategies based on constructivist principles will validate the multiple perspectives, interests, and skills of all students. Finally, in order for Mr. Butler to be successful he will need to pay careful attention to how he structures his cooperative learning groups. He should create diverse groups with approximately four students, who all have stated roles. Mr. Butler would also want to provide a lesson on how to be a good listener and a responsible group member.

Page Ref: 353–354, 357–361

4) Might the use of guided inquiry and/or instructional conversations be helpful to students in this classroom? Are critical thinking skills necessary for success in a high-school chemistry class? Explain.

Answer: Mr. Butler could use guided inquiry techniques by first presenting his students with a puzzling problem in chemistry. Students could design research projects to test their hypotheses about the puzzling chemistry problem. In order to formally test their hypotheses about the discrepant event, Mr. Butler would require his students to state in advance "why would we expect this to happen?". Thus, he would not allow his students to engage in random trial-and-error problem solving approaches. It would be important for the students to develop and test their own questions, rather than relying on questions proposed by Mr. Butler.

In order to be successful in using the instructional conversations approach, Mr. Butler would have to first believe that his students bring expertise in some area relevant to the task. Both Mr. Butler and the student bring important cultural and everyday knowledge and experiences to the situation. In an instructional conversation, Mr. Butler would continually assess the learner's knowledge and be aware of his role in scaffolding the learner to greater understanding of the topic. This is a very different approach than the traditional model of lecturing; however, instructional conversations are considered to be a form of teaching. Instructional conversations have the benefit of keeping student cognitively engaged.

Most likely, all educators would agree one of the outcomes of the teaching and learning process is to engage students in critical thinking. However, not all theorists and educators agree about the order of how to teach lower-order and higher-order (i.e., critical thinking) thinking skills. From an information processing perspective, Mr. Butler would need to first engage students in lower-order thinking skills. From this perspective, Mr. Butler would need to initially identify which terms, principles, or skills should be remembered to the point of automaticity. From a constructivist perspective, it would be important to allow students sufficient time to reflect upon what they have learned and explore new ways to apply their learned chemistry knowledge.

Page Ref: 355-356, 359-361

Chapter 10   Motivation in Learning and Teaching

Multiple-Choice Questions

1) Which one of the following statements is the most accurate definition of motivation?

    A) An inner state that arouses, directs, and maintains a person's behavior

    B) An inner state that causes a person to initiate an action

    C) The level of involvement a person has in a chosen activity

    D) The degree of persistence a person has toward completing an activity

Answer: A

Explanation: A) Motivation is usually defined as an *inner state that arouses, directs, and maintains behavior*. It doesn't "cause" a particular behavior, but creates the conditions that make certain behaviors more or less likely.

Page Ref: 372
Skill: Knowledge
P: .85
D: .21

2) The behavior of which one of the following students best describes the fifth motivation question, which pertains to what the individual is thinking and feeling during an activity?

    A) Anxious Amee, whose worry and anxiety may lead her to make poor choices and procrastinate

    B) Defensive Daleesha who makes poor choices, avoids working on task, procrastinates, and gives up easily

    C) Hopeless Gerardo, who is falling farther behind in his work but causes no management problems

    D) Satisfied Spencer, who is prompt in getting started, The behavior of which one of the following students described in Woolfolk's engaged, persistent, and enjoys the task

Answer: A

Explanation: A) The scenario about *Anxious Amy* reflects only the fifth motivation question (Graham & Weiner, 1996) of what the individual is thinking and feeling during an activity. She is a good student in most subjects but freezes on science tests, and her worry and anxiety may lead her to make poor choices that will only make her more anxious. The scenarios of the three other students demonstrate one of the other four questions about motivation or a combination of several questions.

Page Ref: 372
Skill: Understanding

3) Lashon is very interested in Mrs. Wiley's lesson right now, but he is unlikely to remain so for very long. The type of motivation being evidenced is

    A) cognitive.

    B) social.

    C) state.

    D) trait.

Answer: C

Explanation: C) When viewed as a *state, motivation is regarded as a temporary disposition based on the present circumstances*. Mrs. Wiley's lesson interests Lashon for the moment (state motivation) but may not for long (trait motivation).

Page Ref: 372
Skill: Understanding

4) On Sunday afternoon, Rick spent a couple of hours picking up discarded bottles and cans from a picturesque section of the wildlife refuge, even though he knew he would not get paid anything for his efforts. Rick's motivation is best described as being

    A) attributed.

    B) deferred.

    C) extrinsic.

    D) intrinsic.

Answer: D

Explanation: D) Rick's motivation can best be described as *intrinsic*. He is picking up the bottles because doing so gives him an inner sense of satisfaction and not because it provides extrinsic rewards (e.g., the money).

Page Ref: 373
Skill: Understanding
P: .94
D: .14

5) Being interested in a task because the activity is enjoyable is what type of motivation?

    A) Extrinsic

    B) Intrinsic

    C) State

    D) Trait

Answer: B

Explanation: B) *Intrinsic motivation occurs when we enjoy a task for the pleasure it brings*, without the need for any special incentives (extrinsic reinforcements). State motivation is situational motivation. Trait motivation is relatively stable.

Page Ref: 373
Skill: Knowledge
P: .94
D: .09

6) Ms. Riley tells the class, "If we have a good lesson on fractions, I will credit each of you with a bonus point." She is trying to stimulate what type of motivation?

    A) Extrinsic

    B) Intrinsic

    C) Stable

    D) Trait

Answer: A

Explanation: A) Ms. Riley is trying to stimulate *extrinsic motivation by offering a special reward as an incentive for having a good lesson*. Extrinsic reinforcement is based on external rewards; intrinsic is enjoying the activity without rewards.

Page Ref: 373
Skill: Understanding
P: .96
D: .06

7) Externally imposed reward systems seem particularly appropriate for students who are

    A) interested in the subject.

    B) intrinsically motivated.

    C) not interested in the subject.

    D) self-motivated.

Answer: C

Explanation: C) *Individuals who are* **NOT** *interested in the subject* being taught lack intrinsic motivation. These students are likely to benefit from external or extrinsic motivation.

Page Ref: 373–374
Skill: Understanding
P: .91
D: .23

8) A student's reason for acting is called

    A) extrinsic motivation.

    B) intrinsic motivation.

    C) locus of causality.

    D) self-determined.

Answer: C

Explanation: C) According to the behavioral view of motivation, students are motivated by incentives. *These incentives are frequently extrinsic reinforcers such as good grades, praise, and rewards.*

Page Ref: 374
Skill: Knowledge

9) In most humanistic theories, motivation is based on

  A) extrinsic rewards.

  B) intrinsic needs.

  C) material wealth.

  D) social status.

Answer: B

Explanation: B) As illustrated by Maslow's hierarchy, *humanistic interpretations of motivation stress the role of intrinsic needs such as self–esteem and self–actualization.* This perspective developed, in part, as a reaction against the behavioristic emphasis on reinforcement and extrinsic motivators.

Page Ref: 374
Skill: Knowledge
P: .84
D: .32

10) The concept of self–determination is an important influence in what view of motivation?

  A) Behavioral

  B) Cognitive

  C) Humanistic

  D) Social learning

Answer: C

Explanation: C) *The concept of self–determination is an important influence in the humanistic view of motivation.* Emphasis is placed on people's inborn need to fulfill their potential.

Page Ref: 375
Skill: Knowledge

11) According to behavioral theory of motivation, students are motivated primarily by a(n)

  A) desire for gaining fulfillment for their accomplishments.

  B) desire to gain reinforcers for their behavior.

  C) inherent need to understand what they are learning.

  D) need for social recognition and status.

Answer: B

Explanation: B) According to behavioral theory, the primary motivation for students is *a desire to gain reinforcers for their behavior.*

Page Ref: 374
Skill: Knowledge
P: .66
D: .49

12) Doug's family is very poor, so he often goes to school with no breakfast and a very small lunch packet. According to Maslow, Doug is failing his classes because what type of needs are not being met?

    A) Aesthetic needs

    B) Deficiency needs

    C) Growth needs

    D) Self–actualization needs

Answer: B

Explanation: B) The scenario with Doug illustrates Maslow's *deficiency needs*. He is so poor that his focus is first on his hunger (deficiency need), and he has little or no motivation for learning because he is so hungry.

Page Ref: 375
Skill: Understanding
P: .72
D: .48

13) Jeremy's interest in history has been decreasing lately. According to Maslow's theory, what should the teacher do?

    A) Determine whether his being needs are met.

    B) Determine whether his deficiency needs are met.

    C) Give him less challenging assignments.

    D) Give him more challenging assignments.

Answer: B

Explanation: B) According to Maslow's hierarchy, the teacher should determine whether Jeremy's *deficiency needs* (physiological, safety, love, and belonging) are being met. Otherwise, he is likely to concentrate on them before he concentrates on learning history, a higher–order need.

Page Ref: 374–375
Skill: Understanding
P: .69
D: .48

14) Which one of the following situations is a valid implication of Maslow's hierarchy for education?

   A) Andy, who has low self-esteem, will probably have little motivation to belong to and be liked by a group.

   B) Jennifer, who is feeling ill this week, may show little interest in academic performance.

   C) Robert, who is frustrated in his search for knowledge, may show little interest in his physiological well-being.

   D) Teresa, who fails to satisfy her aesthetic needs, will be prevented from having high self-esteem.

Answer: B

Explanation: B) Maslow's hierarchy is based on the assumption that we first try to satisfy lower-level needs before we attend to higher-level needs. Accordingly, someone like Jennifer who *is feeling ill or unsafe (survival needs) may show little interest in academic achievement.* The other multiple-choice alternatives all depict reverse orderings (higher-level before lower-level needs).

Page Ref: 374–375
Skill: Understanding
P: .78
D: .37

15) In Maslow's hierarchy, self-esteem is considered to be what type of need?

   A) Being

   B) Deficiency

   C) Proficiency

   D) Self-actualization

Answer: B

Explanation: B) Self-esteem is considered a *deficiency need* in Maslow's hierarchy. Deficiency needs require intermittent gratification, but temporarily diminish when satisfied. In contrast, being needs are higher-level needs that involve continually striving for greater knowledge and understanding.

Page Ref: 374–375
Skill: Knowledge

16) Each situation below represents a need in Maslow's hierarchy. Which of the following students demonstrates the most basic need that must be satisfied before any other?

   A) Anne is not included in the "in group" of her class.

   B) Chuck has been threatened by a neighborhood gang.

   C) Dick wants to develop his artistic talents in music.

   D) Joy feels inferior but wants to be important.

Answer: B

Explanation: B) The lowest (most basic) need of the choices given is *safety—Chuck's being threatened by the gang*. That problem (need) would be attended to first before the needs implied by the other response choices, namely, belonging, aesthetic, and self–esteem needs, respectively.

Page Ref: 374–375
Skill: Understanding
P: .86
D: .37

17) Maslow's hierarchy of needs has been criticized because

   A) cognition plays a lesser role than the hierarchy acknowledges.

   B) people frequently attend to needs in different orders than the hierarchy predicts.

   C) survival needs receive too much emphasis relative to safety needs.

   D) the hierarchy overemphasizes the role of reinforcement as a motivator.

Answer: B

Explanation: B) A criticism of Maslow's hierarchy is that *people often do not behave as the theory predicts. Specifically, different levels of needs are often attended to simultaneously or in varied orders depending on the person and the situation.*

Page Ref: 374–375
Skill: Knowledge
P: .85
D: .18

18) The cognitive approach to motivation is illustrated best by people who respond to

   A) events to which they choose to pay attention.

   B) events that have been rewarding in the past.

   C) the objective worth or value of events.

   D) their perceptions of events, not the events themselves.

Answer: D

Explanation: D) Cognitive theories assume that humans have a basic need to understand the environment. Stress is placed, therefore, on *interpretations or perceptions of external events*, rather than on reinforcement as a key motivating factor.

Page Ref: 375–376
Skill: Knowledge
P: .55
D: .25

19) Maria spent many hours trying to complete her geometry proofs. A cognitive interpretation of Maria's motivation is that Maria

    A) knows a good grade will result in a reward from her parents.

    B) is attempting to acquire understanding of how the different theorems work.

    C) is trying to feel fulfilled in her accomplishment in order to raise her self-esteem.

    D) wants her friends to be more likely to accept her than they have so far.

Answer: B

Explanation: B) *Cognitive theories of motivation are concerned with the quest to learn and understand things.* In this case, Maria's behavior in geometry would be explained as interest in understanding her theorems, not in obtaining recognition (social or behavioral theory), rewards (behavioral), or self-esteem (humanistic).

Page Ref: 375–376
Skill: Understanding
P: .81
D: .22

20) According to attribution theory, students who see the causes of their failures as internal and controllable will react to those failures by

    A) assuming things will work out better in the future.

    B) berating themselves for their failure.

    C) exhibiting confusion and anxiety.

    D) finding strategies to succeed the next time.

Answer: D

Explanation: D) Attributing failure to internal and controllable causes is an adaptive mastery-oriented response. *A typical reaction is finding strategies in order to succeed the next time.* The key concept is that the individual believes that eliminating failure is under his/her own power.

Page Ref: 390–391
Skill: Knowledge
P: .80
D: .22

21) Pride or shame for one's own actions is likely to be felt most strongly by those who attribute their actions to

   A) external causes.

   B) internal causes.

   C) stable causes.

   D) unstable causes.

Answer: B

Explanation: B) Pride or shame for one's actions is most likely to be felt most strongly by those who attribute their actions to *internal factors*. Internal attributions make the success or failure the responsibility of the individual, rather than the result of factors beyond his/her control.

Page Ref: 390–392
Skill: Knowledge
P: .88
D: .27

22) Pat believes that the reason for her success in reading is the effort she puts into it. Pat is reflecting what type of locus of control?

   A) External

   B) Internal

   C) Stable

   D) Transitional

Answer: B

Explanation: B) An *internal locus is characterized by the belief of being responsible for one's own fate*. Attributions of success or failure to effort are consistent with that perception, and Pat is viewing her effort as the cause of her success.

Page Ref: 390–391
Skill: Understanding
P: .85
D: .26

23) As Jim looks at his report card, he remarks to Judy, "I got that B because I really didn't work hard in Mr. Wedell's calculus class." According to Weiner, Jim is attributing the cause of his grade to causes that are

   A) external, stable, controllable.

   B) external, unstable, uncontrollable.

   C) internal, stable, controllable.

   D) internal, unstable, uncontrollable.

Answer: C

Explanation: C) Jim appears to have an *internal locus*. He is taking personal responsibility for not working hard in Mr. Wedell's class. If he had an external locus of control, he might try to attribute the low grade to the difficulty of the test.

Page Ref: 390–391
Skill: Understanding
P: .81
D: .24

24) Sara attributes failures to internal causes. Consequently, she is likely to blame her poor mark in science on her

   A) bad luck.

   B) lack of effort.

   C) parents' pressures to succeed.

   D) teacher's difficult tests.

Answer: B

Explanation: B) If Sara has an internal locus, she will look within herself and her behaviors for explanations of success or failure. *Lack of effort might be one reason. She would be less likely to consider external factors such as test difficulty, parental pressures, or bad luck.*

Page Ref: 390–391
Skill: Understanding
P: .36
D: .30

25) Harry is apathetic and certain that he is not able to do the work. He makes poor marks in school and is not inclined to seek help. According to attribution theory, Harry is typical of students who attribute their failures to causes that are

   A) external, stable, and controllable.

   B) external, unstable, and uncontrollable.

   C) internal, stable, and controllable.

   D) internal, stable, and uncontrollable.

Answer: D

Explanation: D) Harry is typical of students who *attribute their failures to causes that are internal,*
                 stable, and uncontrollable. He thinks that he is not able to do the work (internal)
                 so he does not try (uncontrollable) and continues to make poor grades (stable).

Page Ref: 390–391
Skill: Understanding
P: .76
D: .39

26) Participation in communities of practice is emphasized by what theory of motivation?

   A) Cognitive

   B) Humanistic

   C) Constructivist

   D) Sociocultural

Answer: D

Explanation: D) *Sociocultural theory* emphasizes participation in communities of practice as an
                 important source of motivation. People engage in activities in order to
                 maintain their identities and their interpersonal relations within their
                 community, so the concept of identity is central in sociocultural views of
                 motivation.

Page Ref: 376
Skill: Knowledge

27) Anthony said, "I did well because I was lucky." The type of attribution being demonstrated is

   A) external–stable.

   B) external–unstable.

   C) internal –stable.

   D) internal–unstable.

Answer: B

Explanation: B) Students such as Anthony *attribute their successes to external, unstable factors.*
                 Therefore, Anthony did not take any personal responsibility (internal
                 attribution) for his success. He was just lucky.

Page Ref: 390
Skill: Knowledge

28) An "expectancy x value" theory would predict that motivation will necessarily be

    A) close to zero if self-efficacy is low, regardless of goal value.

    B) zero if either expectation to succeed or the perceived value of a goal is zero.

    C) zero if only expectation to succeed and the perceived value of a goal are zero.

    D) zero if self-efficacy and the perceived value of a goal are low.

Answer: B

Explanation: B) Motivation will be zero if *either expectation to succeed or the perceived value of a goal is zero*. This is because social cognitive theory views these variables as interrelated: Motivation = Expectancy X Perceived Value.

Page Ref: 375–376
Skill: Understanding
P: .80
D: .34

29) In expectancy x value theory, the two sources of motivation are

    A) projected future outcomes and the reaction of peers.

    B) projected future outcomes and the value of goals.

    C) social pressures and acquired standards.

    D) social pressures and internal standards.

Answer: B

Explanation: B) Expectancy x value theories view motivation as the product of *projected future outcomes* (the individual's expectations of reaching a goal) and *the value of the goal*. If either is zero, there will be no motivation to succeed.

Page Ref: 375–376
Skill: Knowledge
P: .44
D: .41

30) The type of learning goal that a person will be most motivated to reach is one that is

    A) general in nature and moderately difficult.

    B) general in nature and very difficult.

    C) specific and moderately difficult.

    D) specific and very difficult.

Answer: C

Explanation: C) According to Woolfolk, the type of goal that a person will be most motivated to reach is *one that is specific and moderately difficult*. A specific goal creates clear standards for performance; moderate difficulty goals provide challenge that is reasonable.

Page Ref: 381
Skill: Knowledge
P: .81
D: .28

31) Dennis often cons his best friends into letting him use one of their papers from last semester for his assignment in psychology this semester. In terms of goals, what type of learner does Dennis appear to be?

    A) Ego–involved

    B) Self–directed

    C) Task–involved

    D) Work–avoidant

Answer: D

Explanation: D) Students who are *work–avoidant* do as little as possible. By using someone else's paper, Dennis is evidently more concerned about avoiding work than learning.

Page Ref: 382
Skill: Understanding
P: .56
D: .40

32) Students with performance goals as opposed to learning goals are concerned primarily with

    A) achievement motivation.

    B) looking good in front of others.

    C) bettering themselves in terms of skill competencies.

    D) finishing tasks so that they can seek new challenges.

Answer: B

Explanation: B) Students who have performance goals *want to look good in front of others*. Thus, they are *less concerned with what they learn than with how they appear*.

Page Ref: 381–382
Skill: Knowledge
P: .73
D: .35

33) Fred has wanted to be a chef since he was a little kid, and he used to bake cookies with his mother. The behavioral view expert would say that Fred is motivated to be a chef because

    A) he has a positive cooking self–concept.

    B) he places great value on his cooking ability.

    C) of his early childhood reinforcement history.

    D) of his need for self–actualization.

Answer: C

Explanation: C) A behaviorist would say that Fred's motivation to become a chef is *due the reinforcers given to him during his early childhood*. Fred's motivation stems from his baking cookies with his mother when he was a small child.

Page Ref: 374
Skill: Understanding
P: .56
D: .74

34) Individuals are naturally motivated to learn by

    A) anxiety.

    B) feedback and goal acceptance.

    C) performance goals.

    D) seductive details.

Answer: B

Explanation: B) Natural motivation in individuals arises because of *feedback and goal acceptance*. Receiving helpful feedback and accepting the goal of a task increase our motivation to learn.

Page Ref: 383
Skill: Knowledge

35) Which one of the following quotes exemplifies a learning goal?

    A) "Accomplishing this should make me better prepared for Biology 101."

    B) "If I master this material, I can have some free time."

    C) "I'm going to go for the third assignment option, so that I can receive an A."

    D) "Jason will be impressed if I can learn this laboratory procedure."

Answer: A

Explanation: A) An example of a learning goal is *"accomplishing this should make me better prepared for Biology 101."* Learning goals emphasize learning for self–improvement and to seek challenges. Extrinsic rewards and "looking good" are not as important.

Page Ref: 381
Skill: Understanding
P: .89
D: .20

36) Learning and information processing are influenced by reasoning and problem solving as well as by

    A) cold cognition.

    B) emotions.

    C) involvement.

    D) social interests.

Answer: B

Explanation: B) Learning and information processing are influenced by *emotions* as well as by reasoning and problem solving skills. Cold cognition refers to the reasoning and problem-solving aspects of learning and information processing, while hot cognition refers to the emotional aspects.

Page Ref: 383
Skill: Knowledge

37) As reported by Woolfolk, in Tobias' interpretation of anxiety, the debilitating effects of anxiety are viewed to be due to

    A) attention being diverted from the learning task to a preoccupation with one's feelings.

    B) conditioning in which negative reinforcement obtained from withdrawing from tasks strengthens the anxiety syndrome.

    C) physiological arousal that limits bodily functioning to avoid the anxiety-producing situation.

    D) social effects such as embarrassment for appearing ill at ease or for being too boisterous.

Answer: A

Explanation: A) Tobias' interpretation stresses the cognitive viewpoint that anxiety interferes with information processing by *diverting attention from the material to be learned to one's fears and feelings*. Thus, a high-anxiety student has more information to process, with the learning material often given lower priority than his/her personal worries.

Page Ref: 387
Skill: Knowledge
P: .85
D: .26

38) From the pioneering work of Yerkes and Dodson (1905) to present-day research results, what is the correlation between virtually every aspect of achievement and a wide variety of anxiety measures?

    A) Moderately positive

    B) Negative

    C) Positive

    D) Zero

Answer: B

Explanation: B) Research results strongly support a *negative* correlation between anxiety and achievement.

Page Ref: 387
Skill: Knowledge

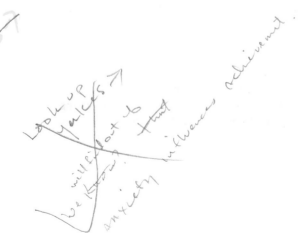

39) An entity view of ability is consistent with what type of goals?

   A) Extrinsic

   B) Intrinsic

   C) Performance

   D) Work–avoidance

Answer: C

Explanation: C) An entity view of ability is consistent with *performance goals*. This view
   assumes that ability is stable and uncontrollable and, therefore, it cannot be
   changed. Given that you cannot change your ability through effort, you might
   as well look for situations in which you can perform effectively.

Page Ref: 380
Skill: Knowledge

40) Whenever Matt appears to be having difficulty in completing his science laboratory work, Ms.
   Butterfield quickly offers to help him and encourages him to continue working. According to
   Graham (1991), Ms. Butterfield's behavior is likely to result in Matt developing

   A) an enhanced sense of self–efficacy.

   B) an incremental view of his ability.

   C) doubts about his ability.

   D) external–unstable attributions.

Answer: C

Explanation: C) Susan Graham (1991) has suggested that when teachers respond to students'
   mistakes with pity, praise, or unsolicited help, the students are more likely to
   attribute their failure to an uncontrollable cause, such as lack of ability. The
   message to students like Matt is that their failures are outside of their control,
   so there is no reason to be held personally responsible. *The result is developing
   doubt about their abilities.*

Page Ref: 388–389
Skill: Understanding

41) Which one of the following notions is consistent with the idea that "practice makes perfect"?

  A) Entity view of ability

  B) External locus of control

  C) Incremental view of ability

  D) Performance goals

Answer: C

Explanation: C) *An incremental view of ability* assumes that ability is unstable and controllable. Therefore, if individuals try hard, they can improve their achievement. This philosophy is consistent with the idea that "practice makes perfect." [This view of ability refers to achievement. Individuals cannot alter their inherent intelligence levels, but they can change their expressions of ability, i.e., their achievements.]

Page Ref: 388–389
Skill: Understanding
P: .78
D: .49

42) Which one of the following quotes is an example of high self–efficacy?

  A) "I am usually good at math, so I will do well in this class."

  B) "I am usually lucky on this type of test, so I should do well on this one."

  C) "The teacher hates me, so I know I will flunk this course."

  D) "The math teacher is easy-going, so I should do well in this class."

Answer: A

Explanation: A) Self–efficacy is our beliefs about our ability to perform at a given level. Thus, the belief that *"I'm usually good at math"* will support the prediction that *"I'll do well."*

Page Ref: 392
Skill: Understanding
P: .90
D: .17

43) Erin is a fifth–grade teacher who has a high degree of efficacy in teaching. Consequently, Erin will most likely

  A) be a fairly easy grader.

  B) be relatively strict with her classroom rules.

  C) have a high sense of "withitness."

  D) try harder when students have learning difficulties.

Answer: D

Explanation: D) Teachers who have a high sense of efficacy in teaching believe that they can succeed and will be persistent about trying. *Thus, Erin will try harder with a student who is having difficulty.*

Page Ref: 392
Skill: Understanding

44) Research on self-efficacy and achievement suggests that school achievement is improved and self-efficacy is increased when students

    A) accredit their successes to luck or to the intervention of others.

    B) advocate controllable activities rather than tasks that are beyond their abilities.

    C) develop high expectations even in the face of difficulties.

    D) receive rewards or other reinforcements based on the quality of their performances.

Answer: D

Explanation: D) When *students receive rewards or reinforcements based on the quality of their performances*, school achievement improves and self-efficacy increases (Graham & Weiner, 1996). Other factors include adopting short-term goals and being taught to use specific learning strategies.

Page Ref: 392
Skill: Knowledge

45) Cognitive evaluation theory explains how praise, criticism, grade assignments, and other events can influence students' intrinsic motivation by affecting their sense of competence and

    A) curiosity.

    B) self-control.

    C) self-determination.

    D) task orientation.

Answer: C

Explanation: C) According to cognitive evaluation theory, two factors explain how praise, criticism, and other events influence our motivation by affecting our sense of competence and *self-determination*.

Page Ref: 378
Skill: Knowledge

46) Cindy faces every classroom situation in exactly the same way: she develops sweaty palms and a rapid heart beat. Cindy is likely to be helped most by

    A) focusing on her feelings.

    B) frequent testing.

    C) highly-structured lessons.

    D) limiting controlling messages.

Answer: C

Explanation: C) For a student such as Cindy who has high anxiety, *highly structured lessons are likely to be helpful*. Such lessons allow students to know what to expect. Both frequent testing and competitive goals place more emphasis on performance and are likely to increase these students' anxiety levels.

Page Ref: 388-389
Skill: Understanding

47) Students who demonstrate "learned helplessness" are likely to

 A) believe that trying harder will improve their results.

 B) find ways to attribute their failures to others.

 C) focus on their failures and not seek assistance.

 D) set easier goals next time in order to increase their chances of success.

Answer: C

Explanation: C) Students who develop learned helplessness begin to believe that nothing can be done to help them succeed. Consequently, they will *focus on their failures and not try to obtain help*.

Page Ref: 392–393
Skill: Knowledge

48) As need for achievement increases in spite of fear of failure, what type of student will be motivated to learn?

 A) Failure-accepting

 B) Failure-avoiding

 C) Mastery-oriented

 D) Socially-oriented

Answer: C

Explanation: C) The type of student whose motivation to achieve increases in spite of possible failure is said to be *mastery-oriented*. Mastery-oriented students accept new challenges and risks.

Page Ref: 381
Skill: Knowledge

49) According to Covington and others, which one of the following would be the strongest indicator of whether an individual will be motivated to accept new challenges and risks?

 A) Desire to avoid failure and seek social acceptance

 B) Drive for achievement and an incremental view of ability

 C) Need for achievement and an entity view of ability

 D) Performance goals that are attainable

Answer: B

Explanation: B) The strongest indicator of whether an individual will be motivated to accept new challenges and risks is the individual's *desire for achievement and an incremental view of his/her own ability*.

Page Ref: 393–394
Skill: Knowledge

50) Students who are mastery-oriented will tend to hold what view of their ability?

    A) Entity and stable

    B) Entity and improvable

    C) Incremental and improvable

    D) Incremental and stable

Answer: C

Explanation: C) *Mastery-oriented students tend to hold an incremental view of ability* that permits them to set moderately difficult objectives, take risks, and cope constructively with failure. Such individuals perform best in competitive situations, learn quickly, are self-confident and energetic, welcome concrete feedback, and are eager to succeed. They develop adaptive strategies in order to succeed. Failure-avoiding individuals employ self-defeating strategies, while failure-accepting individuals are likely to give up and depend on learned helplessness as the excuse for their failure.

Page Ref: 393
Skill: Knowledge
P: .60
D: .43

51) Sally sets unrealistically high goals for herself but is unsure about her abilities. Woolfolk would be likely to label Sally as

    A) failure-accepting.

    B) failure-avoiding.

    C) mastery-elusive.

    D) mastery-oriented.

Answer: B

Explanation: B) *Failure-avoiding* students such as Sally do not want to fail, so they select *goals that are unrealistic.* An example might be a D student setting a goal of scoring 95%, a overly high goal, on the physics exam. When the student does not attain it, no one can blame him/her. In contrast, failure-accepting students are resigned to failure and do not have a need to protect themselves from it.

Page Ref: 393
Skill: Understanding
P: .40
D: .22

52) What type of belief do failure–accepting students have?

   A) Expectation of failure

   B) Expectation of mastery

   C) High fear of failure

   D) Low fear of failure

Answer: A

Explanation: A) Failure–accepting students *expect to fail*. They typically have performance goals, an entity view of ability, and a susceptibility to learned helplessness.

Page Ref: 394
Skill: Knowledge

53) Ms. Kirkendall wants to help students develop more positive self–perceptions. What approach is recommended for her to use?

   A) Curving grades so that more As and Bs than usual will be assigned

   B) Encouraging and helping the students to set high goals for themselves

   C) Providing continual encouragement for students to try harder to succeed

   D) Raising grades based on individual efforts to improve the work assigned

Answer: D

Explanation: D) To develop more positive self–perceptions, students need to recognize that effort will pay off. If Ms. Kirkendall simply provides encouragement or free test points, these strategies will not help students to make this connection. Accordingly, *a better approach would be to give them an opportunity to raise their grades through their personal efforts to improve*.

Page Ref: 393–396
Skill: Understanding
P: .28
D: .24

54) The following sentence is **true** about the relationship between motivation and cultural diversity.

    A) When minority students have culturally relevant materials they can be more motivated to learn and teachers are more likely to "catch and hold" their situational interest.

    B) Some cultures raise children to be more motivated than others.

    C) Regardless of cultural backgrounds, teachers can do little to "catch and hold" students' situational interest.

    D) Students' life experiences really do not influence the learning process in important ways.

Answer: A

Explanation: A) When designing instruction and choosing instructional materials teachers should keep in mind culturally relevant learning materials can influence students' *motivation and situational interest,* which can ultimately effect student achievement.

Page Ref: 403
Skill: Understanding

Completion Questions

1) The interest state that arouses, directs, and maintains behavior is _____.

Answer: motivation
Page Ref: 372

2) The natural tendency to engage in certain types of activities is called _____ motivation.

Answer: intrinsic
Page Ref: 373

3) A temporary characteristic of motivation is called a _____.

Answer: state
Page Ref: 373

4) A relatively permanent characteristic of motivation is called a _____.

Answer: trait
Page Ref: 373

5) Personal freedom, choice, intrinsic motivation, and self-determination are emphasized in _____ theories of motivation.

Answer: humanistic
Page Ref: 374

6) In Maslow's hierarchy, the survival, safety, belonging, and self-esteem needs comprise the general category called _____ needs.

Answer: deficiency
Page Ref: 374-375

7) Cognitive views of motivation developed in response to the _____ of motivation.

Answer: behavioral view
Page Ref: 375–376

8) How an individual's explanations, justifications, and excuses influence motivation is _____ theory.

Answer: attribution
Page Ref: 390–391

9) Individuals who feel that they are responsible for their own successes or failures have a(n) _____ locus.

Answer: internal
Page Ref: 390–391

10) Theories that take into account both the behaviorist's concern with the effects of behavior and the cognitivist's interest in the impact of thinking are characterized as _____ theories.

Answer: expectancy x value
Page Ref: 375–376

11) Even if a student's abilities are underdeveloped and contributions are small, genuine involvement in the group's work is legitimate _____ participation.

Answer: peripheral
Page Ref: 376

12) High concern with how one looks to others is characteristic of people with _____ goals.

Answer: performance
Page Ref: 381

13) Psychological and physical reactions causing a person to be alert, attentive, and wide awake is called _____.

Answer: arousal
Page Ref: 384

14) Students who tend to be anxious in many different situations are said to have _____ anxiety.

Answer: trait
Page Ref: 387

15) Problem solving, emotional management, and avoidance are strategies that people use to cope with _____.

Answer: anxiety
Page Ref: 388

16) Ability is perceived as a stable, uncontrollable trait by people who adopt a(n) _____ view of ability.

Answer: entity
Page Ref: 388

17) Beliefs about our ability to accomplish tasks in a given situation is _____.

Answer: self-efficacy
Page Ref: 392

18) The need to experience choice and control in what we do and how we do it is called _____.

Answer: self-determination
Page Ref: 377

19) Students who come to believe that, no matter what they do, they will not succeed have developed a condition called _____.

Answer: learned helplessness
Page Ref: 392

20) Whereas mastery-oriented students value achievement and success, _____ students try to protect themselves from situations in which they will not look good to others.

Answer: failure-avoiding
Page Ref: 393

21) Students who focus on learning goals because they value achievement and see their ability as being improvable are said to be _____ students.

Answer: mastery-oriented
Page Ref: 381

22) Students whose sense of self-worth and self-efficacy deteriorate become _____ students.

Answer: failure-accepting
Page Ref: 394

23) Sharon believes if she is an outstanding soccer play she will be well liked by her peers. Thus, Sharon place a great amount of _____ value on playing soccer.

Answer: importance or attainment

Explanation: *Importance* or *attainment value* refers to the significance an individual places on doing well on a task.
Page Ref: 396

24) According to Johnson and Johnson, the three types of grouping structures teachers can use are cooperative, competitive, and _____.

Answer: individualistic

Explanation: The three types of group structures are *cooperative, competitive, and individualistic.* The type of group structure a teachers uses influences the goal structure of the class and students' motivation to learn.

Page Ref: 399

True/False Questions

1) Having high motivation as a general personality characteristic is a trait.

Answer: TRUE
Page Ref: 373

2) When individuals are naturally interested in a particular activity, they are intrinsically motivated.

Answer: TRUE
Page Ref: 373

3) Maslow's approach to motivation is a humanistic view.

Answer: TRUE
Page Ref: 374

4) A current reflection of the humanistic perspective is the "self–esteem movement."

Answer: TRUE
Page Ref: 374

5) Attribution theories of motivation describe how an individual's explanations, justifications, and excuses influence motivation.

Answer: TRUE
Page Ref: 390–391

6) Weiner believes that there are two important dimensions that have important implications for motivation: (1) responsibility and (2) stability.

Answer: FALSE
Page Ref: 390–391

7) Viewing a cause of failure as stable is likely to lower aspirations for future success.

Answer: TRUE
Page Ref: 391–392

8) According to the expectancy x value theory, motivation increases as expectancy of success and the value of rewards increase.

Answer: TRUE
Page Ref: 375–376

9) Legitimate peripheral participation means that beginning learners are genuinely involved in the work of the group if their abilities are developed and their contributions are significant.

Answer: FALSE
Page Ref: 376

10) Students who have performance goals are interested in improving their skills, no matter how awkward they may appear in the process.

Answer: FALSE
Page Ref: 381–382

11) Work-avoidant learners feel successful when they do not have to try very hard, when the work is easy for them, or when they can simply "goof off."

Answer: TRUE
Page Ref: 382

12) In addition to having specific attainable goals, task focus, and supportive social relationships, effective goal-setting in the classroom requires feedback and goal acceptance.

Answer: TRUE
Page Ref: 382–383

13) Learning and information processing are influenced by both cold cognition of reasoning and problem solving and hot cognition or emotion.

Answer: TRUE
Page Ref: 383

14) Anxiety tends to be both a trait and a state with primarily affective components.

Answer: TRUE
Page Ref: 387

15) In general, performance is low when the level of anxiety is high.

Answer: TRUE
Page Ref: 387

16) Anxiety can interfere with attention, learning, and testing even at the same time.

Answer: TRUE
Page Ref: 387

17) High needs for self-improvement are consonant with an entity view of ability.

Answer: FALSE
Page Ref: 388

18) Young children are more likely to hold an entity view than an incremental view of ability.

Answer: FALSE
Page Ref: 388–389

19) Self-efficacy refers to individuals' skill at managing their own study behaviors.

Answer: FALSE
Page Ref: 392

20) Individuals with a strong sense of self-efficacy for a given task tend to attribute their failures to lack of ability.

Answer: FALSE
Page Ref: 392

21) Learned helplessness occurs when causes of failure are considered internal, stable, and uncontrollable.

Answer: TRUE
Page Ref: 392

Short Answer Questions

1) Define *motivation,* and differentiate between behavioral, humanistic, cognitive, and sociocultural approaches to the interpretation of motivation.

   Answer: Motivation is defined as a process that energizes and directs behavior. *Behavioral approaches* emphasize the roles of rewards and incentives in motivating behavior. An understanding of student motivation, according to the behavioral views, begins with a careful analysis of the incentives and rewards available in the classroom. B.F. Skinner is a key theorist for the behavioral view of motivation. In contrast, *humanistic theorists* emphasize a belief that people are continually motivated by the inborn need to fulfill their potential. From this perspective, motivating students means to encourage their inner resources their sense of competence, self–esteem, autonomy, and self–actualization. Maslow and Deci are key theorists of the humanistic view of motivation.

   Cognitive theorists believe that behavior is determined by our thinking, not merely by whether we have been rewarded or punished for the behavior in the past. People are viewed to be active and curious and searching for information needed to solve personally relevant problems. Weiner's attribution theory is a good example of the cognitive approach to motivation. Covington is also a key theorist for the cognitive view of motivation. Theories that take into account both the behaviorist's concern with the effects or outcomes of behavior and the cognitivist's interest in the impact of individual thinking can be characterized as *expectancy x value theories.* For example, Bandura's self–efficacy concept is an example of an expectancy x value approach to motivation.

   Sociocultural views of motivation emphasize participation in communities of practice in which people engage in activities in order to maintain their identities and their interpersonal relations within the community. Consequently, students are motivated to learn if they are members of a classroom or school community that values learning. The concept of identity is central to sociocultural views of motivation. People are motivated to learn the values and practices of their community in order to keep their identity as community members. Lave and Wenger are key theorists for the sociocultural view of motivation.

   Page Ref: 371–374

2) List the seven levels of needs as described by Maslow and give a classroom example for each need. What are the implications for learning when students' deficiency needs are not being satisfied? Contrast this situation against one in which the students' being needs are not satisfied.

   Answer: Survival, safety, belonging, and self-esteem are "deficiency" needs in Maslow's hierarchy. When these needs are met, motivation to fulfill them decreases. The need to know and understand (intellectual achievement), aesthetic needs, and self–actualization are "being" needs. When they are met, motivation to seek further fulfillment increases, because being needs are never completely satisfied.

   Page Ref: 374–375

3) Discuss the implications of attribution theory for school achievement in reference to the specific cases in which success or failure is primarily attributed to (a) ability, (b) effort, (c) task difficulty, and (d) luck.

Answer: Attribution theories describe how individuals interpret the causes of success or failure. The importance of such attributions is that they influence students' self-perceptions and future aspirations by treating success as something they can personally control. Attributions vary along the dimensions of internal vs. external, stable vs. unstable, and controllable vs. uncontrollable. Students who view failures as internal ("I am dumb"), stable ("I will remain dumb"), and uncontrollable ("There's nothing I can do to change") risk the danger of becoming resigned to failure and susceptible to "learned helplessness." Teachers need to try to help students perceive that effort (an internal, but controllable factor) can be the primary determinant of their success or failure. Task difficulty and luck are external factors, the former stable and the latter unstable. External attributions that are not controllable may be indicative of resignation to fate or chance (rather than individual effort) as the determinant of success. Attributions are also related to self-determination, as reflected in deCharms' notion of origins (internal orientation) and pawns (external orientation).

Page Ref: 390–391

4) Woolfolk indicates that anxiety generally interferes with learning and performance. Explain the reasons for this effect and suggest ways in which teachers can help high-anxiety students to achieve better grades.

Answer: Anxiety interferes with tests of student abilities. Highly anxious students may be so preoccupied with their symptoms that they are unable to concentrate on the material. Anxious students have trouble learning difficult material, material that relies on intermediate-and short-term memory, and material that is not well-organized. Highly-anxious students are also more likely to drop out of school. Teachers can help anxious students to set realistic goals that allow them to succeed. They can also help students adopt appropriate pacing schedules. Additional strategies include attempting to reduce anxiety about poor performance by providing greater structure and repetition of important parts of lessons.

Page Ref: 384–388

5) Define and differentiate between entity and incremental beliefs about ability. With what types of attributions and goal orientations are each associated?

Answer: Entity beliefs assume that ability is an internal, stable, and uncontrollable trait. Because it cannot be changed, there is little reason to try to improve one's skills. Incremental beliefs, on the other hand, assume that ability is internal, unstable, and controllable. By working hard and applying oneself, ability can be improved and greater success realized. Entity beliefs are usually associated with performance goals ("trying to look good"), whereas incremental beliefs are associated with learning goals ("trying to improve oneself"). Incremental beliefs and learning goals are generally productive of increased feelings of self-efficacy.

Page Ref: 388

6) Suggest and briefly describe some strategies that teachers might use to help failure-avoiding students become more mastery-oriented.

Answer: Failure-avoiding students hold an entity view of ability and tend to set performance goals. They try to protect themselves from failure by engaging in either easy or very difficult tasks. Teachers can help these students become more mastery-oriented by (a) emphasizing the progress they have made rather than simply the grade earned, (b) returning work with specific suggestions for improvement, and (c) having frequent conferences with students in which the connection between effort and improvement is stressed.

Page Ref: 380–383

7) How does Doyle's analysis of academic tasks relate to the TARGETT model for supporting student motivation? Identify Doyle's four general categories of academic tasks and describe the implications of each for student perceptions of risk and ambiguity, and for their motivation.

Answer: Doyle's analysis relates to the "task" element of the TARGETT model. In order to increase student motivation, learning tasks should be attractive and meaningful. Memory tasks require students to recognize or reproduce information that has previously been presented to them. Such tasks have low risk (if easy) and low ambiguity. Procedural tasks involve using a prescribed set of steps to solve a problem. These tasks have high risk (if difficult) but low ambiguity. Comprehension tasks involve transforming or processing information, as in problem solving. Such tasks have high risk (if difficult) and high ambiguity. Opinion tasks ask students to state a preference or attitude and, as a result, have low risk but high ambiguity. In general, low risk and low ambiguity tasks may increase state motivation but decrease long-term or trait motivation for learning, because achievement may not lead to a feeling of increased competence.

Page Ref: 397

8) Beginning teachers have been identified as using four basic types of motivational strategies: (1) rewards/punishments, (2) building confidence, (3) focusing attention, and (4) emphasizing relevance. Differentiate between each strategy in terms of orientation (what they involve) and frequency of use. Which strategies do you believe would be the most and the least effective for focusing attention on tasks? Explain your answers.

Answer: A rewards/punishment strategy calls attention to tangible rewards that students can earn for behaving appropriately. Teachers also frequently give verbal reinforcement for good responses. Attention-focusing strategies motivate students by directing their attention to the task. Examples are turning off the lights until the class is quiet or having the class all work on a challenging problem or special task. Relevance strategies relate what is being taught to past experiences of students. An example might be drawing on the students' participation in a recent field experience in order to introduce a new science topic or using a guest to relate an experience. Confidence-building strategies rely on verbal encouragement or explicit instructions to achieve. Research has shown that the rewards/punishments strategy is used most frequently by teachers; attention-focusing is next, with relevance and confidence-building the least used. Use of relevance strategies was positively correlated with student on-task behavior, while using rewards/punishments was negatively correlated. Woolfolk encourages teachers to use a balance between bounded choices and unbounded choices so that students have a range of task options, which allows them to follow their personal interest while at the same time providing some task structure and explicit expectations.

Page Ref: 396–397, 398

Case Studies

Trina is an average-ability science student, but she is in danger of receiving a failing grade due to her low test scores. "I know the information when I study at home," she said to Mrs. Kirby, "but as soon as you pass out the test, I get so nervous that I can barely remember my name. Then, as I think about how badly I'm going to do, I get even more nervous."

1) How can we interpret the negative effects of anxiety on Trina's test performances? That is, how is anxiety likely to hinder her performances?

Answer: Trina's anxiety is likely to hinder her performance in three ways. First, her negative thoughts do not allow her to focus her attention on the material to be learned. Second, her anxious thoughts can negatively influence her ability to learn new material, especially material that may be disorganized or difficult. Finally, like most highly anxious students, Trina probably has inadequate test-taking skills. Thus, teaching Trina how to relax may not be a sufficient strategy for increasing her test performance. She could also benefit from direct instruction on critical learning strategies (e.g., good note taking skills) and test-taking skills.

Page Ref: 384–388

2) Suggest some strategies that you could use to help Trina to be successful if you were her teacher.

Answer: First you will want to identify what type(s) of coping strategies Trina relies upon when she is anxious. She may engage in problem-solving, emotional management, or avoidance. You could ask her to share her study plan for the upcoming test. If she does not have a plan, more than likely, she is not fully using problem-solving coping strategies. If Trina shares with you that she often talks about her anxious feelings with her family members or friends, then she is using some aspects of emotional management as a coping strategy. You will also want to put Trina in a testing situation in which she cannot avoid taking the test. It may be a good strategy to give her a very short, non-graded test that contains several question types (multiple-choice, essay, true/false, case studies). In terms of testing format, it may also be a useful strategy to provide Trina with a take-home test on occasion.

Page Ref: 388

3) Would you describe Trina as failure-avoiding, failure-accepting, mastery-oriented, or self-determined? Explain why you believe Trina has or does **NOT** have each of these characteristics.

Answer: According to Covington's work, Trina can best be described as failure-accepting. She may get frustrated by her inability to control her anxious thoughts and give up. As a student with a failure-acceptance orientation she may have come to believe "I am just not a good test taker, no matter how hard I try." She does not appear r to be demonstrating failure-avoiding behaviors such as calling in sick to school in order to miss the exam (which would be failure-avoiding). Moreover, failure-avoiding students tend not to care if they fail and Tina appears to still care as indicated by her claims of frustration. If she were mastery-oriented we would have more information that she assumes responsibility for her own learning and decreasing her anxiety. She would also try more strategies in order to see incremental improvement. As a mastery-oriented student she might approach her test anxiety by studying more and asking the teacher and her peers for help.

The fact that Trina is still studying is evidence of her self-determination, which is the need to experience choice and control in a learning situation. She is making the choice to continue to prepare for exams, but she may struggle with the schedules, rules, and deadlines imposed by the examination process.

Page Ref: 377, 380

Although Bill and Elliot are fairly similar in ability, they are as different as night and day in their approaches to school. Elliot seems to care only about how he looks to others. For the school science fair, for example, he selected an extremely easy project on ants that looked fancy and impressive but, actually, had very little substance. He continually makes excuses before taking tests, such as "I'm taking this without any studying." Or he might say, "I'll be happy with a C." After the test, however, he is quick to promote his own good performances when they occur. Bill is quite the opposite. He loves challenges and becomes totally immersed in books and projects. He says that when he gets interested in something, he wants to learn all that he can. He usually earns good grades in his courses, but he seems basically unconcerned about his test scores.

4) Discuss the behaviors of the two boys relative to the distinction made in the Woolfolk text between learning goals and performance goals.

Answer: Elliot's behavior is consistent with students who adopt a performance goal orientation. He is interested in looking good in the eyes of others and may be overly focused on performing better than his peers. In contrast, Bill is generally interested in the subject matter and wants to understand science. While Bill will work hard on non-graded assignments, Elliot is likely to put very little effort into tasks that do not provide him the opportunity to demonstrate his abilities to others. We can also expect that Elliot is likely to frequently ask "will this be on the test?"

Page Ref: 380–383

5) Suppose that the boys' school is holding the annual fund-raising drive. Each student is asked to set goals for selling candy. (Last year the highest total sale was $225.) What is your prediction regarding the nature of the goals likely to be set by Bill and Elliot? Provide a rationale by explaining your predictions.

Answer: Bill is likely to set his goal at raising $225 or a slightly higher amount. Bill is aware that earning $225 is still a challenging task and that he will no doubt encounter difficulties, as this is his first fund-raising experience. Elliot will either set a very low amount, perhaps $100, or an unrealistically high amount of money ($500). By setting a very low amount, he can surpass his goal and beat out other students who might not reach their goal. If he sets an unachievable goal, he believes others will not focus on his poor fund-raising skills because no one could reach that high of a goal. Regardless of whether or not Elliot sets a low or high goal, he continues to focus on himself. In contrast, Bill focuses on the reason why they are holding the annual fund-raising drive.

Page Ref: 380–383

6) Clearly, teachers would prefer students to behave like Bill rather than like Elliot. Suggest some techniques that Elliot's teachers might employ to help him develop more achievement-oriented goals.

Answer: You can encourage Elliot to use deeper processing skills when he is engaged in learning tasks. In addition, it is important to assist Elliot in seeing the value of the learning task. You can point out why the material is interesting, useful, and relevant to his own situation. You will also want to provide Elliot with small but challenging learning tasks that will guarantee him success. By experiencing success he is likely to increase his self-efficacy and confidence. Students with a strong positive sense of self-efficacy are more likely to set learning goals. Finally, as a teacher you should try to minimalize any competitive learning situations in your classroom and provide individual rather than normative feedback.

Page Ref: 380–383

Chapter 11 Engaged Learning: Cooperation and Community

Multiple-Choice Questions

1) Cooperative learning involves the following:

   A) Elaboration, interpretation, and argumentation

   B) Shared values, lack of conflict, and creativity

   C) Cognitive flexibility, competition, and self-respect

   D) Extrinsic rewards, elaboration, and autonomy

   Answer: A

   Explanation: A) Most educators agree that cooperative learning involves situations in which
                   students engage in *elaboration, interpretation, explanation, and argumentation*
                   while doing group activities.

   Page Ref: 417
   Skill: Knowledge

2) Which one of the following elements does **NOT** define a true cooperative learning group?

   A) Collaborative skills

   B) Homogenous grouping

   C) Individual accountability

   D) Positive interdependence

   Answer: B

   Explanation: B) The five elements of cooperative learning listed by David and Roger Johnson
                   (1994) include face-to-face interactions, positive interdependence, individual
                   accountability, group processing, and collaborative skills. *Homogenous
                   grouping is NOT one of the elements of cooperative groups.*

   Page Ref: 417, 420
   Skill: Knowledge

3) Ms. Hackett feels that students in this year's literature class are primarily trying to memorize information and are not thinking deeply or conceptually about what they are learning. What cooperative learning model would appear most desirable for her to use?

    A) ILE

    B) STAD

    C) TARGETT

    D) TGT

Answer: B

Explanation: B) In order for Ms. Hackett to attain her goals for promoting student conceptualization of the material, she should try the *STAD cooperative learning approach*. The STAD model reduces emphasis on competitive evaluation and grading and enhances focus on students' task–involvement as opposed to ego–involvement. ILE is part of the STAD model, while TGT is also a cooperative learning model but one that encourages competitive evaluation.

Page Ref: 419
Skill: Knowledge

4) The five elements of cooperative learning listed by David and Roger Johnson (1994) include positive interdependence, individual accountability, group processing, collaborative skills and

    A) group grading.

    B) large groups of 10 or more students.

    C) single sex groups.

    D) face–to–face interactions.

Answer: D

Explanation: D) The five elements of cooperative learning listed by David and Roger Johnson (1994) include *face–to–face interactions*, positive interdependence, individual accountability, group processing, and collaborative skills.

Page Ref: 420
Skill: Knowledge

5) In organizing cooperative learning groups, Woolfolk suggests that it is best to

    A) balance the number of boys and girls in each group.

    B) group students of similar backgrounds together.

    C) keep groups together for at least half the year.

    D) make shy or introverted students the group leader.

Answer: A

Explanation: A) Woolfolk suggests that it is best to *balance the number of boys and girls in each cooperative learning group*. Otherwise, when there are just a few girls in a group, they tend to be left out of discussions; when there are only a few boys, they tend to dominate the group.

Page Ref: 420
Skill: Understanding

6) Research findings suggest that students who tend to benefit most from cooperative learning experiences are those who

    A) are active in explaining things to others.

    B) are shy or introverted.

    C) have high goal expectations.

    D) receive individual tutoring from others.

Answer: A

Explanation: A) Research suggests that the benefits of cooperative learning largely depend on how actively students participate in interacting verbally with others in the group. Specifically, *students who are active in giving explanations seem to learn more than those who are passive and do not participate verbally.*

Page Ref: 420
Skill: Understanding

7) Which one of the following students is playing the role of reflector in a cooperative learning group?

    A) Amanda makes certain that the questions of all group members are asked and answered.

    B) Gary makes sure that the group is aware of its progress or lack of progress toward the group goal.

    C) Helen is responsible for keeping the noise level of the group at a reasonable pitch.

    D) Lawrence solicits equal participation of group members and restrains dominance by any group member.

Answer: B

Explanation: B) The role of *reflector* in a cooperative learning group is illustrated by Gary, who makes sure that the group is aware of its progress, or lack of progress, toward the goals. Amanda plays the part of the *question commander*, Helen is the quiet captain, and Lawrence is the *gatekeeper*.

Page Ref: 421
Skill: Knowledge

8) In cooperative learning groups, the role of the student who makes certain no one dominates the group is called the

    A) checker.

    B) coach.

    C) gatekeeper.

    D) taskmaster.

Answer: C

Explanation: C) The student who makes certain that no one person dominates the group is played by the *gatekeeper*. Other roles include the *checker*, who checks for the group's understanding of the material being discussed, the *coach*, who helps with academic content and explains concepts, and the *taskmaster*, who keeps the group focused on the task.

Page Ref: 421
Skill: Knowledge

9) In using cooperative learning, it is recommended that teachers

    A) do not assign any roles in advance.

    B) assign roles only to one or two students.

    C) use the assignment of roles as a way to encourage participation.

    D) grade students based on how well they performed their role.

Answer: C

Explanation: C) *Assigning roles is an effective way for teacheres to insure that students fully participate and cooperate with each other.* Roles can be focused on developing students' social skills or complex learning. If focusing on social skills, students can be assigned to roles that support listening, encouragement, and respect for differences. Roles focused on complex learning might include sharing of explanations and insights, probing, and brainstorming.

Page Ref: 421–422
Skill: Understanding

10) Marible was assigned the role of making sure her group understands the learning task. Her role is referred to as the

    A) reflector.

    B) quite captian.

    C) checker.

    D) gatekeeper.

Answer: C

Explanation: C) The *checker is to make sure the group understands* the task or the problem. The checker may frequently ask questions in order to monitor the group's understanding of the situation.

Page Ref: 421
Skill: Knowledge

11) In a cooperative learning situation, the role of the *encourager* is to

    A) encourage all students to participate.

    B) encourage the group to monitor its progress.

    C) encourage the group to use all of its resource materials.

    D) encourage the group to develop a concrete plan.

Answer: A

Explanation: A) The *encourager monitors group members' participation.* The encourager will pay special attention to shy or reluctant students to make sure they are participating. In a caring way, the encourager will try to actively involve non–participating students.

Page Ref: 421
Skill: Understanding

12) In their writing group, Aron has become the expert on how to write an introductory sentence. When students teach other students about the part in which they have expertise, they are engaged in what type of cooperative learning structure?

    A) Jigsaw

    B) Group work

    C) Reciprocal questioning

    D) Service learning

Answer: A

Explanation: A) The *Jigsaw* format is a cooperative learning structure in which each student is responsible for teaching the other group members on one section of the material Thus, each student becomes an "expert" of their assigned or selected content.

Page Ref: 425
Skill: Knowledge

13) Jigsaw, an early format for cooperative learning, emphasizes what relationship among group members?

    A) High dependence

    B) High interdependence

    C) Low dependence

    D) Low interdependence

Answer: B

Explanation: B) The early format of Jigsaw for cooperative learning groups emphasized a high degree of *interdependence among group members.* This means that group members must rely on each other's cooperation in order to achieve success on an assigned task.

Page Ref: 423
Skill: Knowledge

14) According to a large study on bullying,

   A) teachers report there are more incidents of moderate or frequent bullying than students.

   B) the reported frequency of bullying acts are exaggerated due to the media coverage after several severe school violence incidents which were covered in national news.

   C) bullying is quite common in schools and can involve teasing and harassment.

   D) students need to be taught how to be more thick-skinned about their feelings about teasing.

Answer: C

Explanation: C) Depending on the study, *moderate or frequent bullying* is experience by 33% to 60% of students in the school setting.

Page Ref: 428
Skill: Understanding

15) Which one of the following is **NOT** a recommending strategy for dealing with potentially harmful teasing in the school setting:

   A) Be careful using humor.

   B) Remind students they may need to accept some level of teasing if they tease others.

   C) Instruct students how to read the body language of others so they can see if they have hurt another person's feelings.

   D) Learn how to read if someone is having a bad day because teasing him or her has the potential to get them out of a bad mood.

Answer: D

Explanation: D) Students need to remember when it is appropriate to tease another person. If someone is having a *bad day or seems agitated, this is not a good time to tease* someone.

Page Ref: 428
Skill: Knowledge

Completion Questions

1) When all students are required to participate, this is referred to as _____.

   Answer: cooperative learning
   Page Ref: 417

2) Mo is able to rehearse and elaborate her knowledge as a result of her cooperative learning experiences. This explanation of the benefits of cooperative learning is grounded in _____ theory.

   Answer: information processing
   Page Ref: 417

3) In cooperative learning, students interact _____.

Answer: face-to-face
Page Ref: 418

4) Based on a Vygotskian perspective, the ideal size for a cooperative learning group is _____ students.

Answer: two
Page Ref: 418

5) In addition to tolerance, some argue teachers should develop a sense of _____ within their students by providing character education.

Answer: compassion
Page Ref: 430

6) If a cooperative learning group is functioning at a high level and support each other, they are said to have _____.

Answer: positive interdependence
Page Ref: 420

7) The *quiet captain* in a cooperative learning group is responsible for maintaining the _____.

Answer: noise level
Page Ref: 421

8) William is charged with making sure introverted students participate in his cooperative learning group. William was assigned the role of the _____.

Answer: encourager
Page Ref: 421

9) The role of the _____ in a cooperative learning group is to explain concepts when needed.

Answer: coach
Page Ref: 421

10) When the teacher provides students with question stems and then asks students to answer the questions in pairs, he/she is involving the students in _____.

Answer: reciprocal questioning
Page Ref: 423

11) Dansereau's method of having students take turns summarizing and critiquing material is called _____.

Answer: scripted cooperation
Page Ref: 424

12) The _____ format requires each member of a cooperative learning group to teach their other members one section of the material.

Answer: Jigsaw
Page Ref: 425

13) Dansereau's method of having students take turns summarizing and critiquing material is called _____.

Answer: scripted cooperation
Page Ref: 424

14) Johnson and Johnson suggest a true classroom community includes positive interdependence and a shared sense of _____ values.

Answer: civic
Page Ref: 429

15) Ms. Friedberg teaches civic values through her literature curriculum, which is a form of _____.

Answer: character education
Page Ref: 430

16) According to Thomas Likona (2003), honesty, kindness, and self-discipline can and should be taught through _____.

Answer: character education
Page Ref: 431

17) According to Woolfolk, the best answer to school violence is _____.

Answer: prevention
Page Ref: 433

18) Johnson and Johnson have developed a program designed to combat violence, which is referred to as the _____ system.

Answer: Respect and Protect
Page Ref: 434

19) Service learning focuses on academic learning and students' personal and _____.

Answer: social development
Page Ref: 435

20) One of the goals of service learning is to encourage students to reflect upon their own role in _____.

Answer: society
Page Ref: 435–436

21) Richard Sagor's (2003) activity in which teachers evaluate their classroom and curricular materials to determine the extent to which students from different cultures might feel a sense of belonging is referred to as a _____.

Answer: cultural audit
Page Ref: 438

22) A class involved in creating an electronic newsletter for a social service agency is involved in _____, which is a type of service learning.

Answer: virtual volunteering
Page Ref: 437

True/False Questions

1) Based on a large research study involving approximately 20,000 adolescents, Lawrence Steinberg found that 90% of the students reported copying someone else's homework.

Answer: TRUE
Page Ref: 414

2) A teacher can offset some of the effects of being rejected by peers for middle–school students.

Answer: TRUE
Page Ref: 415

3) According to Woolfolk, group work and cooperative learning are simply different terms used for the same instructional approach.

Answer: FALSE
Page Ref: 417

4) According to McCaslin and Good (1996), the advantages of group learning are so superior to individual learning approaches teachers do not need to question the possible disadvantages of group learning.

Answer: FALSE
Page Ref: 418

5) According to McCaslin and Good (1996), one of the potential disadvantages of group learning is that status differences among students may be increased rather than decreased.

Answer: TRUE
Page Ref: 418

6) According to Woolfolk, cooperative learning should be limited to learning situations that involve routine tasks.

Answer: FALSE
Page Ref: 419

7) For very shy children, cooperative learning may be the best instructional approach.

Answer: FALSE
Page Ref: 420

8) In cooperative learning groups, the primary role of the *materials monitor* is to select the material to be studied.

Answer: FALSE
Page Ref: 421

9) Reciprocal teaching is ideal for children but is not an appropriate approach for adolescents.

Answer: FALSE
Page Ref: 423

10) In the Jigsaw method, one student leader is responsible for teaching the material to the group.

Answer: FALSE
Page Ref: 425

11) There is strong agreement within the education community that character education programs should be offered in all schools.

Answer: FALSE
Page Ref: 431

12) Providing students the opportunities to make academic choices can help foster a sense of school belongingness.

Answer: TRUE
Page Ref: 432

13) In his book titled *No One Left to Hate: Teaching Compassion after Columbine,* Elliot Aronson (2000) advocates for searches of student property and web postings.

Answer: TRUE
Page Ref: 433

14) According to Woolfolk's summary of the research, violence in schools is actually decreasing.

Answer: FALSE
Page Ref: 433

15) Service learning refers to problem-based learning projects which are outside of the student's curriculum.

Answer: FALSE
Page Ref: 435

16) One of the reasons Mr. Brakefield assigns students to cooperative learning groups is so that he can rotate leadership roles and opportunities amongst his students. Mr. Brakefield's rationale for assigning groups is a valid one.

Answer: TRUE
Page Ref: 422

17) Teachers who want to encourage dialog in reciprocal questioning should not begin sentences with the word "why."

Answer: FALSE
Page Ref: 423

18) When Tom and Missy take turns summarizing and critiquing the book, they are effectively engaging in scripted cooperation.

Answer: TRUE
Page Ref: 424

19) Some critics challenge character education programs are potentially harmful because they may try to promote specific behaviors rather than encouraging students to think critically about their behaviors.

Answer: TRUE
Page Ref: 431

20) Mr. Savery allows Jim to rationalize or justify his harassing behaviors. Mr. Savery's behavior is considered to be violence-enabling.

Answer: TRUE
Page Ref: 434

21) An increase in risk-taking behaviors is a normal developmental process for early adolescents and should not be considered as an early sign of of violence.

Answer: FALSE
Page Ref: 435

22) Ms. Garcia has noticed that Shawn has frequently stated that he feels disrespected by his classmates. Ms. Garcia should recognize Shawn's comments as an early sign of the potential of violent behavior by Shawn.

Answer: TRUE
Page Ref: 434

23) Mr. Schwab's class engaged in a week-long project to pick up trash around the school grounds. This activity is an example of service-learning.

Answer: FALSE
Page Ref: 437

24) Richard Sagor's (2003) cultural audit is best conducted by a principal or some other external evaluator.

Answer: FALSE
Page Ref: 438

25) According to Richard Sagor's (2003) cultural audit model, the first step is for the teacher to record his or her lesson plans and collect all of the teaching materials used in the classroom.

Answer: TRUE
Page Ref: 438

26) Researchers have found a strong connection between students' feelings of school connectness and student motivation.

Answer: TRUE
Page Ref: 439

27) High standards and expectations will most likely decreased students' feelings of school connectedness.

Answer: FALSE
Page Ref: 439

28) Students who feel connected to school are less likely to demonstrate substance and tobacco use.

Answer: TRUE
Page Ref: 439

Short Answer Questions

1) Discuss some of the ways peers influence each other in the school setting.

Answer: According to Lawrence Steinberg, peers, especially during adolescence, have a tremendous influence on how invested students are in their learning and the effort they will exert to their education. One concern is Steinberg's research finding that one in every five students said that their friends make fun of people who tried to do well in school. In regards to gender, ethnicity, and peer influences there appears to be some general patterns (Graham, Taylor, & Hudley, 1998). Girls across various ethnic groups tend to nominate high-achieving peers when asked to nominate peers they most admire, respected, and wanted to be like. Whereas, African American and boys nominated low-achieving boys as their most admired peer group.

Page Ref: 414–415

2) What are some of the disadvantages of group learning?

Answer: According to McCaslin and Good, some of the disadvantages of group learning can include:
1. Students may come to value speed over good learning.
2. Students may reinforce each other's misconceptions.
3. Off-task socializing may get in the way of learning.
4. Students may become dependent on one student in the group whom they have determined is the "expert."
5. Some students may not "pull their weight" and may look to others to complete the tasks.

In addition, a potential disadvantage of cooperative learning is that is can be time intensive. Compared to a direct instruction approach, cooperative learning can take more time. A final concern is that some parents (and other educators) may view it as simply play time and discredit the value of cooperative learning as a strategy for meeting learning objectives.

Page Ref: 418

3) Ms. Constantine has always identified as an athlete. She was a competitive athlete in her youth and she still competes in age group competitive athletic events. She is proud of the fact that she has designed her sixth-grade classroom around competitive events and activities. All individual and group activities in her class involve a "winning" person or team. She spends a great deal of time finding valued prizes to give as rewards for her competitive activities. What concerns might educators, who call for the creation of learning communities, have with Ms. Constantine's approach?

Answer: Competitive classrooms can sometimes be perceived by learners to be places where they are treated differently based on race, gender, ethnicity, or academic ability. Some research has shown that students in competitive classroom environments are more likely to act out or withdraw altogether. Students who feel they are always compared to others may be more likely to feel a lack of respect from others and adopt a negative attitude towards education. Rather than emphasizing competitive activities, Ms. Constantine might be encouraged to consider use of cooperative learning, problem-based learning, service learning, and non-graded group activities.

Page Ref: 417–419

4) You plan to implement a middle–school mathematics unit on the personal costs of cell phone use. You have decided to teach this curricular unit using cooperative learning. How will you arrange your cooperative learning groups and what factors will you consider in regards to group assignments and membership.

Answer: First, you know it is best for you to assign the group members rather than involve students in this process or conduct a random assignment process. Second, you consider your learning goals which are to engage students in reviewing, rehearsing, and practicing mathematical concepts you have previously covered. Therefore, you determine the ideal group size based on your learning goals is 4 to 5 students. Third, in assigning students to groups you ensure you have gender balance. Finally, knowing your students personalities and temperaments as well as you do allows you to make sure your groups are comprised of a balance of outgoing and introverted or shy students.

Page Ref: 420

5) Discuss three strategies you might take for preventing school violence.

Answer: The following strategies may contribute to the prevention of school violence:
   1.   Encourage your school to adopt a strict anti–weapon policy with search of personal property authority.
   2.   Have clearly stated and communicated policies for students who engage in violent behaviors.
   3.   Treat situations involving bullying and verbal harassment as early warning signs of violence.
   4.   Notify parents if you see any early signs of aggression, bullying, or harassment.
   5.   Pay close attention to students who report feeling neglected or disrespected.
   6.   Teach acceptance and compassion through direct and indirect teaching methods.
   7.   Consider implementing programs such as *Respect and Protect.*
   8.   Take seriously students who enjoy hurting animals.
   9.   Consider using more cooperative learning and service learning in your teaching approaches.
   10.   Be very familiar with the warning signs of the potential for violence.

Page Ref: 433–435

6) Describe how you might conduct a cultural audit of your classroom based on Richard Sagor's model.

Answer: First, you would record and collect all of the curricular materials you used. Your curriculum collection might include print and audio materials, as well as internet resources. Second, you would review and reflect upon all of your lectures, explanations, class discussions, hand-outs, case studies and examples you used to evaluate the extent to which you included examples or illustrations from nonmajority cultures. In the third step, you share your analysis of your materials with your colleagues to see if there is a pattern of using monocultural curricular materials in your classroom or school. In the fourth and final step, you share your materials and findings with external reviewers or collaborators. For example, you might seek input from parents, school patrons, or community leaders who you trust will give you constructive and honest feedback about the extent to which you are incorporating culturally inclusive materials and using multiple perspectives in your classroom.

Page Ref: 438

Case Studies

Your school district recently instituted a new program for students who have demonstrated aggressive behaviors towards teachers or other students. You have accepted responsibility of designing the program to reduce aggression among the students in the program.

1) One approach to preventing aggression among children is to establish a learning community among the students in your classroom. What would you do to create a learning community in your classroom? Give an example of how you would use Johnson and Johnson's three C's of establishing a classroom community.

Answer: Johnson and Johnson's three C's establishing a classroom community are cooperative community, constructive conflict resolution, and civic values. A cooperative community can be established by providing student an opportunity to work together to achieve a mutual goal. For example, your students could conduct a book drive to collect books to send to children who lost their homes during a recent forest fire. In addition to designing an activity designed to increase civic values, a math unit could be build into this unit which would require students to compute the costs associated with mailing the books depending on the distance of the mailing address and the total weight of the books. Knowing that interpersonal conflicts typically arise in group situations, you can anticipate their existence and teach students in advance how to engage in constructive conflict resolution strategies. First, you can inform your students that conflicts are normal and can lead to critical thinking and conceptual change. It may be useful for you to describe a recent conflict you had yourself and the steps you took to positively resolve the situation. You will want to model that while conflicts may be unavoidable, they are best handled when the individual is willing to reflect upon what they and others want out of the situation and why. The chart provided by Woolfolk on healthy conflict resolution (p. 427) and tips related to the use of teasing (p. 428) could be posted in the classroom as a reminder to students on how to handle controversies.

Page Ref: 426–430

Ms. Thomas has been using the Student Teams–Achievement Divisions (STAD) model in her tenth–grade algebra class over the past month. She has been delighted with the results thus far. Students seem to like the cooperative activities and achievement scores are higher than for last year's class. However, this past week has been a trying one for her, as the incidents described below convey. If you were Ms. Thomas, how would you respond to each incident?

2) Sammeria announced that she "has to change teams," because she "absolutely cannot stand Bob." How would you respond to Sammeria?

Answer: First, you will want to utilize your active listening skills and listen for reasons why Sammeria dislikes Bob. This conversation should be conducted privately where other children cannot overhear your discussion. You may need to do some skill building with Sammeria. Perhaps she needs to confront Bob in an appropriate way, or maybe she is misinterpreting Bob's actions. To simply reassign Sammeria does not solve this problem. However, it may be useful to share with Sammeria that one of your goals in using a cooperative learning approach is to encourage students' prosocial and positive behaviors. Ask her how she can personally help you reach your goal of creating a community of learners. Although you know that Sammeria will not be in the same group with Bob much longer because in the STAD model groups are changed every few weeks, you may not want to share this information with Sammeria right away. Instead you may want to focus more strongly on how to resolve the situation between Sammeria and Bob.

Page Ref: 419

Your school district recently instituted a new program for students who have demonstrated aggressive behaviors towards teachers or other students. You have accepted responsibility of designing the program to reduce aggression among the students in the program.

3) A parent has challenged that the new prevention program you have designed to address aggression goes to far and that conflict should be considered a normal part of school life. How would you respond to the parent regarding the issues of conflict management.

Answer: First, you can find a respectful but informative way to share with the parent the fact that researchers have found a link between aggression and student conflict. In some cases, what might initially sound like teasing can potentially turn into harassment and aggression. Moreover, students who do not hear their teacher confront teasing and conflictual disputes may believe the teacher agrees with the insult. One concern is that many students cope with conflict by avoiding, forcing, or threatening the other person. Hence, many schools have adopted a conflict resolution curriculum or provide peer mediation and negotiation programs. Johnson and Johnson have argued all students need to be taught peer mediation strategies. Even if a school does not have a formal training program, Woolfolk suggests teachers can implement their own conflict prevention program in his or her classroom. For example, Esme Codell who is one of the teachers highlighted in Woolfolk's text, teachers her students a simple four–step conflict resolution process: (1) Tell the person what you did not like. (2) Tell the person how the comment or act made you feel. (3) Tell the person what you want in the future. (4) Ask the person to respond to what they can do in the future.

Page Ref: 428–429

Ms. Thomas has been using the Student Teams–Achievement Divisions (STAD) model in her tenth–grade algebra class over the past month. She has been delighted with the results thus far. Students seem to like the cooperative activities and achievement scores are higher than for last year's class. However, this past week has been a trying one for her, as the incidents described below convey. If you were Ms. Thomas, how would you respond to each incident?

4) A parent called to complain that she does not like cooperative learning because her son should not be "getting someone else's grade."

Answer: First, you can thank the mother for coming in to talk with you. Let her know that you welcome her involvement and feedback and that you both share a concern for her son's learning. Also, let her kow that you share some of the same concerns about some types of cooperative learning. Explain and show her the STAD technique you are using. Rather than only focusing on grades, it may be good to share with her your instructional materials and your learning objectives underlying the cooperative learning project. Assure her that using the STAD model, he son's grade will be based on is own achievement and will not be influenced by other student's grades. Share with her your own goal in seeing her son master the material and make improvements based on effort. It may be helpful to show her exactly how you computed her son's individual grade. In fact, you will want to clearly define all terms and concepts. For example, it cannot be assumed the mother has the same understanding of "base score," so you may want to explain her son's base score.

Page Ref: 419

Mr. Hutch placed his students in two teams for a reading contest. The "Eagles" have won a team award for the firth straight time. The "Simpsons" have not won yet.

5) What should Mr. Hutch do about these groups?

Answer: Mr. Hutch may want to look at his team membership. There may be an opportunity for him to change the student groups so that newly created teams are more equal in terms of students' abilities and motivation. By looking at the points earned for the groups, he might discover that the actual differences between the groups' scores is very minimal. This could be a good teaching opportunity to discuss the difference between ranked and non–ranked data (absolute vs. relative points).

Also, Mr. Hutch should consider how he could ensure students are focusing on their improvement rather than group "winning." It will be important for him to remind students about the benefits of individual learning and he may want to consider using the STAD method. He will also want to remind his students of the learning objectives underlying the game. He can point out what about the material to be learned is interesting, relevant, and useful. He can stress to his students how important it is for him to see groups collaborating and not just competing with each other to win. Finally, if the competition becomes so severe and interferes with learning, Mr. Hutch will want to consider eliminating the team competition or at least providing some non–graded group activities in which there are no "winners."

Page Ref: 417–419

6) Ms. Beck, the teacher in the adjacent room, complained that the noise in Mr. Hutch's class (during the group exercises) is too loud and very distracting. If you were Mr. Hutch, how would you handle this situation?

Answer: First, you will want to speak with Ms. Beck directly about the noise situation. This problem may be resolved quickly by simply shutting your classroom door and moving group activities away from the wall connecting your two classrooms. The problem could also be resolved by changing your schedule. Perhaps you could do your cooperative learning exercises while Ms. Beck's class is at lunch or recess. If Ms. Beck also has an activity in which the students get loud, may you could time it so that you do your group activities at the same time.

If you are not assigning students to the role of "quite captain", you may want to do so. If you have quite captains (students who are responsible for monitoring the noise level in their group) you might consider having a quiet captains' team meeting.

If Ms. Beck does not use cooperative learning, it may be useful for him to share with her why and how he is using group work and cooperative learning. He could invite her to observe his class so that she can see the students engaged in a meaningful learning task. Finally, he may need to revise some of your cooperative learning activities. If in fact he is disturbing her class, and the situation cannot be resolved by some of the strategies previously mentioned, he may need to change what he is doing. As noted in previous chapters, the role of attention in learning is crucial. If Ms. Beck's students cannot attend in her class, then he may need to be willing to change some of his exercises.

Page Ref: 417–419

Chapter 12   Creating Learning Environments

Multiple-Choice Questions

1) Classrooms contain many different people with differing values, attitudes, and goals. This is why classrooms are said by Doyle to be

   A) multidimensional.

   B) simultaneous.

   C) unpredictable.

   D) public.

   Answer: A

   Explanation: A) Doyle's concept of *multidimensional classrooms stresses the diversity of students having different values, attitudes, and goals*. This characteristic of classrooms creates challenges for teachers in adapting learning to meet individual needs.

   Page Ref: 444
   Skill: Knowledge
   P: .92
   D: .16

2) Based on Doyle's analysis of classroom characteristics and management needs, the main task for teachers is viewed as

   A) dealing effectively with misbehavior when it occurs.

   B) gaining students' cooperation for learning tasks.

   C) trying to ensure that students will be obedient.

   D) working actively with administrators and teachers.

   Answer: B

   Explanation: B) Doyle's analysis of classroom characteristics and effective management techniques suggests that *gaining student cooperation is the key*. Doing so presents quite a challenge because it requires many different aspects of planning, selecting activities, and delivering instruction. But, once students cooperate, classroom management becomes considerably easier.

   Page Ref: 444
   Skill: Knowledge

3) At what educational level is the direct teaching of classroom rules and procedures most critical for effective classroom management?

    A) Early elementary

    B) High school

    C) Middle elementary

    D) Late elementary to middle school

Answer: A

Explanation: A) *Early elementary students are unfamiliar with their roles.* Therefore, direct teaching of classroom rules and procedures becomes essential at this level.

Page Ref: 444
Skill: Knowledge

4) According to Brophy and Evertson, at what educational level is "maintaining" the management system most important?

    A) High school

    B) Kindergarten

    C) Middle elementary

    D) Preschool

Answer: C

Explanation: C) Children in the *middle–elementary years* are already familiar with their role as students and with classroom routines, according to the research of Brophy and Evertson. Therefore, the task for the teacher becomes maintaining the management system rather than teaching it directly.

Page Ref: 444
Skill: Knowledge

5) According to Woolfolk, one of the best ways to avoid discipline problems is to

    A) have a comprehensive set of rules.

    B) keep the group focused on productive learning.

    C) make the classroom a pleasant environment.

    D) refer problem students to the counselor.

Answer: B

Explanation: B) According to Woolfolk, one of the best ways to prevent discipline problems is to *keep the group focused on productive learning.* When students are interested and engaged in learning, they have much less reason to misbehave.

Page Ref: 444
Skill: Understanding
P: .45
D: .30

6) Which one of the following time measures would generally have the highest correlation with school achievement?

   A) Academic learning time

   B) Allocated time

   C) Class time

   D) Engaged time

Answer: A

Explanation: A) *Academic learning time* is the time when students are working at a high rate of success. Therefore, this time measure should have a higher correlation with academic achievement than allocated time or engaged time. Neither of the latter time measures guarantees that learning is taking place during the respective time periods. For example, students may be actively engaged (engaged time) in a task that they are not understanding or learning in the desired way.

Page Ref: 446
Skill: Understanding
P: .63
D: .37

7) Ms. Rivers has a student, Monika, who has difficulty completing her in–class work. Although Ms. Rivers allows plenty of time for study and Monika is actively working, Monika's efforts appear to be limited by

   A) academic learning time.

   B) allocated time.

   C) class time.

   D) time on task.

Answer: A

Explanation: A) *Academic learning time* is the time when students are working at a high rate of success. Even though Monika is doing the work and "going through the motions," the fact that she is experiencing difficulty (even when Ms. Rivers allows plenty of time) indicates that there is little academic learning time taking place.

Page Ref: 444
Skill: Understanding
P: .42
D: .33

8) Approximately what percentage of a student's time in school is devoted to meaningful, appropriate learning tasks?

    A) 25 percent

    B) 33 percent

    C) 45 percent

    D) 50 percent

Answer: B

Explanation: B) According to the research of Berliner, the amount of time that typical students actually devote to appropriate learning tasks is only *approximately 33 percent*.

Page Ref: 446
Skill: Knowledge

9) Sherry's class knows that different behaviors are expected (and tolerated) during different kinds of activities. It is likely that her class has a good understanding of

    A) each activity's goal.

    B) participation structures.

    C) self-management techniques.

    D) structuring rules.

Answer: B

Explanation: B) *Participation structures* are the rules that define which behaviors are expected during different kinds of activities. Students, such as Sherry, who know the participation structures for a given activity are better able to complete the activity successfully and **NOT** be viewed as a behavior problem by the teacher.

Page Ref: 447
Skill: Understanding
P: .31
D: .37

10) What is the key element underlying participation structures for different classroom activities?

    A) Access to performance goals

    B) Awareness of rules

    C) Providing cognitive activities

    D) Self-management

Answer: B

Explanation: B) The key element underlying participation structures is *awareness of the formal and informal rules for a given activity* so that behavior problems can be avoided. In other words, "prevention is the best medicine."

Page Ref: 447
Skill: Knowledge

11) Mr. Marshall's first two science classes were devoted to demonstrating and explaining rules and procedures in the laboratory. Based on research involving effective management, this procedure will probably result in

    A) loss of student interest and involvement in the subject.

    B) poor understanding of the course material.

    C) rushing through much material to make up the lost time.

    D) time gained over the course of the school year for learning activities.

Answer: D

Explanation: D) During the first few weeks of the school year, effective managers will *explain and review rules and procedures*. Effective managers do **NOT** spend time practicing non-essential routines such as how to be quiet in the hallways or preparing for the dismissal of classes at the end of the day. They also tend to use specific, rather than vague, criticisms when misbehavior occurs. Thus, *Mr. Marshall is using an effective strategy*. His strategy will prove to be a good investment by saving teacher time during the rest of the year that would normally be devoted to disciplinary issues.

Page Ref: 448
Skill: Understanding

12) The essential difference between rules and procedures is that rules are

    A) established by schools; teachers establish procedures.

    B) seldom written; procedures are usually written.

    C) what and what not to do; procedures involve how to do activities.

    D) concerned with behaviors; procedures deal with cognitive activities.

Answer: C

Explanation: C) *Class rules specify appropriate and inappropriate actions—the "do's and don'ts" of classroom life*. They are oriented more toward general behavior than are procedures that deal with the desired ways of completing specific tasks. For example, in a mathematics class, a rule might be: "Listen quietly while others are talking." An example of a procedure could be: "Show your work and underline your answers for all of the problems that you turn in."

Page Ref: 448
Skill: Understanding
P: .72
D: .28

13) When handing in material, Mr. Spark's students pass their work forward to the students in the front row, who then pass the materials from left to right. This approach is an example of classroom

    A) organizational behaviors.

    B) procedures.

    C) protocols.

    D) rules.

Answer: B

Explanation: B) Mr. Spark's students are *following procedures* that, in this case, dictate the proper procedure for students to turn in their work. Rules, in contrast, deal more directly with proper and improper ways of behaving in class; they are less activity–specific than procedures are.

Page Ref: 448
Skill: Understanding
P: .81
D: .28

14) Based on Woolfolk's recommendations, which one of the following rules seems to be more appropriate for elementary school classes than for secondary school classes?

    A) Do not hit, shove, or hurt others.

    B) Listen while others are speaking.

    C) Obey all school rules.

    D) Respect other people's property.

Answer: A

Explanation: A) Elementary students are expected to follow the rule *"do not hit, shove, or hurt others."* Secondary students, however, are expected to know and obey this rule without having to be told. Essential rules for both elementary and secondary school students would appear to be respecting others' property, listening to others, and obeying all school rules.

Page Ref: 450–451
Skill: Understanding

15) Which one of the following rules, based on Woolfolk's recommendations, seems to be more appropriate for secondary school classes than for elementary school classes?

    A) Bring all materials to class.

    B) Listen attentively when others are speaking.

    C) Obey all school rules.

    D) Respect other students' property.

Answer: A

Explanation: A) The rule to *bring all materials to class* is a more appropriate rule for secondary school than for elementary school. In elementary schools, students have their materials right with them in their desks or assigned cupboards, while secondary students must carry their materials from class to class. The craze in recent years of using backpacks has greatly facilitated having needed materials readily at hand for secondary students (provided that the needed materials have been packed).

Page Ref: 451
Skill: Understanding

16) Although specific consequences may be established for specific misbehavior, Woolfolk suggests a general consequence for many problems. This general consequence is

    A) extra school–related work.

    B) redoing the procedure or activity correctly.

    C) removing all reinforcement.

    D) time–out or detention.

Answer: B

Explanation: B) Woolfolk states that, for many behaviors, *the logical consequence is having to go back and do the action correctly.* This type of consequence usually seems reasonable to students and has the advantage of insuring that proper behavior is being practiced.

Page Ref: 451
Skill: Knowledge
P: .46
D: .33

17) Penny is an eighth-grade student in Mr. James' German class. Whenever Mr. James turns to the chalkboard, Penny pokes the student in front of her. The other students laugh, and it takes time to calm the class down. Which one of the following strategies would be the most appropriate for changing Penny's behavior?

   A) After-school detention

   B) Contact with parents

   C) Exclusion from group activities

   D) Expressions of disappointment

Answer: C

Explanation: C) Penny is obviously being reinforced for her misbehavior by her classmates' attention. An effective discipline strategy, therefore, would be *exclusion from the classroom*. This procedure is often called "time-out." [This is also an effective strategy for misbehavior at home.]

Page Ref: 451–452
Skill: Understanding
P: .58
D: .25

18) Kenneth frequently misbehaves in Ms. Lindquist's biology class. Which one of the following penalties for his misbehavior is based on Weinstein and Mignano's categories of negative consequences?

   A) Having Kenneth stand in the hall or the back of the class

   B) Having Kenneth write an essay about his misbehavior and its effects

   C) Having Kenneth write multiple times what he shouldn't do (e.g., "I should not talk in class.")

   D) Using mild physical punishment with Kenneth whenever he misbehaves

Answer: B

Explanation: B) One of Weinstein and Mignano's categories of penalties is "written reflection on the problem." Therefore, the appropriate penalty for Kenneth's frequent misbehavior is the suggestion of *having misbehaving students such as Kenneth write about what they did and how it affected others*.

Page Ref: 452
Skill: Understanding

19) Weinstein and Mignano found that expert teachers primarily used detention to

    A) assemble misbehaving students so they could be dealt with as a group.

    B) make the consequences somewhat public so that peer pressure to behave may be encouraged.

    C) prevent the student from participating in a desired extra-curricular activity.

    D) talk privately with the student about why the particular misbehavior occurred.

Answer: D

Explanation: D) Weinstein and Mignano found that expert teachers' negative consequences fall into seven categories. *One category, detention, was used primarily for the teacher and the student to talk privately about the misbehavior.*

Page Ref: 452
Skill: Knowledge

20) Which one of the following procedures is recommended for making interest-area arrangements?

    A) Allow students choices according to their spatial needs.

    B) Create at least one "racetrack," typically in the center of the room.

    C) Make partitions high enough to block vision over them.

    D) Once a design has been established and it works well, stay with it.

Answer: A

Explanation: A) Because *students have different spatial needs, they should be permitted choices of interest areas.* Moreover, the area designs should be flexible, partitions should be low enough for the teacher to see over them, and "racetracks" should be avoided.

Page Ref: 454–455
Skill: Knowledge

21) What term did Adams and Biddle use to designate the area in a classroom where the greatest number of verbal exchanges takes place?

    A) Action zone

    B) Fishbowl area

    C) Personal territories

    D) Zone of proximal development

Answer: A

Explanation: A) The term coined by Biddle and Adams to describe the area in a classroom in which the greatest amount of interaction occurs is its *action zone.* These researchers found that verbal interactions among teachers and students were concentrated in the center front of the classroom, in a line directly up the center of the room, or wherever participation was greatest.

Page Ref: 454
Skill: Knowledge

22) Greg was trying to pass Bill a note, but Bill kept his eyes on his own work and thought, "Why does Greg do this to me? Mrs. Pepper will spot him for sure. She never misses anything. You'd think she could read minds." Mrs. Pepper could be described as exhibiting what characteristic?

 A) Assertiveness

 B) Group focus

 C) Movement management

 D) Withitness

Answer: D

Explanation: D) Mrs. Pepper is a *"withit" teacher*. Kounin defined withitness as conveying to students an awareness of everything that is happening in the classroom. Mrs Pepper is one of those teachers who seems to have "eyes in the back of her head."

Page Ref: 460
Skill: Understanding
P: .91
D: .17

23) According to Kounin's strategy for effective management, the key goal is

 A) enforcement of consequences.

 B) preventing misbehavior from occurring.

 C) selecting appropriate punishments and reinforcers.

 D) stating rules.

Answer: B

Explanation: B) *"Prevention is the best medicine,"* according to Kounin's analysis of classroom management. Specifically, effective managers were **NOT** all that much different from ineffective managers in handling discipline problems, but effective managers were much better at preventing problems.

Page Ref: 460
Skill: Knowledge

24) Jeremiah throws his book at Sally, but Mrs. Fox mistakenly reprimands Sally for the disruption. Mrs. Fox has made what kind of error?

A) Movement

B) Selection

C) Target

D) Timing

Answer: C

Explanation: C) Ms. Fox is **NOT** demonstrating withitness because she has made the *target error of blaming the wrong student*. Jeremiah will now escape without consequences, and he (and other students) will question Ms. Fox's awareness of what is happening in her classroom.

Page Ref: 460
Skill: Understanding

25) Kathy's student teacher works well with small groups, but she finds it difficult to keep track of the rest of the class during small group sessions. Kathy should work with her student teacher to develop

A) group focus.

B) movement management.

C) overlapping.

D) withitness.

Answer: C

Explanation: C) Kathy's student teacher needs to work on the *skill of overlapping*. Success in this area depends on being able to keep track of and supervise several activities at a time. The three other concepts are not reflected in this situation.

Page Ref: 460
Skill: Understanding
P: .55
D: .45

26) The purpose of using choral responses is to establish

A) group focus.

B) movement management.

C) overlapping.

D) withitness.

Answer: A

Explanation: A) Choral responses are one way of *establishing group focus*, which means keeping as many students as possible active. Choral responding is when the class responds as a group to a question asked by the teacher. This procedure helps to broaden the focus from one or a few students to the entire class.

Page Ref: 462
Skill: Knowledge

27) In movement management, a major problem is to

   A) avoid abrupt and slowdown transitions.

   B) keep group focus.

   C) demonstrate withitness.

   D) watch for overlapping activities.

   Answer: A

   Explanation: A) Major problems in movement management involve *avoiding abrupt and slowdown transitions*. Keeping group focus, demonstrating withitness, and watching for overlapping activities together with movement management are reflective of an effective classroom teacher.

   Page Ref: 461
   Skill: Knowledge

28) Woolfolk suggests that, as a first step toward dealing with a discipline problem, teachers should

   A) ask the student to state the correct rule or procedure.

   B) give the student a nonverbal signal to stop.

   C) give the student a soft reprimand.

   D) tell the student in a clear, assertive way to stop.

   Answer: B

   Explanation: B) Woolfolk suggests making eye contact or using some other *nonverbal signal as a first step in dealing with a discipline problem*. If the nonverbal signal does not work, more overt interventions should be used, such as reminders and commands to stop.

   Page Ref: 462
   Skill: Knowledge

29) Ms. Summers teaches sixth grade in a rural middle school. Henry, a student in her class, is constantly out of his seat. When Ms. Summers confronts him and asks him to take a seat, Henry becomes angry and acts hostile. Which of the following actions should be considered for dealing with Henry?

   A) Ask other students to intervene in helping to prevent open rebellion.

   B) Send another student immediately to notify the principal's office.

   C) Stand your ground and do not back down; be firm and strong.

   D) Wait for a few minutes for Henry to calm down before taking action.

Answer: D

Explanation: D) Different situations will require different actions. Usually, however, if a student is hostile and angry, he/she *needs a few moments to calm down and relax*. Thus, providing the opportunity can result in both the teacher, Ms. Summers, and the student, Henry, being in better dispositions to discuss the situation constructively. Of course, if the student's hostility is threatening and continuous, severe actions will need to be taken.

Page Ref: 462
Skill: Understanding
P: .65
D: .22

30) Mr. Crain experiences a discipline problem with Joe. In imposing penalties, Mr. Crain should

   A) discuss the situation with Joe immediately after the infraction occurs.

   B) negotiate the level of punishment with Joe.

   C) re-establish a positive relationship with Joe as quickly as possible.

   D) reprimand Joe publicly in order to gain the support of the group.

Answer: C

Explanation: C) Weinstein and Mignano would suggest that Mr. Crain should try to *re-establish a positive relationship with a student after the infraction occurs*. These researchers have specifically warned against having an immediate discussion of the situation (emotions may still be high) or making punishments public. Negotiating with students about the punishments would forfeit teacher control of the situation.

Page Ref: 462–463
Skill: Understanding

31) Wendy, a ninth grader, is very bright and energetic in class. She always knows the right answer and pays close attention. Her only problem is that she rarely hands in homework. Her teacher should

    A) enforce the established consequences for incomplete work.

    B) ignore the problem behavior so that it will extinguish.

    C) place Wendy on a system of token reinforcement.

    D) relax the rules slightly so that she can catch up.

Answer: A

Explanation: A) Because Wendy is a "bright and energetic" ninth grader, it is obvious that she can do the work if she wants to. Therefore, the *consequences for failing to complete her homework need to be enforced* in order to convey to Wendy that the choice of receiving a high or a low grade is her own.

Page Ref: 458, 461, 462–46
Skill: Understanding
P: .50
D: .28

32) What is the best way to deal first with a defiant, hostile student?

    A) Be consistent in applying established consequences.

    B) Give the student a chance to cool down and save face.

    C) Have a conference with the counselor and parents.

    D) Make sure that the school office is aware of the incident.

Answer: B

Explanation: B) The best way to deal with a defiant, hostile student is to *give the student a chance to cool down and save face*. The other response choices are ways that can be used after the student has had the opportunity to cool down.

Page Ref: 464
Skill: Knowledge

33) What is the primary rationale for using the paraphrase rule with a class?

    A) Encourage students to speak in full sentences.

    B) Give students the benefit of the doubt when they break a rule.

    C) Increase students' communication skills.

    D) Promote classroom interactions among students.

Answer: C

Explanation: C) The paraphrase rule is designed to *increase communication skills*. It forces students to try to think and express an idea from another person's perspective.

Page Ref: 467
Skill: Knowledge
P: .77
D: .23

34) What is the purpose of the paraphrase rule?

    A) To clarify understanding

    B) To elaborate the concept idea

    C) To identify a hidden message

    D) To point out a problem

Answer: A

Explanation: A) The *purpose of the paraphrase rule is to clarify understanding*. By stating in one's own words what someone else has just said, the meaning of the communication can be evaluated for accuracy of understanding. The rule requires clarity of understanding before the person receiving the communication is permitted to communicate his/her own thought or question.

Page Ref: 467
Skill: Knowledge
P: .85
D: .22

35) Thomas Gordon stresses that the first step in solving a problem is to determine

    A) if a rule has been broken.

    B) who is at fault.

    C) who owns the problem.

    D) why the problem has occurred.

Answer: C

Explanation: C) In Gordon's system, the first step in solving a problem is to *determine who owns the problem*. The answer to this question determines the teacher's strategy to resolve the problem—being either a counselor if student-owned, or an active problem solver with the student if teacher-owned.

Page Ref: 467
Skill: Knowledge

36) In determining who owns a problem, what basic question should the teacher ask?

    A) "Can I do anything about solving the problem?"

    B) "Does the problem tangibly affect me and disrupt my role?"

    C) "How long has the problem been bothersome to the class?"

    D) "Who is annoyed most by this problem?"

Answer: B

Explanation: B) The primary question for teachers in determining ownership of a problem is: *"Does the problem affect me and disrupt my role as a teacher?"* Simply being annoyed by the problem or helpless to resolve it does NOT, by itself, indicate ownership.

Page Ref: 467–468
Skill: Understanding
P: .62
D: .27

37) An adolescent student approaches a teacher and says, "I can't sleep very well at night and worry about all the mess in my life." Gordon would identify this situation as a(n)

    A) external–stable crisis.

    B) identity crisis.

    C) student–owned problem.

    D) teacher–owned problem.

Answer: C

Explanation: C) The *adolescent's problem of not being able to sleep and worrying is student–owned.* The reason is that it directly affects the student and requires him to find a solution. The teacher, however, can be helpful by acting as a counselor and supporter.

Page Ref: 468
Skill: Understanding

38) If you use empathetic, or active, listening in a discussion with a student, there is likely to be an increase in what type of behavior?

    A) Criticism

    B) Defensiveness

    C) Problem solving

    D) Solution messages

Answer: C

Explanation: C) Empathetic or active listening is designed to build trust and communication between the teacher and the student. The immediate goal is *to facilitate the solving of the problem that precipitated the meeting between them.*

Page Ref: 468
Skill: Understanding
P: .59
D: .20

39) A key element in empathetic listening is

    A) giving students clear prescriptions about what actions to take.

    B) ignoring the students' emotions and attending only to verbal behaviors.

    C) reflecting back to the student what you think that student is saying.

    D) sending students "I" messages in order to change the student's behavior.

Answer: C

Explanation: C) The key element in empathetic listening is to allow the student to find a solution to the problem. It is not the teacher's role to give a prescription or solution. Empathetic listeners try to develop trust and provide support by *reflecting back what they think the other person is saying*.

Page Ref: 468
Skill: Knowledge
P: .66
D: .36

40) Which one of the following teachers is sending an "I" message to a student?

   A) "I feel a little upset right now because I am the only one who disagrees with this position."

   B) "I hear you saying that you do not understand what Mary is saying."

   C) "I like David's suggestion. It shows a lot of imagination, so let's try to use it."

   D) "I think that Sam should be given the benefit of the doubt about this issue."

   Answer: A

   Explanation: A) In "I" messages, people express how they are reacting and feeling toward another group member's immediate "here and now" behavior. This is reflected by the teacher who says *I feel a little upset right now, because I am the only one who disagrees with this position."* The quote "I hear you saying . . ." is a paraphrase. The expression "I like David's suggestion . . ." is a supportive statement, while "I think that Sam . . ." is a task–related behavior involving supplying information or opinion.

   Page Ref: 469
   Skill: Understanding

41) A hostile response style is to assertive discipline as a passive response style is to use

   A) empathetic responses.

   B) "I" messages.

   C) ignoring responses.

   D) paraphrasing messages.

   Answer: B

   Explanation: B) The relationship between a hostile response style and assertive discipline is negative. That is, a hostile response is condemning while an assertive response conveys to the student that the teacher cares too much about the student and about learning to permit inappropriate behavior to persist, Therefore, this analogy requires that *a passive response which does not tell the misbehaving student what to do is to be paired with an "I" message,* which communicates clearly in an assertive but non–judgmental way what the student is doing wrong, how it affects the teacher, and how the teacher feels about it.

   Page Ref: 469
   Skill: Understanding

42) Mr. Blake was unhappy. "Sam, I've told you time and time again. Please try to behave." Mr. Blake's response style can be described as

A) accusative.

B) assertive.

C) empathetic.

D) passive.

Answer: D

Explanation: D) Mr. Blake is being *passive by failing to make his feelings and expectations clear.* In contrast, an assertive response deals directly with the teacher's expectations without showing anger or using "you" statements (e.g., "You always misbehave.").

Page Ref: 469–470
Skill: Understanding

43) Which one of the following behaviors would be considered an "assertive response" to a discipline problem?

A) "If you do that once more, you'll be punished."

B) "If you weren't so slow, we could be finished by now."

C) "Stop talking and return to your seats."

D) "Why do you persist in annoying the class?"

Answer: C

Explanation: C) An assertive response is: *"Stop talking and return to your seats."* This statement clearly communicates what the teacher expects, without becoming sidetracked by threats or accusations. The other statements are either passive responses or threats, neither of which can be expected to be effective.

Page Ref: 469
Skill: Understanding
P: .74
D: .24

44) Which one of the following behaviors is likely to be the most successful method for a teacher to follow in attempting to resolve a conflict with a student?

   A) Give in to the student's demands.

   B) Impose a solution on the student.

   C) Negotiate assertive discipline.

   D) Try Gordon's "no lose" method.

Answer: D

Explanation: D) In attempting to resolve a conflict with a student, the most successful method for a teacher to use is to *try Gordon's "no lose" method*. The other three response options reflect negative ways of attempting to resolve conflict, while no one really loses with Gordon's approach.

Page Ref: 470
Skill: Knowledge

45) Gordon's "no lose" method of dealing with conflicts involves

   A) having both the teacher and the students participate in the solution.

   B) having students vote on the best solution to the problem.

   C) imposing a solution for the problem on the students.

   D) using empathetic listening to help the students discover the solution on their own.

Answer: A

Explanation: A) *Gordon's "no–lose" method has both the student(s) and the teacher participating in the solution.* A solution is determined through discussion, group evaluation, and consensus. Voting is not used.

Page Ref: 470
Skill: Knowledge

46) Which one of the following strategies for managing conflict is **APPROPRIATE** when both the goal and the relationship are important?

   A) Compromise

   B) Confront

   C) Use Force

   D) Withdraw

Answer: B

Explanation: B) When both the goal and the relationship are important in a conflict, the most appropriate strategy to use is *confrontation*. To confront the situation directly strengthens the relationship between the conflicting parties and protects the goals of both parties.

Page Ref: 470–471
Skill: Knowledge

47) If a learning goal is very important and the relationship of the people involved is important, what strategy is recommended for managing the conflict?

    A) Compromise

    B) Confrontation

    C) Force

    D) Withdrawal

Answer: B

Explanation: B) When there is an important learning goal and the relationship between the conflicting parties is also important, the strategy recommended for managing the conflict is *confrontation*. Appropriate use of confrontation will strengthen the relationship, protect the goals of both parties, and lead to conflict resolution.

Page Ref: 470–471
Skill: Understanding

Completion Questions

1) The people, tasks, and time pressures are described by Doyle as reflecting the _____ nature of a classroom.

Answer: multidimensional
Page Ref: 444

2) When students are actively attending to learning material, the process is called _____ time or time on task.

Answer: engaged
Page Ref: 446

3) The time students spend working on learning tasks, while experiencing a high rate of success, is called _____ learning time.

Answer: academic
Page Ref: 446

4) The important goal of classroom management to expand the sheer number of minutes available for learning is called _____.

Answer: allocated time
Page Ref: 447

5) The amount of time spent actively involved in specific learning tasks is often called engaged time or _____.

Answer: time on task
Page Ref: 446

6) The informal rules that define when and how students may interact with one another during given activities are called _____ structures.

Answer: participation
Page Ref: 447

7) In addition to the goals of having time for learning and access to learning, the third goal of any classroom management system is _____.

Answer: self-management
Page Ref: 447

8) Activities that are accomplished in the classroom are described as _____.

Answer: procedures
Page Ref: 448

9) Teachers who appear to have "eyes in the back of their head" due to their awareness of everything that happens in the classroom are considered by Kounin to be skilled in _____.

Answer: withitness
Page Ref: 460

10) Choral responding is used to maintain _____ by keeping the whole class attentive to the lesson activities.

Answer: group focus
Page Ref: 460

11) Keeping track of and supervising several activities at the same time is called _____.

Answer: overlapping
Page Ref: 460

12) To know what is happening in the classroom and to identify what is important are the keys to dealing effectively with _____ problems.

Answer: discipline
Page Ref: 460–461

13) Requiring the next participant to summarize what the preceding speaker has said before being permitted to speak illustrates the _____ rule.

Answer: paraphrase
Page Ref: 467

14) A teacher who listens carefully to a student and then tries to paraphrase what the student is saying and feeling is using _____ listening.

Answer: empathetic
Page Ref: 468

15) Canter and Canter's approach to dealing with behavior problems by making expectations clear and following through with defined consequences is called _____ discipline.

Answer: assertive
Page Ref: 469

16) When teachers make "you" statements that condemn students without stating clearly what the student should be doing, these teachers are using a _____ style.

Answer: hostile response
Page Ref: 471

17) Gordon's approach to resolving conflicts that involves a cooperative effort by the teacher and students to find a solution is the _____ method.

Answer: no-lose
Page Ref: 470

True/False Questions

1) One of the characteristics proposed by Doyle for a multidimensional classroom is predictability.

Answer: FALSE
Page Ref: 444

2) Research has shown that approximately half of the time allocated for school turns out to be academic learning time.

Answer: FALSE
Page Ref: 444-445

3) The number of minutes available for learning is called engaged time.

Answer: FALSE
Page Ref: 446

4) Participation structures help define how students should behave in various types of activities.

Answer: TRUE
Page Ref: 447

5) A limitation of encouraging students to become self-managers is the amount of time required to accomplish this goal.

Answer: TRUE
Page Ref: 447

6) The most effective set of classroom rules is one that specifically spells out as many of the "do's and don'ts" as possible.

Answer: FALSE
Page Ref: 448–449

7) Decisions about penalties and rewards should be made early in the school year so that students will know before they break a rule or use the wrong procedure what the consequences will be.

Answer: TRUE
Page Ref: 451

8) There are three basic ways of organizing space in the classroom: (1) interest areas, (2) personal territories, and (3) teacher territories.

Answer: FALSE
Page Ref: 453

9) A circle seating arrangement is generally inappropriate for whole–group presentations.

Answer: TRUE
Page Ref: 453–455

10) The fishbowl arrangement in the classroom helps to create a feeling of group cohesion.

Answer: TRUE
Page Ref: 454

11) Effective managers communicate rules over time rather than primarily during the beginning weeks of school.

Answer: FALSE
Page Ref: 457–458

12) Kounin has suggested that the key element of effective classroom manager's styles is prevention of misbehavior.

Answer: TRUE
Page Ref: 460

13) A teacher who is skilled in *overlapping* can monitor several classroom events at the same time.

Answer: TRUE
Page Ref: 460

14) Movement management means propelling the class lesson at an appropriate and flexible pace and avoiding abrupt transitions and slowdowns.

Answer: TRUE
Page Ref: 462

15) Of the seven ways suggested for stopping misbehavior quickly, the least intrusive way is the make eye contact with, or move closer to, the offender.

Answer: TRUE
Page Ref: 462–464

16) The most important thing for secondary teachers to do with regard to classroom management is to enforce the established consequences for incomplete work.

Answer: TRUE
Page Ref: 462–464

17) Use of the paraphrase rule is more effective with college–age students than with younger students.

Answer: FALSE
Page Ref: 467

18) If a student tells you that he broke up with his girlfriend last night and was unable to complete his homework, it is the teacher's responsibility to see that the homework gets completed.

Answer: FALSE
Page Ref: 467–468

19) Empathetic listening is an effective strategy for helping students to find solutions to problems by keeping the lines of communication open.

Answer: TRUE
Page Ref: 468

20) Assertive discipline usually serves to make students angrier and more likely to misbehave than other types of management.

Answer: FALSE
Page Ref: 469

21) Both research evidence and classroom practice indicate that assertive discipline is an effective management technique.

Answer: FALSE
Page Ref: 469

Short Answer Questions

1) Doyle discussed the following six characteristics of classrooms: (1) multidimensional; (2) simultaneity; (3) immediacy; (4) unpredictability; (5) publicness; and (6) history. Describe each and indicate what, in your opinion, the implications of these characteristics are for classroom management.

   Answer: Doyle has proposed six characteristics of classrooms. Classrooms are *multidimensional* because of the many activities and different types of individuals involved. Therefore, it is difficult for teachers to know how a particular management strategy will work in a given situation. *Simultaneity* means that everything happens at once. Whom to discipline first and what to attend to at what time must be decided. *Immediacy* deals with the fast pace of classroom life and the multitude of exchanges with students that take place in a single day. Classroom events are often *unpredictable*, meaning that a good manager must be prepared to deal with the unexpected. What is seen by all is, therefore, *public*. Classroom *histories* determine the meaning of actions and events that depend on what has happened before in the classroom. [Implications of these characteristics identified by Doyle will differ from student to student, but the answer/illustrations generated by students should include these five characteristics.]

   Page Ref: 444

2) Describe how procedures differ from rules. Using Weinstein and Mignano's suggestions, identify key areas for which procedures need to be established.

   Answer: Rules specify forbidden and expected behaviors in a class (the "do's and don'ts"). *Procedures indicate how activities are accomplished.* Rules are usually written and posted; procedures are usually communicated orally and demonstrated through practicing the various activities. Weinstein and Mignano suggested that teachers establish procedures to cover administrative routines, student movement, housekeeping duties, routines for accomplishing lessons, interactions between teacher and students, and talk among students.

   Page Ref: 448–449

3) Select either an elementary or secondary teaching situation and discuss the types of rules that need to be established and the procedures for communicating the rules to students. When rules are broken, what types of penalties are appropriate for that age level?

   Answer: At the elementary level, useful general rules are "be polite and helpful, respect other people's property, listen quietly while other people are speaking, do not harm others, and obey school rules." Rules should be posted, explained, and discussed with the class. At the secondary school level, examples of useful rules include "bring all needed materials to class, be in your seat and ready to work, respect and be polite to everyone, respect other people's property, listen and stay seated while someone else is speaking, and obey all school rules." For both elementary and secondary students, a good consequence for not following rules is to "go back and do it right." An example is re-working an assignment that has not been completed properly. [Note: In Woolfolk's text, Weinstein and Mignano also listed seven categories of negative consequences that may be included in students' answers to this question.]

   Page Ref: 450–451, 457–458

4) Room arrangement is an important factor in achieving instructional goals. Discuss why this is true and identify and discuss at least four principles of effective room arrangements.

Answer: The principles of effective classroom arrangements are: (1) take account of fixed features; (2) have easy access to materials; (3) provide clean and convenient surfaces for equipment use; (4) provide quiet work areas; (5) allow for easy supervision of all areas; (6) avoid dead spaces and race tracks; (7) provide choices for various spatial preferences; (8) allow flexibility in rearranging the room; and (9) provide a place for students to keep personal belongings. [Students should discuss at least four of these principles in depth. Specific examples drawn from their own experiences would enhance the value of their answers.]

Page Ref: 452–455

5) Kounin listed four "problem–prevention" skills: (1) withitness; (2) overlapping; (3) group focus; and (4) movement management. Define each skill. Draw an example of each skill from your own experiences.

Answer: Kounin's four problem-prevention skills include: (1) *withitness* — the ability to communicate to students that you, the teacher, are aware of what is happening in the classroom; (2) *overlapping* — the ability to keep track of, or supervise, several activities at once; (3) *group focus* — the ability to keep as many students as possible involved in the class activities; and (4) *movement management* — the ability to keep the lessons and the group moving by making smooth transitions, maintaining an appropriate pace, and using variety when changes are necessary. [Student illustrations will differ, but each example should represent a particular problem–management skill.]

Page Ref: 460–461

6) Using your own examples, differentiate between hostile, passive, and assertive responses to misbehavior.

Answer: The first step in Gordon's management system is diagnosis of "who owns the problem" and why the behavior is troubling to the teacher. If the teacher is affected in a tangible way, and the fulfillment of his/her leadership role is blocked, the teacher owns the problem and must work with the student to solve it. Gordon recommends using "I–messages" and the "no–lose" method of problem solving. If the teacher is not affected, then the student owns the problem, and the teacher should use active listening to act as the student's counsel and support.

Page Ref: 469–470

7) Thomas Gordon described a system for determining what kind of response is needed in different problem situations. What is the nature of this system and what does it suggest that teachers should do to solve these types of problems?

Answer: *Assertive responses* to misbehavior make expectations clear by conveying that there will be consequences if the rules are not followed. Therefore, the student is given a choice of following the rules or accepting the consequences. An example: "Stop talking while I pass out the test. Anyone who talks will have 5 points deducted immediately." *Passive responses* comment on the behavior without telling the students what to do or informing them of the consequences. An example: "Does it seem correct to talk as I pass out the papers?" *Hostile responses* condemn students or threaten them personally, but hostile responses tend to be vague regarding what behaviors are desired. An example: "Sam, you are really going to be in for it now! I've had it with you!" [Students' own examples will differ but should reflect the above characteristics.]
Page Ref: 4469–470

Case Studies

Jason has been a problem in Ms. Johnson's second-grade class throughout the whole year. He always seems to be out of his seat and bothering other children. Ms. Johnson is especially frustrated because these misbehaviors are explicitly forbidden by the classroom rules that she established when school began. She finds herself saying over and over, "Jason, you know the rules; now sit down or you're going to be punished." Jason then sits down, but soon he is up and doing the same things again.

1) Based on your assessment of the situation, what does Ms. Johnson appear to be doing wrong in dealing with Jason?

Answer: Ms. Johnson might first reflect upon her class activities and the extent to which Jason has time to be out of his seat. Perhaps he is finishing the assignment early and does not have any other specific learning tasks to complete. Ms. Johnson believes Jason has a clear understanding of the rules, but this is an assumption. She may want to ask Jason about his understanding of the rules. Given that this is a second-grade class, we must consider the issue of cognitive development. Jason may be concrete in his understanding of the rules and believe that he is following certain rules only for certain activities. Although Ms. Johnson continues to "threaten" punishment, she does not appear to be following through with Jason regarding the consequences of his behavior. Finally, Ms. Johnson will want to communicate with Jason's family and inquire whether he follows rules in the home environment.
Page Ref: 446–447, 451

2) Given that the classroom rules specifically forbid Jason's behaviors, suggest a management strategy that Ms. Johnson could use to deal with Jason effectively. What types of consequences, if any, should she apply and in what order?

   Answer: First, Ms. Johnson could focus on the prevention of the behavioral problems. Jason appears to have a need to get out of his seat and interact with other students. Ms. Jackson may want to consider the extent to which her current instructional practices allow for Jason to meet his movement and interaction needs. Second, Ms. Johnson could involve Jason in a self-management program to decrease his behavioral problems. Rather than focusing on obedience to Ms. Johnson's rule, a self-management program would focus on teaching Jason self-control skills. This approach will require Jason to set behavioral goals, manage his own time, establish consequences for his behavior, and take responsibility for his lack of self-control. Although designed as a self-management system, it would be important to involve Jason's family in the development of the self-regulation plan. One possible consequence Ms. Johnson could arrange is a written reflection on his behavioral problem. Jason could be asked to write a short statement about what he did and how his behavior affected his classmates. Ms. Johnson could meet individually with Jason to review his written statement (this record would need to be available to parents if it is kept on file).
   Page Ref: 446–447

3) Describe how Ms. Johnson might use group consequences as an intervention approach.

   Answer: In this case, group consequences may not be an appropriate intervention strategy. Rather, Ms. Johnson will want to work individually with Jason to increase his positive classroom behaviors and keep him on task for learning. Of greatest importance is the need for Ms. Johnson to follow through with the stated consequences.
   Page Ref: 451

Ellen's face is twisted in an angry sneer and her body is visibly shaking. "I'm not going back to my seat!" she screams at Mr. Fournier (the ninth-grade Spanish teacher). "You're always picking on me. I've had it with being the one who's told to do everything." Mr. Fournier is taken aback but stands his ground, and says, "Ellen, return to your seat right now." "I'm not going to," Ellen replies, "No way, no how."

4) What step would you take next in dealing with Ellen, if you were Mr. Fournier?

   Answer: If Ellen and Mr. Fournier were in the room, then he may want to give her some time to calm down before he initiates a discussion. If this event took place during class, he may want to solicit the assistance of a school administrator so that he can continue teaching the class. Mr. Fournier will want to ask Ellen why she perceives that he is "always picking on her." It will be important for him to intentionally listen, not interrupt Ellen as she is speaking, try not to get defensive, and paraphrase (repeat back to her) a summary of what he thought he heard her communicate. He will want to be sure to use "I" sentences, but he should not be passive in his communications with Ellen. Even though Ellen is engaging in hostile communication, Mr. Fournier will want to use clear, firm, and non-hostile statements (i.e., assertive discipline).
   Page Ref: 451–452

5) Would Mr. Fournier's initial response be classified as assertive, hostile, or aggressive? Provide a rationale for your answer.

Answer: Mr. Fourneir's response can be categorized as assertive. He immediately dealt with her comments (assertive) but did not condemn her or use frequent sentences that begin with "you" statements (e.g., "you have no reason to be angry"). Thankfully, he was not aggressive and did not use any attacking or threatening statements, such as "Ellen, you embarrassed me in front of the class; you will pay for that later." In using an assertive approach, he restated his expectations ("return to your seat"), but did not apologize or engage in negotiations with Ellen. Most importantly, Mr. Fournier confronted the situation and was not passive in addressing Ellen's misbehavior.

Page Ref: 469

6) Discuss how Gordon's "no-lose" method could be used in attempting to resolve the problem with Ellen. Identify the specific steps of the model in your answer.

Answer: In Thomas Gordon's "no-lose" method of communication, both the teacher and the student develop the solution to the problem. Based on mutual respect for themselves and the other person, the parties try to come to an agreement that does not require one person to "give in" completely. This strategy involves a six-step problem-solving approach:

1. *Define the problem.* What do Ellen and Mr. Fournier want?
2. *Generate many possible solutions.* Together, Ellen and Mr. Fournier would brainstorm options without criticizing each other's ideas.
3. *Evaluate each solution.* Both Ellen and Mr. Fournier would have an opportunity to rule-out any of the possible solutions. If no solutions seem plausible, then they return to the brainstorming step.
4. *Make a decision.* Ellen and Mr. Fournier would need to come to a consensus about a solution strategy (note: not a vote).
5. *Determine how to implement the solution.* What will be needed? What are the responsibilities (and time frame for completion) of both Ellen and Mr. Fournier for implementing the parts of the solution?
6. *Evaluate the success of the solution.* Both Ellen and Mr. Fournier should share whether they are satisfied with the outcomes related to their solution strategy. How well is the strategy working, or do they need to modify their plan?

Page Ref: 470

Chapter 13   Teaching for Learning

Multiple-Choice Questions

1) Woolfolk suggests that advanced planning is important primarily because such planning

    A) allows the teacher more time to correct daily work.

    B) dictates course readings and requirements.

    C) eliminates uncertainty in teaching.

    D) influences what students will learn.

Answer: D

Explanation: D) The key factor of advance planning is to *influence what students will learn.* This influence occurs as a result of determining how available time and resources will be transformed into activities and assignments for students. Planning also eliminates some uncertainty in teaching, but that is a secondary benefit relative to influencing student learning.

Page Ref: 478
Skill: Knowledge

2) Which one of the following statements is **TRUE** with regard to instructional planning?

    A) For experienced teachers, daily planning is more important than unit or weekly planning.

    B) It is more critical at the beginning of the year for teachers than at any other time.

    C) It is more critical in elementary grades than in the higher grade levels.

    D) Once plans are devised they should generally be followed without variation.

Answer: B

Explanation: B) Planning appears to be *more critical at the beginning of the year than at any other time,* because many procedures, rules, and routines are established early. Plans should be flexible and initially concentrate on the unit level, followed by weekly and then daily planning.

Page Ref: 478
Skill: Knowledge

3) Which one of the following is likely to be an objective written by a teacher from the **cognitive** viewpoint?

A) Students will list four characteristics of classic drama.

B) Students will define and conjugate ten French verbs.

C) Students will calculate the answers to distance problems.

D) Students will understand "aesthetic distance" in drama.

Answer: D

Explanation: D) Cognitive objectives refer to internal changes, unlike behavioral objectives that stress observable or external changes. An example of a cognitive objective would be *the students will understand aesthetic distance in drama*. Note that this type of outcome is difficult to measure (what does "understand" mean?).

Page Ref: 480
Skill: Understanding

4) Which one of the following objectives illustrates an appropriate behavioral example of the cognitive objective, "Students will be able to understand the concept of correlation"?

A) "Achieve mastery on a quiz dealing with correlation issues."

B) "Appreciate how and when correlation is used."

C) "Comprehend the meaning of the concept of correlation."

D) "Identify instances of positive and negative correlation."

Answer: D

Explanation: D) An appropriate behavioral example of the objective, "The student must understand correlation," is *"can identify instances of positive and negative correlation."* The verb "identify" describes a more observable and measurable outcome than do verbs such as appreciate or comprehend. Further, in alternative "a," simply saying "achieve mastery" is ambiguous (what is meant by "mastery"?).

Page Ref: 480
Skill: Understanding
P: .29
D: .21

5) In order to measure the outcomes of cognitive objectives more easily, the objectives should be

   A) based on test questions.

   B) clarified with specific examples.

   C) conceptualized as a general case.

   D) presented to the class prior to a lesson.

Answer: B

Explanation: B) Cognitive objectives are easier to measure when they are *clarified with specific examples*. This process involves trying to specify the particular behaviors that would be demonstrated if the objective were achieved.

Page Ref: 480
Skill: Knowledge
P: .40
D: .10

6) An advantage of Gronlund's approach to writing objectives over Mager's is

   A) clearer specification of the criterion for evaluation.

   B) easier procedures for writing the statements.

   C) greater flexibility for expressing cognitive learning outcomes.

   D) inclusion of the three major components of valid objectives.

Answer: C

Explanation: C) Gronlund's system is advantageous relative to Mager's for *allowing greater flexibility in expressing cognitive objectives*. Cognitive objectives are difficult to operationalize because they emphasize internal outcomes such as "comprehend," "assimilate," and "understand." Gronlund's system allows the teacher to use these types of verbs supported by a listing of exemplary behaviors. Mager's system is more specific and uses knowledge-level verbs primarily, such as "define," "list," and "identify."

Page Ref: 480
Skill: Knowledge
P: .62
D: .32

7) Which one of the following objectives is complete according to Mager's guidelines?

A) Given colored pictures of fruits and vegetables, students will correctly classify them with a high degree of accuracy.

B) Students will correctly identify the function of the four major organs in the digestive system without using notes.

C) Students will correctly recall the major bones of the human body.

D) Using a calculator, students will solve division problems containing fractions.

Answer: B

Explanation: B) A complete Mager–type objective is *the student will correctly identify the functions of four major organs in the digestive system without using notes*. This objective includes a condition (no notes), behavior (identify), and performance criteria (must correctly identify four organs).

Page Ref: 480
Skill: Understanding
P: .55
D: .23

8) Given the objective "students will be able to write complete sentences using words from a new vocabulary list," identify whether Mager's three criteria for a correctly stated behavioral objective are present or absent in this objective.

Behavior	Condition	Criterion
A) Absent	Absent	Absent
B) Absent	Present	Absent
C) Present	Present	Absent
D) Present	Present	Present

Answer: C

Explanation: C) In the objective presented, *only the behavior and condition elements of Mager's system are present*. The criterion is missing: students will be able to write complete sentences (behavior) using words from a new vocabulary list (condition).

Page Ref: 480
Skill: Understanding
P: .54
D: .45

9) The primary value of Bloom's taxonomy of cognitive objectives is that it can

A) lead educators to think carefully about the objectives they construct.

B) provide a valid hierarchy of learning from simple to complex.

C) provide administrators with an objective means of evaluating the effects of courses.

D) rank different types of learning according to their relative importance.

Answer: A

Explanation: A) Although Bloom's taxonomy may not be completely accurate in classifying the complexity of skills, *it is beneficial in leading educators to think carefully about the objectives they construct.*

Page Ref: 481
Skill: Knowledge

10) Ms. Smith would like to measure her first-graders' mastery of their personal information (address, phone number, spelling of name). What level of Bloom's taxonomy do her questions illustrate?

A) Application

B) Comprehension

C) Evaluation

D) Knowledge

Answer: D

Explanation: D) By measuring her first-graders' mastery of their personal information (address, phone number, spelling of name), Ms. Smith has assessed *knowledge,* remembering something essentially as given.

Page Ref: 481
Skill: Understanding
P: .78
D: .25

11) What level of Bloom's taxonomy is most difficult, if not impossible, to measure with multiple-choice tests?

A) Analysis

B) Comprehension

C) Knowledge

D) Synthesis

Answer: D

Explanation: D) It would be extremely difficult, if not impossible, to use multiple-choice tests for assessing *synthesis skills,* which involve creating something by combining elements. An essay test would provide more opportunity for measurement of synthesis abilities because of its open-ended, more divergent means of expression.

Page Ref: 480
Skill: Knowledge

12) A student in a biology class examines a slide of an unfamiliar cell and describes its major parts and how they interrelate. What element in Bloom's taxonomy is most directly exemplified?

   A) Analysis

   B) Comprehension

   C) Evaluation

   D) Synthesis

   Answer: A

   Explanation: A) The biology student is demonstrating *analysis skills*. Such skills involve breaking something down into its parts (the unfamiliar cell, in this example).

   Page Ref: 480
   Skill: Understanding
   P: .62
   D: .02

13) Larry identifies the names of all present members of the President's Cabinet. What element from Bloom's taxonomy is most directly exemplified?

   A) Analysis

   B) Comprehension

   C) Knowledge

   D) Synthesis

   Answer: C

   Explanation: C) Larry is demonstrating *knowledge skills*. All that he has to do is to name the members of the Cabinet. No understanding or higher–order reasoning is required.

   Page Ref: 480
   Skill: Understanding

14) Whitney presents and defends her personal views on the desirability of having the current president nominate Supreme Court Justices. What level of thinking in Bloom's taxonomy is illustrated by Whitney's task?

   A) Application

   B) Comprehension

   C) Evaluation

   D) Synthesis

   Answer: C

   Explanation: C) Whitney is demonstrating *evaluation skills* by judging the desirability of having the President nominate Supreme Court Justices. Evaluation is a high–order skill that involves forming an opinion on the worth or value of something.

   Page Ref: 480
   Skill: Understanding
   P: .52
   D: .09

15) Indicate the **HIGHEST** level of Bloom's taxonomy in which the following question can be classified: "How should government classes judge the feasibility of a court decision?"

   A) Analysis

   B) Application

   C) Evaluation

   D) Synthesis

Answer: C

Explanation: C) Judging the feasibility of a court decision is at the *evaluation level* of Bloom's taxonomy. At this highest level, students must know enough about the particular decision and the background information to make a judgment or "evaluation" about the feasibility or validity of the decision.

Page Ref: 480
Skill: Understanding
P: .71
D: .39

16) What level of Bloom's taxonomy is represented by the following objective? "Student teachers will design a module of instruction in their own content areas."

   A) Analysis

   B) Application

   C) Knowledge

   D) Synthesis

Answer: D

Explanation: D) By designing a module of instruction in their content areas, student teachers would be demonstrating *synthesis*, which is creating something new by combining elements (in this case, what they have learned about their content area, instructional design, and teaching methods).

Page Ref: 480
Skill: Understanding
P: .39
D: .31

17) After teaching about classical conditioning, Ms. Lennon explained the function of each major component in the model (conditioned response, unconditioned stimulus, etc.). What level of the new cognitive taxonomy is most directly exemplified by Ms. Lennon's apparent instructional objective?

   A) Apply

   B) Create

   C) Remember

   D) Understand

   Answer: D

   Explanation: D) Ms. Lennon is most clearly demonstrating *comprehension* by explaining the meaning of specific material without relating it to anything else.

   Page Ref: 480
   Skill: Understanding

18) What is the taxonomic domain of the following objective? "After learning about the properties of magnetism, students will build a vacuum and observe whether there is magnetic behavior present."

   A) Action

   B) Affective

   C) Cognitive

   D) Psychomotor

   Answer: D

   Explanation: D) Learning about the properties of magnetism is in the cognitive domain. However, the key factor in this situation is *building a vacuum machine* that requires using physical skills in the *psychomotor domain*.

   Page Ref: 482–483
   Skill: Understanding
   P: .63
   D: .56

19) To what taxonomic domain does the following objective belong? "Students will share their reactions about the appeal of a painting after a trip to a local gallery."

   A) Action

   B) Affective

   C) Cognitive

   D) Psychomotor

Answer: B

Explanation: B) Sharing reactions about the appeal of a painting is in the *affective domain*. The key factor is that "reactions", or feelings about something, are being communicated, as opposed to information (cognitive domain).

Page Ref: 482
Skill: Understanding
P: .72
D: .47

20) Which one of the following objectives would probably be the most difficult to measure?

   A) Analysis

   B) Application

   C) Receiving

   D) Reflex actions

Answer: C

Explanation: C) *Receiving would be the most difficult to measure,* because it is an affective outcome that cannot be observed or tested as easily as cognitive (application or analysis) or psychomotor objectives (reflexes) can be tested.

Page Ref: 482
Skill: Understanding
P: .66
D: .36

21) Mrs. Savage is hoping that her students will really appreciate the importance of earthquakes following the unit that she is about to teach. The type of affective response that she should expect to occur FIRST for this outcome is

   A) organizing.

   B) receiving.

   C) responding.

   D) valuing.

Answer: B

Explanation: B) The lowest–level outcome in the affective domain is *receiving*. Before Mrs. Savage's class can appreciate the importance of earthquakes, they must receive the material on earthquakes by being attentive.

Page Ref: 482
Skill: Understanding

22) In the highest level of the affective domain, students are expected to

   A) adopt, and act consistently with, a new value.

   B) be aware of how other people feel.

   C) demonstrate an overt response to an idea or thing.

   D) show a new behavior as a result of experience.

Answer: A

Explanation: A) In the highest level of objectives in the affective domain, students are expected to *adopt, and act consistently with, a new value.* For example, a person might become firmly committed to the love of music and share it with his/her friends.

Page Ref: 482
Skill: Knowledge
P: .44
D: .55

23) For evaluating a student's achievement in psychomotor skills, the most appropriate instrument would typically be a(n)

   A) essay test.

   B) objective test.

   C) checklist or rating scale.

   D) personal interview.

Answer: C

Explanation: C) *A checklist or rating scale is particularly useful in evaluating students' psychomotor skills* because the performance results in a product. The checklist or rating scale evaluates the product by asking "Is the skill being performed?" and "How high is the proficiency on this skill?"

Page Ref: 482–483
Skill: Understanding

24) The constructivist approach to planning learning experiences emphasizes what roles for teachers and students?

    A) Both students and teachers determine the content and activities, but teachers select the learning strategy to be used.

    B) Students and teachers together determine the content, activities, and learning strategies to be used.

    C) Students determine the broad learning goals, while teachers determine the specific learning objectives and activities.

    D) Teachers determine the learning goals, activities, and strategies for optimal learning.

Answer: B

Explanation: B) From a constructivist perspective, planning is shared and negotiated by the teacher and students. *Together, they determine content, activities, and learning approaches.* This orientation contrasts with teacher–centered approaches in which the teacher makes all of the decisions (direct instructional methods).

Page Ref: 484
Skill: Knowledge

25) Recent research evidence suggests that a major element in planning and designing lessons and units of instruction for all grade levels is the use of

    A) behavioral objectives.

    B) hands–on material.

    C) thematic and integrated content.

    D) topic maps.

Answer: C

Explanation: C) The major element in planning and designing instruction today is *teaching with themes and integrated content* from kindergarten (Roskos & Neuman, 1995) through high school (Clark & Agne, 1997). Topic maps, objectives, and hands–on material are all useful tools for implementing thematic and integrated content.

Page Ref: 485
Skill: Knowledge

26) A constructivist approach to assessment, compared to a traditional approach, would include use of

    A) fewer teacher comments about each student's work.

    B) more norm-competitive projects designed by students.

    C) students and teachers sharing authority for evaluating students' work.

    D) teacher-designed projects that students evaluate on the basis of predetermined criteria.

Answer: C

Explanation: C) In constructivist teaching approaches, because they are student-centered, *teachers and students share the authority for evaluating students' work* so that students can explain their thought processes and justify answers. The rationale is that students learn much more through such expression than they do simply by writing answers and receiving check marks on their papers. Moreover, by sharing the choice of assessment methods with their teachers, students will have a vested interest in the total evaluation.

Page Ref: 484–485
Skill: Knowledge
P: .68
D: .30

27) In what type of situation would it be most desirable for a teacher to use the lecture approach?

    A) Application and analysis levels are key cognitive objectives for the material.

    B) Cognitive and affective objectives stress lower-level concepts and develop interest in the material.

    C) Students are relatively low in ability level and have limited experience with the material.

    D) Students differ widely in ability levels and background experiences.

Answer: B

Explanation: B) Lecture seems well suited to situations in which *objectives emphasize low-level cognitive objectives (understanding or comprehension) and affective objectives (valuing or becoming interested in material).* Lecture is **NOT** desirable where there is a wide range of individual differences (pacing cannot be adapted well), low-ability students, or high-level cognitive objectives such as synthesis and evaluation.

Page Ref: 487–488
Skill: Knowledge

28) The **BEST** method by which active learning can be incorporated into lectures is to use

    A) lower-level cognitive objectives.

    B) questioning strategies.

    C) scripted cooperation.

    D) techniques involving small groups.

Answer: C

Explanation: C) The best method to use for incorporating active learning into traditional lectures is the technique of *scripted cooperation*. In this strategy, teachers stop their lecture presentations and have students work in pairs in order to translate concepts and ideas into their own words, to check on their understanding of the lecture material, and to organize their thinking. Questioning strategies and small-group work are also active learning strategies, but use of these methods is usually associated with learning methods other than lecturing. Lower-level cognitive objectives can be involved with any type of learning approach.

Page Ref: 490
Skill: Knowledge

29) Which one of the following strategies is appropriate regarding the use of seatwork?

    A) Seatwork should be counted as part of the course grade.

    B) Seatwork should involve only minimal monitoring by the teacher.

    C) Students should not be permitted to help each other with their seatwork.

    D) Teachers in the U.S. use seatwork relatively infrequently when compared to those in other countries.

Answer: A

Explanation: A) It is generally recommended that seatwork should be checked and the results *counted toward the course grade*. This way, students are held accountable for their work. Students should be allowed to help each other, but teachers need to monitor seatwork activities closely.

Page Ref: 491
Skill: Knowledge

30) A frequent criticism of seatwork as a classroom learning strategy is that it

    A) is often overused.

    B) may require learning skills that students might not possess.

    C) places the student in a passive mode.

    D) tends to reduce student motivation.

Answer: A

Explanation: A) Although there is little research on seatwork, it is clear that seatwork *is often overused*. In fact, American students were found in one study to spend about twice as much time engaged in seatwork as Japanese students.

Page Ref: 491
Skill: Knowledge

31) The heart of the recitation approach to teaching that has been around for many years is

    A) praising.

    B) reacting.

    C) soliciting.

    D) setting a framework.

Answer: C

Explanation: C) The heart or core of the recitation approach in teaching is *soliciting* or asking questions.

Page Ref: 493
Skill: Knowledge

32) The questions on the objective test that you are taking right now are what type of question?

    A) Analytical

    B) Convergent

    C) Divergent

    D) Evaluation

Answer: B

Explanation: B) The types of questions on an objective test, such as the items in the test that students are now taking, are *convergent questions*, because there is only one right answer. Divergent questions have several possible answers.

Page Ref: 494
Skill: Understanding
P: .63
D: .31

33) Which one of the following students is responding to a divergent question?

A) Alice identifies the category name for a group of objects.

B) Dave adds to simple lines as many lines as he wants to make a meaningful figure.

C) Janelle indicates which one of five figures is concealed in a complex figure.

D) Mario gives a word to satisfy a definition and a given first letter.

Answer: B

Explanation: B) Divergent thinking involves creating responses to questions or problems that do not have a single correct answer. The latter situation describes convergent thinking. In this example, the divergent thinker is *Dave, who makes as many lines as he judges appropriate to make a meaningful figure.*

Page Ref: 494
Skill: Understanding
P: .78
D: .32

34) Research on the effectiveness of higher-level questions for learning has shown that such questions

A) are consistently inferior to lower-level questions.

B) are consistently superior to lower-level questions.

C) are equally as effective as lower-level questions.

D) vary in effectiveness depending upon the situation.

Answer: D

Explanation: D) While higher-level questions are more likely than lower-level questions to stimulate divergent thinking and meaningful learning, there is no one best way to question. *The effects of higher-level questions can vary depending on the situation.*

Page Ref: 495
Skill: Knowledge
P: .72
D: .18

35) High-ability students generally appear most likely to benefit from

A) a lower pace with little emphasis on correcting errors.

B) a mixture of factual and higher-level questions.

C) a nurturing atmosphere for learning.

D) highly structured lesson plans.

Answer: B

Explanation: B) High-ability students appear to benefit from a *mixture of factual and higher-level questions, a fast pace, and clear error corrections.* A nurturing atmosphere and highly-structured lesson plans are less important for high achievers than for low achievers.

Page Ref: 495
Skill: Knowledge

36) Research shows that the average amount of time teachers wait for students to answer questions is about

    A) one second.

    B) three seconds.

    C) five seconds.

    D) seven seconds or more.

Answer: A

Explanation: A) Research by Rowe (1974) indicated that, on the average, *teachers wait only one second* for students to answer.

Page Ref: 495
Skill: Knowledge

37) The recommended waiting time while questioning students is

    A) one to two seconds.

    B) three to five seconds.

    C) six to eight seconds.

    D) 10 seconds or longer.

Answer: B

Explanation: B) Research by Berliner (1987), Rowe (1974), and others suggests that, when teachers *wait at least five seconds* before calling on a student, students tend to give longer answers, more sophisticated answers, and participate more frequently if given a little more time.

Page Ref: 495
Skill: Knowledge

38) If a student who is called on to respond to a question gives a partially wrong answer, the recommended procedure is to

    A) ask "does anyone have a different answer?" Then call on the first volunteer.

    B) correct the student's answer and go on with the lesson.

    C) provide a prompt or cue and stay with the student for a little while.

    D) say "that's almost correct" and then call on another student.

Answer: C

Explanation: C) When students' answers are partially correct, it is best to give them an opportunity to come up with a better response, or at least correct any misunderstandings. *One recommended procedure is to provide a prompt or cue and give the students a chance to correct the original answer.*

Page Ref: 496
Skill: Knowledge
P: .91
D: .15

39) Group discussions are most appropriate for use when

    A) questions require convergent answers.

    B) students are young or less mature.

    C) students have difficulty expressing themselves.

    D) the class is well prepared to evaluate and synthesize.

Answer: D

Explanation: D) *Group discussions are most appropriate when students are able and prepared to evaluate and synthesize.* They would **NOT** be a good choice for answering lower-level questions that have convergent answers or when a lot of material needs to be covered in limited time.

Page Ref: 496
Skill: Knowledge
P: .71
D: .44

40) Which one of the following procedures is recommended for teachers when using the discussion method?

    A) Ask another student to summarize the first student's response if uncertain about what that student has said.

    B) Discourage students from mentally rehearsing or writing responses before speaking.

    C) Let shy children decide to participate in the discussions whenever they are ready.

    D) Remain as uninvolved as possible during the discussion period.

Answer: A

Explanation: A) The only correct procedure of those presented for this item is *to ask students to summarize other students' responses, especially when the initial responses are not clear.* Shy children should be directly invited to participate, and it is generally desirable for students to be given time to rehearse mentally or write down their ideas before responding.

Page Ref: 496
Skill: Knowledge

41) Analysis of the relationship between teachers' knowledge of a subject and students' learning suggests that knowledge is

    A) necessary but not sufficient to improve learning.

    B) negatively correlated with students' attitudes about the class.

    C) the best predictor of student achievement.

    D) the most important quality of a good teacher.

Answer: A

Explanation: A) To be a good teacher, *it appears necessary but* **NOT** *sufficient to be knowledgeable about the subject taught in order to improve students' learning,* because many factors other than knowledge influence how well students learn. Knowledgeable teachers are not always effective teachers.

Page Ref: 486
Skill: Knowledge
P: .67
D: .35

42) Which one of the following terms is more desirable than the others for improving clarity?

    A) "More or less"

    B) "Sometimes"

    C) "Therefore"

    D) "Whatever"

Answer: C

Explanation: C) Explanatory links such as *"therefore"* serve to help students connect ideas. In contrast, imprecise terms such as "whatever," "sometimes," and "more or less" convey ambiguous meanings to students.

Page Ref: 487
Skill: Knowledge

43) Warmth and enthusiasm on the part of the teacher have been shown to

    A) be related positively to student attitudes.

    B) cause higher student achievement.

    C) cause increased attention by students.

    D) have little effect on student achievement.

Answer: A

Explanation: A) Research has shown that warmth and enthusiasm by teachers are *related positively to student attitudes.* Because the studies have been correlational, the evidence does not indicate that these traits necessarily cause higher achievement, but a relationship can be inferred.

Page Ref: 487
Skill: Knowledge
P: .40
D: .33

44) Which one of the following is **NOT** a typical component of direct instruction?

A) Cooperative learning

B) Guided practice

C) Independent practice

D) Review of previous day's work

Answer: A

Explanation: A) *Cooperative learning* is **NOT** a typical component of direct instruction. Guided practice, independent practice, and reviewing the previous day's work are essential strategies of direct instruction.

Page Ref: 487–488
Skill: Knowledge
P: .66
D: .49

45) A major criticism of direct instruction is that it

A) has proven ineffective in evaluation studies.

B) is often limited to lower-level objectives.

C) overemphasizes constructivist viewpoints.

D) works well with high-ability students but not with low-ability students.

Answer: B

Explanation: B) A major criticism of direct instruction is that this method is *often limited to lower-level learning objectives*.

Page Ref: 490
Skill: Knowledge
P: .50
D: .53

46) Recent research on the effects of direct instruction suggests that there is ample evidence identifying what to be at the heart of the direct instruction teaching model?

A) Guided and independent practice with feedback

B) Inductive reasoning activities and examples

C) Models of expert performance

D) Student-controlled learning activities

Answer: A

Explanation: A) The heart of the direct teaching model is *guided and independent practice with feedback*. The other three response choices are relevant for student-centered teaching approaches.

Page Ref: 490
Skill: Knowledge
P: .66
D: .32

47) The approach to learning to read and write that is now challenging traditional methods for teaching these subjects is called what method?

    A) Code–based

    B) Meaning–based

    C) Phonics–based

    D) Skills–based

Answer: B

Explanation: B) *Meaning–based approaches* to learning are now challenging the traditional teaching methods for reading and writing.

Page Ref: 502
Skill: Knowledge

48) The literature-based and emergent literacy approaches to teaching reading and writing are similar to what teaching approach?

    A) Code–based

    B) Phonics

    C) Skills

    D) Whole–language

Answer: D

Explanation: D) The literature-based and emergent literacy approaches to teaching reading and writing are similar to the *whole–language method*.

Page Ref: 502
Skill: Knowledge

49) The philosophy of the whole–language teaching approach is best captured in which of the following expressions?

    A) "Language fundamentals and basics first; composition second"

    B) "Hooked on phonics"

    C) "Integrating language learning with everyday learning"

    D) "Structuring language curricular events to ensure proper sequential development"

Answer: C

Explanation: C) *Integrating language learning with everyday learning best captures the whole–language philosophy*. The idea is to introduce new words and language rules in the context of stories and activities that are naturally meaningful to students. The teaching of fundamentals follows, rather than precedes, meaningful language learning.

Page Ref: 502–503
Skill: Understanding

50) Which one of the following activities would be most likely to be advocated in a whole-language writing program rather than in a conventional curriculum?

   A) Composing a sonnet by emulating the style used by Shakespeare

   B) Creating sentences that are evaluated for readability by a computer and then revised

   C) Writing an essay on one of three standard themes randomly selected by the teacher

   D) Writing stories about school activities to be published in a class newspaper

Answer: D

Explanation: D) A whole-language writing program would emphasize using writing in meaningful situations. An example is *having students write stories about their school activities for publication in the school newspaper*. The other response choices describe structured or artificial writing activities that would be less natural and less student-centered.

Page Ref: 502–503
Skill: Understanding
P: .49
D: .47

51) Which one of the following children would profit most from training in phonemic awareness?

   A) Ben in preschool

   B) Cassie in first grade

   C) Dexter in third grade

   D) Frances in fifth grade

Answer: A

Explanation: A) *Ben in preschool* is the student who would be most likely to profit from training in phonemic awareness. The principle here is that the younger a child is, the more the child will profit from phonemic awareness training.

Page Ref: 504
Skill: Understanding

52) Which one of the following examples of mathematics learning is the **MOST** compatible with a constructivist view?

   A) Converting from Fahrenheit to Celsius temperatures by experimenting with actual thermometer reading

   B) Simplifying an equation by following the steps listed in the textbook

   C) Using a drill-and-practice computer program dealing with factoring numbers

   D) Using flash cards to teach both addition and subtraction facts

Answer: A

Explanation: A) The constructivist approach to teaching mathematics uses real-life events as a basis for making concepts understandable and interesting. An example is *learning temperature conversion formulas by experimenting with actual thermometer readings*. This approach contrasts with learning math by means of drill-and-practice exercises.

Page Ref: 505–506
Skill: Understanding
P: .68
D: .52

53) The Center for Early Reading describes 10 principles that reflect what approach(s) to teaching?

   A) Code-based and phonics instruction.

   B) Explicit decoding skills and whole-language instruction.

   C) Phonemic awareness and word identification instruction.

   D) Whole-language and meaning-based instruction

Answer: B

Explanation: B) The 10 principles proposed by the Center for Early Reading are based on *explicit decoding skills and whole-language instruction.*

Page Ref: 504
Skill: Knowledge

54) Which one of the five components of a constructivist approach to mathematics is reflected in the following example: "Ask students to restate the problem in their own words."

   A) Construct a case history of each student.

   B) Develop students' reflective processes.

   C) Intervene to negotiate a possible solution.

   D) Promote students' autonomy and commitment to their answers.

Answer: B

Explanation: B) The example of asking students to restate the math problem in their own words indicates the constructivist component of *developing students' reflective processes.*

Page Ref: 506
Skill: Understanding

55) Which one of the following methods is **NOT** related closely to conceptual change teaching?

   A) Cognitive apprenticeships

   B) Explicit teaching

   C) Inquiry learning

   D) Reciprocal teaching

Answer: B

Explanation: B) Conceptual change teaching has much in common with cognitive apprenticeships, inquiry learning, and reciprocal teaching. *It has nothing in common with explicit teaching or direct instruction.*

Page Ref: 507
Skill: Knowledge

56) The goal of conceptual change teaching in science is to help students

   A) achieve the six stages of learning.

   B) cover the curriculum.

   C) engage in instructional conversations.

   D) work cooperatively in groups.

Answer: A

Explanation: A) The goal of conceptual change teaching in science is to help students *achieve the six stages of learning.* Engaging in instructional conversations with other students and teachers and working cooperatively in groups can lead toward achievement of certain of the six stages, but the goal is to achieve all six stages.

Page Ref: 507
Skill: Knowledge

Completion Questions

1) A clear specification of what a teacher intends students to accomplish on a learning task is called a(n) _____.

   Answer: instructional objective
   Page Ref: 478

2) The type of objective that uses verbs such as tabulate, state, total, and measure is a(n) _____.

   Answer: behavioral objective
   Page Ref: 480

3) The type of objective that uses verbs such as comprehend, design, acknowledge, and address is a(n) _____.

   Answer: cognitive objective
   Page Ref: 480

4) Mager's three-part system for formulating instructional objectives includes student behavior, conditions under which that behavior is to be performed, and _____.

Answer: performance criteria
Page Ref: 480

5) A classification scheme for educational objectives is called a _____.

Answer: taxonomy
Page Ref: 481

6) In Bloom's cognitive taxonomy, the type of objective that involves creating something new out of different ideas is _____.

Answer: synthesis
Page Ref: 481

7) The revised cognitive taxonomy has an added dimension of four kinds of _____.

Answer: knowledge
Page Ref: 482

8) Instructional planning is shared by teachers and students in the _____ approach to learning.

Answer: constructivist
Page Ref: 483

9) Constructivist teaching approaches evaluate students using portfolios, exhibitions, and other forms of _____ assessment.

Answer: authentic
Page Ref: 483–484

10) One way of incorporating active learning into lectures is to use _____.

Answer: scripted cooperation
Page Ref: 490

11) An instructional strategy in which teachers pose questions and students answer is called _____.

Answer: recitation
Page Ref: 492

12) The heart of the recitation method of teaching is _____.

Answer: questioning
Page Ref: 493

13) Questions that ask for many possible answers rather than one answer only are called _____ questions.

Answer: divergent
Page Ref: 494

14) Although similar to the recitation strategy, _____ should be more like instructional conversations.

Answer: group discussion
Page Ref: 496

15) After reviewing about 50 studies of teaching, Rosenshine and Furst concluded that the most promising teacher behavior for future research on effective teaching is _____.

Answer: clarity
Page Ref: 487

16) High levels of teacher interaction with students, clear explanations, and well-organized demonstrations characterize _____ teaching.

Answer: active
Page Ref: 487

17) Teachers who use systematic instruction for teaching mastery of basic skills, facts, and information are using active or explicit teaching, or _____ instruction.

Answer: direct
Page Ref: 487

18) Rosenshine's teacher-centered instruction is called direct instruction or _____.

Answer: explicit teaching
Page Ref: 487

19) Examples of meaning-based approaches to reading and writing include literature-based, emergent literacy, and _____ approaches.

Answer: whole-language
Page Ref: 502

20) Traditional phonemic methods of teaching are the _____ approach.

Answer: code-based
Page Ref: 502

21) The most basic skill in learning to read is _____.

Answer: word identification
Page Ref: 502

22) The method that helps students to understand concepts in science rather than to memorize information is called _____ teaching.

Answer: conceptual change
Page Ref: 507

23) Classrooms that integrate constructivist teaching with needed direct teaching of skills are especially good learning environments for students with _____.

Answer: special needs
Page Ref: 509

24) Mr. Kotter asks his students to explain their science ideas using physical models. Mr. Kotter's learning goal is teaching for _____.

Answer: conceptual change
Page Ref: 508

True/False Questions

1) Teacher plans should be regarded as flexible frameworks as opposed to rigid specifications.

Answer: TRUE
Page Ref: 478

2) Objectives seem to be most helpful in promoting student achievement with activities that are loosely rather than highly structured.

Answer: FALSE
Page Ref: 479

3) In the constructivist perspective, it is important for students to have a role in designing objectives for learning.

Answer: TRUE
Page Ref: 483

4) The revision of Bloom's Cognitive Taxonomy has an added dimension of four levels of conceptual knowledge.

Answer: TRUE
Page Ref: 481

5) The quality of a performance skill demonstration can be assessed by means of numerical rating scales.

Answer: TRUE
Page Ref: 482

6) Constructivist teaching methods can be incorporated into any educational situation or setting.

Answer: TRUE
Page Ref: 483–484

7) Development and use of a topic map becomes most important during the planning stage of instruction.

Answer: TRUE
Page Ref: 484

8) A checklist is a useful tool for guiding the assessment of thematic teaching outcomes.

Answer: TRUE
Page Ref: 485

9) In constructivist approaches to learning, teachers make the decisions about content and teaching strategies, and students plan the activities.

Answer: FALSE
Page Ref: 483–484

10) Rather than using specific objectives to guide planning, constructivist teachers have overall goals to guide learning.

Answer: TRUE
Page Ref: 483–484

11) Lecturing is an appropriate and economical method for teaching a large amount of material to students.

Answer: TRUE
Page Ref: 487

12) Scripted cooperation is a learning strategy for pairs of students to take turns summarizing material and criticizing their summaries.

Answer: TRUE
Page Ref: 490

13) An effective approach for teaching basic skills to low achievers is to use lecture presentations with minimal homework and seatwork.

Answer: FALSE
Page Ref: 491

14) Questions dealing with concrete facts are divergent questions.

Answer: FALSE
Page Ref: 494

15) In productive group sessions, a student's questions and comments are directed to another student.

Answer: TRUE
Page Ref: 496

16) Teaching experience is considered to have the strongest relationship with student learning of all the characteristics noted by Woolfolk.

Answer: FALSE
Page Ref: 486

17) Teacher clarity is a characteristic that is fairly simple to define objectively.

Answer: FALSE
Page Ref: 487

18) When instructional goals involve affective development and critical thinking or problem solving, direct instructional strategies are recommended.

Answer: FALSE
Page Ref: 487–489

19) Research on using code-based approaches in teaching reading indicates that being able to identify many words as students read depends on using context to guess meanings.

Answer: FALSE
Page Ref: 502

20) The importance of authentic writing tasks was recognized early by Vygotsky.

Answer: TRUE
Page Ref: 502

21) Under a whole-language perspective, a school is likely to have separate designated periods for reading, writing, and communication skills.

Answer: FALSE
Page Ref: 502-503

22) Both explicit decoding skills and whole-language instruction are employed by effective primary school teachers.

Answer: TRUE
Page Ref: 502-503

23) Research studies indicate the whole-language and constructivist approaches to learning appear to be effective across most subject areas.

Answer: FALSE
Page Ref: 502-503

24) Reciprocal teaching is an instructional approach for increasing student's creativity and innovation.

Answer: FALSE
Page Ref: 503

25) Teachers who are highly committed to covering all of the required information and curriculum are most interested in the goal of teaching for conceptual change.

Answer: FALSE
Page Ref: 507

Short Answer Questions

1) Write three possible cognitive objectives for your teaching specialty, using Mager's and Gronlund's approaches. Each objective should address a different level in Bloom's taxonomy.

Answer: The example objectives will vary in students' answers, but look for each objective to address a different level of Bloom's cognitive taxonomy. If Mager's approach is used, the objective should include student behavior, conditions of performance, and performance criteria. If Gronlund's approach is used, both a general objective and specific examples should be included.
Page Ref: 480

2) Demonstrate your understanding of Bloom's taxonomy for the cognitive domain by listing and describing each level. Be sure to list the levels in order and explain the significance of the sequence.

Answer: Bloom's revised taxonomy includes six levels of cognitive thinking categories. *Knowledge*: Remembering or reorganizing something without necessarily understanding, using, or changing it. *Understanding*: Comprehending the material. *Application*: Using or applying the information to solve a problem. *Analysis*: Breaking something down into its parts. *Evaluation*: Judging the value of materials or methods as they might be used in a given situation. *Creating (Synthesis)*: Making something new by combining elements into a whole. The revision also recognizes that cognitive processes must process or act on four types of knowledge: factual, conceptual, procedural, and metacognitive. Students' responses should also include explanations of the significance of the taxonomy's sequence for teachers. [Note: The above sequence does not represent a true hierarchy, but it generally reflects increasing levels of complexity. The taxonomy serves to help teachers consider different types of learning that lessons can be used to promote.]
Page Ref: 481–482

3) From your own experiences, identify at least one example of objectives in the psychomotor and affective domains that you have for yourself.

Answer: Students' examples of objectives that can be classified as psychomotor and affective will, of course, differ because of their own varying experiences. However, their psychomotor objectives should reflect the characteristics of at least one level in the psychomotor domain. Their affective objectives should also reflect the characteristics of at least one level of that domain.

Page Ref: 482–483

4) What is direct instruction? List its characteristics and describe a situation in which it would be the most appropriate method to use with students. Explain why your situation is appropriate for direct instruction.

Answer: Direct instruction is a system that combines several principles that have been found in traditional forms of teaching. The direct instruction models were identified by researchers who compared teachers whose students learned more than was expected (based on entering knowledge) with teachers whose students performed at an expected or average level. Effectiveness was usually defined as average improvement in standardized test scores for an entire class or school. Therefore, direct instruction models, such as Rosenshine's explicit teaching, Good's active teaching, Ausubel's expository teaching or meaningful verbal learning, and Hunter's Mastery Learning Program apply best to the teaching of basic skills. This approach does not stress comprehension or ensure that students understand what is being taught. Constructivist approaches are better geared to facilitating comprehension. Students' explanations of why direct instruction is appropriate for the situations they created will vary but should include the reasons why this method would be suitable.

Page Ref: 485, 487–491

5) Compare and contrast situations in which the following instructional methods would be most appropriate: (a) direct instruction; (b) group discussion; and (c) computer-based instruction.

Answer: Students' answers will differ for this question but their representative situations should reflect the principles of each of the three methods of instruction. Direct instruction, or explicit teaching, is a system that combines several principles that have been found in traditional teaching methods. Students' answers should elaborate on these principles, and illustrate the procedures. Direct instruction seems best for younger students and for teaching basic skills. Group discussion methods serve to make students more involved and active in their learning activities. These methods also provide students with the opportunity to ask for clarification and to take responsibility for their own learning. Disadvantages of these methods include the fact that they are time–consuming and unpredictable, involve preparing students in advance, may be threatening to shy students, and are often unwieldy to handle.Computer–based instruction is an excellent vehicle for student-centered learning because of its features of self-pacing, instructional adaptation, and utility applications (e.g., word processing). Although programs in the past were almost exclusively drill–and–practice types, today's systems include many more tutorial and simulation programs. Communications networks, videodisc encyclopedias, and microworlds are becoming increasingly available to students by means of the Internet and CD Rom applications.

Page Ref: 485, 496, 514

6) Describe the two types of expectation effects that can occur in the classroom. How can these expectation effects influence student learning? What can you, the teacher, do to combat the negative effects and promote the positive effects of these expectations? Provide specific illustrations of both types of outcomes.

Answer: Two types of teacher-expectation effects have been identified: the self-fulfilling prophecy, or Pygmalion effect, and the self-sustaining expectation effect. In the first instance, a teacher's beliefs about students' abilities have no basis in fact, but student behavior tends to match the initially inaccurate expectation. In the second instance, teachers' unchanging expectations sustain students' achievement at the expected levels. Good and Weinstein (1986) identified six dimensions of teaching that can communicate expectations to students: (1) a Task Environment Curriculum that includes procedures, task definition, pacing, and qualities of the environment; (2) grouping practices; (3) locus of responsibility for learning; (4) feedback and evaluation practices; (5) motivational strategies; and (6) quality of teacher relationships. Students should demonstrate their understanding with concrete illustrations of positive and negative ways of dealing with these expectation effects.

Page Ref: 496–498

7) Describe and differentiate between teaching methods and lesson structures that would be appropriate for low-ability vs. high-ability classes.

Answer: Low-ability students need multiple segments of presentations mixed with seatwork in each class period. Presentations should be fairly short, with frequent periods of practice interspersed within the lesson. In general, these students need small doses of information with opportunities to practice the skills being developed. Low achievers also need to be kept aware of grades and their progress in learning. The atmosphere of the class should be friendly and supportive. Direct teaching of metacognitive skills is recommended. High achievers profit from a rapid class pace and challenging tasks. Both factual and higher-level questions should be asked of high achievers. Presentations and demonstrations can be longer and guided practice shorter than those for low achievers. Less review and independent practice are needed for high-ability students, and, in general, more autonomy can be given to individual students. A major issue here is to adapt direct instruction to students' needs. However, direct instruction has been criticized by educators and psychologists who hold a cognitive view of learning. These people believe that the "basics" approach to teaching low achievers tends to underestimate students' capabilities, to postpone challenging and interesting work for too long (or forever, in some cases), and to deprive students of a meaningful, motivating context for learning or using the skills that are taught. Means and Knapp disparage the "basics" approach to teaching low achievers and propose several principles for moving beyond the basics. [See page 501 in the Point-Counterpoint Section for the entire list.] The Center for the Improvement of Early Reading Achievement (CIERA) has reviewed the research on learning to read that are useful for all children. The strongest research findings were drawn into 10 principles and an expanded version is available on its Web site: www.ciera.org. [See page 510 in Woolfolk's text for a list of the 10 principles.]

Page Ref: 487–491, 504

Case Studies

Juanita Phillips, an expert health and science supervisor for Kensington County Schools, has been asked by the school board to design a sex education course to be offered by all middle schools in the system. Juanita was given only general goals, together with the freedom to develop the course as expertise dictates. The following are the general goals given to Juanita: (1) "Students should understand basic reproductive processes," and (2) "Students should be aware of ways to prevent contracting the AIDS virus."

1) Describe the process that Juanita might employ to develop specific objectives from the general goals.

Answer: Ms. Phillips is an expert teacher in part because she engages in extensive planning – by the year, term, unit, week, and day. She has a clear vision of what she wants to cover and she is able to articulate her goals, outcomes, and standards for student learning. For her sex education course she has developed instructional, behavioral, and cognitive objectives. One of her instructional objectives is that students will be able to accurately state the number of people their age who contract the AIDS virus. One of her behavioral objectives is observing students practice how to calculate a young person's chances of contracted a sexually-transmitted disease if they engage in unprotected sexual activities. She has her students write an essay about "it would never happen to me" in order to assess the extent to which her students meet her standards of higher–level thinking operations (i.e., cognitive objectives). Together, her objectives require students to understand, recognize, create, define, list, find, and apply. Her general goal is that her students will have sufficient knowledge and skills to lead a healthy life. She develops her specific learning objective from this general goal. For example, one of her objectives is to ensure her students have the assertive skills needed to state to partners what they do and do not want to happen in intimate physical situations.

Page Ref: 478, 480, 486

2) Present your views on the desirability of using Mager–type vs. Gronlund–type objectives for the course. Which would you personally prefer? Explain your choice.

Answer: The primary difference between the two is that Mager recommends starting with specific objectives, whereas Gronlund suggests that objectives first be stated in general terms. They both focus on behavioral objectives, which are instructional objectives that are stated in observable behaviors. While both approaches are useful, Gronlund's approach has recently received some favorable attention from prominent educational psychologists and educators because having a small number of objectives has practical utility for teachers. A select set of objectives can help the teacher focus on instructional and assessment methods. If a teacher has too many small–scope objectives, they may lose their value. In addition to broad behavioral objectives, Gronlund believes teachers need to write a few select broad cognitive objectives (e.g., "understand", "appreciate").

Page Ref: 480

3) Are Juanita's objectives likely to be restricted to Bloom's cognitive domain? Why or why not?

Answer: Juanita's objectives can be adapted to fit Bloom's taxonomy. For example, her instructional goal of ensuring students have an understanding of the basic reproductive processes can include objectives written for all six of Bloom's taxonomy for the cognitive domain. Specifically, she will want objectives that include memory and reasoning objectives based on the following skills: knowledge, comprehension, application, analysis, synthesis, evaluation. A *knowledge objective* would involve asking students to identify the various parts of the female reproductive system. An *application objective* might require students to discuss how a healthy lifestyle can prevent cervical cancer in young fertile women. As a final example, Juanita could ask her students to state a metaphor for how the male and female reproductive systems work, which would involve a *synthesis objective* (i.e., creating something new by combining different ideas).
Page Ref: 481–482

As the bell rings, Ms. Chavez takes her place in the front of the room. With a somber and serious expression, she announces in a soft monotone, "Today, we will discuss factors that influence climate in the United States." She continues by saying, "It seems that differences are attributable to global variations due to the earth's axial rotation and solar revolution. However, some scientists disagree." Her lecture continues in this vein for 30 minutes, after which Ms. Chavez asks for questions, gives the homework assignment, and concludes the class. Ms. Chavez' seventh graders do not like her science class. They find the instruction difficult to understand.

4) Based on the brief description above, analyze Ms. Chavez's weaknesses in presenting material and in her choice of approaches (give her lecture skills).

Answer: Ms. Chavez may want to begin her lesson by communicating enthusiasm for her subject matter and the day's lesson. She could state why this information is useful, important, or relevant to her students' situation. Although she mentions that scientists disagree about what factors influence climate in the United States, she did not use this debate to solicit student interest. She could present brief biographical sketches on the various scientists and present their arguments. She does not use questioning to involve students. She could weave questions into her lecture that call upon students to remember points made earlier, apply what they have learned, or make value judgments about what they are learning. Although she allows students to ask questions at the end of her lecture, she does invite students to ask questions as they arise. Thus, students may hold misconceptions that are carried throughout the lecture. Ms. Chavez could benefit from including more active teacher approaches. For example, she could incorporate some scientific demonstrations related to the major concepts in her unit Students could also benefit from the inclusion of scripted cooperation, which requires them to pair up with another student and take turns summarizing the material and criticizing the summaries.
Page Ref: 492–493, 490

5) What are the strengths and limitations of Ms. Chavez's direct instruction approach?

Answer: One of the strengths of direct instruction (i.e., explicit teaching) is that you can cover a large amount of material for a large number of students over a short period of time. For lower level objectives, such as Bloom's knowledge objectives, direct instruction can be an appropriate approach. If the objective requires students to be able to understand and remember, a well delivered lecture can be effective. As noted by Linda Anderson, this is particularly true if the teacher is adept at making good links among main ideas and providing very clear explanations. However, some educators remain critical of explicit teaching methods primarily because they frequently do not involve students in active learning. Some argue that teachers who lecture are merely "transmitting" knowledge rather than requiring students to construct their own knowledge. Also, given the limitations of the cognitive system, especially working memory, we can expect some students will not be able to attend to all of the information in the lecture. Finally, as noted by Noddings, some content just does not lend itself well to a direct instruction approach. For example, some topics in literature require students to ask questions, solve difficult problems, and translate ideas into their own words. This type of content can require teachers to use problem-based learning approaches and/or cooperative learning. Also, much of what students learn requires an application of knowledge and students need practice with real-life manipulative materials.

Page Ref: 481–490

6) Suppose Ms. Chavez approached you for some advice for improving her direct instruction skills. What would you recommend she do and why? What if she also asked you for some guidance regarding whether or not she should include seat work in her lectures. Would you encourage her to incorporate seat work when she has completed her lecture?

Answer: You could recommend that she consider Rosenshine's six teaching functions, which could guide her lectures:
1. *Review and check the previous day's work.*
2. *Present new material.*
3. *Provide guided practice.*
4. *Give feedback and correctives based on student answers.*
5. *Provide independent practice.*
6. *Review material weekly and monthly.*

You could recommend to Ms. Chavez that she break up her lecture by providing her students with some seatwork. Seatwork is beneficial in that it involves students in the learning process. Moreover, it can be a way to quickly assess and misconceptions from the previous day. Ms. Chavez could begin her unit by asking students to respond to a question or two, or she could ask them to complete a concept map. During the seatwork, Ms. Chavez will want to walk around the room and provide careful monitoring. Students can be encouraged to ask Ms. Chavez, or other students, for assistance during the seatwork time. Seatwork has the advantage over homework assignments because students can get immediate help if they have a question. If Ms. Chavez decides to include seatwork, she will want to make sure the assignment connects to material covered in her lecture. Seatwork (or homework) is not useful if it is considered to be meaningless busywork. Seatwork can precede and follow Ms. Chavez's direction instruction. However, as in any instructional approach, the learning objectives of seatwork should be clearly communicated to students.

Page Ref: 488–491

Chapter 14   Standardized Testing

Multiple-Choice Questions

1) Ms. Powell has always been critical of standardized tests, however, now because of No Child Left Behind she realizes she must use more standardized tests because of the realities related to making

   A) her principal and school superintendent happy.

   B) sure parents are involved in classroom activities.

   C) sure portfolios become the assessment method of choice for her school district.

   D) Adequate Yearly Progress

   Answer: D

   Explanation: D) Under the law No Child Left Behind, *Adequate Yearly Progress* refers to the number of students who are "passing" standardized tests. There are severe consequences under the law for schools who do not demonstrate Adequately Yearly Progress.

   Page Ref: 521
   Skill: Understanding

2) How are the processes of evaluation and measurement related?

   A) Evaluation procedures assign quantitative values to measurements.

   B) Evaluation is influenced by the standard error of measurement (SEM).

   C) Measurement procedures assign quantitative values to evaluations.

   D) Measurement procedures involve more judgment than evaluation procedures.

   Answer: C

   Explanation: C) Measurement is the process that *assigns quantitative values in evaluations.* Quantitative measurement cannot be done in all instances, but when possible, quantitative measurement can increase the objectivity of the evaluation data obtained.

   Page Ref: 522
   Skill: Understanding
   P: .62
   D: .68

3) The fundamental purpose of educational assessment is to

   A) determine the quality of the outcomes being judged.

   B) identify which programs or people are superior to others.

   C) obtain objective data that express performances in quantitative terms.

   D) provide information to support decision-making.

Answer: D

Explanation: D) The fundamental purpose of educational assessment is to *provide information to support decision-making*. This is largely a subjective process based on values, although obtaining quantitative data through measurement can increase the objectivity of the decision.

Page Ref: 522
Skill: Knowledge
P: .67
D: .53

4) Paper-and-pencil exercises, direct observations of performances, development of portfolios, and creation of artifacts are all methods of

   A) assessment.

   B) evaluation.

   C) measurement.

   D) testing.

Answer: A

Explanation: A) The term *assessment* is used now because it is broader than testing and measurement to include all types of techniques used to observe people's behaviors. Consequently, assessment includes measurement, testing, and evaluation techniques.

Page Ref: 522
Skill: Knowledge

5) Which one of the following situations requires a norm–referenced evaluation?

A) Assessing whether an individual has been drinking too much to drive

B) Certifying whether a newly graduated education student can perform satisfactorily as a teacher

C) Hiring one manager from a pool of ten applicants for a large department store

D) Reporting to parents about how much students have learned during the semester

Answer: C

Explanation: C) The situation requiring norm–referenced testing is *hiring one manager from a pool of ten applicants*. The purpose here is to measure aptitude or achievement by comparing individuals. In contrast, criterion–referenced testing is used to assess how well individuals have mastered specific skills.

Page Ref: 523
Skill: Understanding
P: .64
D: .37

6) A local high school developed a math achievement test and used the results to determine the selection of students for an advanced placement course with a limited number of seats. What type of test should be used?

A) Criterion–referenced

B) Diagnostic

C) Norm–referenced

D) Standardized

Answer: C

Explanation: C) The local high school should use *norm–referenced assessment* for determining the selection of students for an advanced placement course. Because norm–referenced assessment compares individuals to one another (or to norms), it is especially useful in selecting individuals where space is limited.

Page Ref: 523
Skill: Understanding
P: .61
D: .34

7) A teacher who is interested in finding out how well a student is doing in class compared to students in other schools should use what type of test?

  A) Criterion–referenced

  B) Diagnostic

  C) Norm–referenced

  D) Teacher–designed

Answer: C

Explanation: C) Whenever comparisons among individuals are to be made, *norm–referenced assessments must be used.* In this case, students in one school are to be compared to students in other schools, so a norm–referenced standardized test would be appropriate. Criterion-referenced tests are used to assess specific objectives against a preset criterion of acceptability. Diagnostic tests are intended to identify strengths and weaknesses of individuals, and teacher-designed measures could be either for norm–referenced or criterion–referenced purposes.

Page Ref: 523
Skill: Understanding
P: .84
D: .20

8) Criterion–referenced tests are used primarily to assess

  A) achievement of general instructional goals.

  B) each student's achievement compared to other students.

  C) mastery of specific objectives.

  D) the range of achievement in a large group.

Answer: C

Explanation: C) Criterion–referenced tests are used to measure the *mastery of specific objectives* by indicating what the students can and cannot do. Such tests do **NOT** compare students directly to others or measure attainment of general goals. Evaluation addresses the latter need.

Page Ref: 523
Skill: Knowledge
P: .71
D: .46

9) A school administrator wants to identify the top 10 percent of the senior students in order to recommend them for scholarship competition at the highest rated university in the state. What testing purpose would serve the administrator's purpose?

   A) Criterion-referenced

   B) Diagnostic

   C) Norm-referenced

   D) Standardized

   Answer: C

   Explanation: C) A school administrator who wants to identify the top 10 percent of the senior class for scholarship competition has a *norm-referenced purpose* for making the selection. Students would have to assess individual differences by comparing students to one another, and the 10 percent with the highest achievement would be selected for the competition.

   Page Ref: 523
   Skill: Understanding

10) For which one of the following situations would a criterion-referenced test be the most appropriate measure to use?

   A) Assessing the range of abilities in a large, mixed-ability group of students

   B) Comparing students' general ability in specific subject areas such as English, algebra, or general science

   C) Measuring mastery of basic competencies in addition and subtraction

   D) Selecting candidates for a teaching position when only a few openings are available

   Answer: C

   Explanation: C) A criterion-referenced test would be most appropriate for *measuring mastery of basic competencies in addition and subtraction*. In contrast to norm-referenced tests that involve comparisons between people, criterion-referenced tests assess what skills individuals have and have not mastered (regardless of others' performances).

   Page Ref: 523–524
   Skill: Understanding
   P: .73
   D: .43

11) Which one of the following student outcomes is **MOST** likely to be the result of a criterion-referenced assessment tool?

   A) Anita was the first student to complete the test.

   B) Ben answered 10 out of 12 questions correctly.

   C) Randy scored at the eighty-ninth percentile.

   D) Sonia ranked fifteenth in French and ninth in music.

Answer: B

Explanation: B) Criterion-referenced tests would yield information such as Ben *answered ten out of twelve questions correctly*. Note that this information indicates exactly what Ben was able to do. If nine out of 12 correct was considered to constitute mastery, we could judge Ben to have mastered the objective concerned. [The other multiple-choice alternatives all support judgments of performance relative to other people.]

Page Ref: 524–525
Skill: Understanding
P: .71
D: .40

12) The most important attribute of a norming sample is that it should be

   A) completely random.

   B) large and diverse.

   C) limited in size.

   D) similar to future test-takers.

Answer: D

Explanation: D) The most important attribute of a norming sample is that the sample is *similar to future test-takers*. The reason is that the future test takers' scores will be judged in comparison to those of the norming sample. That comparison would obviously be flawed if the two groups were dissimilar.

Page Ref: 524
Skill: Knowledge
P: .73
D: .49

13) What is the arithmetic mean of the following set of scores? Scores: 0, 13, 15, 16, 16

   A) 12

   B) 13

   C) 14

   D) 15

Answer: A

Explanation: A) The mean is equal to *12*. This mean was determined by summing the scores (60) and dividing that sum by the number of scores (5).

Page Ref: 525
Skill: Understanding

14) Rob scored exactly in the middle of his class on the social studies exam. A valid interpretation of Rob's performance is that he scored exactly at the

　　A) center of a symmetrical frequency distribution.

　　B) mean of the class.

　　C) median of the class.

　　D) mode of the class.

Answer: C

Explanation:　　C) *Rob scored at the median of the scores,* the fiftieth percentile or midpoint of the distribution of scores. The mode is defined as the most frequently occurring, most popular score. The numerical average is the mean. It cannot be assumed that the distribution of the raw scores is normal in shape. If the raw scores are distributed normally, the three measures of central tendency will be equal.

Page Ref: 525
Skill: Understanding

15) What is the median for the following set of scores? Scores: 66, 66, 74, 96, 98

　　A) 66

　　B) 74

　　C) 78

　　D) 80

Answer: B

Explanation:　　B) The median is *74 because it is the middle score*—the score that divides the distribution in half. That is, there are two scores above 74 and two scores below 74. [The mean (average) is 80 and the mode (most frequently occurring) score is 66.]

Page Ref: 525
Skill: Understanding
P: .80
D: .40

16) The relationship between the standard deviation and test scores is that the larger the standard deviation, the

   A) greater the variability in the distribution.

   B) higher the central tendency.

   C) lower the variability in the distribution.

   D) narrower the distribution of scores.

Answer: A

Explanation: A) The larger a standard deviation is relative to the number of items in a test, *the greater the variability will be among the test scores.* Central tendency refers to the center of a distribution and is not influenced directly by the variability of scores. Comparisons among the three measures of central tendency determine the shape of a distribution, not its variability. [If the distribution is normal, all measures of central tendency will be equal.]

Page Ref: 526
Skill: Understanding
P: .84
D: .20

17) A standard deviation is a measure of

   A) how well the students met the tested objectives.

   B) the distance between the median and the extreme scores.

   C) the spread of scores around the mean.

   D) the level of validity for the test.

Answer: C

Explanation: C) The *standard deviation is a measure of the spread or variability of scores relative to the mean;* specifically, how far scores deviate *from the mean.* For a given set of scores, the larger the standard deviation is, the greater the variability there is in the distribution.

Page Ref: 526
Skill: Knowledge
P: .89
D: .18

18) The Algebra I class mean and standard deviation are 80 and 10, respectively. The Biology II class mean and standard deviation are 79 and 4, respectively. Kristen scored 90 in Algebra I and 87 in Biology II. The most valid conclusion to be drawn from these data is that Kristen

   A) scored better relative to her class in Algebra I than in Biology II.

   B) scored better relative to her class in Biology II than in Algebra I.

   C) should earn an A in Algebra I and a B in Biology II.

   D) would be served better by criterion–referenced grading than by norm–referenced grading in both courses.

Answer: B

Explanation: B) Kristen did better *relative to her class in Biology II than in Algebra I*. This conclusion is supported by the fact that her z–score in Biology II is +3 (indicating that she is 3 standard deviations above the mean), while her score in Algebra I is only +1 standard deviations above the mean. [Note: To determine the z–score, first subtract the class mean from the student's score and then divide the result by the standard deviation of the class.]

Page Ref: 525–526
Skill: Understanding
P: .80
D: .32

19) Mr. Skiebert gave the same physics test to each of his three senior classes. Analysis of the data revealed the following descriptive statistics:

Class	Mean	Standard Deviation
One	59	7.5
Two	68	6.2
Three	62	6.9

Compared to the two other classes, Mr. Skiebert can infer that students in Class One exhibit

   A) a narrow distribution of scores.

   B) greater variability.

   C) higher central tendency.

   D) lower variability.

Answer: B

Explanation: B) Mr. Skiebert can infer that *students in Class One exhibit greater variability than do students in the other two classes*. The standard deviation was highest (s = 7.5) for Class One. Class Three was the next most variable class (s = 6.9), while Class Three was the least variable (s = 6.2).

Page Ref: 525–526
Skill: Understanding
P: .79
D: .33

20) On the midterm, Ms. Gomez' first-period class had a mean of 79.5 and a standard deviation of 5. Her third-period class had a mean of 81.7 and a standard deviation of 17. Given only this information, what inference can be made?

A) The first period is more difficult to teach than third period.

B) The midterm was probably too difficult for both classes.

C) The third period is more difficult to teach than first period.

D) The two classes seem to be fairly equal in abilities.

Answer: C

Explanation: C) The best inference is that Ms. Gomez' *third-period class is more difficult to teach* than her first-period class. Even though its mean performance is slightly higher than that for the first period, the standard deviation for the third-period class is much larger—over three times that of first period. Thus, the abilities (and learning needs) of the third-period class are substantially more variable than those of students in the first period.

Page Ref: 526
Skill: Understanding

21) Approximately what percentage of the scores in a normal distribution is higher than one standard deviation above the mean?

A) 2.5 percent

B) 16 percent

C) 34 percent

D) 68 percent

Answer: B

Explanation: B) Approximately *16 percent* of the scores in a normal distribution are higher than one standard deviation above the mean. Similarly, 16 percent are lower than one standard deviation below the mean.

Page Ref: 526
Skill: Knowledge
P: .58
D: .57

22) In a normal distribution of scores, approximately what percent of the z-scores will be negative?

   A) 0

   B) 25

   C) 50

   D) Cannot determine from the information given.

   Answer: C

   Explanation: C) In a normal distribution, approximately *50%* of the z-scores will be negative
                   because half of the scores will fall below the mean and half above the mean.
                   [Why not **exactly** 50%? All scores exactly equal to the arithmetic mean will
                   have a z-score of 0.]

   Page Ref: 529
   Skill: Understanding
   P: .73
   D: .18

23) In a normal distribution, which one of the following measures of central tendency will have
    the highest value?

   A) Mean

   B) Median

   C) Mode

   D) The central tendencies will be equal.

   Answer: D

   Explanation: D) In a normal distribution, the distribution of scores is symmetrical, and the
                   mean (arithmetic average), median (middle score), and mode (most popular
                   score) fall exactly at the center of the distribution. Therefore, *all central
                   tendency statistics are equal*.

   Page Ref: 526
   Skill: Understanding
   P: .72
   D: .36

24) A percentile rank score of 70 means that the student

 A) answered a majority of the questions correctly.

 B) had 70 correct answers on the test.

 C) scored as well as or better than 70 percent of all the test–takers.

 D) scored at the seventh–grade level compared to other students.

Answer: C

Explanation: C) Percentile ranks indicate the percentage of scores that fall at or below a given score. In this case, the student *scored as well as or better than 70 percent of the examinees who took the same test*.

Page Ref: 527
Skill: Understanding
P: .82
D: .26

25) Jennifer, a seventh grader, received a percentile rank of 90 on a standardized vocabulary test. This percentile rank indicates that she

 A) exceeded the eighth–grade performance level.

 B) is as advanced as a ninth grader.

 C) scored above the average for seventh graders.

 D) should be assigned a grade of A for her performance.

Answer: C

Explanation: C) Jennifer's percentile rank of 90 indicates that she *scored above the average for seventh graders*, the norming group to which she is being compared. In fact, she scored extremely well, surpassing 90 percent of the norming sample.

Page Ref: 527
Skill: Understanding
P: .60
D: .28

26) Martin scored in the top 15 percent of his remedial reading class. If the norming group had included the regular and advanced students in his school, Martin's percentile rank would have been

   A) higher.

   B) lower.

   C) similar.

   D) unpredictable.

Answer: B

Explanation: B) Even though Martin was in the top 15 percent of his remedial reading class, *the addition of regular and advanced students to the norm group would lower Martin's position relative to the larger and stronger variability of the total group.* [The higher-achieving students would force the position of Martin's score to be lower when he is compared to all students.]

Page Ref: 527
Skill: Understanding
P: .73
D: .26

27) Sam, a seventh grader, received a grade-equivalent score of 9.2 on a standardized vocabulary test at the end of the spring term. This result indicates that Sam

   A) achieved about the same level as the average ninth graders in the norms group.

   B) knows as much vocabulary as the typical ninth grader in the norms group.

   C) scored above average compared to seventh graders in the norm group.

   D) should be awarded a grade of A for his achievement in vocabulary.

Answer: C

Explanation: C) *Sam scored above the average for seventh graders.* Grade equivalent scores (GE) do not indicate that someone can perform at the grade level supposedly indicated by the size of the GE score (9.2 in this case). Moreover, school grades should not be based on standardized test scores.

Page Ref: 528
Skill: Understanding
P: .52
D: .14

28) The *Public Speaking Aptitude Test* (PSAT) scores are reported for four students from their respective high schools. However, different standard scores were reported for each. Assuming that all scores were based on a raw score normal distribution, which student has the highest score?

   A) Angie: T–score = 57

   B) Bart: z–score = +1.33

   C) Kris: stanine = 5

   D) Larry: SAT–type score = 550

Answer: B

Explanation: B) *Bart has the highest score, because his z–score of 1.33 places him 1.33 standard deviations (s.d.) above the mean.* Angie's T–score is 0.7 s.d. above the mean, Kris scored in the middle stanine, and Larry's SAT score is 0.5 s.d. above the mean. [These values are based on the characteristics of the respective standard scores.]

Page Ref: 529
Skill: Understanding
P: .69
D: .36

29) In a normal distribution, a T–score of 60 is equal to approximately what percentile rank?

   A) 60

   B) 84

   C) 95

   D) 99

Answer: B

Explanation: B) In a normal distribution, a T–score of 60 is approximately equal to a percentile rank of *84*. Consider that a T–score of 60 equals a z–score of 1.00 ($T = 10 z + 50$). A z–score of +1.00 is exactly one standard deviation above the mean, which in a normal distribution accounts for 84 percent of the scores (50 + 34 = 84).

Page Ref: 529
Skill: Understanding
P: .57
D: .55

30) What score–reporting method decreases competition among students by representing the widest range of raw scores?

    A) Percentile ranks

    B) Stanines

    C) T–scores

    D) z–scores

Answer: B

Explanation: B) By consisting of only nine possible scores, *each stanine represents a wide range of scores*. This has the advantage of reducing competition and comparison, because fine distinctions between individuals cannot be made.

Page Ref: 529
Skill: Understanding
P: .50
D: .40

31) The following raw scores were obtained for Bill on four tests, together with the group mean and standard deviation for each test:

Test	Mean	s.d.	Bill's score
Reading	69	3	75
History	53	9	62
Math	37	4	49
Science	49	12	74

In relation to the groups for which the means and standard deviations were computed, on which test did Bill score highest?

    A) History

    B) Math

    C) Reading

    D) Science

Answer: B

Explanation: B) Bill scored the *highest on the math test*. Given the standard deviation of 4 and the class mean of 37, Bill's score of 49 in math was 3 standard deviations above the mean: $(49 - 37)/4 = 3$. On the other tests, Bill scored fewer standard deviations above the class mean.

Page Ref: 526
Skill: Understanding
P: .69
D: .35

32) Assuming that the raw scores are distributed normally, which one of the following standard scores indicates the best performance relative to the group being tested?

   A) Percentile rank of 60

   B) Stanine score of 8

   C) T–score of 59

   D) z–score of +.76

Answer: B

Explanation: B) The *8th stanine* indicates the best performance relative to the group being tested, because the 8th stanine is equal to about 1.5 standard deviations above the mean. [The highest stanine score is 9, with an overall average stanine score of 5.] The other scores are all lower, with the next highest being $T = 59$ (or .9 s above the mean), followed by the z–score (+.76) and then the percentile rank of 60. [These scores are directly comparable when the raw scores are distributed normally.]

Page Ref: 529
Skill: Understanding
P: .71
D: .46

33) Kathy took the *Stanford Achievement Test* on Monday and again on Friday. Her two scores differed by only three points. These results may indicate a good level of what type of reliability?

   A) Alternate–form

   B) Internal consistency

   C) Split–half

   D) Test–retest

Answer: D

Explanation: D) Kathy's performances are indicative of good *test–retest reliability*, a measure of consistency of performance on the same test taken at different times.

Page Ref: 530
Skill: Understanding
P: .84
D: .24

34) The *precision* of a test refers to test reliability as measured by what method?

A) Alternate–form

B) Internal consistency

C) Split–half

D) Test–retest

Answer: B

Explanation: B) The precision of a measurement tool refers directly to *internal consistency reliability*. Alternate–form reliability measures the degree of equivalence between two forms of a measure, while split–half reliability measures the degree to which the two halves of a test are equivalent. Test–retest reliability looks at the degree to which an individual is consistent over time with regard to what is being measured.

Page Ref: 530
Skill: Knowledge

35) One of the most efficient and effective ways to increase the reliability of a test is to

A) have more than one person grade the test.

B) keep the test brief.

C) lengthen the test.

D) provide ample response time.

Answer: C

Explanation: C) Reliability of a test can usually be increased effectively by *lengthening the test to include additional items that measure the objectives of instruction*. Adding items to a test will provide a more accurate picture of a student's "true" performance if the additional items are content relevant (that is, if they measure the same objectives as the other items).

Page Ref: 530
Skill: Understanding
P: .66
D: .40

36) Which one of the following definitions best describes "true score"?

   A) Confidence score if the test were perfectly reliable

   B) Hypothetical score on a student's best day

   C) Observed raw score plus the confidence score

   D) Obtained raw score minus measurement error

Answer: D

Explanation: D) The "true scores" for individuals represent their *obtained raw score minus measurement error*. The reverse way of conceptualizing this relationship is to think of *raw scores as reflecting hypothetical true scores plus testing (measurement) error*. In practice, standard errors of measurement are placed both above and below an individual's raw score to form confidence levels in which the true score is expected to lie. By adding one standard error to both sides of a score, it is expected that the true score will be in this error band approximately two out of three times (66 percent confidence level). Adding two error bands increases the confidence interval to 95 percent; adding three error bands virtually assures that the true score lies within this band (99.9 percent).

Page Ref: 531
Skill: Knowledge
P: .81
D: .21

37) Jerry scored 81 on a test. The mean of this test was 70, the standard deviation was 10, and the standard error of measurement was 2. Given these data, we can be reasonably certain (2 times out of 3) that Jerry's true score would be in the range from

   A) 71 to 91.

   B) 75 to 85.

   C) 77 to 87.

   D) 79 to 83.

Answer: D

Explanation: D) By adding one standard error to both sides of Jerry's score of 81, a reasonably certain conclusion (two times out of three) is that *Jerry's "true score" would fall in the range from 79 to 83.* Thus, the confidence band represents a range of scores in which the person's true score is likely to lie. The range from 77 to 85 represents the addition of two error bands and increases the probability of having the true score in this range to approximately 95 percent. [Response "a" and "b" represent adding two ("a") or one ("b") standard deviations to Jerry's score.]

Page Ref: 531
Skill: Understanding
P: .75
D: .39

38) A newspaper publishes the results of a stratified random survey of 2,500 adult Americans intended to assess the popularity of the President. The poll shows that he has an approval rating of 65 percent with an error of + or − 5 percent. This statistic is an example of a

   A) confidence band or interval.

   B) reliability estimate.

   C) standard deviation.

   D) standard error of measurement.

Answer: A

Explanation: A) A margin of error is often reported for the results of opinion polls, such as this newspaper poll, that reflects the *confidence band or interval for the results*. Therefore, the approval rating for the President in this poll ranged from 60 percent to 70 percent, including the margin for error (the standard error of measurement).

Page Ref: 531
Skill: Understanding
P: .55
D: .20

39) On standardized tests, a difference of a few points between two raw scores is likely to be insignificant due to the

   A) central limits theorem.

   B) confidence interval for the scores.

   C) equivalence reliability of the tests.

   D) probability of chance.

Answer: B

Explanation: B) Two scores that differ by only a few points may be reflective of similar abilities by the students concerned. Specifically, the *confidence bands, or confidence intervals, for the two scores are likely to overlap*, thus allowing for the possibility that the students' "true scores" fall close to the same value.

Page Ref: 531
Skill: Understanding

40) The validity of any test is related directly to the

A) difficulty of the test.

B) evaluation of expert reviewers.

C) length of the test.

D) purpose of the test.

Answer: D

Explanation: D) *A test is valid for a specific purpose.* Length of a test is related to its reliability, and test difficulty will influence the results. Expert reviews refer to the quality of an instrument, but all three of these alternatives are not concerned directly with test validity.

Page Ref: 531–532
Skill: Understanding
P: .50
D: .33

41) When a test actually measures what it purports to measure, the test is said to be

A) credible.

B) reliable.

C) usable.

D) valid.

Answer: D

Explanation: D) The definition of *validity* is that the test actually measures what it purports to measure. By comparison, reliability represents the consistency of test scores across repeated administrations of a test.

Page Ref: 531–532
Skill: Understanding
P: .82
D: .32

42) If a thermometer measured an oven's temperature as 400°F for five days in a row when the temperature was actually 350°F, this measuring instrument would be

    A) both reliable and valid.

    B) both unreliable and invalid.

    C) reliable but not valid.

    D) valid but not reliable.

Answer: C

Explanation: C) In this example of thermometer readings, the fact that the oven's temperature was consistently measured to be 400° Fahrenheit reflects reliability of measurement, but the true temperature was 350°, which raises a validity issue. Therefore, *the thermometer used was reliable but not valid.*

Page Ref: 531–532
Skill: Understanding
P: .64
D: .38

43) After administering a standardized test of reading comprehension, scores are compared to teacher estimates of reading comprehension for each student. What particular technical concern of measurement is involved in this comparison?

    A) Commonality

    B) Discrimination

    C) Reliability

    D) Validity

Answer: D

Explanation: D) When information comes from two different sources (test scores vs. teacher estimates) the relationship represents the *technical issue of validity.* In this case, the specific validity issue is criterion–related validity.

Page Ref: 531–532
Skill: Understanding
P: .58
D: .26

44) The evidence for validity that concerns whether the test measures the trait in question rather than some other trait is what type of evidence?

A) Construct–related

B) Content–related

C) Criterion–related

D) Test–retest

Answer: A

Explanation: A) *Construct validity concerns whether a test successfully measures a specific psychological characteristic or "construct" rather than some other construct.* This is the most difficult type of validity to assess and is considered to be the broadest category of validity, encompassing all other types of validity.

Page Ref: 532
Skill: Knowledge

45) What type of validity is currently thought to include all other types of validity?

A) Content–related

B) Construct–related

C) Criterion–related

D) Prediction–related

Answer: B

Explanation: B) *Construct–related* evidence of validity concerns how well a given instrument or procedure measures a specified psychological trait or set of traits. *Construct–related validity is now considered the broadest type of validity that encompasses all other specific types of validity, including content–related and criterion–related validity.*

Page Ref: 532
Skill: Knowledge

46) The connection between validity and reliability can be best expressed by the statement that validity

A) is essentially the same as reliability.

B) requires and may be assured through reliability.

C) requires but cannot be assured through reliability.

D) requires only a limited reliability.

Answer: C

Explanation: C) *Validity requires reliability, but cannot be assured by it.* Even though scores are consistent (reliable), suggesting a stable assessment, they still may not be measuring the construct desired. An example would be using jumping ability (a measure likely to be reliable) as an indicator of basketball aptitude (a construct that involves many more skills than jumping).

Page Ref: 532
Skill: Understanding

47) What types of standardized tests are teachers most likely to use today?

    A) Achievement and aptitude

    B) Aptitude and diagnostic

    C) Diagnostic and achievement

    D) Interest and aptitude

Answer: A

Explanation: A) The types of standardized test that teachers are most likely to use are
                achievement and aptitude tests. Diagnostic tests are a special type of achievement
                test that is used to identify an individual student's strengths and weaknesses
                in cognitive skills, while interest tests are classified in the aptitude category.

Page Ref: 536
Skill: Knowledge

48) Fred made 103 and Frank made 96 on an achievement test with a confidence interval of 4.
    These results indicate that

    A) Fred's true score is definitely higher than Frank's true score.

    B) measurement error can account for the differences in their scores.

    C) the true scores of each student are probably very close.

    D) the test used to generate these scores must be very reliable.

Answer: B

Explanation: B) A confidence interval represents a "standard error band" that encompasses a
                student's actual score. With a confidence interval of 4, Fred's score of 103 falls
                in the range from 99 to 107, whereas Frank's 96 falls within the range from 92
                to 100. Given the overlap between these intervals, *measurement error could
                account for the differences in their scores*.

Page Ref: 531
Skill: Understanding
P: .74
D: .25

49) On a standardized achievement test, Nicki's local percentile score is 63 and her national percentile rank is 75. It can be concluded accurately that

   A) Nicki answered 63 percent of the local questions correctly.

   B) Nicki did fairly poorly on the standardized test.

   C) the local norming sample scored lower than the national norming sample.

   D) the national norming sample scored lower than the local norming sample.

Answer: D

Explanation: D) Based on Nicki's percentile scores, it can be concluded that the *national norms sample scored lower than the local norms sample*. We know this because Nicki's national percentile score is higher than her local percentile score. Therefore, competition at the local level was greater (remember the meaning of percentile scores).

Page Ref: 538
Skill: Understanding

50) Mr. Roberts administered an individual standardized reading inventory to his fourth-grade students in order to assess where they are having problems in reading comprehension. What specific type of test should he have used?

   A) Criterion-referenced

   B) Diagnostic

   C) Norm-referenced

   D) Standardized

Answer: B

Explanation: B) Mr. Roberts is using a *diagnostic test*. The purpose of such tests is to identify the specific problems students are having (in this case, in reading comprehension). A diagnostic test may yield norm-referenced data that compare an individual to others or criterion-related data that compare an individual to preset criteria. In addition, a diagnostic test may be standardized.

Page Ref: 538
Skill: Understanding
P: .61
D: .33

51) Tests that are designed to predict future performance are what type of tests?

   A) Achievement

   B) Aptitude

   C) Diagnostic

   D) High–stakes end–of–school tests

Answer: B

Explanation: B) *Aptitude* tests (and ability tests) are designed to predict future performance, as opposed to assessing or diagnosing present achievement in some area. Diagnostic tests are designed to identify weaknesses and strengths in specific academic areas. High–stakes tests are designed to assess achievement of basic skills for the purpose of being qualified for high school graduation.

Page Ref: 538
Skill: Knowledge

52) IQ scores are normally distributed with a mean of 100 and a standard deviation of 15. Based on properties of the mathematical normal curve, which one of the following statements is **TRUE**?

   A) Approximately 90 percent of the scores fall between 85 and 115.

   B) A score of 70 is equally as probable as is a score of 130.

   C) There are more scores above 130 than below 85.

   D) There are more scores above the mean than below the mean.

Answer: B

Explanation: B) Given the properties of the normal curve, a *deviation IQ score of 70 would be equally as probable as one of 130*. Both are 30 points, two standard deviations from the mean (100; standard deviation of 15). Because the normal curve is symmetrical, scores at the identical positions above and below the mean occur with the same frequency. Only approximately two–thirds of the scores fall between scores of 85 and 115 (mean plus/minus one standard deviation).

Page Ref: 538
Skill: Understanding

53) What is the major issue underlying high–stakes testing?

    A) A decreased emphasis on standardized testing in favor of authentic testing

    B) An increased dependence on standardized tests for decision making

    C) The relatively high expense of testing large numbers of students

    D) The lack of validity of many standardized tests in use today

Answer: B

Explanation: B) High–stakes testing refers to the *increased dependence on standardized tests for decision–making*. The result is more pressure on teachers and administrators for students to improve on these tests.

Page Ref: 540
Skill: Knowledge
P: .74
D: .36

54) Molly is preparing to take a standardized test that will be used by administrators to evaluate the type of school placement she should have. What type of assessment is Molly involved in?

    A) Criterion–referenced

    B) High–stakes testing

    C) Norm–referenced

    D) Standardized aptitude testing

Answer: B

Explanation: B) The type of assessment that Molly is involved in is *high–stakes testing*, because the administration plans to use her results to determine what kind of curriculum Molly should have. Diagnostic assessment would provide a clearer picture of Molly's strengths and weaknesses that could be used to promote her strengths and overcome her weaknesses, but diagnostic assessment is not a response option for this item.

Page Ref: 540
Skill: Understanding
P: .86
D: .19

55) A test or any assessment instrument is objective to the extent that it

 A) is free of biases of the test administrators and scorers.

 B) measures only a very few variables at a time.

 C) predicts an important and realistic criterion.

 D) yields the same score each time an individual takes it.

Answer: A

Explanation: A) *Objectivity in assessment refers to the extent to which assessment is free of the biases of test administrators and scorers.* Objectivity is related to fairness of assessment and has nothing to do directly with prediction, measuring only a few variables, or yielding consistent scores.

Page Ref: 524
Skill: Understanding
P: .75
D: .35

56) Research on bias in testing indicates that standardized tests predict school achievement

 A) equally well for all groups of students.

 B) equally well for white, English-speaking students.

 C) very accurately for only a small percentage of students.

 D) very accurately for high SES students in all ethnic groups.

Answer: A

Explanation: A) Research on bias in tests indicates that standardized tests predict school achievement *equally well for all groups of students.* Nevertheless, there are good reasons to believe that such tests place minority group students at a disadvantage, particularly with regard to educational opportunities.

Page Ref: 532
Skill: Knowledge

57) Students from minority groups in deprived socioeconomic backgrounds who have taken culture-fair tests have generally performed

 A) better than other minority groups on standardized tests.

 B) better than their non-deprived peers but worse than non-minority groups.

 C) on par with or even worse than their own performances on other types of standardized tests.

 D) worse than their non-deprived peers if the test was individually administered.

Answer: C

Explanation: C) Efforts to develop culture fair tests have **NOT** been very successful. Students from low-income backgrounds have generally performed *on par with or even worse than their own performances on other types of standardized tests.*

Page Ref: 534
Skill: Knowledge

58) Which one of the following strategies is most likely to improve standardized test scores directly?

   A) Drills of vocabulary words

   B) Familiarity with the test–taking procedures

   C) Practice in quick computation

   D) Use of mnemonic memory aids

Answer: B

Explanation: B) One type of training that appears likely to improve standardized test scores directly is *familiarization with the process of testing*. Much of the advantage for some students may be due to greater confidence and practice with the answering procedures.

Page Ref: 533
Skill: Knowledge

59) Alicia is taking the revised math subtest of the *Scholastic Assessment Test* (SAT) test. What will she be asked to do that her older brother Fred did not have to do on a former SAT math subtest?

   A) Answer analogy questions.

   B) Construct responses.

   C) Read passages.

   D) Solve math problems.

Answer: B

Explanation: B) Alicia, in taking the new SAT test, will be *constructing responses* on both the math and writing sections. Her brother, Fred, only had to "bubble in" multiple–choice responses when he took a previous version of the test.

Page Ref: 532
Skill: Understanding

60) Mr. Garren has been emphasizing authentic testing in his social studies class. Which one of the following will be a likely result of this emphasis?

   A) Fewer essay tests

   B) More exhibitions by students of their work

   C) More mastery grading of performances

   D) More reliable grading of students

Answer: B

Explanation: B) Mr. Garren is likely to *have students give exhibitions of their work*. Exhibitions and portfolios are two commonly used authentic assessments.

Page Ref: 545–546
Skill: Understanding
P: .78
D: .36

61) Many states are now requiring procedures that include tests featuring a response format that will require

    A) convergent thinking and higher-level responses.

    B) divergent thinking and higher-level responses.

    C) higher-level recognition responses.

    D) problem-solving recognition responses.

Answer: B

Explanation: B) Many states are now responding to the call for constructed-response formats in their state-wide testing programs under the assumption that constructed-response formats will *encourage divergent thinking and higher-order learning*. Constructed-response items can require these types of learning, but there is no guarantee that, just because students must construct the answers, the items will necessarily require higher-order learning responses and divergent thinking responses. Consequently, constructed-response items require very careful creation by the item writer.

Page Ref: 546
Skill: Knowledge

Use this information for the following question(s). The following descriptive statistics are given for an educational psychology examination administered to 323 students (N). There were 60 multiple-choice items (k) on this test. The items in this set are classified as **Use of Knowledge** (U) items and are referenced to pp. 526–532 in Chapter 14.

Descriptive Statistics

$k = 60$	High score = 56
$N = 323$	Low score = 20
Mean = 40.45	$r_{alpha} = 0.78$
s (S.D.) = 7.45	$s_m = 3.40$

62) The reliability of this test was fairly weak.

    A) The conclusion in this item's statement is **NOT** supported by the above data.

    B) The conclusion in this item's statement is supported by the above data.

    C) There are insufficient data presented to warrant this conclusion.

    Answer: A

    Explanation: A) Because the reliability coefficient for this test is 0.78, it is interpreted as being quite strong (especially for a classroom test). Therefore, *the conclusion that the reliability of the test is weak is NOT supported by the data.* [Further evidence for this conclusion is presented in the feedback for Item 14.83.] Evidence for the stability of the test items could be obtained by administering this same instrument to another group of similar students and comparing the results for the two groups of students. [Actually this comparison was conducted the following semester with another large group of educational psychology students, and the internal reliability estimate was very similar in magnitude. However, because five or six items were substituted in the second test, a direct comparison between the two test administrations could not prove stability reliability for each item on the test.]

Page Ref: 530–531
Skill: Understanding
P: .68
D: .25

63) The amount of measurement error in the score distribution is acceptable.

   A) The conclusion in this item's statement is **NOT** supported by the above data.

   B) The conclusion in this item's statement is supported by the above data.

   C) There are insufficient data presented to warrant this conclusion.

Answer: B

Explanation: B) When test reliability is strong, the amount of measurement error (indicated here by 3.40 items) can be judged as acceptable. There is an inverse relationship between reliability and measurement error: the stronger the reliability, the less error of measurement. Therefore, *the data do support this conclusion*. [Another way to look at these data is to relate the standard error of measurement to the score range (variability): s_m divided by range (R) or $3.40/46 = 0.07$; or 7 percent error in the range of scores. Any error to range ratio less than 10 percent can be viewed to be acceptable, but the less error there is, the greater the reliability of the test.]

Page Ref: 531
Skill: Understanding
P: .72
D: .25

64) There are 5.30 standard deviation units in this distribution of scores.

   A) The conclusion in this item's statement is **NOT** supported by the above data.

   B) The conclusion in this item's statement is supported by the above data.

   C) There are insufficient data presented to warrant this conclusion.

Answer: A

Explanation: A) *The conclusion that there are 5.30 standard deviation units in the range of scores is not supported by the data*. The distance between the mean of 40.45 and the highest obtained score in the distribution (56) is 15.55 units ($56 - 40.45 = 15.55$). This value (15.55) divided by the observed size of the standard deviation (7.45) indicates that there are 2.08 standard deviations above the mean (mean $= 20.45 + 2.08$ *s.d.*). The distance between the lowest observed score (20) and the mean is 20.45 units ($40.45 - 20 = 20.45$). Therefore, the number of standard deviations below the mean is $20.45/7.45 = 2.75$ s.d. Adding the number of standard deviations above and below the mean yields $2.08 + 2.75 = 4.83$ standard deviations in this range of scores. Another way to determine this result is simply to divide the Range of scores (36) by the size of the standard deviation (7.45) $= 4.83$.

Page Ref: 526
Skill: Understanding
P: .67
D: .28

65) The central tendency of the score distribution indicates a symmetrical distribution.

   A) The conclusion in this item's statement is **NOT** supported by the above data.

   B) The conclusion in this item's statement is supported by the above data.

   C) There are insufficient data presented to warrant this conclusion.

   Answer: A

   Explanation: A) *The conclusion for this item is NOT supported by the data*. This distribution is **NOT** shaped symmetrically. There are more standard deviations below the mean (2.75) than above the mean (2.08), and the distance between the mean score and the lowest observed raw score is larger (20.25 points) than between the mean and the highest observed raw score (15.55 points).

   Page Ref: 525
   Skill: Understanding
   P: .48
   D: .28

66) The validity of this test is relatively strong.

   A) The conclusion in this item's statement is **NOT** supported by the above data.

   B) The conclusion in this item's statement is supported by the above data.

   C) There are insufficient data presented to warrant this conclusion.

   Answer: C

   Explanation: C) *There are insufficient data presented to support or refute the conclusion that the validity of this test is relatively strong*. Even though most of the test items were taken from the *Assessment Package* for the Woolfolk book, there is no direct evidence presented in the data to support the conclusion that the test represented even content validity. A behavior–content matrix, or test blueprint, would have been helpful for evaluating content validity, but even an apparently relevant behavior–content matrix is still no guarantee of content validity. Moreover, there was no evidence of criterion–related validity in the data.

   Page Ref: 531
   Skill: Understanding
   P: .63
   D: .38

67) A raw score of 33 places a student one standard deviation below the mean.

    A) The conclusion in this item's statement is **NOT** supported by the above data.

    B) The conclusion in this item's statement is supported by the above data.

    C) There are insufficient data presented to warrant this conclusion.

Answer: B

Explanation: B) By subtracting one standard deviation from the raw score mean of 40.45, the result is a score of 33. Therefore, *the data do support the conclusion that a raw score of 33 places a student one standard deviation below the group mean.*

Page Ref: 526
Skill: Understanding
P: .57
D: .40

Completion Questions

1) The process that includes many kinds of ways to sample and observe students' skills, knowledge, and abilities is _____.

Answer: assessment
Page Ref: 522

2) The process in assessment that provides a numeric description of a characteristic or event is _____.

Answer: measurement
Page Ref: 522

3) A test designed to measure differences in achievement among students is _____.

Answer: norm–referenced
Page Ref: 523

4) When test performances are compared to standards rather than to scores of others, the test is said to be _____ referenced.

Answer: criterion
Page Ref: 523

5) A large group of people representing a given grade level across the nation make up the _____ for a standardized achievement test.

Answer: norming sample
Page Ref: 524

6) A bar graph for a frequency distribution is called a(n) _____.

Answer: histogram
Page Ref: 525

7) The midpoint or middle score of a distribution is called the _____.

Answer: median
Page Ref: 525

8) A distribution of scores that contains two scores with the same highest number of examinees is _____.

Answer: bimodal
Page Ref: 525

9) The spread of scores around the mean is the _____.

Answer: standard deviation
Page Ref: 526

10) In a normal distribution, the type of derived score that has unequal units is _____.

Answer: percentile rank
Page Ref: 527

11) A standard score that directly expresses how many standard deviations a raw score is above or the below the mean is a _____.

Answer: z-score
Page Ref: 529

12) The type of standard score that represents the broadest range of raw scores is the _____ score.

Answer: stanine
Page Ref: 525

13) If scores of individuals are consistent over time, the test is said to have high _____.

Answer: reliability
Page Ref: 530

14) A test that measures what it is supposed to is considered to be _____.

Answer: valid
Page Ref: 531

15) When teachers want to identify specific strengths and weaknesses of students, a _____ test is appropriate.

Answer: diagnostic
Page Ref: 538

16) The type of standardized test that is used to predict future academic behavior is the _____ test.

Answer: aptitude
Page Ref: 538

17) In discussing standardized test results with students and their families, teachers should avoid reporting _____ scores.

Answer: grade-equivalent
Page Ref: 528

18) When critical decisions are made from test scores, the process is called _____ testing.

Answer: high-stakes
Page Ref: 540

19) Current interests in evaluating meaningful products of learning have led some states to develop alternative or _____ assessments to replace paper-and-pencil tests.

Answer: authentic
Page Ref: 545

20) Authentic "real-life" assessments are also called direct, alternative, and _____ assessments.

Answer: performance
Page Ref: 546

21) The format used in many of the new standardized tests used for college admission purposes is the _____ format.

Answer: constructed-response
Page Ref: 546

True/False Questions

1) Assessment is the term used to describe the process of gathering information about students' learning outcomes.

Answer: TRUE
Page Ref: 522

2) Measurement is the quantitative component of evaluation.

Answer: TRUE
Page Ref: 522

3) Norm-referenced tests are used to indicate progress toward specific competency levels.

Answer: FALSE
Page Ref: 523

4) Criterion-referenced assessment is valuable in determining mastery of basic skills.

Answer: TRUE
Page Ref: 525

5) The median is the score that occurs most often in a distribution.

Answer: FALSE
Page Ref: 526

6) Raw score distributions with large standard deviations have greater variability in the scores than distributions based on fewer items that have small standard deviations.

Answer: FALSE
Page Ref: 527

7) A percentile rank score of 60 means that a student is performing better than the majority of those taking the test.

Answer: TRUE
Page Ref: 527

8) A grade-equivalent score of 8.3 means that a student is capable of performing as well as an average eighth-grader in the third month of school.

Answer: FALSE
Page Ref: 528

9) A T-score distribution has a mean of 50 and a standard deviation of 10.

Answer: TRUE
Page Ref: 529

10) Reliability is the degree to which a test measures what it is supposed to measure.

Answer: FALSE
Page Ref: 530

11) The standard error of measurement is related inversely to test reliability, i.e., the smaller the SEM is, the higher the reliability coefficient is.

Answer: TRUE
Page Ref: 531

12) Content-related validity refers to the degree to which the test items cover the appropriate topics.

Answer: TRUE
Page Ref: 532

13) A test must be both reliable and valid in order to be useful.

Answer: TRUE
Page Ref: 532

14) Standardized ability and aptitude tests are less fair as predictors of school success than are teachers' grades.

Answer: FALSE
Page Ref: 536

15) High-stakes testing is what some educators use to make important decisions about students, teachers, and schools.

Answer: TRUE
Page Ref: 540

16) Authentic assessments are procedures that directly assess student performances in "real-life" situations.

Answer: TRUE
Page Ref: 545

17) Performance standards are criteria that specify the expected quality or level of student learning.

Answer: TRUE
Page Ref: 546

Short Answer Questions

1) Compare and contrast norm-referenced and criterion-referenced tests and identify situations where each would be appropriate.

Answer: *Norm-referenced (NR) tests:* Individuals are compared to the average or norm of a large group of people (class, school district, and nation) similar to the individuals being tested. NR tests are used in measuring overall achievement, to identify the range of abilities within a group, and to screen applicants for positions with a limited number of openings. *Criterion-referenced (CR) tests:* Individuals are compared to a predetermined set of performance standards. Criterion-referenced assessments are needed for measuring affective or motor skills and for evaluating whether students have mastered basic cognitive skills and are prepared for advancement to a new position or new level of achievement.
Page Ref: 523–524

2) Identify the three common measures of central tendency. Which one of the three measures do you believe to be the most informative for assessing the typical performance of a group of students? Explain your selection.

Answer: The three measures of central tendency are the mean, median, and mode. The mean is the numerical average of the scores. It is calculated by adding the scores and dividing the total by the number of scores in the distribution. The median is the middle score in the distribution; it is determined by finding (or calculating) the score that divides the distribution in half. The mode is the score that occurs most frequently (the most popular score) in the distribution. [The mean is generally the most useful measure because it is affected by the actual size of all of the scores. Change any score and the mean will change; this is not true of the median or mode.]

Page Ref: 525

3) Define and distinguish between reliability and validity. Is it necessary for a test to be valid in order for it to be reliable? Is it necessary for a test to be reliable in order for it to be valid? Explain your decisions.

Answer: Test reliability means that the test yields consistent and stable scores. For example, if you took an aptitude test this week and the same aptitude test next week, you should obtain similar scores. Reliability is assessed as test–retest reliability, alternate–form reliability, and split–half or internal consistency reliability. If a test is reliable, however, it may not be valid, which means assessing what the instrument is supposed to measure. Validity is represented as content–related validity (appropriate topics), criterion–related validity (predictor of performance), and construct–related validity (assessing the trait in question). Construct–related validity is now viewed as the overall concept of validity under which all other types are subsumed. In order to be valid, an assessment tool must be reliable. However, a reliable measure is not necessarily a valid measure.

Page Ref: 530–531

4) Woolfolk discusses three basic types of standardized tests in her text. Identify the three types of tests and describe how they differ. Are there any similarities among them? Is so, what are the similarities?

Answer: *Achievement measures:* Assess learning in specific content areas, usually norm–referenced, may help with diagnostic purposes as well.
Diagnostic measures: Individual tests given by specialists to identify problem areas, more commonly given to younger students than to older students. Some diagnostic measures are designed for administration to groups of individuals.
Aptitude measures: Attempt to predict future performance and can be focused on scholastic performance (or vocational interests). [However, vocational interest tests, attitude scales, and personality inventories are usually descriptive measures rather than predictive of future performance.]

Page Ref: 536–539

5) Discuss current changes in the conceptions and practices of testing. Address the specific issues of authentic assessments in your answer.

Answer: Today, the growing trend in the practice of testing is decreased satisfaction with conventional standardized paper–and–pencil tests of students' achievement. Such tests are viewed as assessing fairly low–level skills under artificial conditions. Opportunities for students to demonstrate problem-solving skills or creativity are minimal or nonexistent on typical standardized tests. The authentic assessment movement advocates increased use of assessments that require performance on complex tasks in realistic contexts. These tests would emphasize meaningful problems and constructed–response formats such as demonstrations, essays, problem solutions, graphs, diagrams, projects, etc. The result would be the ability to measure higher level and divergent thinking, as opposed to convergent thinking through selection of specific correct answers (as on multiple–choice tests). An example of these changes is the revision of the SAT, which uses constructed responding in math and writing subtests. In addition, *Praxis II* and *Praxis III* of the new National Teacher Examination require realistic, constructed–response productions from pre-service teachers. However, reliability and validity issues associated with authentic assessment tools and techniques must be addressed. To date, standards for performance quality are determined arbitrarily by individual teachers and others who use these measures in educational and business settings.

Page Ref: 539–543

Case Studies

An angry parent corners Mr. Watson, the assistant principal of Cummings Elementary School, in the hallway. "Look at Jennifer's State Achievement scores," the mother said. "I had asked at the beginning of the year that Jennifer should skip seventh grade and be put into the eighth grade. These scores tell me that I was right." Mr. Watson examines the scores and sees the following:

Jennifer Smith 7th Grade: November 13,1997

Subject	T–Score	G–E Score
Math	55	8.0
Language Arts	52	7.8
Social Studies	60	8.8
Science	48	7.3
Writing	53	8.1

1) Define and identify uses of T–scores and grade–equivalent (GE) scores. What are their advantages and limitations?

Answer: Jennifer's T–scores indicate she is above average in all subjects with the exception of science. The mean for the T–distribution is 50 (with a standard deviation of 10), therefore, we can see Jennifer is not far below the expected average score for science. The greatest benefit of T–scores is that they are standardized scores meaning we can compare scores derived from scales in which the mean can represent varying values. T–scores are based on the standard deviation; therefore, a difference of 5 points has the same meaning everywhere on the scale. T–scores can be easier to interpret than z scores because they cannot have a negative value.

Jennifer's *G–E* scores are based on the average of scores based on comparison with norming samples from both the seventh and eighth grade. For example, her language arts G–E scores = 7.8, which can be interpreted as the average performance of a seventh grader and the decimal stands for the tenths of a year (typically interpreted as months). G–E scores can be challenging to interpret and are frequently misleading. For example, Jennifer's G–E score of 8.8 in social studies does not necessarily mean she should be advanced to an eighth-grade social studies class. It is important to note the norming sample procedure. Different forms of tests are used at different grade levels, so Jennifer may not have had the items that would be given to eighth graders. We only know that she did well on items given to seventh graders. Another caution regarding the use of G–E scores is that educators will want to have very detailed information about the norming sample utilized in the investigation.

Page Ref: 529, 536–537

2) Interpret Jennifer's T–score of 60. Based on normal curve properties, what is her approximate percentile rank? Describe how you determined her percentile rank.

Answer: Jennifer's T–score of 60 in social studies reveals that she scored 1 standard deviation above the mean. The mean and standard deviation for the T–score distribution is 50 and 10, respectively. Based on the properties of the normal curve, we can see that Jennifer scored at the eighty-fourth percentile. That is, 84 percent of the other students scored at or below her test score. The figures on page 521 and 522 illustrate how to find the percentile rank by first locating Jennifer's score, which is 1 standard deviation above the mean.

Page Ref: 527–528

In Hillcrest County, schools are held accountable for student learning through the requirement that every student take the *Northern States Achievement Test* (NSAT). Results are examined by district administrators and published in the local newspaper. At Dexter Elementary, a new reading program was implemented in the primary grades this year, and it was found to raise student performance on individually–administered reading tests by a full standard deviation. Ms. Manetti, the school principal, noted that there was no gain on the NSAT reading scores for those classes. Therefore, she decides to discontinue the new reading program.

3) How would the state test the Hillcrest individual reading tests differ with regard to the type of information obtained about reading performance? Assuming that both are well–constructed tests, which one would be likely to provide the more valid information? Explain.

Answer: The two types of tests differ in regards to how test scores are interpreted. The Hillcrest individual reading test is based on interpreting an individual's change in test scores. Whereas the state test (NSAT) is a norm–referenced achievement test, which means a child's score is compared to the scores of other children in the norming sample. It is always important to obtain information about the norming sample (size of sample, school funding, cultural background of students) used for the investigation. One of the issues in standardized testing is that teachers may not be teaching the exact same content as that covered in the test. In addition to content, the two types of tests may differ greatly in how the test is administered. Standardized tests are often administered in a group setting, whereas many locally developed tests are administered individually to children because they are often used for diagnostic assessment purposes.

Page Ref: 523–523

4) Do you agree with Ms. Manetti's decision? Explain your answer.

Answer: Ms. Manetti's decision is understandable given the widespread use of standardized testing in the United States. As noted by Woolfolk, all US states require some type of standardized testing based on multiple-choice questions. One concern is that some tests rely overly much on multiple-choice test items, as evidenced by the fact than only 18 states have student-constructed or essay-type items. As noted in Chapters 14 and 15, developing valid and reliable items and tests is not an easy task. We would not recommend educators make high states decisions based on the results from one type of tests. While we may not agree with Ms. Manetti's decision to eliminate the new reading program, we can see the benefits of many types of tests that serve different purposes and provide different information regarding student learning.

Page Ref: 545–546

5) Evaluate the situation at Dexter Elementary relative to the issue of high-stakes testing. Explain how standardized achievement tests can influence the curriculum at schools using high-stakes tests.

Answer: One of the benefits of standardized achievement tests is that they can hold teachers, schools, and administrators accountable for student learning outcomes. As noted in the new legislation (i.e., No Child Left Behind Act), teachers and schools will need to make their learning objectives explicit and develop plans for assessing students' progress through grade levels. Another benefit to standardized testing programs is that it gets parents, legislators, and educators engaged in dialog about student learning. However, there are also many cautions regarding the use of such high-stakes assessment. While we may agree with the benefits of using data to make good decisions, we must recognize how costly and difficult it is to gather high quality data (based on valid and reliable test scores). High-stakes tests do run the risk of forcing teachers to "teach to the test" and can limit a teacher's innovation and expertise. Also, when schools are labeled as a "failing school" due to low scores on standardized tests, we must be concerned about implications of such labeling for teacher morale and teacher self-efficacy.

Page Ref: 524, 534, 539–54

Chapter 15   Classroom Assessment and Grading

Multiple–Choice Questions

1) "We will have weekly quizzes, but your final grade will be based only on the midterm and final exam." This decision implies that the quizzes are to be used for what type of evaluation?

   A) Criterion–referenced

   B) Formative

   C) Norm–referenced

   D) Summative

   Answer: B

   Explanation: B) Evidently, the quizzes are to be used for *formative evaluation*, because they will be used to help students and the teacher gauge the level of success, without using the results for grading purposes. The latter function would be part of summative evaluation.

   Page Ref: 554
   Skill: Understanding
   P: .71
   D: .49

2) What type of test would provide the most useful information for the following question: "Are students making satisfactory progress in learning the metric system?"

   A) Diagnostic

   B) Formative

   C) Placement

   D) Summative

   Answer: B

   Explanation: B) *Formative tests* would provide the most useful information for determining students' progress in learning the metric system. Unlike summative tests, which assess "final" performance, formative tests are used to provide information about how students are achieving while working on a unit of study.

   Page Ref: 5545
   Skill: Understanding
   P: .80
   D: .39

3) What type of test would provide the most useful information for the following question: "Are the learning outcomes for the new unit sequenced appropriately?"

   A) Diagnostic

   B) Formative

   C) Placement

   D) Summative

Answer: B

Explanation: B) *Formative evaluation* would be most appropriate for assessing whether the learning outcomes for a new unit are sequenced appropriately. One purpose of formative tests is to determine how well instruction is working while it is being tried out and before it is placed in "final" form.

Page Ref: 554
Skill: Understanding
P: .75
D: .17

4) At the beginning of the semester, Mr. Rumstead gave a formative test for the purposes of setting objectives. At the end of the course he gave the same test to determine grades. The second time this test was given, it was used as what type of test?

   A) Aptitude

   B) Diagnostic

   C) Formative

   D) Summative

Answer: D

Explanation: D) Mr. Rumstead is using the results for *summative purposes*, i.e., to evaluate the effectiveness of instruction after it has been delivered. In contrast, formative test information is used to help teachers in planning and refining instruction.

Page Ref: 554
Skill: Understanding
P: .83
D: .28

5) A major difference between formative and summative tests is the

    A) format of the test items.

    B) interpretation of the test data.

    C) preparation of the test directions.

    D) role played by content validity in the two tests.

Answer: B

Explanation: B) A major difference in the construction of norm–referenced and criterion–referenced testing is in the *interpretation of the results.* Norm–referenced tests require items that are "discriminating" and, therefore, they have a moderate degree of difficulty. For criterion–referenced tests, accuracy in measuring the desired skill, not the difficulty of the item, is the main concern.

Page Ref: 554
Skill: Understanding
P: .75
D: .22

6) The concept of using cumulative questions in classroom assessment as a key to effective learning is illustrated best in which one of the following situations?

    A) Ms. Ames gives frequent short tests to students in her algebra class.

    B) Mr. Connors uses many items from his previous tests for his final examination on civics.

    C) Ms. DeSilva requires her ninth–grade students to apply information learned to new problems.

    D) Mr. Worland uses a great variety of test item types to evaluate his students' understanding of science concepts.

Answer: C

Explanation: C) *By requiring her students to apply information learned to new problems, Ms. DeSilva is illustrating the most powerful use of summative assessment. In order to solve new problems, students must understand what they have previously learned. Such is not the case in Mr. Connors' simple repeating of questions that he asked on previous tests, Ms. Ames and her short tests, and Mr. Worland using a variety of item types to evaluate science concepts (the items may or may not measure understanding).*

Page Ref: 554
Skill: Understanding
P: .34
D: .32

7) The term *objective* as used in objective testing refers to the

    A) content goals of the items.

    B) goal(s) of the test.

    C) type of material covered.

    D) way the test is scored.

Answer: D

Explanation: D) The term *objective* in objective testing refers to the *manner in which the test is scored*. Objective means "not open to many interpretations." An example is a multiple-choice test that is scored correct or incorrect.

Page Ref: 556
Skill: Knowledge
P: .72
D: .36

8) A test or rating scale is objective to the extent that it

    A) is free of biases of the administrators and scorers.

    B) measures only one, or only a very few variables.

    C) predicts an important and realistic criterion.

    D) yields the same score each time an individual takes it.

Answer: A

Explanation: A) A test or rating scale is objective to the extent that the instrument is *free of scorer or administrator biases*. [Response options *b* and *c* refer to validity concerns, and *d* refers to reliability.]

Page Ref: 557
Skill: Knowledge
P: .88
D: .28

9) Which one of the following actions is a *limitation* of multiple-choice tests?

    A) Allow for bluffing

    B) Are difficult to grade

    C) Can be difficult to prepare

    D) Cannot measure higher-order learning

Answer: C

Explanation: C) The only limitation of multiple-choice items among those actions listed is that items *can be very difficult to construct when higher-order thinking skills are to be assessed*. Multiple-choice items do not permit bluffing nor are they difficult to grade, but they can measure high-level skills.

Page Ref: 557
Skill: Understanding
P: .53
D: .32

10) What guideline for writing multiple-choice items is violated in the following item stem? "A norm–referenced test is..."

   A) Each alternative must fit the grammatical form of the item.

   B) Item stems should be stated in simple terms.

   C) The stem should include a complete question.

   D) Unessential details should be omitted in the item stem.

Answer: C

Explanation: C) The item stem in this multiple–choice question *should include a complete question* so that knowledgeable students could answer the item correctly without having to read the response choices. In other words, the item would then function as a short–answer or completion item. "Each alternative should fit the grammatical form of the item" is incorrect because no response choices were even presented. Moreover, "unessential details were omitted from the item" would be an incorrect answer because the exact opposite is true: not enough information is presented in the item stem. The stem certainly is presented in simple terms but much too simple!

Page Ref: 557–558
Skill: Understanding

11) When you write multiple–choice items, you should use

   A) as much wording as possible in the distractors.

   B) distractors that require fine discriminations.

   C) "none of the above" less frequently than "all of the above."

   D) stems that present a single problem.

Answer: D

Explanation: D) The stems in multiple–choice items should *present a single problem*. Also, nonessential details should be left out. The result is a clearer and more readable question. It is also advisable not to repeat words in the alternatives that could be included in the stem, and distractors that require very fine discriminations should be avoided. Finally, use of "all of the above" and "none of the above" should be avoided.

Page Ref: 557–558
Skill: Knowledge

12) What is the most serious problem in the multiple–choice test item that you are now reading?

   A) Distractor responses should be clearly incorrect.

   B) Students should not have to discriminate between the alternative choices.

   C) The response choices include two distractors that essentially have the same meaning.

   D) The stem does not present a single, straightforward problem.

   Answer: D

   Explanation: D) The most serious problem in this item is that *there is no clear, straight–forward problem stated in the stem*. Unless the four response options were presented, students would have no idea how to answer the question. This is similar to the problem with item 15.20, but the presentation of a no clear stem option was not given. [The other choices are **NOT** good choices.]

   Page Ref: 558, 560
   Skill: Understanding
   P: .72
   D: .34

13) The most important use of essay tests is to

   A) measure simple learning outcomes.

   B) measure complex learning outcomes.

   C) reduce grading time.

   D) sample a wide variety of learning outcomes.

   Answer: B

   Explanation: B) The main advantage of essays is providing the *potential for the most valid test of complex learning outcomes*. Therefore, essay tests should be reserved for measuring high–level thinking skills. Essay tests are less efficient than objective tests, however, with regard to grading time, assessing simple learning outcomes, and in assessing a wide variety of learning outcomes.

   Page Ref: 559
   Skill: Knowledge
   P: .89
   D: .20

14) All of the following statements are true of essay tests **EXCEPT:**

    A) Each question should give students a precise task.

    B) Less material can be covered in essay than in multiple–choice tests.

    C) Students should be able to answer the questions in a few words for the sake of efficiency.

    D) Questions should measure the higher–level objectives.

Answer: C

Explanation: C) Because the main purpose of essays is to measure higher–level objectives, such as analysis, synthesis, and evaluative thinking, it would not make sense to construct questions that *could be answered in a few words*. Such questions might be more appropriately presented as multiple–choice items.

Page Ref: 559–560
Skill: Knowledge
P: .84
D: .19

15) Starch and Elliot's classic 1912 experiments dealing with the extent of teachers' personal values and biases in scoring essay tests demonstrated what measurement issue that still plagues essay scoring today?

    A) Objectivity

    B) Relevance

    C) Reliability

    D) Validity

Answer: C

Explanation: C) The results of Starch and Elliot's classic 1912 study of the effects of teachers' personal views and biases on their scoring of essay tests demonstrated the problem of *scorer reliability*. This issue still is a major problem today with scoring essay tests and with the authentic (performance or alternative) assessment techniques.

Page Ref: 559–560
Skill: Understanding

16) The most important result of the series of studies conducted by Starch and Elliot in 1912 and 1913 is that the problem of grading was

   A) influenced by certain qualities of the essays themselves.

   B) motivated by rewarding linguistic style over content.

   C) not confined to any particular subject area.

   D) rewarding quantity of the product rather than its quality.

Answer: C

Explanation: C) Starch and Elliot's 1912 and 1913 studies highlighted the fact that unreliability of scoring was *not limited to any particular academic subject*. The same wide variability in grading was found in 1913 for mathematics (geometry) and history as was found by their initial study of English examination papers.

Page Ref: 559
Skill: Knowledge

17) Studies on subjectivity in grading essays have indicated that English teachers tend to score

   A) complex, lengthy answers more highly than simple answers.

   B) most essay examinations reliably and accurately.

   C) neatly written, brief answers more highly than lengthy answers.

   D) simple, direct answers more highly than complex answers.

Answer: A

Explanation: A) Research by Fiske (1981) found that higher scores on essay tests are generally given by English teachers to *neatly written, lengthy, complex answers than to the simple, straightforward language that most teachers claim is the goal for good writing*. These results emphasize the need to specify clear scoring rules (score rubrics) and procedures. Gronlund (2000) has proposed strategies for alleviating the problems of subjectivity and inaccuracy.

Page Ref: 559
Skill: Knowledge
P: .80
D: .35

18) What is the major problem in scoring essay tests?

   A) Difficulty with establishing time limits for responding

   B) Limiting the content covered compared to objective tests

   C) Restricting the tasks to more complex learning outcomes

   D) Subjectivity in assessing the learning products

Answer: D

Explanation: D) The major problem in scoring essay tests is *subjectivity in assessing the learning products*, which leads to lack of reliability in scoring by different scorers.

Page Ref: 559–560
Skill: Knowledge

19) The most defensible practice for scoring essay tests is to evaluate

A) all parts of one student's paper before going on to the next student's paper.

B) each one of the items for all students with reference to its respective model answers.

C) each question as acceptable or unacceptable and assign equal weight to each question.

D) the response for each question with regard to content, organization, and mechanics, with each factor weighted equally.

Answer: B

Explanation: B) The most defensible practice for grading essay tests is to *evaluate each of the questions with reference to its respective model answer*. The model answers provide a framework or guide for scoring that should increase the objectivity and reliability of the evaluation process.

Page Ref: 560
Skill: Knowledge
P: .60
D: .46

20) Which one of the following strategies does **NOT** tend to increase the *reliability* of essay test grades?

A) Base your ratings on a model answer that you have constructed.

B) Grade all essay items for each student in turn based on a pre–established point system.

C) Have students place their names on the back of their test papers.\

D) Score all responses to one essay item before moving on to the next item.

Answer: B

Explanation: B) *Grading all essays for students in turn based on a pre–established point system would* **NOT** *increase the reliability of essay scores*. By the time the teacher graded the second student's essay, he or she would probably forget the grading standards used on the same essay question for the first student. A better procedure is to grade a given essay item for all students before grading the next essay item.

Page Ref: 559–560
Skill: Understanding
P: .53
D: .35

21) Identify the type of objective test item that is most appropriate for measuring the following specific learning outcome: "Select the best reason for a specific action from a given list of alternatives."

    A) Essay

    B) Multiple–choice

    C) Short–answer

    D) True–false

Answer: B

Explanation: B) The best item for measuring "selects the best reason for a specific action from list of alternatives" would be *multiple–choice*. Multiple–choice items provide choices (alternatives) from which the student is asked to select the correct or best answer.

Page Ref: 557–558
Skill: Understanding
P: .72
D: .23

22) Objective tests are generally more reliable than essay tests because objective tests can

    A) be corrected for guessing a response correctly.

    B) contain more independent items measuring achievement.

    C) eliminate subjective judgment in their preparation.

    D) measure almost any important educational attainment.

Answer: B

Explanation: B) Objective tests are generally more reliable than essay tests because they *contain more independent measures of achievement*. Specifically, whereas essay tests can contain only a few questions, an objective test can contain many items, each of which is scored objectively.

Page Ref: 556–558
Skill: Understanding
P: .68
D: .30

23) The key feature of authentic assessments is

    A) development of tests by professional evaluators.

    B) high test–retest reliability.

    C) testing in a realistic context.

    D) use of essays as the primary form of testing.

Answer: C

Explanation: C) The key feature of authentic assessment is testing in a realistic context so that students can be judged on their performances (thinking, creative, or other) on real–life tasks as opposed to scores on paper–and–pencil tests. The primary purpose of requiring students to prepare portfolios of various samples of their work is *to demonstrate students' abilities in areas other than test results*. Portfolios are regarded as evidence of authentic performances or work samples of student achievements. A major problem with portfolios is determining the reliability and validity of portfolios. To date, college admissions personnel do not require student portfolios for college admission purposes (too cumbersome, probably), nor do most prospective employers. However, preservice teachers in many colleges are now being asked to prepare portfolios representing some of their college achievements for use in interviewing for teaching positions.

Page Ref: 561–562
Skill: Knowledge
P: .68
D: .38

24) What type of test purpose is most likely to emphasize a constructed–response format?

    A) Authentic

    B) Formative

    C) Norm–referenced

    D) Summative

Answer: A

Explanation: A) *Authentic assessments* are designed to test complex, higher–level, and real–life outcomes as opposed to lower–level skills as reflected in many standardized and teacher-made tests. One way of doing this is to *make greater use of constructed–response formats* in which students create responses rather than simply select them. [However, the constructed response tasks must be designed to measure higher-order skills.]

Page Ref: 562
Skill: Knowledge

25) Which one of the following procedures best reflects performance assessment?

   A) Making a class presentation that utilizes more than one medium to demonstrate the steps to follow in designing a specific communication

   B) Performing well enough on the SAT to obtain a combined Verbal and Quantitative score of at least 1080

   C) Submitting a journal that will be evaluated on the basis of whether it contains notes for each class meeting

   D) Writing an essay on the "Republican Revolution" in the 1994 elections, citing primary social, economic, and political forces that led to this event

Answer: A

Explanation: A) The best example of a performance assessment in the alternatives presented for this item is *making a class presentation utilizing more than one medium to demonstrate the steps to follow in designing a specific communication*. This task requires actual performance on the part of a student and reflects at least the analysis and synthesis levels of Bloom's cognitive taxonomy. Writing an essay and earning a combined SAT Verbal and Quantitative score of 1080 are clearly traditional cognitive tasks that do **NOT** require students to make a personal performance. Writing and submitting a journal can be viewed as an alternative assessment technique but one that requires merely a checklist to assess whether a journal contains class notes. Therefore, this task is not a good example of a performance assessment procedure.

Page Ref: 562–564
Skill: Understanding
P: .71
D: .26

26) Based on Woolfolk's description of authentic testing, it can be inferred that such assessments could prove

   A) difficult to compare student products to established standards.

   B) effective in providing reliable and equitable outcomes for all students.

   C) relatively easy to grade reliably, but subjectivity will still be a problem.

   D) unpopular among educators who champion constructivist views.

Answer: A

Explanation: A) Because authentic assessments evaluate student performance in context, such assessments *are difficult to compare student products to established standards*. Providing equitable and reliable outcomes for all students is a major problem for authentic assessments. They are very difficult to grade reliably which means that subjectivity is always a problem. However, many consider the advantages of testing in real contexts to outweigh these limitations.

Page Ref: 562–564
Skill: Understanding
P: .78
D: .27

27) The two most serious limitations of essay test items are

    A) organization and reliability of grading.

    B) reliability and validity.

    C) reliability and representativeness.

    D) validity and objectivity.

Answer: C

Explanation: C) The two most serious limitations of essay questions are *reliability because the grading is subjective and representativeness because only a few questions can be asked*, as opposed to many questions on the full range of the instructional material.

Page Ref: 559–560
Skill: Understanding
P: .56
D: .26

28) Which one of the following sources would be the **LEAST** likely product to be found in a student's portfolio?

    A) Artistic products

    B) Peer comments

    C) Standardized test results

    D) Written products

Answer: C

Explanation: C) *Standardized test results* are the products that are **LEAST** likely to be found in student portfolios. Artistic products, peer products, and other written products are examples of authentic assessments that are very likely to be found in student portfolios.

Page Ref: 562–566
Skill: Knowledge

29) Exhibitions differ from portfolios because exhibitions

    A) are authentic assessments.

    B) involve an immediate audience.

    C) use criterion–referenced standards.

    D) use norm–referenced standards.

Answer: B

Explanation: B) Exhibitions differ from portfolios in that exhibitions *involve an immediate audience*. Like portfolios, they comprise a form of authentic testing and require criterion–referenced grading. Moreover, exhibitions also have similar reliability and validity problems. Examples of these problems are reflected by the scoring of figure skating, gymnastics, cheerleading and other similar championships.

Page Ref: 562
Skill: Knowledge

30) Which one of the following statements is **TRUE** regarding the use of portfolios in assessment?

A) Criterion-referenced rather than norm-referenced grading should be used.

B) Only positive samples of student performances should be selected for a portfolio.

C) Portfolios work best with older students (middle or high school).

D) Teachers rather than students should select the work to be included in the portfolio.

Answer: A

Explanation: A) Assessments of portfolios and other authentic tests should be *criterion-referenced by focusing on the quality of the products rather than comparisons with other students.* Students should be involved in selecting the work that will make up the portfolio or exhibition.

Page Ref: 566-567
Skill: Knowledge
P: .66
D: .29

31) Which one of the following procedures would improve the reliability and validity of grading short essay tests, thus refuting the complaint of sensitivity to bias and variability in grading?

A) Administering more pretests

B) Grading on the curve

C) Implementing a contract system

D) Using a scoring rubric

Answer: D

Explanation: D) The reliability and validity of grading short essay tests would be improved by *using a scoring rubric*. A rubric provides a set of directions for scorers to follow. Woolfolk provides a set of guidelines for developing a rubric in this chapter.

Page Ref: 567
Skill: Knowledge

32) A recommended procedure for authentic assessment is

A) grading on the curve in order to determine overall performance scores.

B) having students participate in developing the rating scales and scoring rubrics to be used in evaluation.

C) using authentic testing initially with higher-achieving students, with gradual integration of other students.

D) using only clearly defined, highly structured tasks or problems.

Answer: B

Explanation: B) One recommended procedure for authentic testing is to *permit student participation in developing scoring rubrics and rating scales to be used in evaluation*. Authentic assessments should **NOT** use grading on the curve or be restricted to certain students (all should participate). Moreover, using only clearly-defined tasks is incorrect (ambiguous tasks are encouraged).

Page Ref: 562–564
Skill: Knowledge

33) The basic difference between rating scales and scoring rubrics is that

A) rating scales provide general descriptions of overall performance, while scoring rubrics provide specific feedback.

B) rating scales provide norm-referenced interpretations of performance, while scoring rubrics provide criterion-referenced interpretations.

C) scoring rubrics provide criterion-referenced interpretations of performance, while rating scales provide norm-referenced interpretations.

D) scoring rubrics provide general descriptions of overall performance, while rating scales provide specific feedback.

Answer: D

Explanation: D) The basic difference between rating scales and scoring rubrics is that *scoring rubrics provide general descriptions of overall performances and rating scales provide feedback on specific features of a performance*. The issue of norm-referenced evaluation strategies does not really apply to authentic assessments, except perhaps in competitive performances such as gymnastics or figure skating when judges evaluate not only quality of performance but also comparisons among competitors. [Even though the rating scales that judges use are focused on quality features, competitive aspects do creep in; for example, note the relationship between a contestant's country of origin and that country's judge in Olympic gymnastics and figure skating competitions.]

Page Ref: 567
Skill: Knowledge

34) A scoring rubric that permits raters to use a 50-point scale compared to using a five-point scale will tend to yield

   A) higher reliability.

   B) lower reliability.

   C) reduced variability in scoring.

   D) restricted validity in scoring.

Answer: B

Explanation: B) The wider the range of score points permitted by a rubric, the *lower the reliability of scoring* will be. By forcing decisions to be made within a narrow scoring band, such as scores from one to five, the greater the chance of scorers agreeing on the value of the product. When a large range of possible points is provided, scores will tend to be spread out over the entire range and, therefore, agreement among scorers will be less than it would be when only a small score range is permitted.

Page Ref: 567–568
Skill: Knowledge

35) Do evaluations of portfolios, exhibitions, and other types of authentic assessment products have the same measurement concerns as those for classroom and standardized tests?

   A) No, because authentic assessments are constructed by the students themselves.

   B) No, because authentic assessments are inherently valid and fair to students.

   C) Yes, because authentic assessments have the same potential for invalidity and unfairness.

   D) Yes, because authentic assessments promote learning better than paper-and-pencil tests.

Answer: C

Explanation: C) *Yes, authentic assessments have the same potential for invalidity and unfairness as do other tests*. The evaluation of authentic tests must be done reflectively and carefully. Moreover, merely because an assessment is "authentic" does not necessarily mean it is reliable and valid. For example, the context for the authentic testing situation may not be representative of usual, appropriate, or real-life contexts (if the context is not valid, the evaluation is certainly not fair or reliable). The technical concerns of reliability, validity, and fairness are extremely important issues in authentic assessments, just as they continue to be for traditional assessment tools and procedures.

Page Ref: 567–568
Skill: Understanding
P: .69
D: .28

36) In a study by Margaret Clifford, the participants who were best prepared to deal with failure were those who had experienced what percent success on a previous task?

  A) 10

  B) 25

  C) 50

  D) 100

Answer: C

Explanation: C) In a study by Margaret Clifford, students who succeeded only *fifty percent of the time* before a failure experience performed the best. It appears that these students were used to succeeding in spite of failure, while those who succeeded 100 percent or zero percent of the time were not.

Page Ref: 571–572
Skill: Knowledge

37) With regard to the practice of retaining or "holding back" students with failing grades, Woolfolk's general recommendation is that

  A) promotion should include resource room assignments as well as one–to–one tutoring when needed.

  B) promotion underscores the idea that poor performances bring negative consequences.

  C) retention is usually better for self–esteem and performance than undeserved promotion.

  D) students should be promoted with their peers but provided with extra help in the summer or the next year.

Answer: D

Explanation: D) Research evidence suggests that retaining students in grades is usually detrimental and certainly **NOT** advantageous. Consequently, it is recommended that, if at all possible, *students should be promoted with their peers but then given extra guidance and support in the summer or following year to help them succeed.*

Page Ref: 572–573
Skill: Knowledge

38) In Kelly's 1999 study of the effects of failing an entire grade, the results indicated what percentage of high school seniors had repeated at least one grade since kindergarten?

    A) 10 percent

    B) 20 percent

    C) 25 percent

    D) 40 percent

Answer: B

Explanation: B) Kelly found that *20 percent of seniors* in the study had repeated at least one grade in school (usually one of the primary grades). However, researchers also found that seniors who had been held back performed no differently in high school than did seniors who had not been retained.

Page Ref: 572
Skill: Knowledge

39) Feedback appears to be most helpful when it tells students

    A) their overall test grades.

    B) when they are wrong.

    C) why they are right.

    D) why they are wrong.

Answer: D

Explanation: D) Feedback is most effective when it tells students *why they are wrong*. With the corrective information, students will have much clearer direction for learning appropriate learning strategies.

Page Ref: 573
Skill: Knowledge
P: .63
D: .27

40) Ms. Bateman writes "the answer is just great" as the only comment on a student's paper. Based on Woolfolk's discussion of feedback, this type of feedback is

    A) less appropriate if Ms. Bateman is a tenth-grade teacher than a fourth-grade teacher.

    B) more appropriate if Ms. Bateman is a tenth-grade teacher than a fourth-grade teacher.

    C) more appropriate for an essay test than for a multiple-choice test.

    D) rarely appropriate regardless of grade level or type of test.

Answer: D

Explanation: D) Feedback such as Ms. Bateman's "the answer is great" is *rarely appropriate regardless of grade level or test type*. Brief written comments on test papers are useful as feedback but more so for elementary than secondary students.

Page Ref: 573
Skill: Understanding
P: .53
D: .19

41) What strategy is recommended instead of assigning a failing grade to students' poor work?

   A) Consider the work to be incomplete.

   B) Give students support in revising the work.

   C) Maintain high standards for students' work.

   D) Take responsibility for the students' poor work.

Answer: B

Explanation: B) Instead of assigning a failing grade to the poor work of students, teachers
                 should *give students support in revising their work*. The work could be
                 considered to be incomplete, but this response option does not include what
                 should be done about the incomplete work. It is extremely important that
                 students be given the opportunity to revise their work with assistance from
                 the teacher (and/or others). High standards should be maintained, but this
                 response choice does not really answer the question. Finally, it is not the
                 teacher who should take responsibility for a student's poor work!

Page Ref: 573–574
Skill: Knowledge

42) Grades should be tied to meaningful course objectives so that

   A) high–ability students will be motivated to pursue worthwhile goals.

   B) low–ability students will be motivated to pursue worthwhile goals.

   C) students do not have to choose between learning and making a grade.

   D) the course objectives can be tested fairly and reliably.

Answer: C

Explanation: C) Grades should be tied to meaningful course objectives so that *students do* **NOT**
                 have to choose between learning and making a grade. If tests focus on irrelevant
                 information or over–emphasize memorization, students may decide to
                 sacrifice meaningful learning in order to earn a good grade.

Page Ref: 573–574
Skill: Knowledge
P: .52
D: .22

43) Julie looked over her paper. She had a C- in spite of the fact that she tried as hard as she could to write an innovative paper. There did not seem to be any marks for mechanical errors on the paper. When she questioned her teacher about the grade, he told her, "You did not write your review of the story in the same way as the other students." The **LEAST** likely result of the teacher's actions will be to

   A) decrease Julie's attempts to be more creative.

   B) develop a poor self-concept in Julie.

   C) increase Julie's efforts to be creative.

   D) make Julie give up studying for this class.

Answer: C

Explanation: C) Grading gives feedback to students about their performance and influences their motivation. *By being penalized for writing her review differently from other students, Julie will* **NOT** *be likely to increase her efforts to be creative in the future.* This teacher's actions will tend to decrease Julie's creative efforts and possibly have a negative influence on her self-concept. Whether or not Julie would give up studying for this class is uncertain; she may or may not stop studying (she probably would not stop studying but may not like doing so as well as she did).

Page Ref: 573-574
Skill: Understanding
P: .64
D: .31

44) Which one of the following procedures is recommended for reducing the detrimental effects of grading on students?

   A) Favor norm-referenced over criterion-referenced grading.

   B) Give ungraded assignments in order to increase exploration.

   C) Stop giving partial credit for "almost" correct answers.

   D) Use only one type of item (multiple-choice or essay) on a given test.

Answer: B

Explanation: B) In order to reduce the detrimental effects of grading on students, *ungraded assignments are recommended to increase exploration.* Ungraded assignments remove the pressure to get high grades, which would also be affected by norm-referenced comparative grading. Giving partial credit for "almost" correct answers would probably encourage motivation.

Page Ref: 574-578
Skill: Knowledge

45) One of the most difficult tasks a teacher must accomplish is to

A) determine what type of tests are needed to assess course goals.

B) prepare for individual conferences with students' families.

C) score the results of criterion-referenced and norm-referenced tests.

D) translate descriptions of students' performances into meaningful grades.

Answer: D

Explanation: D) *Translating descriptions of students' performances into letter grades is probably the most difficult task a teacher must undertake.* All grading systems can produce distortions and unfairness in grades when several sources of data having unequal numbers of items, points, and/or values are involved. One way of correcting this problem is to convert the data to T-scores, so that each source of information has a mean of 50 and a standard deviation of 10. Then, the standard scores can be weighted or simply averaged, depending on how much each data source is considered to be important. Students could be asked for their input on this crucial issue, rather than the teacher alone arbitrarily determining how valuable each data source is to be.

Page Ref: 573–574
Skill: Understanding
P: .72
D: .25

46) A typical criterion-referenced report card that reports student learning tends to be

A) complex and time-consuming for teachers.

B) constructive for group comparisons.

C) convenient but not helpful for many students.

D) practical for elementary grades but not for high school.

Answer: A

Explanation: A) A criterion-referenced report card format for reporting individual students' achievements would be *complex and very time-consuming*. Imagine how much time it would take a teacher to complete 30 to 35 of these reports every grading period. In junior and senior high schools, the total number of reports could escalate into perhaps 150 to 200!

Page Ref: 574
Skill: Knowledge

47) In comparing norm-referenced and criterion-referenced standards for grading, Frisbie and Waltmen recommend assigning what grade to a criterion-referenced standard of "demonstrated ability to use basic skills but lacks a few pre-requisites for later learning"?

   A) Above class average (B)

   B) At the class average (C)

   C) Below the class average (D)

   D) Far below class average (F)

Answer: B

Explanation: B) Frisbie and Waltmen recommended that *a grade of C should be assigned to the criterion-referenced standard of "Demonstrated ability to use basic skills."* This C-R standard was viewed as "average" performance.

Page Ref: 574
Skill: Knowledge

48) On five tests that involve different numbers of items, Bill's total raw score was 430, and Diane's total raw score was 440. Under what type of grading system is the possibility greatest that Bill could earn an A and Diane only a B?

   A) Criterion-referenced grading

   B) Norm-referenced using average T-scores

   C) Percentage grading

   D) Point system

Answer: B

Explanation: B) The possibility for Diane's raw score total of 440 to end up being assigned a grade of B while Bill's total of 430 is an A could occur if *the raw scores for each of the individual sources of information were translated into T-scores and averaged*. It is very possible that the sources of information used for the overall final grade contain different numbers of items or points and different degrees of reliability for the data sources. Merely cumulating raw score points (a point system) assumes that all data sources are equally reliable and equally representative of course objectives. Percentage scoring and other criterion-referenced strategies also assume equal reliability and representativeness.

Page Ref: 574-575
Skill: Understanding
P: .76
D: .46

49) When teachers want to give different weights to tests and assignments, it is most appropriate to use a what type of grading system?

    A) Criterion-referenced

    B) Normal curve

    C) Percentage

    D) Point or norm-referenced

Answer: D

Explanation: D) The *norm-referenced and point systems* provide a means of weighting evidence in order to meet whatever criterion has been set for each source of information to be included in final grades. Percentages can be used in norm-referenced assessment (although not recommended) and are the typical reporting method for criterion-referenced mastery measures, but percentages cannot be averaged or weighted. Arbitrarily forcing individual differences to be spread out when the raw score data source does not reflect normal curve properties is a poor and unfair technique, but its use of standard scores does permit weighting.

Page Ref: 574
Skill: Knowledge

50) A popular grading system to use for combining grades from many assignments is to use

    A) an average of the grades from all sources.

    B) an average of all of the norm-referenced scores.

    C) a point system.

    D) percentage grading.

Answer: C

Explanation: C) A popular grading system that is often used to combine grades from many assignments is *a point system*. Averaging grades from all sources, percentage grading, and even most norm-referenced grading have built-in disadvantages. [These issues are discussed well in the text.]

Page Ref: 575
Skill: Knowledge

51) Ms. Smith's students vary somewhat but, as a group, they do very well on their unit test on World War II. She assigns the grade of B to each student. Ms. Smith appears to be using what type of grading system?

A) Dual marking

B) Norm-referenced

C) Percentage correct

D) Standard score

Answer: C

Explanation: C) Ms. Smith could be using *percentage-correct grading*. This type of grading establishes score categories for the different letter grades (e.g., 90–100 = A; 80–89 = B, etc.). If all students attain the highest level, all would receive the highest grade. In contrast, normal curve and certain other norm-referenced systems would include some type of ranking of students and award the full range of grades according to students' position in the class. For example, the middle two-thirds of students in a normal distribution are demonstrating "average" performances. Under a strict system, they might be assigned Cs, while under more lenient systems, they might receive Bs, depending on the nature of the group. Students who are average in an honors class would deserve a B, while the average student in a typical class would earn a C.

Page Ref: 576
Skill: Understanding

52) Mr. Anderson observes that the high anxiety level of his students about their grades is hindering their learning in his English class. What grading system would be his best choice for promoting learning?

A) Contract

B) Norm-referenced

C) Percentage

D) Point

Answer: A

Explanation: A) Mr. Anderson would be advised to consider the beneficial effect of contract systems for *reducing student anxiety about grades*. A possible reason is that contracts give students more control over the grades they earn than occurs with other systems. Students are given the option of earning particular grades based on the amount of work they are willing to perform. A-level work, for example, might involve all the requirements for a B, plus additional work. Students contract to work for grades on an individual basis. This type of system would lessen the anxieties of students about grades, but such a system could lead to grade inflation. However, contract systems allows for giving more emphasis to quantity rather than quality. The reason is that higher grades are typically earned for doing more work, not necessarily better work.

Page Ref: 577
Skill: Understanding

53) What marking system is most likely to reduce students' anxiety about grades?

   A) Adjusted norm-referenced system

   B) Contract system

   C) Percentage grading

   D) Point system

Answer: B

Explanation: B) The marking system that is most likely to reduce students' anxieties about grades is a *contract system*. In contract systems, students have input into what the contract contains and, therefore, are less likely to be anxious or fearful about fulfilling their contracts.

Page Ref: 577–578
Skill: Knowledge

54) The purpose of the revise option in contracting is to

   A) adjust the grade distribution in conformity with desired standards.

   B) allow students to improve the quality of their work.

   C) permit students to adjust their contracts upward or downward.

   D) reduce the possibility of grade inflation.

Answer: B

Explanation: B) The purpose of the revise option in contract systems is to *give students the opportunity to improve the quality of their work*. This addresses the frequent limitation of contracts in focusing more on quantity rather than quality of work, but it can also lead to grade inflation. The revise option gives students a chance to improve their work and receive credit for doing so. The credit is usually less than the full amount that would be given for originally completed work of the same quality. [This option also places an increased load on the teacher!]

Page Ref: 577
Skill: Understanding

55) Individual learning expectation (ILE) refers to a

   A) grade distribution.

   B) grading orientation.

   C) halo effect.

   D) student attribution.

Answer: B

Explanation: B) Individual learning expectation (ILE) is a *grading orientation* that awards points
                to students based on the degree of improvement demonstrated on a test
                relative to their base (average) scores.

Page Ref: 579
Skill: Knowledge
P: .41
D: .40

56) Ms. Deeg is grading a paper written by one of her seventh–grade English students, Randy. She
has been trying to get him to be more creative in his writing but, until today, she has not seen
much improvement. Today, Randy's paper contains several novel and exciting ideas.
Unfortunately, it is poorly written in a mechanical sense. What should Ms. Deeg do?

   A) Combine the mechanics and creativity into one grade.

   B) Grade the mechanics and give extra credit for creativity.

   C) Ignore the creativity and grade mechanics only.

   D) Ignore the mechanics and assign a grade for creativity.

Answer: B

Explanation: B) A good strategy for Ms. Deeg would be to *grade the mechanics and give extra
                credit for creativity*. This way, Randy would receive feedback and an
                appropriate grade while being reinforced for his creativity.

Page Ref: 579
Skill: Understanding
P: .51
D: .43

57) The type of skills that would be most effective for teachers to have in conducting conferences with students and their families is skill in

   A) academic knowledge.

   B) communication.

   C) creativity.

   D) problem solving.

Answer: B

Explanation: B) Teachers' *communication skills* are most effective in preparing and carrying out family conferences. Academic knowledge, problem solving, and creativity are also important skills to have. However, effective communication skills are necessary first in order for the other skills to be demonstrated.

Page Ref: 579–580
Skill: Knowledge

58) The Buckley Amendment of 1974 provides that

   A) certain information in school records must be kept confidential.

   B) no federal monies may be used for testing minority students.

   C) parents may review or challenge material in school records.

   D) placement tests given to minorities must be culture–fair.

Answer: C

Explanation: C) The Buckley Amendment of 1974 provides that *parents may review or challenge all material in school records.* This means that teachers and schools must be careful about the grades given to students (and comments made about them), because they can be held accountable for their accuracy and validity.

Page Ref: 582
Skill: Knowledge

Completion Questions

1) A general term for the type of testing that is used to guide planning and identify students' needs is _____ assessment.

   Answer: formative
   Page Ref: 554

2) Formative assessment can include teacher–designed pretests, diagnostic tests, and _____ instruction or curriculum–based assessment.

   Answer: data–based
   Page Ref: 554

3) A general term for the type of testing that is used to determine final achievement in a course is _____ assessment.

Answer: summative
Page Ref: 554

4) Tests in which the scoring of items does not require interpretation are said to be _____.

Answer: objective
Page Ref: 556

5) The incorrect answers in a multiple-choice question are called alternatives or _____.

Answer: distractors
Page Ref: 557

6) Tests that are objective and relatively simple and tend to be the most reliable are composed of _____ items.

Answer: selection-type
Page Ref: 557

7) The challenges in evaluating essay tests include being clear with students about the _____ for grading and then applying them fairly and consistently.

Answer: criteria
Page Ref: 559

8) A general term for tests designed to assess performances in realistic contexts is _____ testing.

Answer: authentic
Page Ref: 562

9) Because authentic assessments require students to perform, it is perfectly logical to _____, because the whole point of instruction is for students to do well on these tasks.

Answer: teach to the test
Page Ref: 562

10) A type of authentic assessment in which students' work is collected to demonstrate progress and achievement in a particular area is a(n) _____.

Answer: portfolio
Page Ref: 562

11) Portfolios often include work in progress, revisions, the student's reflections on what he/she has learned, and student _____.

Answer: self-analyses
Page Ref: 562

12) When a general description of overall performance is desirable, the most appropriate type of assessment tool to use is called _____.

Answer: scoring rubrics
Page Ref: 566

13) Margaret Clifford's advice to teachers is that there must be a tolerance for error-making in every classroom and that the yardstick by which learning is judged should be _____ rather than continual success.

Answer: gradual success
Page Ref: 571–572

14) The type of grading that has the advantage of relating judgments about a student to the achievement of others is _____.

Answer: norm-referenced
Page Ref: 574

15) The grading system that does not permit the mathematical averaging and/or combining of test scores, homework assignments, and other measures of student performances is _____.

Answer: criterion-referenced
Page Ref: 574

16) A grading system that combines and weighs scores from many assignments is called a(n) _____ system.

Answer: point
Page Ref: 575

17) A grading system in which, for example, a score from 70–79 percent would earn a C, 80–89 percent a B, and 90–100 percent an A, is called a(n) _____ system.

Answer: percentage
Page Ref: 576

18) A grading system in which students agree to do certain types of work for a particular grade is the _____ system.

Answer: contract
Page Ref: 577

19) The tendency to view particular aspects of a student's work based on an overall general impression is called the _____.

Answer: halo effect
Page Ref: 579

True/False Questions

1) A diagnostic pretest is a type of formative measurement.

   Answer: TRUE
   Page Ref: 554

2) Data–based instruction uses testing on a monthly schedule for an overall assessment of progress.

   Answer: FALSE
   Page Ref: 554

3) Multiple–choice questions may be used to test higher–level objectives.

   Answer: TRUE
   Page Ref: 557

4) It is generally best to put as little wording as possible into the stem of a multiple–choice question relative to the distractors.

   Answer: FALSE
   Page Ref: 557

5) A multiple–choice item format is preferable to a matching format when related concepts are to be linked.

   Answer: FALSE
   Page Ref: 557

6) It is considered desirable to grade one essay question for the entire class before grading the next one for any student.

   Answer: TRUE
   Page Ref: 559

7) Establishing scoring standards is more difficult for making norm–referenced decisions than for making criterion–referenced decisions.

   Answer: FALSE
   Page Ref: 560

8) Common types of authentic assessments include portfolios and exhibitions.

   Answer: TRUE
   Page Ref: 562

9) Authentic tests are generally easier than conventional tests to grade objectively.

   Answer: FALSE
   Page Ref: 562–566

10) In a student portfolio, the teacher should determine what evidence of work should be included.

Answer: FALSE
Page Ref: 563

11) Descriptive rating scales are a type of scoring rubric.

Answer: TRUE
Page Ref: 566

12) Having students assist in the development of rating scales and scoring rubrics can lead to improved learning.

Answer: TRUE
Page Ref: 567

13) Criterion-referenced grading is more appropriate than norm-referenced grading for authentic assessments.

Answer: TRUE
Page Ref: 574

14) Research on the effects of written feedback indicate that teachers should make positive suggestions for improvement and avoid making comments about errors or faulty strategies.

Answer: FALSE
Page Ref: 573

15) Both criterion-referenced and norm-referenced report cards indicate student progress toward specific goals.

Answer: FALSE
Page Ref: 574

16) Grading on the curve is an example of a criterion-referenced system.

Answer: FALSE
Page Ref: 574

17) When individual differences in achievement are to be reported, a norm-referenced grading system is appropriate.

Answer: TRUE
Page Ref: 574

18) Criterion-referenced grading systems use standards of subject mastery and learning to determine grades.

Answer: TRUE
Page Ref: 574

19) A useful, but not always reliable, system for combining grades from multiple assignments is the point system.

Answer: TRUE
Page Ref: 575

20) The influence of a halo effect increases the reliability of criterion-referenced grades.

Answer: FALSE
Page Ref: 579

21) Using any grading system requires the teacher to be able to defend the grades assigned to students.

Answer: TRUE
Page Ref: 579

22) The main implication of the Buckley Amendment is greater protection for teachers against parents' questioning a teacher's grading system.

Answer: FALSE
Page Ref: 582

Short Answer Questions

1) Compare and contrast formative and summative measurements. Identify the different uses of formative and summative tests in your answer.

Answer: Formative tests are used to determine pre-instruction ability levels and to gauge the progress of instruction. Pretests are formative tests that can be used to set proper objectives and indicate possible teaching strategies. Diagnostic tests are formative tests that identify strengths and weaknesses; rarely, if ever, are teacher-designed diagnostic tests used to compare individual differences. Summative tests are used to measure final achievement. Unlike formative and diagnostic measures, summative tests are used to determine grades.

Page Ref: 554

2) In what situations is the use of multiple–choice items desirable? Suggest some guidelines for how such items should be constructed.

Answer: Multiple-choice items can be used to test higher–level learning objectives (comprehension, analysis, synthesis) as well as knowledge. For such objectives, however, essay questions should also be strongly considered and may be more effective. Many more multiple–choice questions than essay questions can be answered in a single class period. Therefore, objective tests can represent a much larger content domain than can essay tests. Moreover, objective tests are more reliable than essay tests. Guidelines for multiple–choice item construction include (a) favoring positive over negative phrasing, (b) limiting the amount of wording in the distractors relative to the stem, (c) making all alternatives grammatically consistent with the stem, (d) not making the correct answer stand out by its length, and (e) not overusing categorical words such as "always" and "never" in distractors.

Page Ref: 556–557

3) In order to judge how well your students can analyze the elements of a play, you administer an essay test. Why is this appropriate and how can you try to ensure that the test is well–written and graded correctly?

Answer: Essay tests are expected to assess high–level thinking skills, although many teacher-designed essay tests do measure lower–lever thinking skills. Well–designed essay items can be excellent for testing higher–order objectives such as analysis, synthesis, and evaluation. The essay test should set a clear and precise task and indicate how the answers will be evaluated. Because there is room for teacher bias in grading, it is best to read all the answers for a single question consecutively, and shuffle the papers between different essay items. Using a scoring rubric for each item would enhance reliability, and a point system could be used for grading based on the total points assigned for the scoring rubrics for all items. It is clearly best to grade students in *random order on each essay question*. Otherwise, the same people might be graded first or last, thus creating a greater possibility for bias in question scores and overall scores. It would not increase objectivity in grading to give students a choice of essay questions. That procedure would tend to make grading very confusing and unreliable. Suggested procedures are to construct a model answer, grade all responses to a given question before moving to the next question, and have students write their names on the backs of their answer sheets.

Page Ref: 559–560

4) Compare authentic testing to conventional testing with regard to philosophy, procedures, student roles, types of evaluation, grading, and situations that favor the use of each category of assessment procedures.

Answer: The philosophy of authentic assessment is that tests should be viewed in similar ways as performances. That is, students should be given opportunities to demonstrate what they have learned in realistic or "authentic" contexts. This view contrasts with that for conventional tests that evaluate students under highly-controlled conditions, usually limited to paper-and-pencil modes of expression. Two common forms of authentic tests are portfolios and exhibitions. The former involves collecting the student's work over a period of time and evaluating it relative to established standards. Criterion-referenced rather the norm-referenced grading should be used. Exhibitions are similarly graded, but consist of public performances in which the student displays his/her work. It should be noted, however, that these types of assessments are difficult to evaluate objectively; consequently, the reliability of grades for authentic tasks is difficult to determine.

Page Ref: 562

5) Compare and contrast criterion-referenced, norm-referenced, and percentage grading.

Answer: Criterion-referenced grading evaluates students on the basis of achieving certain standards, such as learning a list of vocabulary words or demonstrating a specific skill. Comparison to the criterion, not to other students, determines the grade. Norm-referenced grading evaluates students according to their relative position or ranking in a class, such that the top 20 percent might receive As, the next 20 percent receive Bs, and so on. Percentage grading involves establishing specific percentage score ranges (e.g., 80–89 percent; 90–100 percent) to be associated with the various letter grades. However, these types of norm-referenced grading systems are very arbitrary.

Page Ref: 574

6) Teachers frequently think of grading as focusing on achievement (test scores). What are some other qualities or criteria on which grading might be based and how might they be incorporated fairly in an overall grading system?

Answer: Grading can be based on improvement and effort, as well as on test scores, especially on information sources such as essay tests, homework, and projects. One example is the *individual learning expectation* (ILE) system in which students earn points for improvement relative to their base scores. Another system is the *dual marking approach* that assigns two grades, one for actual level of achievement and the other for the amount of effort demonstrated. A grade of B1, for example, would indicate B work with an outstanding effort; a grade of B3 would indicate B work with relatively poor effort. Another norm-referenced system involves evidence obtained from the students themselves to determine whether students differ significantly from each other and, therefore, should be assigned grades differentially. This system uses the group's mean and standard deviation, with the mean score plus/minus one-half standard deviation defining "average" performance. Then, the range from the mean plus one-half standard deviation to one and one-half standard deviations above the mean comprises the "above average" group; the mirror image of this range below the mean describes the "below average" group. Scores higher than the above-average range (higher than the mean plus 1.5s) constitutes superior performance, and scores less than the below-average range are very poor or failing performances. Application of one standard error of measurement below the cut-off points decreases the possibility of erring on the side of being too strict in identifying the various grade groups, and students are pleased that missing a grade cut-off point by only a few points is avoided. This system does *not* force normal-curve grading, and it makes the assignment of grades dependent on whether students who earn As truly demonstrate higher achievement than students whose scores earned them Bs (or Cs, etc.).

Page Ref: 574–579

Case Studies

Howard Williams teaches a college course in educational foundations to preservice teachers. The course is intended to expose students to the historical roots of education, key philosophers, and current issues in teaching and education. 90 percent of students' grades in his course are determined by a midterm and a final exam, both consisting of 75 multiple-choice questions. The remaining 10 percent is attendance. One question on the midterm, for example, was: "The first normal school in Tennessee was established in . . ." followed by four alternatives. A question on the final was: "The philosopher identified with the progressive movement was . . ."' followed by four alternatives. When asked about the course after they had graduated, students often described it as "well taught, but meaningless."

1) What type of testing plan would you recommend to improve the validity of Dr. Williams' course?

    Answer: In regards to objective testing, Dr. Williams could improve his tests by using multiple-choice items that rely on more than identification of facts (i.e., declarative knowledge). Although difficult, it is possible to write multiple-choice items that also require students to compare and contrast information or apply the knowledge they have learned. Dr. Williams could also expand his objective tests to include more types of items than multiple-choice type items. He could also include true/false, completion, and short-answer items. Given that he only administers a midterm and a final, an essay question may improve the quality of his tests. If he chooses to include an essay, he will want to develop a model answer prior to grading any answers. As noted by Gronlund, a model answer (and asking students not to put their name on their essay) helps to ensure reliability and fairness in grading.

Page Ref: 556–560

2) Identify how authentic testing could be used in a course of that type. Specifically, what types of authentic "performances" might be evaluated and how could they be evaluated?

Answer: While objective tests are useful for assessing mastery of content knowledge, they are limited in their ability to assess students' skills and abilities as they would be applied in real-life situations. Authentic assessment requires students to apply their skills and abilities and are good to use when the goal is to assess students' ability to write, speak, listen, create, do research, solve problems, and/or apply knowledge. The type of authentic assessment Dr. Willams might choose to include would probably be influenced by the number of students in his class. For example, if he had over 50 students in his class, it would be a substantial work load to ask students to complete both a portfolio project and the creation of a video tape. One type of authentic assessment available to Dr. Williams is asking groups of students to create a thematic web site that they could use during their student teaching experience. The web site would contain content, teaching resources, connections to state teaching standards, activities for the learner, and plans for evaluating student learning. As noted by Woolfolk, this type of authentic assessment requires that the teacher provide students with clear structure, time lines, and task instructions. This type of project should not be "graded on the curve" and students should know the evaluation criteria in advance For example, Dr. Williams may set the criteria that the web site must minimally contain 10 links to other curriculum materials available through the Internet. Finally, Mr. Williams will want to be careful not to turn this assignment into a competitive one. He can explicitly state that he expects all web sites will be different from each other and not necessarily better than each other.

Page Ref: 556, 574–577

3) React to Dr. Williams' grading system. How might it be improved to be more motivating and valid?

Answer: Dr. Williams may want to consider providing more frequents tests or other types of evaluation. Students can benefit from early and frequent feedback. Also, when only two tests are included in a course, this situation can be particularly problematic for students with high test anxiety. Course grades based only on a small number of tests can potentially encourage students to overly engage in a performance goal orientation , which may or may not include any type of learning goals. Dr. Williams may want to consider adding a group project and/or some type of authentic assessment to his course (i.e., student presentations or learning portfolios). There are also some meaningful experiences Dr. Williams could add to his course which would add to students' overall points in the course. For example, he could require the prospective teachers to observe an expert teacher and write a short reaction paper. This type of assignment could be graded for completion and thoroughness rather than the ability to state a "correct answer."

Page Ref: 573

4) Given that Dr. Williams will probably continue to use at least some multiple-choice testing, suggest some guidelines regarding when and how to use this testing format. Specifically, what objectives should multiple-choice questions test? How should items be constructed to improve their content validity for course objectives?

Answer: The first decision Dr. Williams may need to make is whether or not to construct his own multiple-choice test or use the test bank provided by the publisher of the textbook. Ready-made tests have the advantage that items are reviewed by experts in the field and norming samples allow for extensive item analyses. Also, ready-made test items typically match the language and objectives of the accompanying textbook.

If Dr. Williams decides to write his own multiple-choice items, he will want to first consider the nature of the content he is assessing. If he is interested in having students connect concepts, a matching strategy may be a better item format. Dr. Williams wants to make sure that he is testing students' knowledge rather than their test taking or guessing skills. In developing the question (referred to as the stem), he should write the question to only measure one key concept. Item stems should not be overly wordy, yet they should contain as much wording as possible so that phrases will not have to be repeated in each alternative (i.e., possible answers). In writing alternative answers he should carefully include distractors, which can distract students who may only have partial knowledge of a concept. In addition, the alternative answers should follow the same grammatical form of the stem, so that no answers can be ruled out for obvious reasons. Items should vary in content and instructions. For example, test developers should not overuse "all of the above" or "none of the above" in the answer alternatives. Similarly, the categorial words of "always" or "never" should be avoided in question stems because highly skilled test takers are aware things are "always true."

Page Ref: 556–558

Ms. Rogers uses a grading system in her high school Spanish class in which students who average 60–69 percent receive a D, 70–79 percent a C, 80–89 percent a B, and 90–100 percent an A. Ms. Rogers has the reputation of being an excellent "expert" teacher. This year, 18 of her 24 students earned a final grade of A and the other six students earned a B. Her new principal criticizes Ms. Rogers for using "an apparently invalid grading system that fails to provide adequate differentiation between students."

5) Identify the type of grading system that Ms. Rogers is using. What are its general advantages and disadvantages?

Answer: Ms. Rogers is using a criterion-referenced grading system, which involves grading each student's mastery of her course objectives. This type of grading system has the advantage that it can be directly connected to the teachers' instructional goals and the student's learning goals. Given that the case study states Ms. Rogers is considered to be an expert teacher, we can assume that she has developed well-defined instructional objectives and goals. She may even include these objects on student's report cards next to their grades. One limitation of the criterion-referenced grading system is that it can be very difficult to develop clear instructional goals and corresponding grading criteria for all material to be learned. This can be especially true for novice teachers.

Page Ref: 574

6) Would her grading system be considered norm-referenced? Why or why not?

Answer: Her grading system is not consistent with a norm-referenced system, which assesses student's learning and achievement in relation to one another. The practice frequently referred to as "grading on the curve" has been found to negatively impact student-to-student and student-to-teacher relationships. If her system were to be norm-referenced, we would know more about the average scores and the distribution of scores. A concern is that a student could have demonstrated some understanding of basic knowledge (perhaps a "C" on Ms. Rogers' grading scale) and yet receive a failing grade of a D if all of the other students scored exceptionally high on the exam.

Page Ref: 574

7) React to the principal's arguments. Do you believe that the grading system is inappropriate? Explain your rationale.

Answer: The principal's concerns may be unwarranted. Given that Ms. Rogers, who is an expert teacher, has clear and thorough instructional objectives, she should in fact be recognized for her ability to effectively teach the material to her students. The extent to which students can master the Spanish language is of more concern than if the course differentiates students' abilities.

Page Ref: 581–582

APPENDIX 2

A: PERFORMANCE ASSESSMENT PROCEDURES

What Is a Rationale?

Frequently, authentic assessment tasks may require a rationale that presents a justification for a proposed solution to a problem or for a recommended set of procedures. A rationale can be based upon three generalized criteria: (1) **value**; (2) **scientific theory or evidence**; and (3) **effectiveness**. Thus, problem solutions and procedures are considered to be good when they achieve valuable outcomes (i.e., they have value), when they are scientifically sound (i.e., they conform to the most current theoretical formulations or research evidence in the field), and when they provide more efficient ways of dealing with the problem (i.e., they are very effective). The primary source for a rationale is the science and theory of psychology and education. A rationale should emphasize first the scientific soundness of the solutions and/or procedures, followed by attention given to the effectiveness dimension. The value dimension probably should receive the least amount of emphasis, because, it is probably most appropriate to use when dealing with philosophical issues.

For the Individual Problem (IP) that requires integration of selected concepts, principles, and theories, you may be asked to construct a set of instructional procedures for educators, therapists, supervisors, or other personnel to follow when faced with a specific task or problem. You will be expected to identify a specific problem in which you are interested and for which reasonable solutions can be proposed based upon the concepts and principles of psychology and education.

COMPONENTS OF A RATIONALE

How should a rationale be written? Your task is to explain why the instructional procedures and/or group solutions recommended in your individual or group projects are, in fact, theoretically sound. Therefore, you must use the key concepts, principles, and theories learned in this course and in your selected supplementary readings. Many rationales/justifications are much too general. For example, someone might include this statement: "The teacher used self-disclosure." Such a statement is inadequate, because it simply identifies a procedure (self-disclosure) but does not explain why it was used or what its effect was. It would be much better to use a statement something like this: "In order to establish trust with the group, the leader used self-disclosure by sharing information about why he/she decided to become a teacher and how important it was to be a good teacher." Notice that this last statement not only explains why self-disclosure was used but also describes the kind of information that the teacher disclosed. You could also explain how the teacher's self-disclosure procedure should increase the probability of students using the self-disclosure procedure. In all instances, you should cite references to support your statements. Four general principles should be followed in developing a rationale:

- ☐ As you develop the rationale, continually ask yourself why you used or recommended a particular instructional learning or motivation procedure.

- ☐ Try to employ as many different theoretical concepts and principles in your discussion (the rationale) as possible.

- ☐ When making reference to a theoretical term (e.g., self-disclosure, motivation, reinforcement, validity, etc.) include a concrete example of the use of that concept in your project and, wherever possible, refer to the page in your project report where that example appears.

- ☐ Cite specific references and include a bibliography at the end of your report.

The "name of the game" for a rationale is providing answers to the constant question of "For what reason do I (or we) want to use this procedure, to implement that solution, or to make this recommendation?" *A rationale provides the reasons why.* Also, do not forget that the rationale, like all of your work, should conform to the rules for correct usage of standard English. Good Luck!

General Instructions for
Authentic Assessment Problems

An individual problem may be your integrated summative assessment measure in this course. One obvious purpose of your problem is to demonstrate your understanding of the various considerations, techniques, and theories that you have learned. However, the less obvious but more important purpose of this activity is for you to integrate and synthesize your new knowledge for yourself, utilizing it as a professional in your field.

In general, the suggested problems are broad problems with which you can work. It is up to you to select a specific problem (e.g., a student, client, trainee, curricular area or classroom, therapy, or supervisory situation) that is of particular interest to you. The specific problem you use, while narrow enough to be discussed in **approximately 10 typewritten double-spaced pages**, should be complex enough to allow you to use concepts, principles, and theories from at least two content areas of Educational Psychology with which you have dealt this semester. Such examples include group dynamics, physical/personal/social development, learning theories and processes, motivation, individual differences, classroom management, and traditional and authentic assessment procedures.

Each problem requires theoretical analyses, justification (rationale), and/or critiques. Therefore, be sure to substantiate your statements with references to specific concepts, principles, and theories. The references listed in the bibliography presented in Anita Woolfolk's textbook are excellent reference sources, but avoid referring solely to these sources and other introductory materials. Demonstrate your ability to utilize the professional literature available in the campus library.

TASK PROCEDURES

The five steps presented below are either directly required or indirectly implied by the instructions for each problem. In doing your project, ensure that each step has been included.

Step 1: Problem Statement

Select or create a specific problem in which you are interested and for which possible solutions can be proposed utilizing relevant concepts, principles, and theories of Educational Psychology. Limit the scope of the problem. Develop a specific problem statement.

Step 2: Theoretical Analysis

Analyze the problem from at least two or more theoretical perspectives.

Step 3: Plan/Solution

Design a program/plan/solution for the problem you have chosen. The program should incorporate techniques related to the theories you used in analyzing the problem.

Step 4: Justification/Rationale

Explain and justify your plan in terms of the theories that you utilized in designing the plan. Present any possible criticism of the plan that might be made by theorists holding views differing from those you used. Be certain to cite relevant references!

Step 5: Implementation and Critique

If possible, implement your plan. In any case, critique its effectiveness from a theoretical perspective.

Note: You may find it useful to analyze the problem (Step 2) and structure the solution (Step 3) from one theoretical perspective (e.g., constructivism) and then to incorporate other theoretical perspectives (e.g., behavioral theory and/or humanist theory) into your evaluation of the solution (Steps 4 and 5).

Checklist for Submitting Authentic Problems

Before submitting the Authentic Assessment Problem to your instructor, check to see that your document conforms to the following guidelines:

☐ Written narrative materials (problem statement, theoretical analysis, justification, and critique) should total a minimum of 8-10 pages.

☐ The rationale, or justification, should be based on the criteria presented in "What Is A Rationale?" on pages 529-530.

☐ Submit all instructional materials that you have developed: lesson outlines, tests, objectives, etc. Also submit any tapes, rating scales, etc., that comprise a record of a learner's or your performance. In other words, the instructor needs to see clearly what you have done and how well you have done it.

☐ Cite specific references and include a bibliography at the end of your project.

☐ Make your work as professional as possible in appearance, presentation, and quality.

☐ Your name (and section number, if applicable) should be on each page of your document, or the document should be bound in such manner that there is no danger of pages being separated.

☐ **Always make a second (back-up) copy of your document!** Your instructor may request that you turn in two copies of your project. [On the other hand, you might spill coffee on it, your dog might chew it up, or your computer might crash when you are trying to make corrections or changes!] It is ALWAYS WISE to have at least one back-up copy of any material that you create.

Authentic assessment tasks help you to integrate what you have learned in this course and allow you to demonstrate your understanding of what educational psychology is all about. An important component of learning is motivation, and two important components of motivation are relevance and interest. Accordingly, assist your own learning by making your project relevant and interesting to yourself. Be as creative in planning and carrying out your chosen task, and remember that good writing skills are valued in all professions!

APPENDIX 2

B: SELECTED AUTHENTIC ASSESSMENT TASKS

Designing a Self-Selected Task

An important component of any learning is the relevance and interest of the subject matter for the learner. Although the Individual Problems presented in the following pages provide a wide variety of opportunities, some people may not find them to be relevant to their needs. For example, Public Relations and Advertising make use of many principles of Educational Psychology, and it would be reasonable for the people in those fields to produce a project related to their own area. In addition, persons in the areas for which the projects that follow are directed may be highly interested in applying what they have learned to a specific problem that we have not suggested. How can you make Educational Psychology relevant to your own interests? The purpose of this task is to apply the techniques and theories of Educational Psychology to the development and evaluation of an individual problem in your own professional area

TASK PROCEDURES:

1. Identify a specific problem in which you are interested and for which a realistic solution can be proposed utilizing concepts and principles of Educational Psychology. Develop a specific problem statement. Limit the scope of the problem. For example, "the development of an advertising campaign to combat smoking" is very general and broad, but "the development of a sixty-second commercial designed to persuade people to stop smoking" could produce an appropriate project.

2. Analyze the problem from a particular theoretical approach. Consider any of the following perspectives: Behaviorist, Cognitivist, and/or Constructivist Principles and Theories. Measurement Theory is also appropriate for some problems. In your analysis, include any of the content areas presented and discussed in this course that you believe to have relevance for your chosen problem.

3. Design a program/plan/solutions for the problem that you have chosen. The program should incorporate techniques related to the concepts, principles, and theories that you used in analyzing the problem. Be creative!

4. Explain and justify your plan in terms of the concepts, principles, and theories that you utilized when designing it. Present any possible criticism of the plan that might be made by theorists holding views differing from those you used.

5. For some problems, such as working with an individual student or managing a health therapy problem, it may be possible to implement your plan, even if only briefly. Describe what happened when you implemented the plan. In any case, critique the effectiveness of your proposed plan or project from a theoretical perspective (part of a rationale).

6. Turn in your completed task to the instructor.

As always, make certain that you demonstrate your ability to deal with complex problems and issues that relate to your future profession. You may be surprised to find that your professional world is even more demanding than your academic world is right now. Working cooperatively with others and solving complex problems will become a way of life in your professional world. Whatever you can do for yourself now to prepare well for that future world will serve to make you a more complete professional.

Developmental Analysis of a Learning Problem

The students comprising a learning group are a mixed lot, differing from one another in every aspect of functioning. Time constraints force us to gear instructional activities toward persons near the middle of the range of differences. At times, we must make additional plans for persons at the extreme ends of the spectrum -- those who are either especially advanced or especially slow in their cognitive, affective and/or psychomotor development. How do we analyze learning difficulties in terms of developmental levels? What recommendations can be made for helping persons with such difficulties? The objectives for this task are (1) to apply developmental principles in analyzing learning problems, and (2) to employ techniques and theories of Educational Psychology in suggesting ways to correct learning problems

TASK PROCEDURES:

1.   Contact a professional in your field and arrange to observe an individual who is having learning problems. Observe the person in the learning group for **8-10 hours**. Record your observations systematically. Because of your time constraints, concentrate upon his/her performance in one area, such as reading, physical education, social interaction, on-the-job skills, etc. Summarize your observations of and information about the individual. Based upon this information, develop a specific problem statement.

2.   Analyze the problem from a developmental perspective. Is it a problem of cognitive, affective or psychomotor development, or of some combination of the three? At what developmental level is the learner? How does this level compare to the "usual" level of people in this age or school grade? What aspects of the person's background (both hereditary and environmental) may have influenced his/her developmental level? Base your analysis upon the views of at least one developmental theorist.

3.   Design a detailed plan for working with the individual in order to help correct or to compensate for his/her learning problem. Your plan should utilize techniques that are derived from a specific theoretical perspective (behaviorism, cognitivism, need theory, etc.) and that directly relate to your analysis of the problem.

4.   Write a theoretical justification explaining why your plan should be beneficial to the learner and outlining the anticipated outcomes and any potential problems.

5.   Present your analysis, plan and justification to the teacher, therapist, or supervisor of this individual. Discuss how practical and successful the teacher, therapist, or supervisor thinks the plan would be. Evaluate his/her criticisms and suggestions from both theoretical and "common sense" perspectives. [Although implementation of the plan is beyond the scope of this project, you may wish to note whether the teacher, therapist, or supervisor wishes to use it, or any part of it, and report any progress in the learner's abilities at the time of your final write-up.]

6.   Turn in your completed task to your instructor.

Developing a Learning Activity
(Contributed by Dr. Elizabeth M. Penn, Thomas More College)

PROBLEM:

Construct a learning activity and/or learning materials for your specific grade(s) or age group and content subject. Your learning activity must be based on a specific learning theory or theories. A 3-5 page typewritten paper that explains how the activity and/or materials implement the selected theory/principles must accompany the project.

FORMAT OF PAPER:

Your paper must include a cover sheet that identifies the Theory and the Elements of the Theory implemented in your activity. For example, you might choose to create a project for secondary social studies that incorporates all seven of Gardner's Multiple Intelligences through the use of learning centers.

Project: Learning Center Activities for Women's History

Theory: Gardner's Multiple Intelligences

Elements: **Linguistic**

Imagine that you are a female school teacher in 1960. You have just learned that the male faculty members with very similar credentials to yours are making substantially more money than you for the same experience level. Write a letter to a friend describing your feelings and anticipated actions.

Logical-Mathematical

Using the computer, create a chart that illustrates the relative salaries of men and women and indicates how the respective salaries have changed during the last three decades.

Note: For this problem, the student would continue creating activities until each of the seven elements of this theory has been addressed. The materials for all activities must be submitted with the paper itself.

In addition to submitting the project and paper to the instructor, students will have an opportunity to present and defend their work. They will be asked (1) to explain what they did, (2) to defend why a particular methodology was selected, and (3) to respond to questions from a panel of practitioners and peers. Panel members will use the following rubric or scoring guide to assess students' projects, and these assessment forms will be given back to individual students.

ASSESSMENT RUBRIC

MASTER TEACHER

Activity is worth the time of the teacher and students.
Materials are legible, attractive, and durable.
Activity is developmentally appropriate.
Accurate explanation of theory is presented.
Presentation interests and motivates the audience.

APPRENTICE TEACHER

Activity is worth the time of the teacher and students.
Materials are legible and durable.
Activity is developmentally appropriate.
Accurate explanation of theory is presented.
Presentation is clear and well-organized.

NOVICE TEACHER

Activity is not worth the time of the teacher and students.
Materials are legible.
Accurate explanation of theory is presented.
Presentation is well-organized.

COMMENTS FROM PANEL MEMBERS:

This rubric is intended to be used in a holistic manner. Points are not awarded for individual components of the project, but panel members may make written comments that are shared with students. The scoring rubric can be converted to letter grades if necessary. For example, the Master Teacher rating = 4.0 (or *A*); the Apprentice Teacher = 3.0 (or *B*), and the Novice Teacher = 2.0 (or *C*). [It is assumed that students will be permitted to revise their papers, activities, and/or presentations until they reach their desired criterion level.]

Designing a Self-Concept Enhancement Program

For each behavior of an individual, there is some underlying reason or drive that influences both the form and the content of the action. We want our students and clients to be motivated to utilize the assistance, instruction and experience that are provided. Unfortunately, many people are not so motivated; often this lack of motivation is related to a problem with self-concept or self-image. For example, a female who has incorporated into her self-concept the traditional feminine stereotype that females are poor in science may not be motivated to learn in science courses. On the other hand, a male who has learned that the macho-type male should not be interested in artistic endeavors may not be motivated to participate in humanities courses. How can we help others develop self-motivation toward behaviors beneficial to them? How might their self-concepts be changed to support such motivation? The purposes of this task are (1) to employ the techniques and theories of motivation and self-concept enhancement in the development and evaluation of a Self-Concept Enhancement Program and (2) to implement (if possible) your plan and evaluate its effectiveness

TASK PROCEDURES:

1.   Identify and describe a specific motivational problem that you have, or someone you know has, that can be defined as a problem of poor self-concept. The problem could be related to scholastic, personal, social, occupational, or with other concerns. Write a specific problem statement.

2.   Analyze the problem in terms of the cognitive, behavioral, cognitivist, and constructivist learning theorists. Which theory seems to account most adequately for the problem? Explain. Be sure to consider the current level of motivation, possible conflicting motivations, and how the motivational problem relates to the subject's specific self-concept.

3.   Develop a program designed to enhance the subject's self-concept and, thus, promote self-regulation and self-motivation. The program should relate directly to the problem behaviors, and it should be based upon the techniques of the theoretical position that most adequately explains the problem.

4.   Justify your program in terms of your chosen theoretical perspective. Critique the program from the viewpoint of at least two alternative theories.

5.   If possible, implement the program. Be sure to pre-test and post-test the client in order to assess his/her behavioral and attitudinal changes. Evaluate the effectiveness of your program, using the assessment results and the reactions of the client and yourself. Relate this evidence and the reactions to theoretical perspectives.

6.   Turn in the entire "package" to your instructor for evaluation.

Designing a Group Management Plan

"Order," "self-control" or "classroom management" -- however a teacher, therapist, or supervisor may view discipline, it remains an integral part of effective learning and instruction. Freedom to learn encompasses restrictions on behaviors that interfere with the learning activities of other group members. How can a teacher, therapist, supervisor, or others design a management plan that enhances the education of the group without harming the individual? The purposes of this task are (1) to design a management plan for a specific group of individuals that reflects an integration of management techniques based on theoretical perspectives and (2) to use the theories of development, individual differences, self-concept, and learning in evaluating the management plan

TASK PROCEDURES:

1. Identify a specific group management problem likely to occur with a group in the grade level or other setting in which you expect to teach. Limit the scope of the problem.

2. Write a specific problem statement.

3. Analyze the problem from at least two theoretical perspectives.

4. Design a management plan to handle the problem you have analyzed and described. The plan should be in two parts: (a) Prevention of Misbehavior and (b) Correction of Misbehavior. In developing your plan, use any one or a combination of the following: general principles and concepts of development; behaviorist, cognitivist, and/or constructivist theories of learning; motivation theory; and classroom management strategies. The techniques that you choose should correspond to those used in analyzing the problem.

5. Justify your plan from your chosen theoretical perspective(s) and critique it from a differing theoretical viewpoint.

6. Have at least two persons who are appropriate for your intended group or who have had experience in teaching or working with such a group review and discuss the plan with you. How effective do they think it would be? Why? Summarize their comments and your responses.

7. Evaluate your management plan. What would be its effect upon both learning and personal development for the intended group? How well would it actually work in promoting discipline and enhancing learner self-concept and self-regulation? Criticize and support your plan in terms of the relevant motivational, developmental, and learning theories.

8. Turn in your completed task to the instructor.

Working with Special Needs Students

Identify your future professional role and the type of situation in which you will be working. The purpose of this task is to develop specific plans for working with each individual difference or special need student(s) listed in the Task Procedures section.

TASK PROCEDURES

1. Identify your future professional role and situation (e.g., high-school industrial arts teacher, assembly plant supervisor, speech therapist in a hospital, dietitian for a college housing unit, etc.).

2. Develop two specific suggestions or plans for working with each of the following individual differences or special needs situations:

Situation #1 **The group of people with whom you are working (students, clients, subordinates, etc.) is 50 percent Caucasian, 20 percent Hispanic-American, 20 percent Black-American, 7 percent Native American, and 3 percent Asian-American.**

1. List four specific examples of factors (environmental, personal, interpersonal, etc.) that you need to take into account when working with this group.

2. Describe one behavioral and one cognitive constructivist motivation technique that you, the teacher/manager/therapist, can use to modify an instructional sequence for the above students.

3. Explain why each of these motivational techniques should work with these students.

4. Outline a general plan for motivating students like these. Which theoretical perspective of motivation is most reflected in your plan?

Situation #2: One person in your group is educationally blind and mildly retarded.

1. List at least four specific examples of factors (environmental, personal, interpersonal, etc.) that you need to take into account when working with this individual.

2. Describe two motivational techniques that you, the teacher/manager/therapist, can use to modify an instructional sequence for the above students. Base one technique on behavioral perspectives and the other on humanistic perspectives.

3. Explain why each of these motivational techniques should work with these students.

4. Outline a general plan for motivating students like these. Which theoretical perspective of motivation is most reflected in your plan?

Situation #3: Three gifted individuals in the group are from low SES families.

1. List four specific examples of factors that you must take into account when working with this situation.

2. Describe two motivation techniques that you, the teacher/manager/therapist, can use to modify an instructional sequence for these gifted students. Base one technique on constructivist perspectives and the other on the behavioral or humanistic perspective.

3. Explain why each of these motivational techniques should work with these students.

4. Outline a general plan for motivating students like these. Which theoretical perspective of motivation is most reflected in your plan?

Situation #4: Several of the people in the group speak a Black English dialect.

1. List four specific examples of factors that you must take into account when working with this group.

2. Describe two motivation techniques for this group that you have not used for the other group situations. These motivational techniques may represent any two of the three motivational perspectives.

3. Explain why each of these motivational techniques should work with these students.

4. Outline a plan for motivating learners (students, clients, etc.). Relate each part of your plan to the theoretical perspective it represents. Which theoretical perspective of motivation is most reflected in your plan?

Note: Turn in your completed plans for these four situations to the instructor.

An Information Processing Problem

Prepare a brief lesson plan based on the information-processing model for learning that is organized according to Gagné's instructional events. Incorporate specific memory techniques in your plan. Identify effective procedures intended to help an individual memorize a vast amount of unfamiliar material in a very short time. Explain how time can influence learning. The purpose of this task is to demonstrate your understanding of the information-processing learning model.

TASK PROCEDURES

1. Describe a scenario for your lesson, including the specific environment for instruction, the learners' ages, ability level(s), social status, special needs, and other factors that are relevant for this particular instructional event.

2. Select a topic that you could teach in this scenario. The topic should be simple and easily taught in a short lesson; yet, it should require more than rote memorization of facts. Possible topics might include:

    How to program a calculator   Benefits of exercise
    Need for computers in education   Using video equipment
    Effects of slavery on today's society   Effects of smoking
    Aftermath of the Gulf War   The Vietnam Era

3. Prepare an outlined lesson for your topic that incorporates each of Gagné's instructional events and is based on information-processing theory. Include specific memory techniques that would be applicable to this problem (e.g., advance organizers, mnemonic devices, ways to increase meaning, etc.)

4. Compare and contrast the information processing approach to learning with those of discovery learning and expository learning. Suggest at least three specific changes that you would need to make in this lesson plan if you were to use discovery or expository learning techniques for this lesson.

5. Discuss the effects of time on learning. Include relevant factors of meaning, retention, interference and massed or "cram" practice sessions. What implications can you draw about how learners should study for exams?

6. Turn in the completed task to your instructor.

A Discovery Learning Task

Outline a set of instructional and learning procedures based on Bruner's discovery learning principles to facilitate comprehension of instructional material in your professional area. The procedures should include activities designed for the instructional events described by Gagné, with special emphasis upon the first five events: **gaining attention, informing learners of the objective(s), stimulating recall, presenting the material, and providing guidance during the learning process.** The purpose of this task is to demonstrate your understanding of discovery learning strategies and how they can be used to design instructional events for student learning.

TASK PROCEDURES

1. Your task is to develop a lesson plan using discovery learning principles for one of the following topics or a task that is relevant for your own professional area:

The Civil War	Skeletal system
First aid	Prime numbers
Color wheel	Periodic Table
Using the Internet	Bulimia
How to send photos via e-mail	Civil rights

2. List the objective(s) for your lesson and explain how learners will be informed of these objectives. Identify any relevant sources underlying the means you choose.

3. Brainstorm and select specific activities to gain the attention of learners. Place an asterisk (*) beside the activity (or possibly two activities) that you believe would offer the best possible solution for gaining learner attention. Explain your choice(s).

4. Identify necessary prerequisite information and suggest specific strategies for stimulating recall of such prerequisites. Place an asterisk (*) beside the activity, or activities, that you think would be the best for identifying prerequisite information and stimulating recall of the prerequisite information. Explain your selection(s).

5. Brainstorm and select specific activities for presenting the material and, most importantly, providing learning guidance. Place an asterisk (*) after the activity, or activities, that you believe to be the best strategies for presenting the material and providing learning guidance. Explain your selection(s). This should be the most comprehensive and important section of your procedural outline.

6. Brainstorm and select activities for eliciting performance, providing feedback and assessing performance. Again, identify the most promising strategies activities for eliciting the desired performance, providing appropriate feedback, and assessing the quality of the performance. Explain your selections.

7. Brainstorm and select activities designed to enhance retention and transfer of the newly learned information. Identify the most promising strategies and explain your choices. Be sure to make use of principles of meaningful learning and interference theory..

8. Turn in your completed task to the instructor.

Enhancing Problem-Solving Skills

Many years ago, someone concluded that living is a continuous problem-solving activity. Each day that we live presents us with numerous problem situations for which we must seek solutions. Some daily problems are relatively easy for us to solve; others are very complex and difficult to solve. Problem-solving behavior is not innate; it is learned. Consequently, it is important for us as teachers and other professionals to encourage the development of problem-solving skills in our students, clients, or trainees. Moreover, problem solving frequently requires creativity. In order to encourage creativity in others, we must demonstrate creativity in our professional work. The purposes of this task are (1) to design activities that are intended to encourage the problem-solving skills of learners; (2) to develop an action plan (or lesson plan) for teaching problem-solving skills; and (3) to incorporate strategies and activities for promoting creative thinking skills in an action or lesson plan

TASK PROCEDURES

1. Identify the learners for your lesson. Describe them in some detail, including age range, subject area, level(s) of ability, gender make-up of the group, whether there are learners with disabilities in the group, and any other characteristics of the learners that might have impact on your deciding what strategies to use to promote their learning.

2. Decide upon a lesson and describe it as completely detailed as possible. Identify the learning problem that is involved in the lesson.

3. "Brainstorm" possible problem-solving activities for the lesson and rank them for their potential value for carrying out a successful solution to the problem.

4. Select the two highest-ranked activities and explain how and/or why these activities would encourage learner problem-solving skills.

5. Develop an outline of your problem-solving action/lesson plan that will create a realistic learning environment.

6. Incorporate activities for promoting creativity into your action/lesson plan. Explain how these activities would provide a positive, realistic environment for your learners.

7. Turn in the completed task to your instructor.

Guidelines for Generalization and Transfer

Several guidelines have proven to be effective in encouraging and promoting generalization and transfer of learning with learners of different ages and different learning styles.

1. Make certain that all learners have adequate opportunity to master basic skills.

2. Aid learners in using and improving reading, writing, and math skills.

3. Relate the content being learned to the future needs of the learners.

4. Make certain that learners have mastered all basic skills and relevant material.

5. Provide practice in a wide variety of situations for using the new material or skill.

Critical thinking skills are also essential for solving problems, enhancing study skills, and increasing generalization and transfer of learning to new situations and problems. Critical thinking often follows the basic problem-solving model. [Consult the Woolfolk text for a discussion of critical thinking skills.]

TASK PROCEDURES

1. Describe briefly how people usually study for a test.

2. Critique these current study habits with respect to the type of transfer each study technique can facilitate or impede. Do these present study habits tend to facilitate recall and transfer of learning? What could you do to enhance the chances for recall, generalization and transfer?

3. Brainstorm a list of suggested study activities designed to promote (a) recall and (b) positive transfer, both specific and general. Generate specific activities designed to counteract, or reduce the potential influence of interference. Identify which activities should facilitate each type of transfer and which activities should counteract the effects of interference.

4. Write out your best suggestions in a sequence of "cookbook" study directions. Label each direction with the type of transfer that it is expected to enhance and the type of interference that it is expected to counteract.

5. Turn in the written task to your instructor.

A Critical Thinking Hierarchy
(Contributed by Dr. Jean Strait, Augsburg College)

Outcome statements are currently being drafted and mandated for many educational programs. Critical thinking is high on the list of competencies developed by educators. According to Brookfield (1987) *critical thinking* is defined as reflecting on assumptions underlying actions and considering new ways of looking at the world and how people live in it. It is an engaging, productive process that enables people to be more effective and innovative in every aspect of life and work. Teaching critical thinking is important because we teach students skills required for analyzing information, questions, or problems in order to understand them more fully and solve them more effectively. Because critical thinking is a process and not an outcome, Brookfield viewed it in stages or phases. The first of these stages is known as the *trigger event*. The basic starting point for critical thinking, this unexpected event, prompts a sense of inner conflict. In order for people to deal with this inner discomfort, they travel into the second stage of critical thinking, that of *appraisal or self-examination*.

Once people can identify the issue of conflict and recognize it, they can then begin to search for others with the same discrepancy that leads them into the third stage known as *exploration*. Arising out of the testing and exploring of alternatives comes an awareness for *developing alternative perspectives*. In this fourth stage, people begin to comprehend and appreciate their own situation as well as that of others. Finally, having decided on the worth, accuracy, and validity of new ways of thinking, people begin to integrate these new ways of thinking into their own lives. This *integration* involves transforming attitudes and assumptions as well as establishing a renewed conviction for existing stances. The *resolution* appears when a person is "ready" to accept it.

Keeping this paradigm as a basis, it is reasonable to turn to the *Minnesota Transfer Curriculum on Critical Thinking* and examine four sub-competencies in parallel fashion. Evaluation of each of these sub-competencies can be placed on a process scale to denote student progress and mastery of each of the phases. Many courses have a portfolio component. The process scale can be used to assess individual projects or artifacts within a portfolio, specific sections of the portfolio, or student generated reflections written about a section of the portfolio. When instructors begin to use the scale, everyone rates the same 10 student products together in order to achieve inter-rater reliability. When students are introduced to the scale, they are shown samples of superior, adequate, and needs improvement types of work and are encouraged to classify their own current assignments according to the scale. Suggested grade assignments are presented in parentheses by the qualitative description for each set of criteria. A brief explanation of the assessment of a sample student product for each sub-competency is included.

Sub-competency A: Gather factual information and apply it to a learning experience assignment in a manner that is clear, comprehensive, and conscious of possible bias in the information selected. [This sub-competency includes the *trigger event*, *self-examination*, and *exploration* phases in Brookfield's paradigm.]

Superior (A)

Identifies problems, analyzes them, and provides alternatives for problems--looks at components, relationship, and how everything interacts together.

Process shows discoveries or flexible solutions.

Uses reference materials to draw conclusions and present assertions.

Integrates information from a variety of sources.

Adequate (*C*)

Gathers research and identifies problems.

Does some analysis of these problems (components and relationships).

Process evident but mechanistic, little flexibility

Uses reference materials independently.

Revises for clarity, adding reasons and examples (second draft)

Needs Improvement (*NI*)

Gathers information and identifies components only.

Wrong issues are addressed and problems are solved inappropriately.

Little or no variety, flexibility, breadth, or depth.

Uses reference materials to locate information only with guidance.

Revises by recopying or makes no revision.

Sub-competency B: Imagine and seek out a variety of possible goals, assumptions, interpretations, or perspectives that provide alternative meanings or solutions for a given assignment or learning experience. [This sub-competency highlights *exploration* and *alternative searching* aspects of Brookfield's paradigm in addition to others mentioned in sub-competency A.]

Superior (*A*)

Seeks out the best solutions for the situation, simulates a workable or practical problem, and extends the solution to other problems.

Wrestles with key issues using various resources -- tries to learn new ways or approaches to resolving issues or solving problems.

Interacting with alternatives -- discusses key issues -- modifies value system.

Multidimensional

New ways of thinking are evident -- new conceptual framework.

Adequate (*C*)

Seeks out a variety of alternatives and determines which is the best solution that may apply to a similar problem.

Uses limited resources -- wants simplistic answers that can be understood easily.

Personally reflects on issues but may be narrow in focus.

504

Appropriate insights but only a few details or examples are evident.

New ways of thinking may begin to emerge and a need for change may be expressed.

Needs Improvement (*NI*)

Seeks out every alternative but does not distinguish which ones are workable or practical.

Frustrated by complexity -- may see few or no solutions.

Basic retelling with no evidence of reflection -- usually unrelated topics appear and are unclear

Single focus

New ideas emerge but no attempt is made to demonstrate understanding of them.

Sub-competency C: Analyze the logical connections among the facts, goals, and implicit assumptions relevant to a problem or claim; generate and evaluate implications that result from the connections. [This competency contains *developing alternative perspectives* and *exploration* phases of Brookfield's paradigm in addition to those mentioned in sub-competencies A and B.]

Superior (*A*)

Effectively addresses the topic and all parts of the task.

Is well organized and developed.

Uses clearly appropriate details to support a thesis or illustrate ideas.

Displays consistent use of appropriate language.

Demonstrates appropriate syntax and semantics -- clear and comprehensive.

Adequate (*C*)

Addresses the topic but may slight parts of the task.

Is adequately organized and developed.

Uses some details to support a thesis or demonstrate an idea.

Adequate but inconsistent usage and syntax.

May contain errors that occasionally obscure meaning -- sometimes unclear.

Needs Improvement (*NI*)

Organizes or develops the topic inadequately and shows insufficient details to support or illustrate generalizations.

Shows little organization; ideas are not fully developed.

Uses inappropriate word choice and provides few details to support contentions.

Includes an accumulation of errors in sentence structure and/or usage.

Many errors -- meaning is unclear and not focused.

Sub-competency D: Recognize and articulate the value assumptions that underlie and affect decisions making, interpretations, analyses, and evaluations made by ourselves and others. [This sub-competency highlights *assessing alternative perspectives, integration and conflict resolution* phases in addition to those mentioned for the other three sub-competencies.]

Superior (*A*)

Identifies all the value assumptions pertinent to problems or issues.

Comprehensively analyzes the nature of the value assumptions and their implications for the problem.

Synthesizes new value assumptions with existing knowledge structures.

Adequate (*C*)

Identifies some of the value assumptions.

Partially analyzes the value assumptions.

Recognizes new value assumptions; may integrate into existing knowledge structures.

Needs Improvement (*NI*)

Fails to address key value assumptions or any of the existing value assumption pertinent to the issues or problem.

Analyzes value assumption inaccurately.

Uses only existing schema and value assumptions to solve problems -- recognizes no new information or fails to integrate information into existing knowledge structures.

Working with One Student, Trainee, or Client

Although some students in Educational Psychology may be as many as two years away from real-life instructional experience, there are alternative methods for beginning to practice the techniques you have learned in this course. One method involves tutoring an individual who is having trouble with a particular subject area. Another approach involves working with someone who is having difficulty staying on a diet or stopping smoking. Some other person may need to have a special physical fitness program designed because of a particular health problem. How can you use the techniques and theories of learning, motivation, development, and assessment in order to help someone overcome a particular kind of learning problem? The purposes of this task are to develop, implement, and evaluate an instructional plan or health-enhancement program for an individual student, trainee, or client that is based on principles and theories of learning and motivation

TASK PROCEDURES:

1. Find someone who is having problems with a particular content area or who needs to solve some health-related problem. Some possible sources for locating a person are local public and parochial schools, adult education programs, teachers of courses on English for foreign students, Upward Bound Programs, management training programs, the local adult Reading Academy, senior citizens in your neighborhood, or your own friends and neighbors.

2. Arrange to work with the person for approximately 8-10 hours over at least a two-week period (for example, three-four hours per week for a period of two weeks.) Because of time constraints, concentrate on only one particular learning skill or health problem area. Negotiate with your instructor regarding how extensive and concentrated this problem area should be. State specifically what the problem of concern is.

3. Analyze the problem from at least two (2) theoretical perspectives.

4. Plan the tutoring or training sessions as you would plan instruction for a class. You will need to use the same aspects of instruction: pre-assessment (formal or informal), objectives, instructional sequencing, feedback and so on. In developing your tutoring plan or health-enhancement program, utilize relevant techniques and theories of Educational Psychology. You may find it easiest to develop your plan or program from a single theoretical perspective (e.g., behaviorism, cognitivism, or constructivism).

5. Write a theoretical justification for your instructional program. Critique your program from a different perspective. At the end of the tutoring or training experience, gather information on the effectiveness of your instruction. Examine behavioral changes in the student, trainee or client between the pretest and posttest (summative) assessment of the student. Meet with your student's teacher or other appropriate person in order to discuss whether he/she has noted any improvements. Discuss with the student, trainee, or client the effectiveness of your instruction. Try to judge your own performance objectively. Summarize these various indicators of the success of your instructional plan or health program.

6. Evaluate the overall instructional plan or health program. Did it succeed as you anticipated in your theoretical justification? What were its strengths and weaknesses? What criticisms or analyses of its weaknesses might be presented from a theoretical viewpoint other than the one you utilized in your plan? What improvements can you suggest and justify theoretically?

This particular problem may be of particular interest to students who are planning to work in special education, health promotions, or related programs. Tutoring an individual is becoming an increasingly important activity for pre-service, and even in-service, teachers. Most college and university education programs are now requiring field-based experiences as part of the required curriculum. One way to gain such experience is to work with a single individual on learning problems. The directions for this activity can be helpful in guiding students thinking about planning, implementing, and evaluating such a field-based task.

Designing Effective Instructional Questions

Asking questions is undoubtedly the oldest strategy employed in instruction. It was used in ancient China, Syria and Egypt. More recently (413 B.C.!), questioning was the procedure used to evaluate the results of learning when approximately 7,000 Athenian survivors of the ill-fated attempt to conquer Sicily were questioned regarding their ability to recite verses of Euripides. Nearly all of these survivors remained imprisoned and were required to work the quarries near Syracuse because they were unable to respond correctly to the questions presented.

Unfortunately, many questions (if not most) require mere parroting responses. Such questions do not require learners to think; they merely require repeating back whatever has been read or heard. Questioning as an effective teaching strategy, however, can assist learners to imagine future happenings or to imagine what might have happened if past events were changed. Questioning also can help learners to organize material efficiently and to generalize and transfer new learning. This unit is designed in order to facilitate the design of thought-provoking and divergent questions. Such questions can then be a vehicle for enhancing memory, retention, creativity, generalization of learning, and transfer of learning.

Frequently overlooked in instructional design is the strategy of designing effective questions, especially those requiring higher-order thinking. Asking questions often appears to be an easy task. However, designing effective instructional questions requires considerable skill if they are to be used to foster critical thinking and creativity and to promote generalization and transfer of learning.

Most people find it relatively easy to ask questions that require "right" or "best" answers. Typically, such answers reflect low-level thinking on the part of the responders. Questioning that requires learners to think is a much more difficult strategy. The concept of "thought" involves at least two types of thinking: convergent and divergent. Convergent thinking is directed toward the usual right-wrong concept, no matter how complex the thinking required might be. Convergent questions require answers that can then be evaluated as right or wrong.

In creative learning and teaching, however, it is important to design a set of questions that require learners to extend their thinking beyond the conventional (**convergent thinking**) in order to see new relationships and to look for new implications of old ideas. This type of thinking is called **divergent thinking** and **creativity**. The two basic approaches to thinking, convergent and divergent, can be expressed schematically with respect to what direction the product of each type of thinking usually takes: **Critical thinking** skills are thought to include both divergent and convergent thinking skills. **Divergent (creative) thinkers** may be the persons who are the most satisfied with their lives, because they are able to envision new and different solutions to the crises in life that all persons inevitably face. If this speculation were proven to be true of many people, we would be committing a terrible disservice to our learners if we do not try to foster or enhance divergent (creative) thinking.

Several types of divergent-creative thinking questions have been proposed: (1) **open-ended questions**, (2) **hypothetical questions**, and (3) **creative questions**. These three types of questions are illustrated as follows:

1.   **Open-ended Questions:** How many different, unconventional ways can you use a stone?

2   **Hypothetical Questions:** If you were a bird (or other living creature) how would you feel about communicating and traveling with people?

3.   **Creative Questions:** How could living creatures possibly survive in an active volcano?

The purpose of this task is to design thought-provoking, critical-thinking, and divergent questions for a subject area of your choice.

TASK PROCEDURES

1. Select a section of material in your text (or other source). This material will serve as a common stimulus if you are working in cooperative groups for generating thought-provoking, convergent thinking questions. If you are working individually, select a topic that is familiar to you.

2. Construct a set of 8-10 thought-provoking, *convergent thinking* questions based upon the text material. Identify the cognitive taxonomic level reflected in the type of thinking expected by each question.

3. The stimulus material for writing *divergent thinking* questions could be taken from the following list of topics or create your own topic(s):

   uses of illumination or darkness   measures of temperature
   types of communication   non-effective teachers
   insects, reptiles or mammals   computer uses

4. Construct as many *divergent, unconventional* questions as you can (i.e., "brainstorm" questions), using your selected topic(s) as the stimulus material. Examples of all three types of divergent questions should be generated: *open-ended*, *hypothetical*, and *creative*.

5. Critique the group's questions (or your own list) and select the two most unusual, divergent questions in each of the three categories. Asterisk these six questions.

6. Evaluate the advantages and disadvantages of asking students such provocative questions as those you have created.

7. Turn in the completed task to your instructor.

Using Motivational Theories

Teachers, therapists, and supervisors sometimes encounter people who are not motivated to learn or to behave in appropriate ways. Although these students, clients, or employees are often thought of as unmotivated, their motivation lies in areas that are either irrelevant to or inconsistent with the desired behaviors. The ability to know what to do in these situations is an important part of becoming a teacher, therapist, supervisor, parent, or anyone else who works with people. The purpose of this task is to employ theories of motivation in the analysis and design of activities that will increase a student's, client's, or employee's motivation for learning or behaving appropriately.

TASK PROCEDURES

1. Create a list of at least five motivational problem situations encountered by professionals in your area. Use ideas from your own experiences, experiences that others you know have had, or situations you expect to face in the future. Examples of such situations are:

    A. An employee who, while otherwise efficient, seldom gets to work on time.

    B. A student who is known to have a high IQ but daydreams and does below average work.

    C. A student who never studies for tests usually flunks.

    D. A client who will not do prescribed therapeutic exercises.

    E. A patient who, after four months on a strict diet, is obviously starting to stray back into old eating habits.

    F. An employee who spends more time chatting with fellow employees than working.

    G. While attempting to meet a deadline, a professor plagiarizes a colleague's work and the deed is discovered.

2. Choose two of these situations (or create two of your own) that seem to you to be the most important or that you think you will be likely to face in the future. Try to choose the situations so that *two* different theoretical viewpoints (e.g., Maslow's hierarchy of needs, achievement motivation theory, attribution theory, or social learning theory) are represented.

3. Specify as much detail as possible about each situation (e.g., the person's sex, age, background, behaviors, and feelings).

4. For each situation, develop an outline of the steps that you would use to solve the particular motivational problem. Be as consistent as possible with the theory for each situation. If you feel it is necessary to combine theoretical positions in your solutions, be sure to identify the aspects of your strategy that are related to each theory.

5. Turn in your completed task to the instructor.

A Contemporary Motivational Task

In today's American society, many people are confronted with a motivation problem concerning personal health. A parent, friend, or health professions educator (physical educator, dietician, nurse, etc.) is frequently called on to deal with the problem of motivating an individual to start and/or maintain a physical fitness, recreational, or dietary program. For example, an individual may know all the facts about a good dietary program but not be able to motivate himself/herself to keep on the program. This situation is a motivational problem, rather than a learning one. Consequently, it requires a motivational solution, rather than one employing techniques of teaching verbal information. The purpose of this task is to describe motivational activities based on behaviorist, humanist, and constructivist points of view that facilitate initiating and maintaining a physical fitness, recreational, or dietary program

Define the problem presented in the scenario below according to constructivist, behaviorist, and humanist perspectives. Propose a set of solutions to the problem based on each of these three theoretical positions.

SCENARIO

Imagine that you and/or your group provides a dietary and physical fitness counseling service. A mother, her son, and a concerned teacher come to you for counseling. The son, Jeff, is 17 years old and 100 pounds overweight for his age and height. Jeff has tried numerous diets but does not stay on any of them. The mother indicates that her son started to gain weight five years ago, shortly after the death of his father. He is an only child.

The teacher indicates that Jeff's schoolwork is above average, although he is isolated from school peers and seems to have few, if any, close friends. Further, Jeff's mother indicates that Jeff returns home immediately after school, goes to his room and studies until time for dinner. After dinner, he watches TV, snacks all evening and does light studying.

Today you are having a preliminary meeting with Jeff and his family in order to define the problem, identify further information needed, and outline possible solutions. The "stage is now set" for creating an effective solution to this motivational problem.

TASK PROCEDURES

1. Assume that your counseling group decides that the major problem is motivational. Further, you believe the teenager needs a physical fitness, dietary, or recreational program.

2. Identify and list as many different possible "facets" of the problem as you can. Define the problem from constructivist (achievement motivation or attribution theory), humanistic (Maslow), and behaviorist (reinforcement and extrinsic motivation) perspectives..

3. What additional information do you need in order to gain a specific definition of the problem? List the types and sources of information that you would like to have, considering the constructivist, behaviorist, and humanist points of view.

4. "Brainstorm" many different possible solutions to the problem, considering each of the different perspectives that one could take regarding the problem. Clearly label the solution sets in terms of whether they represent constructivist, behaviorist, or humanist perspectives.

5. Select the solutions (actions) that would be most likely to solve the problem. Explain your choices.

6. Turn in the completed task to your instructor.

Solving a Behavioral Problem

Select one of the following behavioral problems (or construct your own) and develop an approach designed to modify the behaviors involved according to techniques advocated by behavioral theorists. Some possible options are presented with each problem. Make adaptations as necessary to fit your future career.[Note: You will need to identify the appropriate assumptions, constraints and facts regarding age, occupation, grade level, etc.]

1. Jennifer, a student or employee, takes longer each day to complete assignments; some are never completed.

2. Scott participates in class or meetings only if directly called upon and he never joins in voluntarily.

3. Karl failed all academic subjects during the first half of the year. Although he has an average IQ as measured by a group ability test, his parents and teachers have been unable to encourage him to study, despite threats and punishments.

4. Kim is frequently 3 to 5 minutes late each day to her 5th-hour class, work, or therapy appointment.

5. Ms. Tanaka's students (or employees or clients) are often at her desk (or office) without a valid reason.

6. Theo makes negative statements about himself, such as "I am dumb" and "I can't do it." He gives up on most projects before he even gets started.

7. During a speech-therapy session, Laura talks about irrelevant topics and acts impulsively in order to avoid working on therapy assignments.

8. In Home Economics class, the students follow the teacher's directions about one-half of the time. Instructions concerning clean- up, use of utensils, following recipes, and conduct are frequently ignored. (This situation could be revised to describe the adult employees at a restaurant, hospital cafeteria, or food manufacturing plant.)

TASK PROCEDURES

1. Select one of the problem situations described in the above section and adapt it to fit your future professional situation. Describe the adapted situation, including any relevant constraints, assumptions, and facts.

2. Determine the probable reinforcement or "payoff" of the specific inappropriate behavior. Why is it occurring?

3. State exactly what the negative behavior is and under what conditions it occurs. Use your imagination.

4. Describe specifically some mild, preliminary steps you might take to extinguish the negative behavior when it first appears.

5. Assume that the preliminary steps are not successful. Specify exactly the desired substitute behavior(s) in the form of a behavioral objective.

6.   Determine appropriate reinforcers to use in encouraging the desired behavior(s).

7.   Design specific behavioral procedures, based of behavior modification techniques, for extinguishing

8.   the negative behavior and developing the desired behavior(s). Possible procedures include one or a combination of the following: positive and negative reinforcement, punishment, shaping, vicarious reinforcement, modeling, group responsibility, token reinforcement, contingency-contracting, and self-management. Be sure to describe the schedule(s) of reinforcement to be used.

9.   Turn in your completed task to the instructor.

APPENDIX 2

C: TOOLS FOR EVALUATING AUTHENTIC ASSESSMENT PRODUCTS

Self/Peer Scoring Rubrics for Authentic Tasks
(Contributed by Dr. Dianne Horgan, University of Memphis)

Analyzing case studies provides one means by which students can demonstrate understanding of the concepts and principles of Educational Psychology. These analyses can be accomplished by students working on their own or by working cooperatively in small groups. These rubrics can be adapted for other student performance tasks such as a training plan, lesson/unit plans, individual problems, or any writing task that requires a rationale. The purpose of this task is to analyze an assigned case study (or other performance task) by applying concepts of educational psychology from different perspectives

TASK PROCEDURES

These scoring rubrics can be used in different ways. One strategy is to ask students to assess their own drafts using the self-assessment form. The draft can be evaluated by the instructor who would indicate on students' self-assessment forms whether or not the instructor agrees with their self assessment and provide specific feedback as to why there is disagreement or agreement. On the draft, a specific grade is not given, rather simply a "+". "-."or "❏ " next to the scores they gave themselves. Only the final paper is graded. Usually the peer reviews are graded in order to ensure that the reviews are done with care. (Left to their own devices, many peers are quite reluctant to give feedback.) Four levels of scores for the peer reviews are given:

Excellent	In addition to filling out the form, peers wrote useful and insightful margin notes to the author.
Good	The form is completely filled out, and there are some useful margin notes for the author.
Minimal	The form is completely filled out, but no useful margin notes are included.
Unacceptable	The form is not fully filled out.

The authors then revise their case analyses, using the instructor's feedback and the feedback from their peer reviewers. At least a week should be allocated for the revisions.

GRADING THE FINAL DRAFTS

A scale ranging from 90 - 100 = A, 80 - 89 = B, 70 - 79 = C, etc. can be applied to the final documents. Both a global rating and a rating for each of five specific criteria can be utilized. The highest possible score for each individual criterion is 20 points. The results of the global rating are added to or subtracted from the ratings for the five criteria.

In grading students' final drafts, it is recommended that reference is made to the original self-assessment form, looking especially for indications as to whether or not the author made use of the feedback. An overall rating is assigned based on the extent to which students attended to their individual feedback. These points are added to or subtracted from the total from each of the five individual criteria.

QUALITATIVE/QUANTITATIVE RATING SCALE

Excellent (+ 8 to 10 points): Student attended to almost all of the appropriate feedback, and the final paper is substantially improved.

Good (+5 to 8 points): Student attended to much of the appropriate feedback and the final paper is improved. Or, the first draft was excellent and the student attended to any minimal feedback that was necessary.

Satisfactory (+2 to 4 points): Student attended to some feedback, and the final paper is improved.

Minimal (0 to - 1 point): There were suggestions for change, yet very few changes were made based on feedback.

Unsatisfactory (-2 to -6 points): Substantial changes were suggested but most were not made.

SPECIFIC CRITERIA RATINGS

In deciding what level of performance should yield how many points, it is important to take into consideration how much exposure students have had to case analysis tasks. One recommendation is having students conduct oral cases before they write their case analyses. During the oral presentations, the instructor can guide students to attend to the first four criteria: (1) use of theory/research/concepts; (2) attention to different perspectives; (3) advice offered to individuals involved in the case; and (4) the level of analysis. Therefore, a higher level of sophistication can be expected than when this task is a student's first attempt at a case analysis (theoretical paper or whatever the task may be). Moreover, the level of sophistication expected will depend on the preparation level of the students. With these considerations in mind, the following is a guide to assigning criterion points:

I.   **Use of theory/research/concepts:**

Excellent (18-20 points): Student cites at least 3 theories or theorists, at least 3 studies, and a least 5 concepts; demonstrates full understanding of those cited.

Good (16-17 points): Student cites at least 3 theories or theorists, at least 3 studies, and least 5 concepts and demonstrates adequate understanding of most of those cited.

Acceptable (14-15 points): Student cites a good number of theories, studies, and concepts, but there is considerable confusion with regard to how some of the theories, studies, or concepts apply to this case.

Minimal (12-13 points): Student cites a good number of theories, studies, and concepts, but there is no real indication that the student understood them.

Unsatisfactory (11 or fewer points): Student cites only a few theories, studies, or concepts. There is little to demonstrate understanding of how the theories, studies, or concepts apply to the case.

II. Attention to different perspectives:

Excellent (18-20 points): Student identifies the major stakeholders and is able to articulate each position accurately and sympathetically.

Good (16-17 points): Student identifies the major stakeholders and is able to see most of their perspectives.

Acceptable (14-15 points): Student identifies most of the major stakeholders and acknowledge different perspectives, but is not able·to fully appreciate all sides.

Minimal (12-13 points): Student recognizes there are different perspectives, but overlooks some or does not see the validity of important stakeholders' positions.

Unsatisfactory (11 or fewer points): Student fails to see beyond his or her own perspective or perhaps fails to identify different stakeholders.

III. Advice:

Excellent (18-20 points): Student offers a number of appropriate, practical, specific, related to the course, and useful pieces of advice that take into account the needs of all the major stakeholders. Different cases offer different numbers of opportunities for advice; so the number necessary to earn this rating will vary from case to case.

Good (16-17 points): Student offers some appropriate, practical, specific, course-related, and useful pieces of advice that take into account the needs of the major stakeholders. At this level, there are either fewer pieces of advice or lower quality advice than what earns an "excellent" rating.

Acceptable (14-15 points): Student offers some advice, some of which is based on course content or takes into account the needs of major stakeholders.

Minimal (12-13 points): Student offers limited advice that is not based on course content or does not take into account the needs of major stakeholders.

Unsatisfactory (11 or fewer points): Student fails to offer any advice that is based on course content or fails to offer advice that meets the needs of different stakeholders.

IV. Level of Analysis: If a student has done poorly on criterion I, he or she will necessarily do poorly on this section.

Excellent (18-20 points): Student goes beyond citing theories and research and shows a sophisticated understanding of the dynamics of the case. The student gives a good analysis of how the problem developed, seeing its multiple causes and the contributions of various stakeholders. The student sees the "big picture" and articulates how the specific problem fits with larger issues and problems. Student uses the course concepts to amplify his or her analysis.

Good (16-17 points): Student appreciates how more than one stakeholder contributed to the problem and sees that the problem did not develop in a vacuum. The student is able to articulate how concepts from the class can help understanding of the case.

Acceptable (14-15 points): Student is able to see multiple roles and has some understanding of the dynamics, but has only limited understanding of how course concepts apply.

Minimal (12-13 points): Student's appreciation of the problem is narrow. Appreciates some of the complexity, but has difficulty using course concepts to discuss the case.

Unsatisfactory (11 or fewer points): Student fails to go beyond the superficial. May blame one stakeholder for the problem or fail to see how multiple events lead to the problem. The student Is not able to apply course content to the case.

V.   Style/grammar/spelling:

Because students receive feedback on their drafts that includes attention to their errors, this section should be evaluated rigorously.

Excellent (18-20 points): Well-written, very few errors.

Good (16-17 points): Well-written, but some minor errors.

Acceptable (14-15 points): No major problems but contains a number of errors and perhaps some awkward writing.

Minimal (12-13 points): Some major grammatical problems, a number of errors, weak writing skills.

Unsatisfactory (11 or fewer points): Major grammatical and spelling errors and, overall, poor writing skills.

PEER ASSESSMENT FORM FOR CASE ANALYSIS

Score each criterion from 1-20

I.   **Use of theory/research/concepts**

     The student referred to *theories or theorists* _____ times. (Should be at least 3.)

     The student referred to *research studies* _____ times. (Should be at least 3.)

     The student referred to *concepts* from the text or lecture _____ times. (Should be least 5.)

                                                 Total Score: _____

II.   **Attention to different perspectives**

     The student considered the perspective of the following people or groups:

     1. _____   2. _____

     3. _____   4. _____

     5. _____   6. _____

                                                 Total Score: _____

III. **Advice**

     Did the student make SPECIFIC suggestions? _____   How many? _____

     Were they based on information related to this class? _____

     Were the suggestions practical? _____

     Did the student consider the multiple perspectives listed above? _____

                                               Total Score: _____

IV. **Level of analysis**

     Did the student go beyond a superficial analysis? _____

     Did the student consider the multiple perspectives listed above? _____

     Did the student go beyond blaming people for the problem? _____

     Did the student use theories/concepts/research to help explain how the problem developed? _____

     Did the student see more than one problem? _____

     Did the student see more than one person as contributing to the problem(s). _____

                                               Total Score: _____

V.   **Style/grammar/spelling**

     Mark each error. Found ___ grammar; ___ spelling errors.
     [None or 1 minor error = 20; many errors = zero.]

                                               Total Score: _____

Final Assessment: I predict this paper will receive (add I-V) _____points.

Performance Checklist for Written Products
(Contributed by Dr. Gary G. Brannigan, State University of New York – Plattsburg)

Frequently, students do not take advantage of opportunities to read more extensively about topics presented in textbooks. Therefore, in order to encourage them to "engage" with the material they are studying and "bring it to life," writing projects can be assigned with the following instruction: Apply a specific concept, idea, or procedure in the chapter to a situation that you have experienced personally, professionally, or vicariously (e.g., from a case study). In addition to the solid foundation provided by Woolfolk's *Educational Psychology (2007),* students should choose from among three alternatives in selecting supplementary readings to provide a more in-depth understanding of the topic:

1. Conduct a library search and identify a source.

2. Choose a source from the Instructor's Research Manual of Woolfolk's *Educational Psychology, 10/e.*

3. Choose a section from an anthology or supplementary text dealing with research. Branningan (1996) provides a centralized source of in-depth, lively accounts of applied research in major areas of education (see references).

Students should be encouraged to use their imagination and creativity in the choice of experiences to examine. Among the many possibilities are the following: apply Vygotsky's ideas in an interview; develop mnemonic strategies; conduct behavioral analyses; examine attribution styles; develop cooperative learning paradigms; modify behaviors; and even design authentic performance assessments. Topics generally can be covered in 500 to 1000 words. The number of topics assigned and the length of each assignment can be adjusted to the demands of individual courses.

These activities permit students to demonstrate what they have learned by applying their knowledge to novel situations. They also must develop and organize their thoughts and present them in a manner that others will clearly understand. The following Checklist, including feedback criteria, was adapted from the model of Spandel and Stiggin (1990). This Checklist is focused on the skills of knowledge and application, development and organization of ideas, and written expression.

PERFORMANCE CHECKLIST

Strengths

_____ Knowledge of topic clearly evident

_____ Knowledge applied in relevant manner

_____ Interesting

_____ Well focused

_____ Clear

_____ Detailed, complete, rich

_____ Written from experience

Weaknesses

_____ Faulty knowledge base

_____ Inaccurate application of knowledge

_____ Lacking in purpose or theme

_____ Rambling

_____ Unclear muddle

_____ Broad, general, vague

_____ Not believable, boring

Organization and Development of Ideas

Strengths

_____ Good introduction

_____ Good placement of details

_____ Smooth transitions

_____ Smooth, easy pace

_____ Reader doesn't have to think about organization

_____ Strong conclusion

_____ Starts somewhere - goes somewhere

Weaknesses

_____ Details seem out of place

_____ Introduction boring, predictable

_____ Transitions absent, weak, too obvious

_____ Doesn't go anywhere

_____ Wanders aimlessly

_____ Stops abruptly

_____ Drags on; Bogs down in trivia

Conventions of Writing

Strengths

_____ Correct spelling

_____ Interesting word patterns

_____ Good phrasing

_____ Paragraphing enhances organization

_____ Paragraphs start appropriately

_____ Varied sentence length

Weaknesses

_____ Spelling faulty

_____ Short, choppy sentences

_____ Long, rambling sentences

_____ Little or no paragraphing

_____ Paragraphs start in wrong place

_____ Repetitious structure patterns

_____ Varied sentence structure	_____ Same sentence structure throughout
_____ Varied sentence beginnings	_____ Same paragraph beginnings
_____ Punctuation works with sentence structure	_____ Punctuation is inconsistent with sentence structure
_____ Correct grammar	_____ Grammatical problems
_____ Sound usage	_____ Faulty usage
_____ Attention to details (i.e., dotted *i*, crossed *t*)	_____ Careless, hasty errors
_____ Easy to read	_____ Hard to read

Summary Assessment of Written Products

Skill	5	3	1
Application of Knowledge	Successful	Reasonably Successful	Not Successful
Organization and Development of Ideas	Well Organized and Developed	Fairly Well Organized and Developed	Not Organized or Developed Well
Writing Conventions	No Significant Mistake	Several Significant Mistakes	Many Significant Mistakes

Teacher Rating Scales for Authentic Assessments
(Contributed by Dr. William Gnagey, Illinois State University)

This set of four rating scales can be utilized in a variety of situations, but they are intended primarily for use in field-based settings. Students who have a direct observation component in their pre-service (or in-service) curriculum should find these forms to be easy to use, and the criteria included on each scale will help students to focus on pertinent concepts and issues.

TEACHER CHARACTERISTICS RATING SCALE

Rate the teacher you have observed on each of the seven characteristics listed below. Use the following scale: 5 = Superior; 4 = Excellent; 3 = Average; 2 = Poor; 1 = Incompetent; NO = Not Observed. In the space under each rated characteristic, describe one specific event that supports your rating.

_____ 1. Knowledge of the subject matter being taught

      Specific Event:

_____ 2. Skill in organizing ideas and materials

      Specific Event:

_____ 3. Skill in communicating clearly and understandably

      Specific Event:

_____ 4. Use of effective methods of teaching

      Specific Event:

_____ 5. Enthusiasm about teaching the material

      Specific Event:

_____ 6. Warm and caring attitude toward students

      Specific Event:

_____ 7. Flexibility in making instructional changes when indicated

      Specific Event:

CONSTRUCTIVIST RATING SCALE*

Rate the teacher you have observed on each of the six practices listed below. Use the following scale: 5 = Almost Always; 4 = Frequently; 3 = Sometimes; 2 = Occasionally; 1 = Hardly Ever; NO = Not Observed. In the space under each practice, describe one specific event that supports your rating.

_____ 1.   Makes sure that students are attending to the lesson.

Specific Event:

_____ 2.   Helps students focus on the most important information.

Specific Event:

_____ 3.   Helps students connect new information with that already learned.

Specific Event:

_____ 4.   Provides for repetition and review of information.

Specific Event:

_____ 5.   Presents material in a clear, well organized way.

Specific Event:

_____ 6.   Focuses on meaning, not memorization.

Specific Event:

MASLOVIAN HUMANIST TEACHING RATING SCALE *

Rate the teacher you have observed on each of the seven practices listed below. Use the following scale: 5 = Almost Always; 4 = Frequently; 3 = Sometimes; 2 = Occasionally; 1 = Hardly Ever; NO = Not Observed. In the space under each practice, describe one specific event that supports your rating.

_____ 1.   Helps students fulfill their survival (physiological) needs.

        Specific event:

_____ 2.   Helps students fulfill their security (safety) needs.

        Specific Event:

_____ 3.   Helps students fulfill their belonging (social) needs.

        Specific Event:

_____ 4.   Helps students fulfill their esteem needs.

        Specific Event:

_____ 5.   Helps students fulfill their intellectual achievement needs.

        Specific Event:

_____ 6.   Helps students fulfill their aesthetic appreciation needs.

        Specific Event:

_____ 7.   Helps students fulfill their self-actualization needs.

        Specific Event:

ERIKSONIAN TEACHING RATING SCALE*

Rate the teacher you have observed on each of the five practices listed below. Use the following scale: 5 = Almost Always; 4 = Frequently; 3 = Sometimes; 2 = Occasionally; 1=Hardly Ever; NO = Not Observed. In the space under each practice, describe one specific event that supports your rating.

_____ 1.   Promotes trust between students and teacher and/or among students.

Specific Event:

_____ 2.   Promotes student autonomy.

Specific Event:

_____ 3.   Promotes student initiative.

Specific Event:

_____ 4.   Promotes student industry.

Specific Event:

_____ 5.   Facilitates students' search for identity.

Specific Event:

APPENDIX 2

D: TEACHER-DESIGNED ASSESSMENT TASKS

Planning a Classroom Test

One of the most important functions of any educator (teacher, college professor, nutrition specialist, parent, manager, clinician, etc.) is to make decisions about what to teach and how to specify the criteria of acceptable performance. The first step in this decision process is to translate broad learning goals into manageable instructional units on which specific behavioral objectives can be based. Called **task analysis**, this procedure is a useful first step for making decisions about what to teach and what is to be evaluated.

The next stage of the decision process involves stating learning goals as behavioral objectives. Clearly stated behavioral objectives facilitates specification of the criteria for acceptable performance and identifies what is to be taught. A **table of specifications** (TOS) as a "blueprint" for instruction that is based on a taxonomy of behavior is an effective tool to employ in making specific decisions about what to teach and what is to be evaluated. The purposes of this task are (1) to write behavioral objectives that reflect accurately the requirements of one approach to writing objectives, and (2) to construct a Table of Specifications (TOS) based upon one taxonomic domain (cognitive, affective, or psychomotor) for an instructional sequence

CONSTRUCTING A TABLE OF SPECIFICATIONS

After the goals and objectives have been determined for a particular instructional unit, the next stage in the sequence of instructional design usually is to identify the series of tasks to be undertaken. However, having in mind a final model of what is to be attained is extremely helpful in planning the sequence of instructional activities. Some type of diagram or chart that includes the objectives and content to be learned will be very helpful. Many instructors have found that a two-dimensional table, representing the content to be learned on one axis and the type of thinking required on the other axis, can be very helpful in identifying instructional emphasis.

This two-dimensional table (behavior-content matrix) is often called a **Table of Specifications (TOS)**. Regardless of whether the TOS is detailed or simple, the first step in constructing a TOS is to identify the goals. Next, the specific objectives designed to accomplish the goals are written and sequenced according to their content. When these have been determined, the TOS can be developed. An elaborated TOS will reflect the importance of each behavioral level in a taxonomic domain and of each sub-topic content area. Sometimes a few cells in the TOS will be empty, indicating that the particular content/behavior category does not have an objective.

The use of a TOS has at least three advantages. First, many of the potential problems found in using behavioral objectives can be avoided, such as the use of trivial objectives that lead to the "spoon-feeding" of learners. Second, seeing all of the objectives for a unit (or course) of instruction in one place makes it convenient to organize them into logical sequences. A third significant advantage of using a TOS is that it provides the basis for developing the means (a **test blueprint**) by which learning outcomes are to be measured and evaluated. When the test, or other measurement tool, is designed to reflect the TOS for a given unit, the instrument will have content validity. In other words, the instrument truthfully reflects what is to be learned.

531

TASK PROCEDURES

1. Construct a specification chart that includes at least 10 well-written behavioral objectives distributed across the levels of one taxonomic domain (cognitive, affective, or psychomotor).

2. Select a topic for a short lesson and sub-divide the topic into at least four sub-categories.

3. Briefly describe the learners.

4. State the broad goal(s) of the lesson.

5. Identify which approach to writing objectives will be followed.

6. Working individually, write 3-4 objectives that reflect at least three levels of the taxonomic domain (cognitive, affective, or psychomotor) involved in your goals.

7. As an individual or as a group, develop a Table of Specifications that relates the behavioral outcomes (objectives) to the content of the lesson. Judge the emphases (percent of time to be spent) to be given to the various content areas and taxonomic levels. (The number of objectives reflected in the TOS may vary, depending upon the nature of the goal and the learners.)

8. Critique the objectives prepared by individual group members with respect to how well they fulfill the Table of Specifications (TOS). List the 10 best objectives and label them according to your TOS decisions made in Step 6. If your TOS calls for an objective that was not written by any group member, write it (them) as a group, and label it (them) as a group-prepared objective.

9. Turn in the task to your instructor. If you are in a cooperative learning group, include your own initial set of 3-4 objectives.

Developing and Analyzing a Teacher-Designed Test

The two major purposes of an assessment tool are to identify what individuals have learned and to judge the effectiveness of instruction. In addition, of course, tests are used to determine course grades that, in turn, have far-reaching effects on various aspects of students' lives. What steps can be taken to ensure that a test is a fair and accurate assessment of both learning and instruction? How can the effectiveness of the test itself be gauged and improved?

OBJECTIVES:
* To design an effective and efficient measure of classroom learning
* To administer the assessment instrument to a small group of examinees (at least 10 persons)
* To analyze the results of the instrument and interpret the data accurately

THE PROBLEM:

Your assignment is to construct an objective test, administer it, analyze the results, revise your test, and assign grades to your examinees. You may choose any topic and group of examinees that interest you. You are, however, responsible for gaining access to your chosen population to administer the test. Projects for this assignment may include tests for: reading, spelling, math, science, or social studies at the elementary-school level; U. S. government, algebra, biology, chemistry, foreign language, or literature at the secondary level; or fraternity history and house rules, volleyball rules, college trivia (i.e., for tour-guides), library information, or any other topic approved by your instructor. Be creative!

CRITERIA FOR EVALUATING/GRADING ASSESSMENT PROJECTS:

* Appropriateness of your choice(s) given the topic area and testing population you select

* Accuracy with which you classify educational objectives and test items

* Evidence of your ability to calculate and interpret the indices for test and item quality

* Your ability to revise your test and test items given the data you receive

* Appropriateness of your evaluation of the examinees in terms of the method of evaluation you use, given the results of your test and item analyses and the grades that you assign to individuals.

When choosing a test purpose, for instance, you must identify your selection (i.e., norm-referenced or criterion-referenced purpose), the evidence you used to make that choice (i.e., the levels of thinking and/or the objectives that you want to test in the cognitive domain), and the text and other expert source material (i.e., other textbooks, journal articles, material from another class/professor) that support your work. Remember that, if your course objectives are mastery-oriented, you must plan on constructing two or more equivalent forms of your test, because it is highly probable that some of your students will not meet your mastery criterion on their first attempt. It is not an easy task to create equivalent forms of a test, but it is necessary to do so if mastery of subject content is the learning goal. Also, remember that only a few objectives should be measured in a test designed to assess mastery.

TASK PROCEDURES:

Specific guidelines for this project are presented below. You are to follow these guidelines precisely, omitting no step, and including all relevant issues, concerns, and concepts! These guidelines are also relevant (with minor variations) for the development, analysis, and evaluation of other types of assessment tools, including rating scales, scoring rubrics, and other authentic projects.

1. Describe as thoroughly as possible the student group for which your instrument is intended. Include such information as grade level, subject matter area, typical ability level, degree of variability in the group, socioeconomic status of the group, etc. Identify all constraints or limitations that impinge upon your project (e.g., time constraints, need to use someone's class, age of subjects, etc.). Make certain that you describe the general nature of the instructional strategies that were employed.

2. Identify the nature of the subject content to be tested. Outline the topic content. What is the overall purpose of the test, norm-referenced or criterion-referenced? Explain your choice. How difficult should the test items be for your purpose? Explain.

3. State precisely the specific behavioral objectives that the test purports to measure. Prepare behavior-content matrix or test blueprint that relates objectives to subject content.

4. Decide on the item format(s) to be used and explain why it was chosen. Construct test items that reflect the behavior-content matrix. Carefully follow the rules for good item construction.

5. Prepare the test. Describe the administration and scoring issues that should be considered, including ways of preparing examinees for the test.

6. Administer the test to your examinees, and score the tests carefully. Present the data graphically (histogram or frequency polygon) in addition to the usual high to low distribution of scores reported by scoring services or created by hand.

7. Before analyzing/interpreting the test data, focus upon item analysis and evaluation. Analyze and evaluate each test item. Describe the effectiveness of the items as a set. Do the item data support your test purpose? Thoroughly evaluate and discuss all items that (a) are difficult for your students and/or (b) do not function effectively for your group..

8. Analyze and interpret the overall test results, with respect to each of the problem issues. Derive and explain statistical relationships that help you to interpret the data.

9. Assign letter grades to test performances on the basis of an appropriate grading practice. Defend your choice of the grading procedure.

10. Summarize the study and make recommendations for improving the effectiveness of the test. Turn in the original and one copy of your project. The original will be returned to you with instructor comments.

This performance task will be evaluated in terms of the overall thoroughness and accuracy with which the above steps are handled. Such qualities as neatness, correct grammar and logical organization of ideas also will be considered. Use relevant terminology but do not assume that your reader can "fill in the gaps."

Interpreting a Set of Test Data

The following set of test data was obtained for Exam I administered to 334 students in an introductory educational psychology course in the fall semester of 1996. The testing condition for this exam was in-class, closed book. The test included 60 multiple-choice items designed to measure knowledge, understanding, and application of assigned content topics.

Group mean (M):	**40.58**
Standard deviation (s):	**7.78**
Range of scores (R):	**38**
Average item difficulty:	**67%**
Alpha reliability:	**0.82**
Error of measurement (s_m):	**3.31**
Number of s in R:	**4.88**
Percent of error in score range:	**9%**

PROCEDURES

1. Given the above set of test results, interpret the data thoroughly with regard to:

   * measures of central tendency
   * measures of variability
   * shape of the distribution
   * measures of relationship (reliability and error)

2. Describe the shape of the distribution of scores.

3. What percentage or proportion of the maximum possible is the observed range? Does this finding support the perceived test purpose? Explain.

4. How many standard deviations are above the mean? Below the mean?

5. Interpret the reliability coefficient. What does the reliability estimate suggest about this exam? How much measurement error is there in the observed range of scores?

6. What is the average difficulty level of the test? What test purpose does it reflect?

7. Speculate about how the individual test items functioned.

8.   What kind of test data are these? NR or CRM? Explain your decision.

9.   Speculate about how the individual test items would have functioned. Explain the basis for your position.

10. Describe the overall quality of this exam.

11. Would it be appropriate to assign letter grades to the distribution of scores? Why? Why not? If appropriate, how would you assign grades to the scores from this exam?

12. Describe how you would report these or your own test results to your students? Could you defend your assignment of letter grades to students' performances to their parents or guardians? Explain your answer.

Feedback for Test Data Interpretation Problem

Measures of Central Tendency

For this 60-item exam, the mean score of 40.58 (the central tendency of the score distribution) indicates that the average difficulty level of the exam is approximately 67%. This measure of central tendency, the arithmetic center of the score distribution, strongly suggests that the data are potentially norm-referenced. The average student who took this exam was successful on 67% of the items in the exam. This average difficulty level indicates that the exam is not a mastery exam; mastery would require an average difficulty level of approximately 90% or higher.

Measures of Variability

The least precise measure of the variability among student performances is the range of scores in the distribution. For this exam, the range was 38 items, or 63.33% (39/60) of the total number of items in the exam. The larger a range of scores is, the larger will be the number of individual differences in performance. As a rule of thumb, the score range for norm-referenced results should be at least 40% of the total items in a test, in order to demonstrate a sufficient number of individual differences in performance for making tentative decisions concerning student achievement levels.

The most precise measure of variability is the standard deviation (σ, s, or S.D.). This statistic is used to identify how far away each individual score is from the center of the distribution (the mean). As a point of reference, a perfectly normal distribution of scores has at least six s units in its range, representing approximately 99.9% of the total number of people being measured. However, usually approximately 500 or more persons must be involved in the assessment procedure in order to have as much variability as that found in the theoretical normal distribution. The distribution of scores for the 334 students who took this exam is not a perfectly normal distribution, even though it has the general shape of a normal distribution There are only 4.88 s units in this distribution, but this number of s units represents as much variability as could be expected for this sample size.

Reliability and Error of Measurement

The estimate of internal test reliability of 0.82 (Cronbach alpha r) is reasonably high for this exam, indicating that the test items tended to function very consistently. This reliability estimate also suggests a strong relationship between how students responded to individual items and their total test scores. Because the overall test reliability is strong, we can also infer that there was rather strong discrimination power in the items on this exam (ability to differentiate among levels of achievement).

The standard error of measurement (s_m) was 3.31 items, indicating that individual students can expect their scores to vary by this number of items (increase or decrease the score) should they take this same test again (assuming no new learning takes place in the meantime). However, knowing the size of the measurement error is not especially meaningful in a practical sense, but when the standard error is divided by the range of scores, we can obtain an estimate of how many individual scores in the range can be attributed to measurement error. For this exam, the ratio of measurement error to range of scores was 3.31:38. This ratio indicates that less than 9% of the 334 scores might not reflect accurate levels of achievement. As a rule, 10 percent or less error in a score range is viewed to be acceptable. Obviously, even less error or no error at all (perfect reliability) would be ideal!

Item Analysis Data Interpretation Task

Given the Item Analysis Summary Table presented below, interpret the overall functioning of the test items as a group. These item summary data were obtained from a large multiple-division undergraduate educational psychology course in the fall of 1996. There was a total of 334 students who took the 60-item multiple-choice test designed to emphasize use of knowledge rather than factual information. The testing condition was the traditional in-class, closed-book administration.

ITEM ANALYSIS SUMMARY CHART

P \ D	++++ 1.00 -.80	+++ .79 -.60	++ .59 -.40	+ .39 -.20	Non ± .19	Neg -.20 +	Total
Easy 1.00 to .75	0	0	3	10	8	0	21
Average .74 to .26	0	2	15	20	2	0	39
Hard .25 to 0.00	0	0	0	0	0	0	0
Total	0	2	18	30	10	0	60

TASK PROCEDURES

1. Describe the efficiency and effectiveness of the 60-item Exam 1 designed for students in a basic undergraduate Educational Psychology course.

    *   Does the purpose of this test look as though it was intended to be norm-referenced or criterion-referenced mastery?
    *   How appropriate is the item difficulty level for the apparent test purpose?
    *   How appropriate for the test purpose is the discrimination power of the items?

2. Summarize the overall effectiveness of this test for assigning grades to individuals in this class. Are there sufficient individual differences to warrant differential grade assignments?

Feedback for Item Analysis Interpretation Task

Difficulty of Test Items

Analysis of the difficulty of the items on this exam indicates that 35% of the items were easy for students (answered correctly by 75% or more of the subjects), while the remaining 65% were average in difficulty level (P values ranging from 26% - 74%). Students found no hard item on this exam. Because of the large number of easy items, the overall difficulty of this test can be described as "high average." Sometimes, we might want to have a few hard items that would challenge the best achievers in the class. It is fun, however, to report to students that they did not find any really difficult item on the exam, especially after hearing complaints (sometimes quite bitter ones) about how difficult the educational psychology exams are. The evidence for this exam (and all of the other educational psychology exams) contradicts such complaints!

Discrimination Power of Test Items

The item analysis summary data provide rather strong evidence for the power of these items to differentiate among levels of student achievement. Fifty items (83%) demonstrated significant discrimination power, with 20 of these items as strong discriminators (D values of 40% or higher). Thirty-seven (62%) of the discriminators were average in difficulty level, a finding that is not surprising because it is more difficult for easy and hard items to discriminate than it is for average items. In other words, when most students answer an item successfully (say 80% or more students answering correctly), there is little "room" for any significant difference to occur between the high and low-scoring criterion groups, and the same concept is true for hard items (answered successfully by 25% or fewer examinees). Eight of the easy items (38%) and only two of the average items (3.3%) were non-significant discriminators (but all of these were in the positive direction).

Fortunately, there were no apparent problem items on this test; that is, there were no significantly negative discriminators. If any significantly negative discriminator were to be found, it is important to determine why low scorers were more successful than high scorers. Miskeying of items is a frequent source of negative discrimination. Another possible cause includes ambiguity in item content and/or structure. Perhaps clues to the correct answer for some specific items were given inadvertently in a review session for the exam that may have been attended by students who were less prepared than others. In any case, it is important to track down the reason(s) for significantly negative discriminators. All difficult items (success by only 25% or fewer students) and even non-discriminating average difficulty items should also be examined in depth in order to identify why these items functioned as they did.

Summary Interpretation of Item Data

These item data strongly support the conclusion that these norm-referenced results reflect a high-average overall difficulty level and strong discrimination power for identifying individual differences in achievement levels among students. Therefore, assigning differential to student performances is valid. Moreover, these item data strongly suggest that the overall test is reliable, because discrimination power influences test reliability (the more individual differences, the greater the reliability and. hence, the less measurement error).

In-Depth Analysis of a Multiple-Choice Test Item

Often a teacher needs to look in depth at certain test items that the Item Analysis Summary Table indicates potential problems. Such items did **NOT** function as the teacher wanted them to function; i.e., some items may have been too difficult and the teacher wants to know why they were difficult. Other items may be negative discriminators. Again, the question is why did the correct response draw significantly more low scorers than high scorers. Something is wrong with such items, and an in-depth look at how each alternative choice functioned is warranted. The purpose of this task is to conduct an in-depth analysis of a sample item in order to see how this type of analysis works. You may need to review the effective "short-cut" procedures for calculating item difficulty and item discrimination indices.

TASK PROCEDURES

Given the distribution of responses for students who scored high (High Scoring Group) and those who scored low (Low Scoring Group), calculate the difficulty index (P) and the discrimination index (D) for the sample item presented below. The correct response is marked with an asterisk (*) and bold-face type.

* Evaluate the distribution of responses for the alternative (distractor) choices for the item and identify all nonfunctional alternatives.

* Evaluate whether the item functioned appropriately for (a) a norm-referenced purpose or (b) a criterion-referenced mastery purpose. Defend your selection.

* Critique the construction of this item and revise the item as needed.

Sample Item: *Math students should be able to translate verbal problems into mathematical statements. This objective is probably intended to be in what level of Bloom's Taxonomy?*

1. Comprehension
2. Application
3. Synthesis
4. Analysis

Alternative Response Choices

	A*	B	C	D	Omit	Total
High Group	20	0	0	0	0	20
Low Group	10	6	1	3	0	20

Feedback for In-Depth Item Analysis Task

The difficulty index for the sample multiple-choice item is: $P = 20 + 10 = 30/40 = 0.75$, interpreted as a borderline Easy Item. Therefore, a majority (75%) of the students in this class were able to recognize that comprehension skills in Bloom's taxonomy include translating from one context to another -- in this case, translating verbal math problems into mathematical statements. The discrimination index, the power of an item to distinguish between students who achieved high scores on the total test and students who scored low, is: $D = 20 - 10 = 10/20 = .50$, interpreted as a moderately strong degree of discrimination power. In other words, twice as many high scorers than low scorers were successful on this item. Therefore, even though this item was rather easy for the group as a whole, it was successful in identifying individual differences in achievement with regard to this item.

Distractor responses for an item should function in the direction opposite to the correct response. That is, distractors should identify students who are confused about the concept being assessed or who simply do not understand what is being asked (and students who simply did not prepare well for the test). All of the high-scoring students selected the correct response, so all distractor responses functioned as they should for the high-scoring group. For those in the low-scoring group who answered this item incorrectly, response B had significant negative discrimination power ($-6/20 = -.30$), which is how a response should function for students who do not know or understand the question.. For responses C and D, the discrimination power was not significant ($-1/20 = .05$ and $-3/20 = 1.15$, respectively) but was in the appropriate direction (negative). Finally, no one in either high or low criterion groups omitted this item; apparently, no one was confused by the item or at least everyone had a chance to answer the item.

Because of the discrimination power of this item, it was probably intended for a norm-referenced test. Even though it was rather easy ($P = 0.75$), the item was still not easy enough for a criterion-referenced mastery test. For mastery tests, all or nearly all P values should be above 0.80, or above whatever criterion level has been set for mastery. For norm-referenced tests, P values can vary but most will demonstrate average difficulty and a few items may be easy (as motivators for low-achieving students) or difficult (as challenges for high-achieving students). The goal of norm-referenced assessments is *to identify individual differences if there are individual differences*. Evidence of individual differences is necessary if assessments are to be used for differential grading purposes. The goal of criterion-referenced mastery assessments is to demonstrate that all students have achieved mastery of specific cognitive or psychomotor skills. Consequently, evidence of achieving/mastering those skills is needed. Differential grades are irrelevant in mastery assessments, even though teachers are often required to assign letter or percentage grades to mastery achievements. Some schools are now providing qualitative descriptions of mastery achievement rather than letter grades.

Examination of the construction of this item suggests that the item is grammatically correct, and there does not seem to be unnecessary verbiage in the item. However, the response alternatives need to be ordered alphabetically in order to avoid patterns among the keyed responses. This is an easy strategy to implement in writing items without having to use a table of random numbers. [Some computer programs are available that are capable of random ordering of item response choices, but alphabetizing will accomplish the same purpose.] When students are made aware that all item response alternatives are ordered alphabetically, they will know not to look for response patterns.

Analyzing Criterion-Referenced Mastery Items*

A number of methods have been proposed for analyzing items designed to measure mastery of basic skills. However, most of the methods are cumbersome and difficult for classroom teachers to use. An easy method proposed by Hopkins and Antes‡ (1989) and patterned after the simple 1927 Truman Kelly model. Only the definition of the criterion groups is changes. Instead of the High-scoring and Low-scoring Criterion Groups, the Gronlund model identifies the Mastery Group versus the Non-Mastery Group. Difficulty (P) and discrimination (D) indices are calculated in the same way as before: P = percent of students in both criterion groups who responded successfully to the item. D = percent difference between students who mastered the item and those who did not. Thus, the formulas are:

$$P = \frac{\text{\# Successes Mastery (MG) and \# Successes in Non-Mastery (NMG) Groups}}{\text{Total Number in Combined Groups}}$$

$$D = \frac{\text{\# Successes in MG}}{\text{\# Students in MG}} \quad \text{minus} \quad \frac{\text{\# Successes in NMG}}{\text{\# Students in NMG}}$$

For example, if 28 of 30 in MG and 8 of 10 NMG students responded successfully to an item, the P value is 28 + 6/40 = 34/40 = 0.85. The D index is 28/30 minus 8/10 = 0.93 - 0.80 = 0.13, not a significant difference between Mastery and Non-Mastery groups. If an entire test were made up of items that functioned in this same way, there would be *no evidence* to support the conclusion that Mastery students differed from Non-Mastery students with regard to the skills measured by the test.

TASK PROCEDURES

Given the distribution of responses for a set of five items drawn from a test designed to measure mastery of essential subject content (a criterion-referenced mastery test), identify which item best fits each description. The total group of students included **28** students, of whom **22 students met the mastery criterion** and **6 students did not meet the criterion**. Analyze the following set of items derived from this group.

Number of Students Responding Correctly

Item	Above Criterion (N = 22)	Below Criterion (N = 6)
1	22	3
2	19	1
3	18	4
4	21	5
5	22	6
6	20	4
7	11	3

* Reference for Mastery Item Analysis Formulas: Hopkins, C. D., & Antes, R. L. (1989). *Classroom testing: Construction* (2nd ed.). Itasia, IL: F. E. Peacock.

1. Which item seems to be the **ideal** choice for a true mastery test? _____

2. Which item is the **most difficult "easy"** item? _____

3. Which could be the **best "easy"** item for a norm-referenced test? _____

4. Which item has the **lowest positive** discrimination index? _____

5. Which item looks **most** like a norm-referenced item? _____

6. Which item is **least** effective for any test purpose? _____

7. Which item shows **low but significantly positive** discrimination? _____

Question: If you do not conduct item analyses on your own classroom tests now or in the future, what evidence will you use to demonstrate to students, parents, and/or other interested stakeholders that your assessment tools are relevant, reliable, and valid for your students? Defend your position.

Feedback for Mastery Item Analysis Data Set

BASIC ITEM DATA

Applying the difficulty (P) and discrimination power (D) formulas to items intended for mastery assessment (Hopkins & Antes, 1989) yields for following indices for Items 1 - 7:

Item	Difficulty (P) Index	Discrimination Power (D)
1	0.89	.38
2	0.71	.69
3	0.78	.15
4	0.93	.12
5	1.00	.00
6	0.86	.24
7	0.50	.00

a. The ideal item for a true mastery test is Item 5, for which all students demonstrated mastery of the skill/concept being measured.

b. The item that is the most difficult of the easy items is Item 3, which is at the low end of the range for easy items (75 to 100% success). Items 2 and 7 are in the average difficulty range (26 - 74% success).

c. Item 1 is the best easy item that could be in a norm-referenced test because it is a moderately strong discriminator (D = .38), even though it is an easy item. Although Item 6 is a bit easier than Item 1, its discrimination power is much lower.

d. The item with the lowest positive discrimination power is Item 4 (D = .12).

e. Item 2 looks most like a good norm-referenced item with its P value of 71% and its very strong D index of 69%. The P index for Item 7 is appropriate but it has no discrimination power.

f. The least effective item for any testing purpose is Item 7 because it is too difficult for a mastery test and has no discrimination power for s norm-referenced test.

g. The lowest significantly positive discriminator is Item 6 (D = .24). Items 3 and 4 are positive discriminators but they are not significant; the difference between mastery and non-mastery groups is 20% for each item.

Testwiseness Practice Test

Directions: This set of 8 items is a hypothetical test on which you could answer every item correctly merely by knowing some of the pitfalls in item construction. See how many correct answers you can find.

1. The purpose of the cluss in furmpaling is to remove

   a. cluss-prags.
   b. tremalis.
   c. cloughs.
   d. plumots.

2. Trassig is true when

   a. lusps trasses the vom.
   b. the viskal flans, if the viskal is donwil or zortil.
   c. the belugl frulls.
   d. dissles lisk easily.

3. The sigia frequently overfesks the trelsum because

   a   all siglas are mellious.
   b   siglas are always votial.
   c.   the trelsum is usually tarious.
   d.   no tresla are feskable.

4. The fribbled breg will minter best with an

   a. derst.
   b. morst.
   c. sortar.
   d. ignu.

5. Among resons for tristol doss are

   a   the sabs foped and the foths tinzed.
   b.   the kredges roted with the orts.
   c.   few racobs were accepted in sluth.
   d.   most of the polats were thonced.

6.   Which of the following is/are always present when trossels are being gruven?

    a.   rint and vost
    b.   vost
    c.   shum and vost
    d.   vost and plone

7.   The mintering function of the ignu is most effectively carried out in connection with

    a.   a razma tol.
    b.   the groshing stantol.
    c.   the gribbled breg.
    d.   a frally sush.

8.   What is the answer to this question?

    a.   _____
    b.   _____
    c.   _____
    d.   _____

[Source: Anonymous]

Have you figured out the clues? The answers all reflect what is known as **"testwiseness,"** meaning that we have learned to identify correct answers even though we may know little or nothing about what is being measured. Check your answers with your instructor.

Feedback for Testwiseness Test

Each "correct" response represents one or more faulty item writing rules. Item construction must be undertaken with care and diligence in order to avoid violating construction rules. Even in writing fairly simple knowledge-level objective test items, it is not always easy to avoid giving clues to the correct/keyed answer. Writing short-answer and essay items is also burdened with potential construction faults. [See Gronlund & Lind, 2000, for details concerning item construction rules for all types of item formats.]

Keyed Answers:

1. = *a.* In this item, response *a* contains a word (cluss-prags) that is in the stem. This repetition of the same word is a clue to the keyed answer.

2. = *b.* Response *b* is noticeably longer that the other three choices. Often the longest response choice is the keyed answer.

3. = *c.* For this item, use of such qualifiers as "all," "always," and "no" are clues for avoiding these responses as the keyed response. The qualifier "usually" is not as strong as the others.

4. = *d.* The use of "an" in the item stem points to the choice of *d* as the keyed answer, because this response is the only one that begins with a vowel.

5. = *a.* The verb "are" in the stem calls for two or more objects in the keyed answer. Only response *a* contains two objects.

6. = *b.* For this item, the grammatical structure of response *b* differs from that of the other three choices. In multiple-choice items, consistent grammatical structure is an important item construction feature.

7. = *c.* For this item, an answer to a previous question (Item 4) clues the correct answer for this item. The word *ignu* is associated with *gribbled breg* in Item 4 and again here in Item 7.

8. = *d.* The last item which has no response choices reflects a noticeable sequencing of the keyed answer: *a*, *b*, *c*, *d*, *a*, *b*, *c*, and now *d* again.

APPENDIX 3

AN ACTION RESEARCH PROJECT

An Action Research Project
Anita Woolfolk Hoy

Here is an assignment that I often use with my classes when the students have a field placement or when I am working with inservice teachers. The assignment comes in two parts. First, students propose their project using this general framework

Action Research Proposal Format

1. **Statement of the problem**, question, goal, or issue—a paragraph or so.

2. **Rationale:** Why did you select this problem (question, goal, issue)? What is the origin or basis of the problem (where did it come from or what gave you the idea)? Why is this an important problem?

3. **Context of the project**: Describe the students (age, abilities, challenges), classroom, resources, materials, limitations, subject area (if appropriate), students' previous experiences, and any other relevant contextual information.

4. **What exactly will you do?** Describe plans, procedures, timetable.

5. **Data:** How will you gather relevant information about your project? What are your sources of data and how will you keep records. What information will you need to determine if you have met your goals, solved the problem, answered the question, or addressed the issue in question 1 above? Will you observe, interview, use traditional or other testing, videotape or audiotape, examine student work, develop portfolios, use journals, note activity patterns, do sociograms, or use other ways to understand the situation and the changes that follow from your project?

6. **Analyses:** How will you use the information you gather? What will you do with it after you collect it? How will you pull it together to address question 1 above?

7. **Resources and References:** <u>List</u> at least four readings, chapters, or sections of chapters, from this and other courses and from outside sources that you will consult as you complete your project and written report. Your final report must have a summary of this **Supporting Research and Scholarship** that pertains to your problem or question and makes a case for your action plan. Use APA style to list the resources.

Students share these proposals during class or post them to a class bulletin board for feedback. I do not grade this assignment.

Action Research Final Project Format

Students use this format to complete the final written report of their action research project. Together we develop rubric to assess the project.

1. **Clear Statement** of the problem (question, goal, issue), including a **Rationale**: Why did you select this problem or question? Why is it important?

2. **Context of the project**: Describe the students (age, abilities, challenges), classroom, resources, materials, limitations, subject area (if appropriate), students' previous experiences, and any other relevant contextual information.

3. **Supporting Research and Scholarship**: Summarize relevant research and scholarship that pertains to your problem or question. What does the literature suggest about possible solutions or actions? Make a case for your action plan.

4. **Action/Intervention**: What exactly did you do? Describe procedures, interventions, timetable, including how you **gathered relevant information** (your sources of data).

5. **Results:** What happened? What are the actual outcomes or effects of your action?

6. **Reflections:** What are your observations, analyses, new understandings? How would you revise your plan to improve it or to learn more?

7. **Resources and References**: Use APA style to list the resources. Include at least 8.

An adequate paper (B) will be written in APA style, but with some errors. The problem statement and rationale will be clear, but not thoroughly elaborated. The context will paint a brief picture of the situation. The literature review will include several relevant sources and will connect the sources to the problem statement. The action will be clearly described and a minimum of relevant data will be gathered--perhaps only one kind of data will be collected. The results will be briefly described. The reflection will relate readings to the results of the project in order to understand the outcomes and speculate about how the plan could be improved. References will be appropriate to the project, with at least 2 recent journal articles included.

An exceptional paper (A+) will be written in APA style with very few errors. The problem statement and rationale will be clear and thoroughly elaborated such that the reader knows what is being addressed and why. The context will paint a full picture of the situation, and include useful information beyond simple demographics of the class and school. The literature review will include several relevant sources and will connect the sources to the problem statement. This section will be well organized to build toward an argument for the action plan so the reader is educated about a small area of research and convinced that the action plan is solidly grounded. The action will be clearly described and several kinds of relevant data will be gathered in ways that are systematic and carefully documented. The results will be briefly described, using tables, charts, or other visual or graphic presentations as appropriate. The reflection will tie readings to the results of the project in order to understand the outcomes and speculate about how the plan could be improved. The analyses will be thoughtful and will relate the project to readings and discussion in this and other classes. References will be appropriate to the project, with at least 4 recent journal articles included. The references will reflect a targeted but thorough search for pertinent information.

I usually spend part of one class doing peer editing of the first draft of this final report using this guide sheet:

Feedback for _____

by_____

Action Research Final Report Contents: Is there:

_____ a statement of the problem including a rationale?

_____ a description of the context?

_____ a review of the research related to the problem?

_____ a clear description of the action taken?

_____ a set of data/information sources?

_____ an analysis of the information -- results?

_____ a reflection on the project?

_____ a set of appropriate references?

NOTES

NOTES

NOTES

NOTES

NOTES

NOTES

NOTES

NOTES

NOTES

NOTES

NOTES